A-Z SHEFF

C000294154

CONTENTS

REFERENCE

Motorway	**M1**	Map Continuation · Large Scale City Centre	54 · 4
'A' Road	A61	National Grid Reference	385
'B' Road	B6150	Ambulance Station	✚
Dual Carriageway		Car Park (Selection of)	P
One Way Street Traffic flow on 'A' Roads is indicated by a heavy line on the drivers left.	→	Church or Chapel	†
Restricted Access		Fire Station	■
Pedestrianised Road	[----------]	Hospital	⊞
House Numbers 'A' and 'B' Roads only	8 · 13	Information Centre	ⓘ
Railway	Level Crossing · Station	Police Station	▲
County Boundary	+ · + · + · +	Post Office	●
District Boundary	— · — · — · —	Toilet	▽
Posttown Boundary By arrangement with the Post Office		Toilet with Disabled Facilities	⓰
Postcode Boundary (Within Post Towns)	— — —	Viewpoint	※

SCALE

Map Pages 6-141
1:18103 (3½ inches to 1 mile)

Miles 0 — ¼ — ½
Metres 0 — 250 — 500 — 750

Central Area 4-5
1:9051 (7 inches to 1 mile)

Miles 0 — ⅛ — ¼
Metres 0 — 100 — 200 — 300

Geographers' A-Z Map Company Ltd.

Head Office
Fairfield Rd., Borough Grn. Sevenoaks, Kent. TN15 8PP
Telephone 0732 781000
Showrooms
44 Gray's Inn Road, London. WC1X 8LR
Telephone 071-242 9246

An A-Z Publication   Edition 1 1991

454

88

E **95** **F** **G** **H**

1

LAUGHTON EN LE MORTHEN

KIRK CROFT ROAD

Manor Farm

FIRBECK

ORCHARD CL.
JOHN CL.
NEW ST.
Rec. Grd.
KINGSWOOD AV.

GRANGEWOOD RD.
LONGTHWTE RD.
LINGODELL CL.

St. John's Farm

St. John's

E R H A M

2

ROAD

Little Moor

Throapham

OLDCOTES B6463 ROAD

3

LEYS 87

LANE

Sports Ground

Throapham Common

Works Sports Grd.

B6060 LANE

DINNINGTON

f i

BRECK LANE

ANNE ST.
HUNTERS TWY
HUNTRS PK
HUNTRS HUNTERS TER
HUNTS HUNTERS TGN CHASE
CHESTNUT GRO.

MANOR

Recreation Ground

Play. Fld.

White Gates

CHARLES ST.
DUKE ST.
QUEEN ST.

Timber Yard

Wks.

Rother Valley College

Tennis Courts

Tennis Courts

Dinnington Comprehensive Sch.

Lime Kiln Close Plantation

LANE

NINGTON LLIERY

DOE

Sch.

QUARRY LANE

CORONATION AV.

PLANTATION AV.

SOUTH CRES.

ROAD

SCHL
EAST ST.
S EAST STREET
DOE QUARRY TER
SCARSDALE
CLARENCE ST.
VICTORIA ST.
HOWL
THE CRESCENT
HILL

Ty Newydd

LODGE

Tennis Cts.
Bowl Grn.

Miners' Welfare Institute

PATERSON RD.

4

LANE

86

Club
Football Grd.
Cricket Ground

Bowls
CARLISLE TER

Liby
Cemy.

CONSTABLE

ST. JOSEPH'S
Sch.

St. Joseph's R.C. Hall

NEW STREET

ADDISON

LORDENS

LEICESTER RD.

SILVERDALES

Football Grd.

Cricket Grd.

BYRON

KEATS DR.

ATHORPE GRO.
Club
Depot

TILFORD RD.

LAUGHTON ROAD

LEOPOLD ST.

BARLEYCROFT

Hall Farm
Hall Ct.

NEW RD.

LODGE

WESTERN AV.
CENTRAL AV.

EASTERN AV.
EASTERN CL.
AVENUE HIGH

BURNS

NOOK

SHAKESPEARE DR.
OSBORNE
MILTON

BYRON DR.

MILFORD RD.
SHELLEY RD.
ROAD

5

Lodge Plantation

S31

f

Alcove Plantation

MIDDLETON AV.
LEONARD RD.
CARVER DR.
MIDDLETON

FALCON WAY

DINNINGTON

B6060 ROAD

NURSERY ROAD

WALNUT
GLEN EAGLES RD
TROON
SUNNINGDALE
WENTWORTH
TURNBERRY WY

BIRKDALE AV.

BELFRY
MOORTOWN AV.
WAY

WINSTON

Burial Grd.

FURNESS CL.
CARTMEL WLK.

HILL BRANDS

White Wall Plantation

White Walls Farm

6

DEVONSHIRE DRIVE
DEVONSHIRE DR.
SCARBRGH RD
LEEDS RD
DONC RD

NETHERTHORPE WY.

ORCHARD

Anston Park Inf. & Jun. Sch.

BEECH AV.
RYDAL
BUTTERMERE
ENNERDALE CL.
WARWICK WY.

PARK AVENUE

CARTMEL CRES.
LANGDALE
BORROWDALE
APPLEBY WLK.

CONISTON
CAR DIECK
CLEVELAND
KESWICK

LAKELAND

NORTH ANSTON

E **119** **F** **G** **H**

385

54

53

Cricket Ground

E

Park Plantation

F

48

105

G

Junction 31

Bleak Ho.

Four Winds

Fm.

Bung

H

Todwick Common Farm

Mona Terrace

T O D W I C K
C O M M O N

1

Nicker Wood

A57

ON

ROAD

K

Fiddle Neck Farm

Nicker Wood

M1

Upper Common Farm

CARR

LANE

Spts. Grd.

Meadow Ho.

Pav.

2

f

Nickerwood Farm

i

e

l

d

84

Sewage Works

3

11 8

S31

Low Laithes Farm

M O T O R W A Y

ROAD

Playing Field

Kiveton Park Meadows Jun. Sch.

KIVETON PARK

4

Kiveton Park Inf. Schs.

Brooklands Farm

FORGE

HORSE SHOE CL.

STORTH

LANE

Wales Comp. Sch. Play. Fld.

HIGHFIE

Brooklands House

OLD

QUARRY AV.

POPLAR

ASH GRO.

CHESTNUT AV.

MAPLE RD.

WALES

WHEEL

PEVERIL

NHOE

Warehouse

THE BEECHES

RD.

ROOKERY CL.

LIME TREE

MYRTLE GRO.

CEDAR NOOK

Bowl. Grn.

Works

SWOOD
LLAS

SCHOOL CL.
Club

STREET

DR.

CL.

62

STATION

Victoria

83

CHOOL

98

ROAD

WALES

LESTRANGE

228

164

137

B6059

ROAD

COLLIER

The Barracks

FIR TREE DR.

GREEN OAK DR.

Wales Jun. & Inf. Sch.

Play. Fld.

SYCAMORE

187

HIGHMOOR

Hlth. Cen.

Liby.

THOMAS

RAWSON

Kiveton Bridge

5

HERRY TREE

Wood Hill

WALES

Grave Yard

CHURCH CL.

ORCHARD

QUEENS

ROTHER

MOOR AV.

LITTLEMOOR AV.

FESTIVAL CL.

Tennis Courts

Recreation Ground

KIVET (KIVE

High House Farm

Wales Hall Farm

HIGH HOUSE FM. CT.

LONGLANDS

LEDGER

CORONATION AV.

GRNSIDE

NORWOOD

Tennis Courts

Cemetery

STOCKWELL

CHURCH LANE

STOCKWELL AV.

LAMBRELL AV.

NORWOOD CR.

6

M1

COALPIT LANE

82

Norwood Lodge

d Bridge

E

F

127

48

LANE

G

H

Hard Fiel

49

E **F** Sch. **G** Norbriggs **H**

375

Riverdale Park
CARAVAN SITE

Playing
Field

RIVERDALE RD.

BENT LA.

TORIA AV

WHITE RD.

MOOR VIEW RD.

S WORKSOP A619

Sports
Ground

Staveley
Bridge

THE PADDOCKS

NORBRIGGS RD

Play. Fld.

The Farm

Norbriggs
Cottages

BOLSOVER

ROAD

B6419

Woodthorpe
Hall

1

RALPH

ROAD

Playing Field

Netherthorpe Grammar
School

CRANLEIGH
RD.

LINDEN

SPENCER AV

ROAD

WOODTHORPE

Wellsholme
Farm

Bank
House

ROAD

NETHERTHORPE

ETH
FIELDS

MARSHFIELD
GR.

WOODTHORPE

SEYMOUR

BRIDLE

Woodthorpe C. of E.
Primary School

Oxcroft
Junction

Mineral Railway

ROAD

2

Brook

River Doe Lea

Disused Workings

Woodthorpe
Grange

Coal Stocking
Area

Coal Stocking
Area

Mineral Railway

M1

74

L   D

LA.

Coal Stocking
Area

Coal Stocking
Area

3

POOLSBROOK
VIEW

THE GROVE

Seymour
Junction

Coal Stocking Area

Mineral Railway

Coal Stocking Area

Coal Stocking
Area

M

O

T

O

R

W

A

Y

ROAD

POOLSBROOK

POOLSBROOK CRES.

POOLSBROOK

MARKHAM

Opencast
Workings

Woodside

4

POOLSBRK
SQ.

COTTAGE
CL.

CO-OPERATIVE COTTS

CL.

ROAD

Sports
Ground

Opencast
Workings

Woodside

brook Prim.
chool

r

i   **e**   **I**   **d**

LANE

Poolsbrook Miners
Welfare Club

Opencast Workings

BOLSOVER

73

5

EAST

GRO

NORTH

POOLSBROOK

NORTH

WHITTON
PL.

CRESCENT

The Oaks

LANE

Mineral Railway

MARKHAM

WEST CRES.

CRESCENT

MARKHAM

MARKHAM
CT.

DUCKMANTON RD.

Club

Sports
Ground

S44

ROAD

M1

MARKHAM
COLLIERY

Mineral Railway

Mineral Railway

Woodhouse
Farm

6

SOUTH
CRES.

RD.

ROAD

DUCKMANTON

Middle
Farm

Four
Poplars

Reservoir

DE PEVERIL RD.

RECTORY RD.

Depot

M1

MARKHAM

445

Works

WORKS

Sewage
Works

Offices

WORKS

H

B6418

BUTTERMILK LA.

Nether Farm

72

46

E **F** **G** **H**

139

72

E **BRIMMINGTON COMMON**

F

G

H

Manor Inf. Sch.

133

ELIOT CL.

CHESTERTON DRIVE

BROOK ST

41

TAPTON GRANGE

VICTORIA PARK

VICTORIA RD

GROVE WAY

MANOR

GROVE

Lodge Farm

WESTWOOD LA

Allpits Plantation

1

HILL LA

DARK LANE

Oldfield Farm

BARRY RD

MELVILLE CL

WHEATHILL

GRANGE PK

AV.

LODGE CL

S43

ROAD

WESTMOOR LANE

WESTWOOD RD

ORLANDS

f i

Plover Wood

SANDS

EASTWOOD

BLACKSMITH LANE

MANOR RD

l **d**

Plover Hill Farm

HATHERN CL

PARKER LANE

FREEDOM WAY

TERFIELD AND NORTH DERBYSHIRE ROYAL HOSPITAL

TAPTON WAY

PLOVER DRIVE

ALLPITS NORTH

CENTRAL

ROAD

LIME LANE

ROSE GLOVE

BRANGINE

GLOVE

ORCHARD

H

Calow C. of E. Junior School

2

Moor Farm

The Bungalow

MAIN LANE

N O R T H

AVENUE

WILLOW

LAUREL

HEATHER CL

Sports Ground

LANE

71

Dryhurst

Burial Ground

CHURCHSIDE

CHURCH ST.

CHURCH MEADOWS

CHURCH

VILLAS

LAWN

CHESTERFIELD

Eastwood Park

EASTWOOD DR

WORKS

Lodge Farm

CHESTERFIELD

ROAD

TOP

ROAD

Lodge Farm

HARVEY

DARK LANE

CALOW

Oaks Farm

Lodge Farm

3

A632

RD.

S44

Sports Ground

Moortop Farm

Bolehill Plantation

HILL LANE

Top Alley

Spring House Farm

Nursery

Calow Oaks

E A S T

The Croft

4

Moorfi

KENYON RD

BARNES RD

THE CLOUGH

DINGLE

DINGLE BANK

WOOD LANE

Jubilee Cotts.

Oak Tree Cottages

BACK LANE

Bolehill

Hady Plantation

White House Farm

Cock Alley

Riddings House Farm

370

Wrays Hill Farm

HASLAND LANE

Nether House Farm

HEATHCOTE DRIVE

Laurel Farm

Laurel House

BOLE LANE

HALLFLAT LA

Shaft (Dis.)

5

Furnace Hillock

D E R B Y S H I R E

Calowgreen Farm

Calow Green

D

A617

BY-PASS

Moor Farm

Green Farm

Hill Crest

Sycamore House

MOOR LA.

6

HORSE VALLEY RD.

B6039

ROAD

ROAD

Winsick

Manor Farm

Calow Brook

HASSOCKY LANE

B6425

Spring View Farm

69

VENUE

E

F

G

H

42

340

41

42

Hemsworth
WF9
Upton
North Elmsall
South Elmsall
South Kirby
DN6
Askern
Thorne
DN8
143
Skellow
Carcroft
Stainforth
Hatfield
ADWICK LE STREET
Barnby Dun
Dunscroft
DN7
Hatfield Woodhouse
Woodlands
Toll Bar
Kirk Sandall
Great Houghton
Hooton Pagnell
Arksey
Edenthorpe
Thornscoe East
Thurnscoe
Dearne
Hickleton
DN5
BENTLEY
Wheatley
Armthorpe
DN3
Goldthorpe
Cusworth
DN1
DN2
Bolton upon Dearne
Barnburgh
High Melton
Sprotbrough
Hexthorpe
Balby
DONCASTER
Branton
DN9
S63
Warmsworth
DN4
Hyde Park
Cantley
Auckley
WATH UPON DEARNE
MEXBOROUGH
S64
CONISBROUGH
Bessacarr
SWINTON
Denaby Main
Finningley
Upper Haugh
Kilnhurst
DN12
New Edlington
New Rossington
Rossington
RAWMARSH
S65
Ravenfield
Wadworth
DN11
Misson
Thrybergh
Braithwell
ROTHERHAM
Bramley
MALTBY
Tickhill
Bawtry
DN10
Herringthorpe
Wickersley
S66
Harworth
Bircotes
Gringley on the Hill
Moorgate
Whiston
S60
Oldcotes
Ranskill
Treeton
Thurcroft
Laughton en le Morthen
Aughton
Aston
Laughton Common
Langold
Blyth
Beighton
S31
Todwick
Dinnington
Carlton in Lindrick
S81
DN22
S19
North Anston
Waterthorpe
Wales
Woodsetts
Halfway
South Anston
EAST RETFORD
Killamarsh
Harthill
WORKSOP
Renishaw
Barlborough
Manton
Mastin Moor
Whitwell
S80
Staveley
Clowne
Creswell
Elkesley
Duckmanton
Shuttlewood
East Markham
Bolsover
NG20
SCALE
0 1 2 3 4 5 Miles
0 1 2 3 4 5 6 7 8 Kilometres
Tuxford
S44
Langwith
Langwith Junction
Church Warsop
Warsop
Boughton
NG22
Shirebrook
Edwinstowe
Ollerton

INDEX TO PLACES & AREAS

Names in this Index shown in CAPITAL LETTERS followed by their Postcode District(s), are Postal Addresses

HOOD GREEN. (S75).—6A 22
Hood Hill.—5H 51
HOOTON LEVITT. (S66).—6E 83
HOOTON ROBERTS. (S65)
—6G 57
Horner House.—2C 140
Howard Hill.—6A 86
Hoyland Common.—6F 37
Hoyland Lowe.—4G 37
HOYLAND. (S74).—5A 38
Hoyle Mill.—6B 14
Hurl Field.—2A 112
Hyde Park.—1F 47

Ickles.—5B 78
Inkersall Green.—4A 134
INKERSALL. (S43).—5B 134
Intake.—4A 34
(Doncaster)
Intake.—2C 112
(Sheffield)

Jeffrey Green.—6A 96
Jordan.—4H 77
Jordanthorpe.—3F 123
JUMP. (S74).—4C 38

Kelham Island.—6E 87
Kendray.—2C 24
Kexbrough.—5A 6
KILLAMARSH. (S31).—3B 126
KILNHURST. (S62).—6C 56
Kimberworth.—2G 77
Kimberworth Park.—6G 67
Kingstone.—2F 23
KIRK SANDALL. (DN3).—3D 21
KIVETON PARK. (S31).—4A 118
KIVETON PARK STATION. (S31)
—6D 118
Knoll Top.—3E 141
Knowle Top.—5C 84

Lane End.—1E 65
LAUGHTON COMMON. (S31)
—2C 106
LAUGHTON EN LE MORTHEN.
(S31).—6G 107
Lea Brook.—2G 53
Liberty Hill.—6E 85
Lightwood.—6B 112
Listerdale.—5E 81
Little Common.—4G 109
LITTLE HOUGHTON. (S72)
—1G 27
Little Norton.—1E 123
Little Sheffield.—4D 98
Littleworth.—4F 63
Lodge Moor.—4A 96
LONG SANDALL. (DN2).—5A 20
Loundsley Green.—6E 131
Low Barugh.—1B 12
Lowedges.—3D 122
Lower Bradway.—3A 122
Lower Crabtree.—3G 87
Lower Pilley.—6C 36
Lower Walkley.—4A 86
Lowfield.—6E 99
Low Laithes.—3H 25
LOW STUBBIN. (S62).—5C 54
Low Valley.—5D 26
Low Wincobank.—4D 76
Loxley Bottom.—3G 85
LOXLEY. (S6).—3D 84
Lundwood.—4E 15

Lydgate.—2G 97

Malinbridge.—4H 85
MALTBY. (S66).—4G 83
Manor.—4D 100
Manor Park.—3C 100
MAPPLEWELL. (S75).—5F 7
Masbrough.—3B 78
Meadow Hall.—6E 77
Meadow Head.—5D 110
Meadow View.—5B 56
Measborough Dike.—1B 24
Meersbrook.—2F 111
Meersbrook Bank.—2E 111
MEXBOROUGH. (S64).—1E 57
Mickley.—6H 121
Middlecliff.—2A 28
Middlecroft.—2B 134
Middlewood.—5F 73
Millhouses.—3G 27
(Barnsley)
Millhouses.—4B 110
(Sheffield)
Milton.—1A 52
Monk Bretton.—3C 14
Moorgate.—1G 91
MORTHEN. (S66).—4F 93
Mortomley.—6C 50
MOSBOROUGH. (S19).—2D 124

Neepsend.—5D 86
Nether Cantley.—1F 49
Nether Edge.—1C 110
Nethergate.—6C 84
Nether Green.—5E 97
NETHER HAUGH. (S62).—1B 68
Netherthorpe.—6E 105
(Aston, Sheffield)
Netherthorpe.—1E 135
(Chesterfield)
Netherthorpe.—1C 98 & 2A 4
(Crookesmoor, Sheffield)
Newbold.—5F 131
Newbold Moor.—3H 131
New Brimington.—2F 133
New Edington.—3B 60
Newfield Green.—1H 111
Newgate.—2A 130
Newhill.—6D 40
New Lodge.—6A 8
New Rossington.—5C 62
Newton.—6H 31
New Totley.—5E 121
New Village.—5B 18
NEW WHITTINGTON. (S43)
—1D 132
New York.—4C 78
Nook End.—5D 84
Norbriggs.—1F 135
Normandale.—3E 85
Normanton Spring.—1G 113
North Anston.—2G 119
Northfield.—1D 78
NORTON. (DN6).—6F 111
Norton Hammer.—3C 110
Norton Lees.—3E 111
Norton Woodseats.—4F 111
Norwood.—1D 126
Nutwell.—4G 35

OLD DENABY. (DN12).—2F 57
OLD EDLINGTON. (DN12)
—6A 60
Old Haywoods.—3G 141
Old Kirk Sandall.—2B 20

Old Mill.—4A 14
Old Town.—4E 13
Old Wheel.—3B 84
Old Whittington.—1A 132
Onesacre.—2B 72
Orgreave.—2C 102
OUGHTIBRIDGE. (S30).—2D 72
Owlerton.—3B 86
OWLTHORPE. (S19).—5A 114
Oxclose.—3G 125

PARKGATE. (S60 & S62).—4F 69
Park Head.—6D 84
(Stannington, Sheffield)
Parkhead.—4F 109
(Whirlow, Sheffield)
Park Hill.—2H 99
Parkside.—6D 84
Parkwood Springs.—4D 86
Parson Cross.—4D 74
Peakley Hill.—6A 128
Philadelphia.—5D 86
Piccadilly.—4A 56
Pilley.—5B 36
Pilley Green.—6B 36
Pilley Hills.—5A 36
Pismire Hill.—5H 75
Pitsmoor.—4F 87
Platts Common.—4A 38
Plumbley.—3B 124
Pogmoor.—5D 12
POOLSBROOK. (S43).—3E 135
Potter Hill.—6A 50

Quarry Hills.—4G 27
Quoit Green.—2F 129

Rails.—1A 96
Rainstorth.—5A 66
Ranmoor.—4F 97
Ravenfield Common.—1H 81
RAVENFIELD. (S65).—4H 71
RAWMARSH. (S62).—2F 69
Richmond.—5G 101
Richmond Park.—3F 77
RIDGEWAY. (S12).—6G 113
Ringinglow.—3A 108
Rockingham.—4H 67
Rollestone.—3H 111
Roman Terrace.—6C 42
ROSSINGTON. (DN11).—4E 63
Rostholme.—5A 18
ROTHERHAM (S60 to S63 & S65
& , S66).—3D 78
Royd.—5F 141
ROYSTON. (S71).—2E 9
Ryecroft.—1H 69

St Ann's.—2E 79
St Augustines.—5A 138
St Helen's.—1C 14
Sandhill.—1B 28
(Barnsley)
Sandhill.—6H 55
(Rotherham)
Sandygate.—3E 97
SCAWSBY. (DN5).—3G 31
SCAWTHORPE. (DN5).—1G 31
SCHOLES. (S61).—3E 67
Shaftholme.—3D 18
SHAFTON. (S72).—2C 10
Shafton Two Gates.—3D 10
Sharrow.—6B 98
Sharrow Head.—5C 98

Sharrow Vale.—5B 98
Shaw Lands.—6F 13
Shay House.—3D 140
Sheepbridge.—1G 131
Sheffield Lane Top.—5G 75
Sheffield Park.—4A 100
SHEFFIELD. (S1 to S31)
—2E 99 & 3E 5
Shirecliffe.—1C 86
Shiregreen.—3A 76
Slade Hooton.—4G 95
Small Bridge.—1A 48
Smithies.—3A 14
Smithley.—6G 25
Smithy Green.—2H 13
Smithy Moor.—2B 140
Snape Hill.—4E 27
(Barnsley)
Snape Hill.—1E 129
(Sheffield)
SOTHALL. (S19).—5F 115
South Anston.—3F 119
Southey Green.—6D 74
Spink Hall.—4D 140
Spital.—4C 138
SPROTBROUGH. (DN5).—2D 44
Sprotbrough Park.—2E 45
STAINBOROUGH. (S75).—5B 22
Staincross.—3E 7
Stairfoot.—1E 25
STANNINGTON. (S6).—5C 84
STAVELEY. (S43).—1C 134
Steel Bank.—6A 86
Stephen Hill.—2F 97
Sticking Hill.—4D 42
Stockbridge.—5C 18
Stocksbridge.—3D 140
Stonegravels.—6A 132
Storrs.—4A 84
Street.—3G 53
Stubbin.—4F 141
Stubbing.—6C 72
Studfield Hill.—3F 85
Stumperlowe.—5E 97
Summerfield.—3A 98
Sunnyfields.—2F 31
Sunnyside.—5C 20
(Doncaster)
SUNNYSIDE. (S66).—3G 81
(Rotherham)
Swallow Hill.—6E 7
SWALLOWNEST. (S31).—6A 104
Swinton Bridge.—2C 56
SWINTON. (S64).—2B 56

TANKERSLEY. (S75).—1D 50
Tapton.—5C 132
Tapton Hill.—3G 97
Templeborough.—6H 77
The Brecks.—5C 80
The Cross.—2G 75
Thorn Hill.—1C 78
Thorpe Common.—4B 66
THORPE HESLEY. (S61).—2B 66
Throapham.—2F 107
THRYBERGH. (S65).—4D 70
THURCROFT. (S66).—4A 94
Thurnscoe East.—1G 29
THURNSCOE. (S63).—1E 29
Tiltshills.—1A 18
Tinsley.—1B 89
TODWICK. (S31).—2A 118
Tofts.—1C 96
Toll Bar.—2A 18
Totley.—5D 120
Totley Brook.—4E 121
TOTLEY RISE. (S17).—4G 121

INDEX TO STREETS

HOW TO USE THIS INDEX

1. Each street name is followed by its Postal District and then by its map page reference; e.g. Abbey Brook Clo. S8—6C 110 is in the Sheffield 8 Postal District and it is to be found in square 6C on page 110. However, with the now general usage of Postal Coding, it is not recommended that this index should be used as a means of addressing mail.

2. A strict alphabetical order is followed in which Av., Rd., St. etc. (even though abbreviated) are read in full and as part of the street name; e.g. Abbots Rd. appears after Abbotsford Dri. but before Abbott St.

3. Streets & Subsidiary names not shown on the Maps, appear in the Index in Italics with the thoroughfare to which it is connected shown in brackets.

4 The Postcode for any Town or locality used in Postal addresses can be found in the Index to Places on pages 144, 145 & 146 or the Postcode Map on pages 142 & 143

GENERAL ABBREVIATIONS

All : Alley	Cotts : Cottages	Junct : Junction	Rd : Road
App : Approach	Ct : Court	La : Lane	S : Sheffield
Arc : Arcade	Cres : Crescent	Lit : Little	S : South
Av : Avenue	DN : Doncaster	Lwr : Lower	Sq : Square
Bk : Back	Dri : Drive	Mnr : Manor	Sta : Station
Boulevd : Boulevard	E : East	Mans : Mansions	St : Street
Bri : Bridge	Embkmt : Embankment	Mkt : Market	Ter : Terrace
B'way : Broadway	Est : Estate	M : Mews	Up : Upper
Bldgs : Buildings	Gdns : Gardens	Mt : Mount	Vs : Villas
Chu : Church	Ga : Gate	N : North	WF : Wakefield
Chyd : Churchyard	Gt : Great	Pal : Palace	Wlk : Walk
Circ : Circle	Grn : Green	Pde : Parade	W : West
Cir : Circus	Gro : Grove	Pk : Park	Yd : Yard
Clo : Close	Ho : House	Pas : Passage	
Comn : Common	Ind : Industrial	Pl : Place	

Abbey Brook Clo. S8—6C 110
Abbey Brook Ct. S8—6C 110
Abbey Brook Dri. S8—6C 110
Abbey Brook Gdns. S8—6C 110
Abbey Clo. S31—6F 95
Abbey Ct. S8—6C 110
Abbey Cres. S7—6H 109
Abbey Croft. S7—6H 109
Abbey Croft. S41—4C 130
Abbeydale Pk. Cres. S17
 —3F 121
Abbeydale Pk. Rise. S17
 —2E 121
Abbeydale Rd. S7
 —4B 110 to 5E 99
Abbeydale Rd. S. S17 & S7
 —4F 121
Abbeyfield Rd. S4—4F 87
Abbey Grange. S7—6H 109
Abbey Grn. S75—3C 22
Abbey La. S11, S7 & S8—4G 109
Abbey La. S31—4G 95
Abbey La. S71—6E 15
Abbey Sq. S71—3E 15
Abbey View Dri. S8—4E 111
Abbey View Rd. S8—4E 111
Abbey Wlk. DN5—4G 31
Abbey Way. S31—4B 106
Abbotsford Dri. S66—5A 94
Abbots Meadow. S19—6G 115
Abbots Rd. S71—3F 15
Abbott St. DN4—1B 46
Abdy La. S64—3E 55
Abdy Rd. S61—5F 67
Abdy Rd. S62—4C 54
Abell St. S65—5C 70
Aberconway Cres. DN11
 —5C 62

Abercorn Rd. DN2—5A 34
Abercrombie St. S41—1A 138
Aberford Gro. S74—5D 38
Abingdon Gdns. S61—4B 68
Abingdon Rd. DN2—4H 33
Abney Clo. S14—1G 111
Abney Clo. S40—5E 131
Abney Dri. S14—1G 111
Abney Rd. S14—1G 111
Abney St. S1—3C 4 & 2D 98
Abus Rd. DN5—1E 31
Acacia Av. S30—3D 64
Acacia Av. S66—4G 81
 (Bramley)
Acacia Av. S66—4D 82
 (Maltby)
Acacia Cres. S31—3H 125
Acacia Gro. DN12—5C 58
Acacia Gro. S72—3C 10
Acacia Rd. DN4—3D 48
Acacia Rd. S5—5A 76
Acer Clo. S31—4F 119
 (Anston)
Acer Clo. S31—4A 126
 (Killamarsh)
Ackworth Dri. S9—2H 89
Acorn Croft. S61—5B 68
Acorn Dri. S6—5C 84
Acorn Hill. S6—4D 84
Acorn St. S3—6E 87
Acorn Way. S6—5B 84
Acre Clo. DN3—5D 20
Acre Clo. S66—2E 83
Acre Ga. S30—1B 64
Acre La. S30—1A 72
Acres Hill La. S9—2D 100
Acres Hill Rd. S9—1D 100
Acres View Clo. S41—4H 131

Adastral Av. S12—5C 112
Addison Rd. S5—1H 87
Addison Rd. S64—6F 43
Addison Rd. S66—4D 82
Addison Sq. S31—4F 107
Addy Clo. S6—6C 86
Addy Dri. S6—6C 86
Addy St. S6—6C 86
Adelaide Rd. S7—1B 110
Adelaide St. S66—6H 83
Adelphi St. S6—6C 86
Adkins Dri. S5—6C 74
Adkins Rd. S5—6C 74
Adlard Rd. DN2—3H 33
Adlington Cres. S5—5D 74
Adlington Rd. S5—5D 74
Admirals Crest. S61—5D 66
Adrian Cres. S5—5E 75
Adsetts St. S4—2A 88
Adwick Av. DN5—2H 17
Adwick La. DN6—1E 17
Adwick Rd. S64—4D 42 to 1F 57
Agden Rd. S7—5C 98
Agnes Rd. S70—1G 23
Agnes Rd. S75—5C 6
Agnes Ter. S70—1G 23
Ainsdale Av. S63—5F 29
Ainsdale Clo. S71—1D 8
Ainsdale Ct. S71—1D 14
Ainsdale Rd. S71—1D 8
Ainsley Rd. S10—1A 98
Ainsty Rd. S7—6D 98
Ainthorpe Rd. DN5—2H 17
Aintree Av. DN4—1B 48
Aintree Clo. DN5—4F 31
Aintree Dri. S64—5F 43
Aire Clo. S30—1D 64
Airedale Rd. S6—1G 85

Airedale Rd. S75—5A 6
Aireton Clo. S66—4E 81
Aireton Rd. S70—5G 13
Air Mount Clo. S66—5E 81
Aisby Dri. DN11—3E 63
Aisthorpe Rd. S8—4D 110
Aitken Rd. S62—5C 56
Aizlewood Rd. S8—6D 98
 (in two parts)
Akley Bank Clo. S17—4F 121
Alan Rd. S75—5B 6
Alba Clo. S73—3C 26
Albanus Croft. S6—5C 84
Albanus Ridge. S6—5C 84
Albany Av. S30—3F 65
Albany Clo. S73—3G 25
Albany La. DN11—4C 62
Albany Rd. DN4—3A 46
Albany Rd. S7—6D 98
Albany Rd. S30—3D 140
Albany Rd. S62—4B 56
Albany St. S65—3E 79
Albert Av. S43—1D 132
Albert Cres. S72—2H 27
Albert Rd. S8—1E 111
Albert Rd. S12—4B 114
Albert Rd. S62—3F 69
Albert Rd. S63—4G 29
 (Goldthorpe)
Albert Rd. S63—4D 40
 (Wath upon Dearne)
Albert Rd. S64—6E 43
Albert St. S31—6D 124
Albert St. S60—3C 78
Albert St. S63—1E 29
Albert St. S64—1B 56
Albert St. S66—5H 83
Albert St. S70—6H 13

Albert St. S72—4C 10
Albert St. E. S70—6H 13
Albert St. N. S41—2H 131
Albert Ter. Rd. S6—6C 86
Albion Dri. S63—1H 29
Albion Ho. S70—1H 23
Albion Pl. DN1—6E 33
Albion Rd. S40—2H 137
Albion Rd. S60—3E 79
Albion Rd. S71—6E 9
Albion Row. S6—1D 96
Albion St. S6—1C 98
Albion Ter. DN4—2B 46
Albion Ter. S70—1B 24
Alcester Rd. S7—6D 98
Aldam Clo. S17—5E 121
Aldam Clo. S65—2B 80
Aldam Croft. S17—5E 121
Aldam Rd. DN4—5G 45
Aldam Rd. S17—5F 121
Aldam Way. S17—5E 121
Aldbury Clo. S71—1B 14
Aldcliffe Cres. DN4—1F 61
Aldene Av. S6—2F 85
Aldene Glade. S6—2F 85
Aldene Rd. S6—1F 85
Alder Clo. S75—4E 7
Alder Gro. DN4—4A 46
Alder Gro. S73—5D 26
Alder La. S9—2G 101
Alder M. S74—6A 38
Alderney Rd. S2—6E 99
Aldersgate Clo. DN11—6E 63
Aldersgate Ct. S66—4H 83
Alders Grn. S6—2D 84
Alderson Av. S62—6F 55
Alderson Clo. S31—4B 104
Alderson Dri. DN2—6F 33
Alderson Dri. S71—1A 14
Alderson Pl. S2—5E 99
Alderson Rd. S2—5E 99
Alderson Rd. N. S2—5E 99
Alders, The. S42—6A 136
Aldervale Clo. S64—5B 56
Aldesworth Rd. DN4—2C 48
Aldfield Way. S5—2F 87
Aldham Cotts. S73—4A 26
Aldham Cres. S73—3G 25
Aldham Ho. La. S73—5H 25
Aldham Ind. Est. S73—4A 26
Aldine Ct. S1—3F 5
Aldred Clo. S31—1C 126
Aldred Clo. S66—4F 81
Aldred Rd. S10—6A 86
Aldred Rd. S70—6G 13
Aldred St. S65—4E 79
Aldrin Way. S66—3E 83
Aldwarke La. S65—5H 69
Aldwarke Rd. S62—4F 69
Alexander St. DN5—6B 18
Alexandra Clo. S61—1G 77
Alexandra Rd. DN4—3B 46
Alexandra Rd. DN5—5B 18
Alexandra Rd. DN6—1F 17
Alexandra Rd. S2—6F 99
Alexandra Rd. S18—1F 129
Alexandra Rd. S31—5A 104
Alexandra Rd. S64—6F 43
Alexandra Rd. E. S41—3C 138
Alexandra Rd. W. S40—2H 137
Alexandra St. S66—6H 83
Alexandra Ter. S71—1F 25
Alford Av. S30—2D 72
Alfred Rd. S9—4B 88
(in two parts)
Alfred St. S71—1G 9
Algar Clo. S2—6A 100
Algar Cres. S2—6B 100

Algar Dri. S2—6A 100
Algar Pl. S2—6A 100
Algar Rd. S2—6A 100
Alhambra Shopping Centre.
S70—6H 13
Alice Rd. S61—2B 78
Aliott Clo. S65—1H 81
Alison Clo. S31—6B 104
Alison Cres. S2—4D 100
Alison Dri. S31—6B 104
Allan St. S65—3E 79
Allatt Clo. S70—1H 23
Alldred Cres. S64—4A 56
Allenby Cres. DN11—5C 62
Allenby Dri. S8—2C 122
Allendale. S70—4C 24
Allendale Ct. S70—4C 24
Allendale Dri. S74—6A 38
Allendale Rd. DN5—6H 31
Allendale Rd. S65—5A 80
Allendale Rd. S74—6H 37
Allendale Rd. S75—3G 13
(Barnsley)
Allendale Rd. S75—5B 6
(Darton)
Allende Way. S9—5D 88
Allen Rd. S19—5F 115
Allen St. S3—1C 4 & 1D 98
Allerton St. DN1—5D 32
Allestree Dri. S18—2A 128
All Hallows Dri. S66—5E 83
Alliance St. S4—4H 87
Alliss Rd. DN3—3H 49
Allott Cres. S74—4C 38
Allotts Ct. S70—4C 36
Allott St. S74—6C 38
(Elsecar)
Allott St. S74—6F 37
(Hoyland)
Allpits Rd. S44—2F 139
All Saints Clo. S63—5E 41
All Saints Sq. S60—3D 78
All Saints Sq. S64—2C 58
All Saints Way. S31—6D 104
Allsopps Yd. S74—2H 37
Allsops Pl. S41—3H 131
Allt St. S62—3F 69
Alma Cres. S18—6E 123
Alma Rd. S30—6B 50
Alma Rd. S60—4D 78
Alma Row. S60—2A 92
Alma St. S3—6E 87
Alma St. S70—6F 13
Alma St. S73—1F 39
Alma St. W. S40—3G 137
Almholme La. DN5—4E 19
Almond Av. DN3—2F 35
Almond Av. S72—6B 10
Almond Clo. S44—2G 139
Almond Clo. S66—4E 83
Almond Cres. S43—1A 0
Almond Dri. S31—4A 126
Almond Glade. S66—6G 81
Almond Pl. S43—4E 133
Almond Pl. S63—6F 41
Almond Rd. DN4—3D 48
Almond Tree Rd. S31—5E 117
Alms Hill Cres. S11—4F 109
Alms Hill Dri. S11—4F 109
Alms Hill Glade. S11—4F 109
Alms Hill Rd. S11—4F 109
Almshouses. S62—4C 52
Alney Pl. S6—5A 74
Alnwick Dri. S12—2E 113
Alnwick Rd. S12—2C 112
Alperton Clo. S71—2F 15
Alpha Rd. S65—2H 79
Alpha St. DN5—2H 17

Alpine Clo. S30—3C 140
Alpine Rd. S6—6B 86
Alpine Rd. S30—3C 140
Alport Av. S12—3G 113
Alport Dri. S12—2G 113
Alport Gro. S12—2G 113
Alport Pl. S12—3G 113
Alport Rise. S18—1B 128
Alport Rd. S12—2G 113
Alric Dri. S60—2B 90
Alsing Rd. S9—6E 77
Alston Clo. DN4—4B 48
Alston Rd. DN4—5B 48
Alton Clo. S11—5G 109
Alton Clo. S18—3B 128
Alton Clo. S42—5D 136
Alton Way. S75—4E 7
Alum Chine Clo. S41—5C 138
Alvaston Wlk. DN12—2C 58
Alverley La. DN4—1G 61
Alverley View. DN11—2G 61
Alwyn Av. DN5—2G 31
Amalfi Clo. S73—4D 26
Ambassador Gdns. DN3—4G 35
Amber Cres. S40—4E 137
Amberley St. S9—3C 88
Ambler Rise. S31—6A 104
Ambleside Clo. S19—3E 125
Ambleside Clo. S41—4E 131
Ambleside Clo. S60—3A 90
Ambleside Cres. DN5—2C 44
Ambleside Gro. S71—1G 25
Ambleside Wlk. S31—1H 119
Amen Corner. S60—2C & 2D 78
(in two parts)
America La. S62—4B 54
Amersall Cres. DN5—1G 31
Amersall Rd. DN5—1G 31
Amesbury Clo. S41—4G 131
Amory's Holt Clo. S66—2E 83
Amory's Holt Dri. S66—2E 83
Amory's Holt Rd. S66—2E 83
Amory's Holt Way. S66—2E 83
Amos Rd. S9—1D 88
Anchorage Cres. DN5—5A 32
Anchorage La. DN5—5H 31
Ancona Rise. S73—4D 26
Ancote Clo. S75—6C 12
Anderson Clo. S43—1E 133
Anderson La. S43—6F 133
Andover Dri. S3—5E 87
Andover St. S3—5F 87
Andrew La. S3—1G 5
Andrew St. S3—6F 87
Anelay Rd. DN4—4H 45
Anfield Rd. DN4—4C 48
Angel La. S62—5H 53
Angel St. S3—2F 5 & 1F 99
Angel St. S63—2B 42
Angel Yd. S40—2A 138
Angerford Av. S8—3E 111
Anglesey Rd. S18—3E 129
Angleton Av. S2—5E 101
Angleton Gdns. S2—5E 101
Angleton Grn. S2—5E 101
Angram Rd. S30—5B 50
Annat Pl. S30—6A 50
Annesley Clo. S8—2D 122
Annesley Clo. S41—5C 138
Annesley Rd. S8—1D 122
Anne St. S31—2F 107
Anns Rd. S2—6E 99
Anns Rd. N. S2—6F 99
Ann St. S62—4F 69
Ansdell Rd. DN5—5B 18
Ansell Rd. S11—1G 109
Anson Gro. S60—3D 90
Anson St. S2—3H 5 & 2G 99

Ansten Cres. DN4—3C 48
Anston Av. S31—4A 118
Anston Clo. S31—1F 119
Antrim Av. S10—3B 98
Anvil Clo. S6—5E 85
Anvil Cres. S30—1F 75
Apley Rd. DN1—1D 46
Apollo St. S62—6H 55
Apostle Clo. DN4—5G 45
Appleby Rd. DN2—5A 34
Appleby Wlk. S31—6F 107
Applegarth Clo. S12—1C 112
Applegarth Dri. S12—1C 112
Applehaigh View. S71—1C 8
Appleton Way. DN5—1H 31
Appleton Way. S70—4A 24
Appletree Dri. S18—2E 129
April Clo. S71—3D 14
April Dri. S71—3D 14
Aqueduct St. S71—4H 13
Arbour Clo. S41—6D 138
Arbour Cres. S66—5B 94
Arbour Dri. S66—5B 94
Arbour La. S65—4H 71
Arbourthorne. S2—4A 100
Arbourthorne Est. S2—1A 112
Arbourthorne Rd. S2
—6H 99 to 2B 112
Arcade, The. S9—6E 77
Arcade, The. S70—6H 13
Archdale Clo. S2—5D 100
Archdale Pl. S2—5C 100
Archdale Rd. S2—4C 100
Archer Ga. S6—2D 84
Archer Ho. S65—2E 79
Archer La. S7—2B 110
Archer Rd. S8—4B 110
Archery Clo. S66—6F 81
Archibald Rd. S7—1C 110
Archibald Way. S3—3C 98
Arcon Pl. S62—1G 69
Arcubus Av. S31—5B 104
Ardeen Rd. DN2—5G 33
Arden Clo. S40—1E 137
Arden Clo. S65—1H 79
Arden Ga. DN4—1F 61
Ardmore St. S6—6C 88
Ardsley Av. S31—6C 104
Ardsley Clo. S19—5H 113
Ardsley Dri. S19—5H 113
Ardsley Gro. S19—5H 113
Ardsley M. S71—1G 25
Ardsley Rd. S40—2D 136
Ardsley Rd. S70—4C 24
Argyle Clo. S8—2F 111
Argyle La. DN11—4C 62
Argyle Rd. S8—2E 111
Argyle St. S64—6E 43
Argyll Av. DN2—4H 33
Arklow Clo. S41—5B 138
Arklow Rd. DN2—5G 33
Arksey Comn. La. DN5—5E 19
Arksey La. DN5—6B 18
Arkwright Rd. DN5—4H 31
Arley St. S2—4E 99
Arlington Av. S31—5D 104
Armer St. S60—3C 78
Armitage Rd. DN4—4H 45
Armitage Rd. S30—4F 141
Armley Rd. S9—3C 88
Armroyd La. S74—1A 52
Arms Park Dri. S19—3F 125
Armstead Rd. S19—4G 115
Armstrong Wlk. S66—3E 83
Armthorpe La. DN2—4G 33
Armthorpe La. DN3
—1E to 4F 21

Armthorpe Rd. DN2
—4G 33 to 3C 34
Armthorpe Rd. S11—5F 97
Army Row. S71—1F 9
Armytage Ind. Est. S41—3C 132
Arncliffe Dri. S30—1D 64
Arncliffe Dri. S70—1D 22
Arndale Precinct. S66—4G 83
Arnold Av. S12—5C 112
Arnold Av. S71—5B 8
Arnold Cres. S64—5E 43
Arnold St. S65—3H 79
Arnold St. S6—4A 86
Arnside Clo. S41—2F 131
Arnside Rd. S8—2C 110
Arnside Rd. S66—3G 83
Arnside Ter. S8—2C 110
Arran Hill. S65—4D 70
Arran Rd. S10—2H 97
Arras St. S9—6B 88
Arren Clo. DN3—1H 21
Arrowsmith Ho. S65—2E 79
(off Carlisle St.)
Arthington St. S8—1E 111
Arthur Av. DN5—5C 18
Arthur Pl. DN5—5C 18
Arthur Rd. S30—3C 140
Arthur St. DN5—5C 18
Arthur St. S31—6B 104
Arthur St. S60—2C 78
Arthur St. S62—6G 55
Arthur St. S70—4A 24
Artisan View. S8—1E 111
Arundel Av. S60—1E 103
Arundel Av. S65—6B 70
Arundel Clo. S18—2B 128
Arundel Clo. S41—3H 131
Arundel Cotts. S60—1E 103
Arundel Ct. S11—3F 109
Arundel Cres. S60—1E 103
Arundel Gdns. DN5—1H 31
Arundel La. S1—5E 5 & 3E 99
Arundel La. S1—5F 5 & 3F 99
(in two parts)
Arundel Dri. S71—2F 15
Arundel Rd. S30—1E 65
Arundel Rd. S60—1E 103
Arundel Rd. S65—4F 79
Arundel St. S1—6E 5 & 3E 99
Arundel St. S60—1E 103
Arundel View. S74—4C 38
Ascension Clo. S66—5H 83
Ascot Av. DN4—2B 48
Ascot Clo. S64—5F 43
Ascot Dri. DN5—3F 31
Ascot St. S2—4E 99
Ashberry Gdns. S6—6B 86
Ashberry Rd. S6—6B 86
Ashbourne Clo. S40—6C 130
Ashbourne Gro. S13—4H 101
Ashbourne Gro. S30—3E 73
Ashbourne Rd. S13—4H 101
Ashbourne Rd. S71—6C 8
Ashburnham Gdns. DN5—6G 31
Ashburton Clo. DN6—1C 16
Ashbury Dri. S8—5G 111
Ashbury La. S8—5G 111
Ashby Ct. S70—1F 23
Ash Clo. S31—4A 126
Ash Clo. S65—5B 80
Ash Cotts. S73—3G 25
Ash Cres. S30—3F 141
Ash Cres. S31—6G 125
Ash Cres. S64—5C 42
Ashcroft Clo. DN12—4A 60
Ashcroft Cotts. S62—5B 52
Ashcroft Dri. S41—1B 132
Ashdale Clo. DN3—6D 20

Ash Dale Rd. DN4—1B 60
Ashdell. S10—3A 98
Ashdell La. S10—3A 98
Ashdell Rd. S10—3A 98
Ashdene Ct. S64—5B 56
Ashdown Dri. S40—4F 137
Ashdown Gdns. S19—4G 115
Ashdown Pl. DN5—1H 31
Ash Dyke Clo. S75—6F 9
Asher Rd. S7—5D 98
Ashes La. S62—5B 52
Ashfield Clo. DN3—4G 35
Ashfield Clo. S12—3B 112
Ashfield Clo. S75—4E 13
Ashfield Dri. S12—3B 112
Ashfield Rd. DN4—5A 46
Ashfield Rd. S30—3F 141
Ashfield Rd. S41—5D 138
Ashford Clo. S18—3B 128
Ashford Rd. S11—5B 98
Ashford Rd. S18—2B 128
Ashfurlong Clo. S17—2F 121
Ashfurlong Dri. S17—2F 121
Ashfurlong Rd. S17—2F 121
Ashgate Av. S40—2E 137
Ashgate Clo. S10—3A 98
Ashgate La. S10—3A 98
Ashgate Rd. S10—3A 98
Ashgate Rd. S42 & S40—1B 136
Ashgate Valley Rd. S40—1F 137
Ash Gro. DN3—2G 35
Ash Gro. DN12—4C 58
Ash Gro. S10—3B 98
Ash Gro. S31—4G 117
Ash Gro. S62—2H 69
Ash Gro. S66—3H 83
(Maltby)
Ash Gro. S66—4G 81
(Wickersley)
Ash Gro. S70—2D 24
Ash Ho. La. S17—6D 108
Ashland Ct. S7—1C 110
Ashland Rd. S7—1C 110
Ashland Rd. S31—6E 125
Ash La. S30—3G 141
Ashleigh. S72—2G 11
Ashleigh Clo. S41—1B 132
Ashleigh Gdns. S61—5B 68
Ashley Clo. S31—3B 126
Ashley Croft. S71—1D 8
Ashley Gro. S31—6B 104
Ashley Ind. Est. S60—2D 78
Ashley La. S31—3B 126
Ashmore Av. S31—6G 125
Ash Mt. S72—1C 10
Ashover Clo. S70—5A 24
Ashover Rd. S43—5A 134
Ashpool Clo. S13—1A 114
Ash Ridge. S64—3B 56
Ash Rd. S63—6G 41
Ash Rd. S72—3D 10
Ash Row. S71—6C 14
Ash St. S6—5C 86
Ash St. S19—1C 124
Ash St. S73—3G 25
Ashton Av. DN5—1F 31
Ashton Clo. S31—3A 126
Ashton Clo. S40—5E 137
Ash Tree Clo. S40—2E 137
Ashurst Clo. S6—5E 85
Ashurst Clo. S40—6B 130
Ashurst Dri. S6—4E 85
Ashurst Pl. S6—5E 85
Ashurst Rd. S6—4E 85
Ash Vale. S40—2D 136
Ash Vale W. S40—2D 136
Ash View. S30—3D 64

Ash View. S61—4B 68
Ashville. DN11—5E 63
Ashwell Rd. S13—1A 114
Ashwood Clo. S30—5A 50
Ashwood Ct. S70—5B 24
Ashwood Ho. DN6—2E 17
Ashwood Rd. S30—6A 50
Ashwood Rd. S62—3F 69
Ashworth Dri. S61—5F 67
Askam Ct. S66—3H 81
Askam Rd. S66—3H 81
Askern Ho. DN1—1C 46
(off Oxford Pl.)
Askern Rd. DN5—2H 17 to 6B 18
Askew Ct. S30—4E 141
Askrigg Clo. DN4—4D 48
Asline Rd. S2—5E 99
Aspen Clo. DN3—6D 20
Aspen Clo. S31—3A 126
Aspen Rd. S31—6G 125
Aspen Wlk. S66—4C 82
Aspen Way. S64—5A 56
Aspley Clo. S40—6G 131
Asquith Rd. DN5—6B 18
Asquith Rd. S9—5D 76
Aster Clo. S19—4F 115
Aster Clo. S31—3F 119
Aston Clo. S18—6G 123
Aston Clo. S31—4B 104
Aston Ct. S43—1D 134
Aston Dri. S71—1A 14
Aston La. S31—3B 104
Aston Relief Rd. S13 & S31
—5G 103
Aston St. S2—1H 99
Astwell Gdns. S30—1C 64
Athelstan Clo. S13—6D 100
Athelstan Cres. DN3—4D 20
Athelstane Dri. S66—6A 94
Athelstane Rd. DN12—3D 58
Athelstan Rd. S13—4G 101
Athersley Cres. S71—1A 14
Athersley Gdns. S19—5A 114
Athersley Rd. S71—1B 14
Atherton Clo. S2—1B 112
Atherton Rd. S2—1B 112
Atholl Clo. S42—5D 136
Atholl Cres. DN2—4A 34
Athol Rd. S8—3C 110
Athorpe Gro. S31—4E 107
Athron Dri. S65—5A 80
Athron St. DN1—5E 33
Atkin Pl. S2—5E 99
Atlantic Cres. S8—3C 122
Atlantic Dri. S8—3C 122
Atlantic Rd. S8—3B 122
Atlantic Wlk. S8—3C 122
Atlantic Way. S8—3C 122
Atlas St. S4—5H 87
Atlas St. S60—2C 90
Atlow Clo. S40—6D 130
Atrium. S19—5E 115
Atterby Dri. DN11—3E 63
Attercliffe Comn. S9—4C 88
Attercliffe Rd. S4 & S9—6H 87
Attlee Av. DN11—4B 62
Attlee Clo. S66—5H 83
Attlee Cres. S73—6G 27
Attlee Rd. S43—4H 133
Aubretia Av. S60—4D 90
Auburn Dri. DN12—3B 60
Auckland Av. S6—3E 85
Auckland Dri. S19—3D 124
Auckland Rise. S19—3E 125
Auckland Rd. DN2—4E 33
Auckland Rd. S64—6F 43
Auckland's Pl. S40—3A 138
Auckland Way. S19—3E 125

Audrey Rd. S13—6E 101
Aughton Av. S31—4A 104
Aughton Clo. S13—6F 101
Aughton Cres. S13—5E 101
Aughton Dri. S13—5E 101
Aughton La. S31—5C 104
Aughton Rd. S31—5A 104
Augustus Rd. S60—1C 90
Aukley Rd. S8—2D 110
Aunby Dri. S31—5B 104
Austen Av. DN4—5G 45
Austen Dri. S66—4H 81
Austerfield Av. DN5—2A 32
Austin Clo. S6—3E 85
Austin Ct. S6—2E 85
Austwick Clo. DN4—1F 61
Austwick Clo. S75—3E 7
Austwick Wlk. S70—5G 13
Autumn Clo. S66—5C 94
Autumn Dri. S66—3G 83
Avenue 1. S41—5B 138
Avenue 2. S41—5B 138
Avenue 3. S41—5B 138
Avenue 4. S41—5B 138
Avenue 5. S41—5B 138
Avenue 6. S41—5B 138
Avenue 7. S41—5B 138
Avenue 8. S41—5B 138
Avenue Ct. S10—5G 97
Avenue Rd. DN2—4E 33
Avenue Rd. S7—1D 110
Avenue Rd. S41—3A 132
Avenue S63—5G 41
Avenue, The. DN4—2A 48
Avenue, The. DN5—6C 18
(Bentley)
Avenue, The. DN5—1F 43
(Harlington)
Avenue, The. S9—1E 101
Avenue, The. S18—1F 129
Avenue, The. S19—3F 115
Avenue, The. S66—2E 95
Avenue, The. S71—1G 9
Avenue, The. S75—5B 36
Aviemore Rd. DN4—5G 45
Avill Way. S66—6F 81
Avisford Dri. S5—6B 74
Avisford Rd. S5—5B 74
Avoca Av. DN2—5G 33
Avocet Way. S61—1B 66
Avon Clo. S18—6F 123
Avon Clo. S66—3F 83
Avon Clo. S73—2H 39
Avon Clo. S75—4A 12
Avondale Dri. S71—4E 9
Avondale Rd. DN1—6G 33
Avondale Rd. S6—3H 85
Avondale Rd. S40—1H 137
Avondale Rd. S43—5B 134
Avondale Rd. S61—2A 78
Avon Gro. S30—1C 64
Avon Mt. S61—2A 78
Avon St. S71—6A 14
Axholme Ct. DN2—5F 33
Axholme Rd. DN2—4E 33
Axle La. S31—3D 118
Aylesbury Ct. S9—5D 76
Aylesbury Cres. S9—6D 76
Aylesbury Rd. DN2—5H 33
Aylesford Clo. S71—4H 13
Aylsham Rd. S31—6C 104
Aylward Clo. S2—6B 100
Aylward Rd. S2—6B 100
Aymer Dri. S66—5A 94
Ayrsome Wlk. DN4—3C 48
Aysgarth Av. S71—1H 25
Aysgarth Clo. DN4—4D 48
Aysgarth Rise. S41—5A 104

Aysgarth Rd. S6—4A 74
Ayton Wlk. DN5—5A 18
Azalea Clo. S31—4F 119

Babington Cres. S2—6B 100
Babur Rd. S4—5H 87
Backfield Rise. S30—1E 65
Backfields. S1—4D 4 & 2E 99
Back La. DN5—4D 30
Back La. DN12—6A 60
Back La. S10—1F 97
Back La. S17—4F 121
Back La. S30—2A 140
Back La. S31—1G 119
  (Anston)
Back La. S31—5A 124
  (Eckington)
Back La. S44—4H 139
Back La. S62—1C 68
Back La. S65—3D 70
Back La. S66—6A 82
Back La. S71—2C 14
Back La. S72—2B 28
Back La. W. S71—1C 8
Backmoor Cres. S8—5G 111
Backmoor Rd. S8—5G 111
Back Poplar Ter. S71—1G 9
Back Row. DN3—2F 49
Backside La. DN4—5F 45
Bacon La. S9—6A 88
Bacons La. S40—5H 137
Baden Powell Av. S40—4H 137
Baden Powell Rd. S40—3A 138
Baden St. S60—2C 78
Baden St. S70—5B 24
Badger Clo. S13—6C 102
Badger Clo. S42—5D 136
Badger Dri. S13—6C 102
Badger La. S1—3C 4
Badger Pl. S13—6C 102
Badger Rise. S13—6C 102
Badger Rd. S13—6C 102
Badsley Ct. S65—3G 79
Badsley Moor La. S65—4F 79
Badsley St. S65—3F 79
Badsley St. S. S65—4F 79
Badsworth Clo. S73—1H 39
Badsworth Rd. DN4—6F 45
Bage Hill. S42—6A 136
Bagger Wood Hill. S75—6A 22
Bagger Wood Rd. S75—6A 22
Bagley Rd. S4—2H 87
Bagshaw's Rd. S12—1D 112
Bagshot St. S11—5B 98
Bahram Gro. DN11—5C 62
Bahram Rd. DN4—3A 48
Bailey Dri. S31—1C 126
Bailey La. S1—3C 4 & 2D 98
Bailey St. S1—3D 4 & 2E 99
Bainbridge Rd. DN4—2B 46
Baines Av. DN12—4A 60
Baines Wood Clo. S41—3E 131
Bainton Dri. S70—2F 23
Bakehouse La. S31—6D 124
Bakehouse La. S75—4D 12
Baker Dri. S31—3A 126
Bakers Hill. S1—3G 5
Bakers La. S1—2D 4 & 1E 99
Baker St. S9—5B 88
Baker St. S70—6H 13
Bakewell Rd. S43—6A 134
Bakewell Rd. S71—1A 14
Balaclava La. S6—5C 86
Balaclava Rd. S6—5C 86
Bala St. S71—6H 13
Balby Carr Bank. DN4—3C 46
Balby Rd. DN4—3B 46

Balcarres Rd. DN11—4D 62
Baldwin Av. DN5—4A 32
Baldwin St. S9—6B 88
Balfour Rd. DN5—6C 18
Balfour Rd. S9—6D 88
Balk La. S10—1A 90
Balk La. S66—4H 81
Balk La. S70—2C 36
Balkley La. S73—4G 27
Balk, The. DN5—2D 18
Balk, The. S61—3B 68
Balk, The. S75—3G 7
Ballam Av. DN5—6G 17
Ballfield Av. S75—5A 6
Ballfield La. S75—5A 6
Ballfield Av. S13—4A 102
Ballfield Clo. S13—4B 102
Ballfield Cres. S13—4B 102
Ballfield Dri. S13—4B 102
Ballfield Pl. S13—4A 102
Ballfield Rise. S13—4B 102
Ballfield Rd. S13—4A 102
Ballfield Way. S13—4A 102
Ball St. S3—6D 86
Balmain Dri. S6—2H 85
Balmain Rd. S6—2H 85
Balmer La. S41—5C 132
Balmoak La. S41—5C 132
Balmoral Ct. S11—3F 109
Balmoral Cres. S18—1B 128
Balmoral Rd. DN2—5F 33
Balmoral Rd. S13—1C 114
Balmoral Way. S66—3H 81
Baltic Rd. S9—5B 88
Baltic Way. S9—5B 88
Bamford Av. S71—1A 14
Bamford Clo. S75—2A 22
Bamford Rd. S43—6H 133
Bamforth St. S6—4B 86
Bank Clo. S7—1C 110
Bank Clo. S61—6H 67
Bank Ct. S43—3D 132
Bank End Av. S70—4C 24
Bank End Rd. S70—4B 24
Bankfield La. S6—5C 84
Bankfield Rd. S6—3G 85
Bank Ho. Rd. S6—6A 86
Bank La. S30—6G 141
Bank Rd. S41—5A 132
Bank Sq. DN11—5C 62
Bank St. DN1—2C 46
Bank St. S1—2E 5 & 1F 99
Bank St. S31—2F 119
Bank St. S40—2G 137
Bank St. S43—3D 132
Bank St. S64—1E 57
Bank St. S70—2H 23
Bank St. S71—1E 25
Bank St. S72—6B 10
Bank St. S74—6H 37
Bank Ter. S10—2A 98
  (off Parker's La.)
Bank Top Rd. S65—5B 80
Bank View. S12—4C 114
Bank View. S60—2H 91
Bankwood Clo. S14—2H 111
Bank Wood Clo. S41—4D 130
Bankwood Cres. DN11—3B 62
Bankwood La. DN11—2B 62
Bankwood Rd. S14—2H 111
Banner Ct. S11—1H 109
Banner Cross Dri. S11—1H 109
Banner Cross Rd. S11—2H 109
Bannerdale Clo. S11—1A 110
Bannerdale Rd. S11 & S7
  —1A 110
Bannerdale View. S11—1A 110

Bannham Rd. S9—1F 101
Bannister Ho. DN2—3G 33
Bar Av. S75—5H 7
Barbados Way. S66—4A 82
Barber Balk Clo. S61—6H 67
Barber Balk Rd. S61—1H 77
Barber Clo. S31—2A 118
Barber Cres. S10—1B 98
Barber Pl. S10—1B 98
Barber Rd. S10—1B 98
Barber's Av. S62—2F 69
Barber's Cres. S62—2G 69
Barber's La. S31—1B 126
Barber's Path. S64—6D 42
Barber St. S74—5A 38
Barber Wood Rd. S61—2C 76
Barbon Clo. S40—6G 131
Barbot Hall Ind. Est. S61—5D 68
Barbot Hill Rd. S61—5C 68
Bard Ct. S2—3H 5
Barden Cres. S60—3C 90
Barden Dri. S75—4D 12
Bardolf Rd. DN4—2C 48
Bardon Rd. DN3—4D 20
Bard St. S2—2H 5 & 2G 99
Bardwell Rd. S3—5D 86
Barewell Hill. S72—1H 11
Barfield Av. S60—2G 91
Barfield Rd. S74—5A 38
Barholme Clo. S41—4D 130
Barholm Rd. S10—3F 97
Bari Clo. S73—3C 26
Baring Rd. S61—3D 76
Barkby Rd. S9—5C 76
Barker Field. S40—2F 137
Barker La. S40—2F 137
Barkers Croft. S61—4H 67
Barkers La. DN12—4H 59
Barker's Pl. S6—2A 86
Barker's Pool. S1—4D 4 & 2E 99
Barker's Rd. S7—1B 110
Barker St. S64—1C 56
Barkston Rd. S71—1C 14
Bar La. S75—5H 7
Barlborough Rd. S73—2G 39
Barlby Gro. S12—4C 114
Barleycroft La. S31—5F 107
Barley La. S42—6C 130
Barleywood Rd. S9—5E 89
Barlow Dri. S6—5G 85
Barlow Lees La. S18—6C 128
Barlow Rd. S6—5G 85
Barlow Rd. S41—2B 130
Barlow Rd. S43—2C 134
Barlow View. S18—4F 129
Barmouth Rd. S7—2C 110
Barnabas Wlk. S71—4H 13
Barnard Av. S18—6H 123
Barnardiston Rd. S9—6D 88
Barnburgh Ho. DN12—2C 60
Barnburgh La. S63—5G 29
Barnby Dun Rd. DN2
  —2A 34 to 5B 20
Barncliffe Clo. S10—5C 96
Barncliffe Cres. S10—4B 96
Barncliffe Dri. S10—4B 96
Barncliffe Glen. S10—5C 96
Barncliffe Rd. S10—4B 96
Barn Clo. S41—5F 131
Barnes Av. S18—1B 128
Barnes Ct. S2—6G 5 & 3F 99
Barnes Ct. S64—4A 56
  (off Lawrence Rd.)
Barnes Hall Rd. S30—3B 64
Barnes La. S18—5H 121
Barnes Rd. S41—4E 139
Barnet Av. S11—2E 109

Barnet Rd. S11—2E 109
Barnfield Av. S10—2E 97
Barnfield Clo. S10—2E 97
Barnfield Clo. S43—1C 134
Barnfield Dri. S10—3E 97
Barnfield Rd. S10—2E 97
Barnfield Ter. S43—1C 134
Barnfield Wlk. S43—1C 134
Barnham Clo. S40—5D 136
Barnsdale Av. S19—5A 114
Barnsley Av. DN12—3C 58
Barnsley Business &
  Innovation Centre. S75—3D 12
Barnsley Rd. DN5
  —2A 30 to 3G 31
Barnsley Rd. S4 & S5—3F 87
Barnsley Rd. S63
  —6A 52 to 2B 66
Barnsley Rd. S63—4D 28 to
  (Highgate, Goldthorpe) 4G 29
Barnsley Rd. S63—3C 40
  (Wath upon Dearne)
Barnsley Rd. S72—3E to 1H 11
  (Brierley)
Barnsley Rd. S72—1G 15
  (Cudworth)
Barnsley Rd. S73—2D 26
  (Darfield)
Barnsley Rd. S73—4H 25 &
  5A 26
(in three parts, Wombwell)
Barnsley Rd. S74—3H 37
Barnsley Rd. S75—5C 6 to 1A 12
  (Darton)
Barnsley Rd. S75—1B 22
  (Dodworth)
Barnsley Rd. WF4—1H 7
  (Grange Moor)
Barnsley Western Rf. Rd. S70
  —6G 13
Barnstone St. DN4—2A 46
Barnwell Cres. S73—4H 25
Baron St. S1—4E 99
Barrack La. S6—5C 86
Barracks Field Ter. S74—6C 38
Barracks Sq. S40—2A 138
Barratt Rd. S31—6D 124
Barrel La. DN4—5G 45
Barret Rd. DN4—2D 48
Barretta St. S4—2H 87
Barrie Cres. S5—1D 86
Barrie Dri. S5—6D 74
Barrie Gro. S66—5B 82
Barrie Rd. S5—5B 46
Barrie Rd. S5—6D 74
Barrowby Rd. S60—6H 79
Barrow Cottage. S62—4B 52
Barrow Field La. S62—3C 52
Barrowfield Rd. S74—4H 37
Barrow Hill. S62—4A 52
Barrow Rd. S9—5D 76
Barrow St. S43—1D 134
Barry Rd. S43—1F 139
Bartholomew St. S73—6A 26
Bartle Av. S12—3B 112
Bartle Dri. S12—3B 112
Bartle Rd. S12—3B 112
Bartlett Clo. S6—6C 84
Bartlett Rd. S5—5D 74
Bartle Way. S12—3B 112
Barton Av. S71—4A 8
Barton Cres. S40—5C 130
Barton La. DN3—3E 35
Barton Pl. DN12—4D 58
Barton Rd. S8—1E 111
Barugh Grn. Rd. S75—2A 12
Barugh La. S75—2A 12
Basegreen Av. S12—4D 112

Basegreen Clo. S12—4D 112
Basegreen Cres. S12—4D 112
Basegreen Dri. S12—4D 112
Basegreen Pl. S12—4D 112
Basegreen Rd. S12—4D 112
Basegreen Way. S12—4E 113
Basford Clo. S9—4E 89
Basford Dri. S9—6D 88
Basford Pl. S9—6E 89
Basford St. S9—6D 88
Basil Av. DN3—2C 34
Basildon Rd. S63—1E 29
Baslow Cres. S75—2A 22
Baslow Rd. S17
—6B 120 to 4F 121
Baslow Rd. S42—4A 136
Baslow Rd. S71—6D 8
Bassett Pl. S2—3H 99
Bassett Rd. S2—3A 100
Bassey Rd. DN3—3H 49
Bassingthorpe La. S61—6B 68
Bassledene Rd. S2—5C 100
Bass Ter. DN1—6E 33
Bastock Rd. S6—2B 86
Bateman Clo. S72—3F 9
Bateman Rd. S66—5A 82
(in two parts)
Bateman Sq. S63—1E 29
Batemoor Clo. S8—3E 123
Batemoor Dri. S8—3E 123
Batemoor Pl. S8—3E 123
Batemoor Rd. S8—3E 123
Batemoor Wlk. S8—3E 123
(off Batemoor Clo.)
Bates St. S10—6A 86
Bath St. S1—6B 4 & 3D 98
Battison La. S63—1D 54
Batt St. S8—5E 99
Batty Av. S72—1G 15
Batworth Dri. S5—3E 87
Batworth Rd. S5—3E 87
Bawtry Ga. S9—1G 89
Bawtry Rd. S9—1G 89
Bawtry Rd. S60—2A 90
Bawtry Rd. S66—5C 80 to 4B 82
Baxter Av. DN1—5E 33
Baxter Clo. S6—5A 74
Baxter Dri. S6—5A 74
Baxter Ga. DN1—6C 32
Baxter Rd. S6—5A 74
Bayardo Wlk. DN11—6D 62
Baycliff Clo. S71—1D 14
Bay Ct. S31—4A 126
Baysdale Croft. S19—2D 124
Bay Tree Av. S66—3F 81
Bazley Rd. S2—1B 112
Beacon Clo. S9—1B 88
Beacon Croft. S9—1B 88
Beacon Rd. S9—1B 88
Beaconsfield Rd. DN4—2A 46
Beaconsfield Rd. S60—6G 79
Beaconsfield St. S64—6D 42
Beaconsfield St. S70—1G 23
Beacon View. S74—6C 38
Beacon Way. S9—1B 88
Beancroft Clo. DN11—6H 61
Bear Tree Clo. S62—3F 69
Bear Tree Rd. S62—3F 69
Bear Tree St. S62—4F 69
Beauchamp Rd. S61—6H 67
Beauchief Abbey La. S8
—1A 122
Beauchief Clo. S30—4H 141
Beauchief Ct. S8—6C 110
Beauchief Dri. S8 & S17
—2A 122
Beauchief Rise. S8—6A 110

Beaufort Rd. DN2—5H 33
Beaufort Rd. S10—2B 98
Beaumont Av. DN6—1B 16
Beaumont Av. S2—3C 100
Beaumont Av. S70—6D 12
Beaumont Clo. S2—3D 100
Beaumont Cres. S2—3C 100
Beaumont Dri. S65—4H 79
Beaumont Rd. S75—6A 6
Beaumont Rd. N. S2—3C 100
Beaumont St. S74—6F 37
Beaumont Way. S2—3C 100
Beaver Av. S13—5B 102
Beaver Clo. S13—5B 102
Beaver Dri. S13—5B 102
Beaver Hill Rd. S13—5B 102
Beaver Pl. S40—3F 137
Beccles Way. S66—4H 81
Beck Clo. S5—2A 76
Beck Clo. S64—4B 56
Becket Av. S8—3B 122
Becket Cres. S8—3C 122
Becket Cres. S61—5F 67
Becket Rd. S8—3C 122
Beckett Hospital Ter. S70
—1H 23
Beckett Rd. DN2—4E to 2G 33
Beckett St. S71—5H 13
Becket Wlk. S8—3B 122
Beckfield Gro. S63—6D 28
Beckford La. S5—1H 75
Becknoll Rd. S73—3A 40
Beck Rd. S5—2H 75
Beckton Av. S19—5E 115
Beckton Ct. S19—5F 115
Beckton Gro. S19—5E 115
Beckwith Rd. S31—3C 106
Beckwith Rd. S65—2B 80
Bedale Rd. DN5—2F 31
Bedale Rd. S8—1D 110
Bedale Wlk. S72—2C 10
Bedford Clo. S31—6D 106
Bedford Dri. S30—1D 72
Bedford St. S6—6D 86
Bedford St. S66—5H 83
Bedford St. S70—2H 23
Bedford Ter. S71—2A 14
Bedgebury Clo. S19—6H 115
Bedgrave Clo. S31—1D 126
Beecham Ct. S64—4A 56
Beech Av. S62—2H 69
Beech Av. S65—5C 80
Beech Av. S72—5B 10
Beech Clo. S66—4D 82
Beech Clo. S72—2G 11
Beech Clo. S73—3F 39
Beech Cres. S31—6G 125
(Eckington)
Beech Cres. S31—4A 126
(Killamarsh)
Beech Cres. S64—6C 42
Beechcroft Rd. DN4—5G 45
Beechdale Clo. S40—1F 137
Beech Dri. DN3—2H 49
Beeches Av. S2—5G 99
Beeches Dri. S2—5G 99
Beeches Gro. S19—4G 115
Beeches Rd. S31—4F 117
Beeches, The. DN3—3D 20
Beeches, The. S64—3A 56
Beechfern Clo. S30—5B 50
Beechfield Rd. DN1—1D 46
Beech Gro. DN4—5E 45
Beech Gro. DN5—1B 32
Beech Gro. DN12—4D 58
Beech Gro. S31—6F 107
Beech Gro. S66—4G 81
Beech Gro. S70—2F 23

Beech Hill. DN12—3E 59
Beech Hill Rd. S10—3A 98
Beech Ho. Rd. S73—3F 39
Beech Rd. DN3—3F 35
Beech Rd. DN11—5E 63
'Beech Rd. S63—5G 41
Beech Rd. S66—4D 82
Beech Rd. S72—3D 10
Beech St. S43—2G 133
Beech St. S70—1H 23
Beechville Av. S64—4A 56
Beech Way. S18—6E 123
Beech Way. S31—5A 104
Beechwood Clo. DN3—6E 21
Beechwood Clo. S62—6H 55
Beechwood Clo. S62—2F 55
Beechwood Lodge Flats. S65
—2F 79
Beechwood Rd. S6—3H 85
Beechwood Rd. S18—2D 128
Beechwood Rd. S30—1C 64
(High Green)
Beechwood Rd. S30—4D 140
(Stocksbridge)
Beechwood Rd. S60—5G 79
Beechwood Wlk. DN12—4A 60
(off Broomvale Wlk)
Beehive Rd. S10—1B 98
Beehive Yd. S40—3F 137
Beeley Clo. S43—5A 134
Beeley Rd. S30—3E 73
Beeley St. S2—4D 98
Beeley Way. S43—6A 134
Beeston Clo. S18—1A 128
Beeston Sq. S71—5B 8
Beeton Rd. S8—2D 110
Beet St. S3—3B 4 & 2D 98
Beetwell St. S40—3A 138
Beever La. S75—4C 12
Beeversleigh. S65—3E 79
(off Clifton La.)
Beevers Rd. S61—5F 67
Beever St. S63—4H 29
Beevor Ct. S71—6A 14
Beevor St. S71—6B 14
Begonia Clo. S31—3F 119
Beighton Rd. S12—4B 114
Beighton Rd. S13—1C 114
Beighton Rd. S62—5C 56
Beighton Rd. E. S19—4D 114
Belcourt Rd. S65—5B 80
Beldon Clo. S2—6H 99
Beldon Pl. S2—6H 99
Beldon Rd. S2—6H 99
Belford Clo. S66—3G 81
Belford Dri. S66—2G 81
Belfry Gdns. DN4—4E 49
Belfry Way. S31—6G 107
Belgrave Dri. S10—4D 96
Belgrave Pl. S31—6B 104
Belgrave Rd. S10—4E 97
Belgrave Rd. S71—6A 14
Belgrave Sq. S2—5E 99
Belklane Dri. S31—2C 126
Bellamy Clo. S65—4H 79
Bell Bank View. S70—4H 23
Bellbrooke Av. S73—2D 26
Bellbrooke Pl. S73—2D 26
Bellefield St. S3—1A 4 & 1C 98
Belle Grn. La. S72—6C 10
Belle Vue Av. DN4—1G 47
Belle Vue Clo. S43—3D 132
Belle Vue Rd. S64—6E 43
Bellhagg Rd. S6—5H 85
Bellhouse La. S43—1D 134

Bellhouse Rd. S5
—6H 75 to 2A 76
Bellis Av. DN4—3A 46
Bellowes Rd. S62—2F 69
Bellrope Acre. DN3—4F 35
Bellscroft Av. S65—5C 70
Bells Sq. S1—3D 4 & 2E 99
Bell St. S31—6D 104
Bellwood Cres. S74—6G 37
Belmont Av. DN4—2C 46
Belmont Av. S30—2E 65
Belmont Av. S71—2B 14
Belmont Dri. S30—3E 141
Belmont Dri. S43—1D 134
Belmonte Gdns. S2
—6H 5 & 3G 99
Belmont St. S41—3A 132
Belmont St. S61—3A 78
Belmont St. S64—1D 56
Belper Rd. S7—1D 110
Belsize Rd. S10—5E 97
Beltoft Way. DN12—2G 59
Belton Clo. S18—2A 128
Belvedere. DN4—5H 45
Belvedere Av. S40—5G 137
Belvedere Clo. S31—2H 119
Belvedere Clo. S40—5C 136
Belvedere Clo. S72—3C 10
Belvedere Dri. S73—2D 26
Belvedere Pde. S66—2G 81
Belvoir Av. DN5—1G 43
Ben Bank Rd. S75—3A 22
Bence Clo. S75—6C 6
Bence La. S75—5A 6
Ben Clo. S6—2F 85
Benita Av. S64—1G 57
Ben La. S6—2F 85
Benmore Dri. S19—6H 115
Bennett Clo. S62—6H 55
Bennetthorpe. DN2—1E 47
Bennett St. S2—5D 98
Bennett St. S61—3G 77
Bennimoor Way. S40—5G 137
Benson Rd. S2—3A 100
Bentfield Av. S60—6A 80
Bentham Dri. S71—3D 14
Bentham Rd. S40—6G 131
Bentham Way. S75—3E 7
Bent Hills La. S30—1A 72
Bentinck Clo. DN1—1D 46
Bentinck St. DN12—3F 59
Bent La. S43—1E 135
Bent Lathes Av. S60—6A 80
Bentley Av. DN4—1A 46
Bentley Clo. S71—2E 15
Bentley Comn. La. DN5—1C 32
Bentley Moor La. DN5—1G 17
Bentley Rd. DN5—2A 32
Bentley Rd. S6—6G 85
Bentley Rd. S30—4F 65
Bentley Rd. S66—5H 81
Bentley St. S60—6D 78
Benton Ct. S61—2H 77
Benton Ter. S64—4B 56
Benton Way. S61—2H 77
Bents Clo. S11—2E 109
Bents Clo. S30—2E 65
Bents Cres. S11—3F 109
Bents Cres. S18—6G 123
Bents Dri. S11—2E 109
Bents Grn. Av. S11—1E 109
Bents Grn. Pl. S11—2F 109
Bents Grn. Rd. S11—1F 109
Bents La. S18—6G 123
Bents Rd. S11—2F 109
Bents Rd. S17—5C 120
Bents Rd. S61—6H 67
Bents View. S11—2E 109

Benty La. S10—2F 97
Beresford Rd. S66—5H 83
Beresford St. DN5—6C 18
Berkeley Croft. S71—1D 8
Berkeley Precinct. S11—5B 98
Berkley Clo. S70—4H 23
Bernard Clo. S43—3F 133
Bernard Gdns. S2—2H 5
Bernard Rd. DN12—4B 60
Bernard Rd. S2 & S4—1H 99
Bernard St. S2—2G 99
Bernard St. S60—4E 79
Bernard St. S62—6H 55
Berners Clo. S2—1A 112
Berners Dri. S2—1A 112
Berners Pl. S2—1A 112
Berners Rd. S2—1A 112
Berneslai Clo. S70—5G 13
Bernshall Cres. S5—1F 75
Berresford Rd. S11—5B 98
Berrington Clo. DN4—1G 61
Berry Av. S31—6C 124
Berrydale. S70—4B 24
Berry Holme Clo. S30—2E 65
Berry Holme Ct. S30—2E 65
Berry Holme Dri. S30—2E 65
Bertram Rd. S30—3E 73
Berwick Clo. S40—6E 137
Berwick Way. DN2—4A 34
Berwyn Clo. S40—6E 131
Bessacarr La. DN4—5C 48
Bessemer Pl. S9—6A 88
Bessemer Rd. S9—5A 88
Bessemer Ter. S30—2D 140
Bessingby Rd. S6—4A 86
Bethel Sq. S74—5B 38
(off Bethel St.)
Bethel St. S74—5B 38
Bethel Wlk. S1—4D 4
Betjeman Gdns. S10—4A 98
Betony Clo. S31—4H 125
Beulah Rd. S6—2B 86
Bevan Av. DN11—4D 62
Bevan Clo. S74—5C 38
Bevan Cres. S66—3F 83
Bevan Dri. S43—5H 133
Bevan Way. S30—2D 64
Bevercotes Rd. S5—6H 75
Beverley Av. S70—3H 23
Beverley Clo. S31—6B 104
Beverley Clo. S71—6A 8
Beverley Gdns. DN5—4F 31
Beverley Rd. DN2—3G 33
Beverleys Rd. S8—3E 111
Beverley St. S9—5C 88
Bevin Pl. S62—1H 69
Bevis Row. S2—2G 99
Bevre Rd. DN3—1F 35
Bewdley Ct. S71—1F 9
Bewicke Av. DN5—3F 31
Bhatia Clo. S64—6E 43
Bib La. S31—4E 95
Bickerton Rd. S6—1A 86
Bierlow Clo. S73—3A 40
Bigby Way. S66—2H 81
Bignor Pl. S6—4B 74
Bignor Rd. S6—4B 74
Bilby La. S43—2E 133
Billam Pl. S61—6G 67
Billam St. S31—6B 124
Billingley Dri. S63—2E 29
Billingley Grn. La. S72—3B 28
Billingley La. S72—2B 28
Billingley View. S63—1H 41
Bilston St. S6—4B 86
Binders Rd. S61—6G 67
Binfield Rd. S8—2D 110

Bingham Ct. S10—5G 97
Bingham Pk. Cres. S11—5G 97
Bingham Pk. Rd. S11—6G 97
Bingham Rd. S8—5D 110
Bingley La. S6—1A 96
Bingley St. S75—5F 13
Binsted Av. S5—6B 74
Binsted Clo. S5—6B 74
Binsted Croft. S5—6B 74
Binsted Dri. S5—6B 74
Binsted Gdns. S5—6B 74
Binsted Glade. S5—6B 74
Binsted Gro. S5—6B 74
Binsted Rd. S5—6B 74
Binsted Way. S5—6B 74
Birchall Av. S60—2H 91
Birch Av. S30—3E 65
Birch Clo. S31—4A 126
Birch Cres. S66—4G 81
Birchdale Clo. DN3—6D 20
Birchen Clo. DN4—6C 48
Birchen Clo. S18—2B 128
Birchen Clo. S40—6F 131
Birches Fold. S18—5G 123
Birches La. S18—5G 123
Birch Farm Av. S8—1E 123
Birchfield Rd. S66—4H 83
Birchfield Wlk. S75—5D 12
Birch Gro. DN12—3F 59
Birch Gro. S30—3E 73
Birch Ho. Av. S30—3D 72
Birchitt Clo. S17—4A 122
Birchitt Pl. S17—4A 122
Birchitt Rd. S17—4A 122
Birchitt View. S18—6E 123
Birchlands Dri. S31—4B 126
Birch La. S43—2G 133
Birch Pk. Ct. S61—3A 78
Birch Rd. DN4—3D 48
Birch Rd. S9—5A 88
Birch Rd. S70—2D 24
Birch Tree Clo. DN3—1E 21
Birch Tree Rd. S30—4D 140
Birchtree Rd. S61—4B 66
Birchvale Rd. S12—4F 113
Birchwood Av. S62—6F 55
Birchwood Clo. S19—1E 125
Birchwood Clo. S66—3D 82
Birchwood Ct. DN4—6F 49
Birchwood Ct. S40—6H 137
Birchwood Cres. S40—6H 137
Birchwood Croft. S19—1E 125
Birchwood Dell. DN4—6F 49
Birchwood Dri. S65—1H 81
Birchwood Gdns. S19—1E 125
Birchwood Gro. S19—1E 125
Birchwood Rise. S19—1E 125
Birchwood View. S19—1E 125
Birchwood Way. S19—1E 125
Bircotes Wlk. DN11—4F 63
Bird Av. S73—1E 39
Birdholme Cres. S40—5A 138
Bird St. S43—1D 134
Birdwell Comn. S70—5D 36
Birdwell Rd. S4—2B 88
Birdwell Rd. S62—5B 56
Birdwell Rd. S75—3D 22
Birk Av. S70—2C 24
Birkbeck Ct. S30—5B 50
Birk Cres. S70—2C 24
Birkdale Av. S31—5G 107
Birkdale Clo. DN4—5F 49
Birkdale Clo. S72—5C 10
Birkdale Dri. S40—5E 137
Birkdale Rise. S64—3B 56
Birkdale Rd. S71—1D 8
Birkendale. S6—6B 86

Birkendale Rd. S6—6B 86
Birkendale View. S6—6B 86
Birk Grn. S70—2D 24
Birk Ho. La. S70—2D 24
Birklands Av. S13—4G 101
Birklands Clo. S13—4G 101
Birklands Dri. S13—4G 101
Birk Rd. S70—2C 24
Birks Av. S13—1B 114
Birks Holt Dri. S66—6H 83
Birks Rd. S61—6G 67
Birks Wood Dri. S30—3D 72
Birk Ter. S70—2C 24
Birley Brook Dri. S41—5D 130
Birley La. S12—5E 113
Birley Croft. S41—4D 130
Birley Moor Av. S12—4G 113
Birley Moor Clo. S12—4G 113
Birley Moor Cres. S12—4G 113
Birley Moor Dri. S12—5G 113
Birley Moor Pl. S12—5G 113
Birley Moor Rd. S12—2E 113
Birley Moor Way. S12—5G 113
Birley Rise Cres. S6—5A 74
Birley Rise Rd. S6—5A 74
Birley Spa La. S12
—4H 113 to 4C 114
Birley Spa Wlk. S12—3B 114
(off Carter Lodge Dri.)
Birley Vale Av. S12—3E 113
Birley Vale Clo. S12—3E 113
Birley View. S30—4D 72
Birthwaite Rd. S75—1D 6
Birtley St. S66—4D 82
Bisby Rd. S62—1G 69
Biscay Way. S63—5F 41
Bishopdale Clo. S19—6A 114
Bishopdale Rise. S19—1A 124
Bishop Hill. S13—1A 114
Bishops Clo. S8—2F 111
Bishopscourt Rd. S8—2E 111
Bishopsgate La. DN11—6E 63
Bishopsholme Clo. S5—1E 87
Bishopsholme Rd. S5—1E 87
Bishopston Wlk. S66—3E 83
Bishop St. S3—6C 4 & 3D 98
Bishops Way. S71—4C 14
Bisley Clo. S71—2G 9
Bismarck St. S70—2H 23
Bitholmes La. S30—5H 141
Bittern View. S61—1C 66
Blacka Moor Cres. S17—3C 120
Blacka Moor Rd. S17—3C 120
Blackamoor Rd. S64—4E 55
Blacka Moor View. S17—3C 120
Black Bank. DN4—3E 47
Blackberry Flats. S19—2E 125
Blackbird Av. S60—3D 90
Blackbrook Av. S10—4A 96
Blackbrook Dri. S10—4A 96
Blackbrook Rd. S10—4A 96
Blackburn Cres. S30—1C 64
Blackburn Croft. S30—1D 64
Blackburn Dri. S30—2C 64
Blackburne St. S6—4B 86
Blackburn La. S61—3D 76
Blackburn La. S75—5F 13
Blackburn Rd S61
—4D 76 to 5E 77
Blackburn St. S70—4A 24
Black Carr Rd S66—5E 81
Blackdown Av S30 5D 114
Blackdown Av S40—6D 130
Blackdown Clo S19—5D 114
Blacker Grange S74—3H 37
Blacker La. S70—1E 37
Blacker La. S72—2C 10

Blacker Rd. S75—4G 7
Blackheath Clo. S71—6D 8
Blackheath Rd. S71—6D 8
Blackheath Wlk. S71—6D 8
Black La. S6—4D 84
Black La. S74—1D 50
Blackmoor Cres. S66—2B 90
Blackmore St. S4—6H 87
Blacksmith La. S30—1A 74
Blacksmith La. S44—1G 139
Blackstock Clo. S14—5H 111
Blackstock Cres. S14—5H 111
Blackstock Dri. S14—5H 111
Blackstock Rd. S14
—5H to 2H 111
Black Swan Wlk. S1—3E 5
Blackthorn Av. S66—4G 81
Blackthorn Clo. S30—5B 50
Blackthorne Clo. DN12—4A 60
Blackwell Clo. S2—2G 99
Blackwell Pl. S2—3H 5 & 2G 99
Blackwood Av. DN4—5H 45
Blagden St. S2—2G 99
Blair Athol Rd. S11—1H 109
Blake Av. DN2—3F 33
Blake Clo. S66—5H 81
Blake Gro. Rd. S6—6C 86
Blakeley Clo. S71—6E 9
Blakeney Rd. S10—2A 98
Blake St. S6—6B 86
Blandford Dri. S41—4G 131
Bland La. S6—2F 85
(in two parts)
Bland St. S4—3A 88
Blast La. S2—2H 5
Blast La. S4—2H 5 & 1A 6
Blaxton Clo. S19—5A 114
Blayton Rd. S4—3G 87
Bleachcroft Way. S70—2E 25
Bleak Av. S72—3C 10
Bleakley Clo. S72—3C 10
Bleasdale Gro. S71—3B 14
Blenheim Av. S70—1G 23
Blenheim Clo. S66—2G 81
Blenheim Ct. S66—3F 81
Blenheim Cres. S64—6D 42
Blenheim Gdns. S1—2G 109
Blenheim Gro. S70—1G 23
Blenheim Rd. S70—2F 23
Blocks, The. S18—3B 130
Bloemfontein St. S72—1G 15
Blonk St. S1—1G 5 & 1F 99
Bloomfield Rd. S75—4D 6
Bloomhouse La. S75—4C 6
Blossom Cres. S12—4D 112
Blow Hall Cres. DN12—3C 60
Blow Hall Riding. DN12—4D 60
Blucher St. S70—6G 13
Bluebank View. S43—1D 132
Bluebell Clo. S72—3C 10
Bluebell Rd. S5—6B 76
Bluebell Rd. S75—2C 6
Bluebird Hill. S31—1C 116
Blue Boy St. S3—1C 4 & 1D 98
Blundell Clo. DN4—4C 48
Blundell Ct. S71—2D 14
Blunt Av. S43—1A 0
Blyde Rd. S5—2G 87
Bly Rd. S73—3D 26
Blyth Av. S62—2F 69
Blyth Clo. S40—5D 136
Blythe Clo. S60—2B 92
Blythe St. S73—6A 26
Blyth Rd. S66—5J 12
Boardman Av. S62—5C 54
Boat La. DN5—3D 44
Bobbinmill La. S40—3F 137

Bochum Parkway. S8
—2E 123 to 6A 112
Bocking Clo. S8—6B 110
Bocking Hill. S30—3F 141
Bocking La. S8—6B 110
Bocking Rise. S8—1C 122
Boden La. S1—3C 4
Boden Pl. S9—6E 89
Bodmin Ct. S71—4B 14
Bodmin St. S9—5B 88
Bodmin Way. S40—6E 131
Boggard La. S30—3C 72
Boiley La. S31—5A 126
Boland Rd. S8—4B 122
Bold St. S9—4C 88
Bole Hill. S44—4G 139
Bole Hill. S60—6F 91
Bole Hill La. S10—1H 97
Bolehill La. S31—6G 125
Bole Hill Rd. S6—1F 97 to 5H 85
Bolsover Rd. S5—1H 87
Bolsover Rd. S43—1H 135
Bolsover Rd. E. S5—2H 87
Bolsover St. S3—3A 4 & 2C 98
Bolton Hill Rd. DN4—5C 48
Bolton Rd. S63—5A 42
Bolton Rd. S64—2H 55
Bolton St. DN12—1B 58
Bolton St. S3—5B 4 & 3D 98
Bond Clo. DN1—1C 46
Bondfield Av. DN11—5E 63
Bondfield Cres. S73—1E 39
Bondfield Rd. S43—4A 134
Bond Rd. S75—4F 13
Bond St. DN11—6D 62
Bond St. S43—3A 134
Bond St. S73—6B 26
Bonet La. S60—2A 90
Bonington Rise. S66—3E 83
Bonville Gdns. S3—1B 4
Booker Rd. S8—5C 110
Booker's La. S31—3B 106
Bookers Way. S31—4B 106
Booth Clo. S19—5D 114
Booth Clo. S66—5C 94
Booth Croft. S19—5D 114
Booth Pl. S62—6E 55
Booth St. S61—3B 68
Booth St. S74—5B 38
Borough Rd. S6—3A 86
Borrowdale Av. S19—3E 125
Borrowdale Clo. S19—3E 125
Borrowdale Clo. S71—1G 25
Borrowdale Cres. S31—6F 107
Borrowdale Dri. S19—3E 125
Borrowdale Rd. S19—3E 125
Boston Castle Gro. S60—5E 79
Boston Castle Ter. S60—5E 79
Boston St. S2—4D 98
Bosville Clo. S65—4H 71
Bosville Rd. S10—2H 97
Bosville St. S65—1B 80
Boswell Clo. DN11—5C 62
Boswell Clo. S30—5A 50
Boswell Clo. S71—1D 8
Boswell Rd. DN4—4A 48
Boswell Rd. S63—1F 55
Boswell St. S65—4F 79
Bosworth Rd. DN6—1C 16
Bosworth St. S10—1H 97
Botanical Rd. S11—4A 98
Botham St. S4—3A 88
Botsford St. S3—5E 87
Boulder Bri. Rd. S71—3G 9
Boulevard, The. DN3—5C 20
Boulton Clo. S40—6C 130
Boulton Dri. DN3—2F 49

Boundary Av. DN2—2A 34
Boundary Grn. S62—3G 69
Boundary Rd. S2—3H 99
Boundary St. S70—1B 24
Bourne Clo. S43—2E 133
Bourne Ct. S75—3G 7
Bourne Rd. S5—5G 75
Bourne Rd. S70—5H 23
Bourne Wlk. S75—3G 7
Bowden Wood Av. S9—3E 101
Bowden Wood Clo. S9—3E 101
Bowden Wood Cres. S9—3E 101
Bowden Wood Dri. S9—3E 101
Bowden Wood Pl. S9—3E 101
Bowden Wood Rd. S9—3E 101
Bowdon St. S1—5C 4 & 3D 98
Bowen Dri. S65—5D 70
Bowen Rd. S65—1F 79
Bower Farm Rd. S41—1B 132
Bower Ho. S30—6A 64
Bower La. S30—6A 64
Bower Rd. S10—1B 98
Bower Rd. S64—6B 42
Bowers Fold. DN1—6D 32
Bower Spring. S3—1E 5 & 1E 99
Bower St. S3—1E 5 & 1E 99
Bower Vale. DN12—4A 60
Bowfell View. S71—3A 14
Bowfield Clo. S5—5H 75
Bowfield Rd. S5—5G 75
Bowland Clo. DN5—1H 31
Bowland Cres. S70—5H 23
Bowland Dri. S30—2C 64
Bowland Dri. S42—6D 136
Bowlease Gdns. DN4—3C 48
Bowling Grn. St. S3
—1D 4 & 6E 87
Bowman Clo. S12—5B 112
Bowman Dri. S12—5B 112
Bowman Dri. S66—3E 83
Bowness Clo. S18—2C 128
Bowness Clo. S41—4F 131
Bowness Dri. S63—2A 42
Bowness Rd. S6—4A 86
Bowness Rd. S41—4F 131
Bowood Rd. S11—5B 98
Bowshaw. S18—5D 122
Bowshaw Av. S8—4E 123
Bowshaw Clo. S8—4E 123
Bowshaw View. S8—4E 123
Bow St. S72—6B 10
Boyce St. S6—6B 86
Boyd Rd. S63—2F 55
Boyland St. S3—5D 86
Boynton Cres. S5—1E 87
Boynton Rd. S5—1E 87
Boythorpe Av. S40—3G 137
Boythorpe Cres. S40—4H 137
Boythorpe Mt. S40—3H 137
Boythorpe Rise. S40—3G 137
Boythorpe Rd. S40—3H 137
Brackley St. S3—5F 87
Bradberry Balk La. S73—5A 26
Bradbury Clo. S40—2G 137
Bradbury's Clo. S62—4F 69
Bradbury St. S8—1E 111
Bradbury St. S70—6F 13
Bradfield Rd. S6—3A 86
Bradford Rd. DN2—1A 34
Bradford Row. DN1—6D 32
Bradgate Clo. S61—2A 78

Bradgate Ct. S61—2H 77
Bradgate Ho. Clo. S61—2A 78
Bradgate La. S61—2H 77
Bradgate Pl. S61—1A 78
Bradgate Rd. S61—1A 78
Bradley Av. S73—6A 26
Bradley Clo. S43—4E 133
Bradley La. S18—6A 128
Bradley Rise. S62—6G 55
Bradley St. S10—6A 86
Bradley Way. S43—4E 133
Bradshaw Av. S60—2F 103
Bradshaw Clo. S75—5C 12
Bradshaw Rd. S43—5H 133
Bradshaw Way. S60—2F 103
Bradstone Rd. S65—2A 80
Bradway Clo. S17—4H 121
Bradway Dri. S17—4H 121
Bradway Grange Rd. S17
—4A 122
Bradway Rd. S17—4H to 3G 121
Bradwell Av. S75—3C 22
Bradwell Clo. S18—2A 128
Bradwell Pl. S43—4A 134
Bradwell St. S2—1F 111
Braemar St. DN2—6G 33
Braemore Rd. S6—2G 85
Brailsford Av. S5—1E 75
Brailsford Ct. S5—1E 75
Brailsford Rd. S5—1E 75
Brairfield Rd. S12—4C 112
Brairfields La. S30—4C 72
Braithwaite St. S75—4G 7
Braithwell Rd. DN5—4A 18
Braithwell Rd. S65—1H 81
Braithwell Rd. S66—4F 83
Braithwell Wlk. DN12—1B 58
Braithwell Way. S66—3A 82
Bramah St. S71—4E 9
Bramall La. S2—4E 99
Bramall La. S30—1B 140
Bramble Clo. S66—6F 81
Bramble Way. S63—5B 40
Brambling Ct. S41—2C 138
Bramcote Av. S71—5A 8
Brameld Rd. S62—2F 69
Brameld Rd. S64—2H 55
Bramham Rd. DN4—2D 48
Bramham Rd. S9—6D 88
Bramley Av. S13—5H 101
Bramley Av. S31—5C 104
Bramley Clo. S19—2C 124
Bramley Ct. DN12—2B 58
Bramley Ct. S10—2H 97
Bramley Dri. S13—4H 101
Bramley Hall Rd. S13—5H 101
Bramley La. S13—4H 101
Bramley La. S65—1A 82
Bramley Pk. Caravan Site. S31
—6A 124
Bramley Pk. Rd. S13—4H 101
Bramley Way. S66—3A 82
Brampton Av. S66—5H 93
Brampton Clo. DN3—4E 35
Brampton Ct. S19—5A 114
Brampton Cres. S73—2H 39
Brampton La. DN3—4E 35
Brampton La. S31—1F 105
Brampton Meadows.
—5H 93
Brampton Rd. S63—4B 40
Brampton Rd. S66—6H 93
Brampton St. S73—2H 39
Brampton St. S73—3B 40
Brampton View. S73—2H 39
Bramshill Clo. S19—6G 115
Bramshill Ct. S19—6G 115
Bramshill Rise. S40—4F 137

Bramwell Gdns. S3
—2A 4 & 1C 98
Bramwell St. S3—2A 4 & 1C 98
Bramwell St. S65—2E 79
Bramwith La. DN3—1G 21
Bramwith Rd. S11—5F 97
Bramworth Rd. DN4—2H 45
Brandene Clo. S44—2G 139
Brand La. DN5—5B 30
Brandon St. S3—4F 87
Brandreth Clo. S6—6C 86
Brandreth Rd. S6—6C 86
Brands La. S31—6H 107
Branksome Av. S70—6E 13
Branksome Chine Av. S41
—6C 138
Bransby St. S6—6B 86
Branstone Rd. DN5—1D 44
Branton Clo. S40—4H 137
Branton Ga. Rd. DN3—1H 49
Branton Ter. DN3—3H 49
Brantwood Cres. DN4—2D 48
Brathay Clo. S4—2B 88
Brathay Rd. S4—2B 88
Bray St. S9—6C 88
Bray Wlk. S61—5E 67
Brealey Clo. S43—2C 134
Brearley Av. S30—4F 141
Brearley Av. S43—1D 132
Breckland Rd. S40—5D 136
Brecklands. S60—5A 80
Brecklands. S66—5E 81
Breck La. S31—3F 107
Brecks Cres. S65—5C 80
Brecks La. DN3—3D 20
Brecks La. S65—2B 80
Brecon Clo. S19—5G 115
Brecon Clo. S40—6E 131
Brendon Av. S40—1E 137
Brendon Clo. S73—3H 39
Brent Clo. S40—6E 131
Brent La. S43—1E 135
Brentwood Av. S11—1B 110
Brentwood Rd. S11—1B 110
Bressingham Clo. S4—5G 87
Bressingham Rd. S4—5G 87
Bretby Clo. DN4—4D 48
Bretby Rd. S40—5C 130
Brett Clo. S62—5C 54
Bretton Clo. S75—5A 6
Bretton Gro. S12—4F 113
Bretton Ho. DN1—1C 46
(off St James St.)
Bretton Rd. S75—5A 6
Bretton View. S72—2G 15
Brewery Rd. S63—4F 41
Brewery St. S41—2B 138
Breydon Av. DN5—4G 31
Briar Clo. S41—6G 131
Briar Ct. S66—6F 81
Briardene Clo. S40—6B 130
Briarfield Av. S12—4C 112
Briarfield Cres. S12—4C 112
Briarfield Rd. S12—4C 112
Briarfields La. S30—4C 72
Briar Gro. S72—2G 11
Briar Rise. S70—5A 24
Briar Rd. DN3—1E 35
Briar Rd. S7—1C 110
Briars Clo. S31—4B 126
Briar View. S43—4E 133
Briary Av. S30—6B 50
Brickhouse La. S17—1C 120
Brickhouse Yd. S40—2G 137
Brick Kiln Croft. S43—4F 133
Brick St. S10—1H 97
Brickyard, The. S72—4C 10
Brickyard Wlk. S40—2A 138

Bridby St. S13—1D 114
Bridge Gdns. S71—4H 13
Bridgegate. S60—2D 78
Bridge Gro. DN5—4H 31
Bridge Hill. S30—2D 72
Bridgehouses. S3—1F 5 & 6E 87
Bridge Inn Rd. S30—1E 65
Bridge Rd. DN4—2A 48
Bridge Stile Clo. S19—2C 124
Bridge St. DN4—1B 46
Bridge St. S3—1F 5 & 1E 99
Bridge St. S31—2B 126
Bridge St. S40—5A 138
Bridge St. S60—2D 78
Bridge St. S63—6F 29
Bridge St. S64—2C 56
Bridge St. S71—5H 13
Bridge St. S75—4C 6
Bridle Clo. S30—1E 65
Bridle Cres. S31—6D 114
Bridle Rd. S43—2F 135
Bridle Stile. S19—2C 124
Bridle Stile Av. S19—2B 124
Bridle Stile Clo. S19—2C 124
Bridleway, The. S62—6A 56
Bridport Rd. S9—6D 88
Brier Clo. S19—6D 114
Brierfield Clo. S75—5E 13
Brierley Rd. DN4—4B 48
Brierley Rd. S72—5F 11
  (Grimethorpe)
Brierley Rd. S72—3D 10
  (Shafton)
Brierley Rd. S72—1E 11
  (S. Hiendley)
Brierly Dri. S65—6C 70
Brier St. S6—3A 86
Briery Wlk. S61—4B 68
Briggs St. S71—4E 9
Brightmore Dri. S3
          —3A 4 & 2C 98
Brighton St. S9—3D & 2D 88
Brighton St. S72—6G 11
Brighton Ter. Rd. S10—1A 98
Brightside La. S9—4A 88
Bright St. S9—2D 88
Brimington Rd. S41—1B 138
Brimington Rd. N. S41—2A to
  (in two parts)   3A 132
Brimmesfield Clo. S2—6A 100
Brimmesfield Dri. S2—5A 100
Brimmesfield Rd. S2—6A 100
Brinckman St. S70—1A 24
Brincliffe Clo. S40—4D 136
Brincliffe Cres. S11—6A 98
Brincliffe Edge Clo. S11
          —1A 110
Brincliffe Edge Rd. S11
          —1H 109 to 2C 110
Brincliffe Gdns. S11—6A 98
Brincliffe Hill. S11—6H 97
Brindley Clo. S8—3E 111
Brindley Ct. S31—3A 126
Brindley Cres. S8—3E 111
Brindley Rd. S41—5A 132
Brindley Way. S43—1D 134
Brinkburn Clo. S17—3F 121
Brinkburn Ct. S17—3F 121
Brinkburn Dri. S17—3F 121
Brinkburn Vale Rd. S17—3F 121
Brinsford Rd. S60—2C 90
Brinsworth Hall Av. S60—3B 90
Brinsworth Hall Cres. S60
          —3B 90
Brinsworth Hall Dri. S60—3B 90
Brinsworth Hall Gro. S60
          —4B 90
Brinsworth La. S60—3B 90

Brinsworth Rd. S60—3B to
  (in three parts)   5C 90
Brinsworth St. S9—5B 88
Brinsworth St. S60—3C 78
Bristol Gro. DN2—3G 33
Bristol Rd. S11—4A 98
Britain St. S64—1D 56
Britannia Clo. S70—1H 23
Britannia Ct. S30—2E 65
Britannia Ho. S70—1H 23
Britannia Rd. S9—1E 101
  (in two parts)
Britannia Rd. S40—6B 138
Britland Clo. S75—5C 12
Britnall St. S9—5C 88
Briton Sq. S63—1G 29
Briton St. S63—1G 29
Brittain St. S1—6F 5 & 3F 99
Britten Ho. DN2—3G 33
Broachgate. DN5—1G 31
Broadcarr Rd. S74—3B 52
Broadcroft Clo. S19—4G 115
Broad Dyke Clo. S31—5B 118
Broad Elms Clo. S11—3F 109
Broad Elms La. S11—4E 109
Broadfield Rd. S8—1D 110
Broadgorse Clo. S40—6H 137
Broadhead Rd. S30—4F 141
Broad Inge Cres. S30—2C 64
Broadlands Av. S19—5A 114
Broadlands Clo. S19—5B 114
Broadlands Croft. S19—5B 114
Broadlands Rise. S19—5B 114
Broad La. S3 & S1—3B 4 & 2D 98
Broadley Rd. S13—6E 101
Broad Oaks. S9—6B 88
Broad Oaks La. S9—1B 100
Broad Pavement. S40—2A 138
Broad Riding. DN12—4D 60
Broad St. S2—2G 5 & 1F & 1G 99
  (in two parts)
Broad St. S62—4F 69
Broad St. S74—5H 37
Broad St. La. S2—2H 5 & 1G 99
Broadwater. S63—1G 41
Broadway. S60—4B 90
Broadway. S64—3H 55
Broadway. S65—2H 79
Broadway. S70—6D 12
Broadway. S75—4F 7
Broadway Av. S30—3F 65
Broadway Clo. S64—3H 55
Broadway Ct. S70—6D 12
Broadway E. S65—2H 79
Broadway, The. DN4—6H 45
Brocco Bank. S11—5A 98
Brocco La. S3—2C 4 & 1D 98
Brocco St. S3—2C 4 & 1D 98
Brockfield Clo. S70—4A 24
Brockhill Ct. S43—3F 133
Brockhole Clo. DN4—4D 48
Brockholes La. DN3—4H 49
Brockhurst Way. S65—5D 70
Brocklehurst Av. S8—1G 123
Brocklehurst Av. S70—3D 24
Brocklehurst Piece. S40
          —3F 137
Brockwell Ct. S40—5F 131
Brockwell La. S40—5D 130 to
  (in two parts)   6E 131
Brockwell La. S42—4B 130
Brockwell Pl. S40—1G 137
Brockwell Ter. S40—1G 137
Brockwell Wlk. S40—6F 131
Brodsworth Ho. DN1—1C 46
  (off St James St.)
Bromehead Way. S41—4F 131
Brompton Dri. DN5—2E 45

Brompton Rd. S9—4C 88
Bromwich Rd. S8—5C 110
Bronte Av. DN4—5H 45
Bronte Clo. S71—4B 14
Bronte Gro. S64—5F 43
Bronte Pl. S62—6H 55
Brookbank Av. S40—1F 137
Brook Clo. S30—6A 64
Brook Clo. S31—6C 104
Brook Croft. S31—2F 119
Brook Dri. S3—2B 4 & 1D 98
Brooke Dri. S43—6F 133
Brooke Dri. S65—3D 42
Brooke St. DN1—4D 32
Brooke St. S74—5H 37
Brookfield Av. S40—3C 136
Brookfield Av. S64—3B 56
Brookfield Clo. DN4—4F 35
Brookfield Rd. S7—6D 98
Brookfield Ter. S71—5E 9
Brook Hill. S3—3A 4 & 2C 98
Brook Hill. S61—3B 66
Brookhouse Clo. S12—4B 114
Brookhouse Ct. S12—4B 114
Brookhouse Hill. S10—6C 96
Brookhouse La. S31—5E 95
Brookhouse Rd. S31—1B 116
Brooklands Av. S10—6B 96
Brooklands Cres. S10—6B 96
Brooklands Dri. S10—6B 96
Brook La. S3—3B 4 & 2D 98
Brook La. S12—4B 114
Brook La. S30—1A 74
  (Grenoside)
Brook La. S30—2C 72
  (Oughtibridge)
Brook La. S66—3H 81
Brooklyn Dri. S40—1F 137
Brooklyn Pl. S8—2E 111
Brooklyn Rd. S8—2E 111
Brook Rd. DN12—3F 59
Brook Rd. S8—2D 110
Brook Rd. S30—1C 64
Brook Rd. S65—1H 79
Brook Row. S30—4E 141
Brookside. DN12—4E 59
Brookside. S64—4H 55
Brookside. S65—4A 80
Brookside Bar. S40—3B 136
Brookside Clo. S12—4B 114
Brookside Ct. S62—5D 68
Brookside Cres. S63—6B 40
Brookside Dri. S70—3D 24
Brookside Glen. S40—3B 136
Brookside La. S6—4A 84
Brook Sq. DN12—4E 59
Brook St. S60—2H 91
Brook St. S62—4G 69
Brook Vale. S40—3G 137
Brookvale. S71—4D 14
Brookview Ct. S18—6E 123
Brook Way. DN5—6D 18
Brook Yd. S40—2G 137
Broom Av. S60—5H 79
Broombank Rd. S41—1F 131
Broom Chase. S60—5F 79
Broom Clo. S2—4D 98
Broom Clo. S41—4F 131
Broom Clo. S63—6D 28
  (Bolton-upon-Dearne)
Broom Clo. S63—1G 55
  (Wath upon Dearne)
Broom Clo. S70—3D 24
Broom Ct. S60—5G 79
  (Broom Rd.)
Broom Ct. S60—5F 79
  (Wade Clo.)

Broom Cres. S60—5F 79
Broomcroft. S75—3D 22
Broom Dri. S60—6H 79
Broome Av. S64—2B 56
Broomfield Av. S41—6D 138
Broomfield Clo. S70—1D 22
Broomfield Ct. S30—3F 141
Broomfield Ct. S71—1F 9
Broomfield Gro. S30—4F 141
Broomfield Gro. S60—5F 79
Broomfield La. S30—4E 141
Broomfield Rd. S10—3B 98
Broomfield Rd. S30—3F 141
Broom Gdns. S43—4F 133
Broom Grange. S60—5G 79
Broom Gro. S31—4F 119
Broom Gro. S60—4F 79
Broomgrove Cres. S10—3B 98
Broomgrove Hall. S10—3B 98
Broomgrove La. S10—3B 98
Broomgrove Rd. S10—3B 98
Broomhall Pl. S10
          —6A 4 & 3C 98
Broomhall Rd. S10
          —6A 4 & 4C 98
Broomhall St. S3—6A 4 & 3C to
  (in three parts)   3D 98
Broomhead Ct. S75—5F 7
Broomhead Rd. S73—2H 39
Broomhill. DN12—1B 58
Broomhill Clo. S31—6B 124
Broom Hill Dri. DN4—4D 48
Broomhill La. S63—6G 27
Broomhill Rd. S41—1H 131
Broomhill View. S63—2H 41
Broomhouse La. DN12 & DN4
          —4B 60
Broom La. S60—5G 79
Broom Riddings. S61—5B 68
Broom Rd. S60—4F 79
Broomroyd. S70—5B 24
Broomspring La. S10
          —5A 4 & 3C 98
Broom St. S10—6A 4 & 3C 98
Broom Ter. S60—4F 79
Broomvale Wlk. DN12—4A 60
Broom Valley Rd. S60—4E 79
Broomville St. S64—2C 56
Broomwood Clo. S19—4G 115
Broomwood Gdns. S19—4G 115
Brosley Av. DN3—1H 21
Brotherton St. S5—5F 87
Brough Grn. S75—4D 22
Broughton Av. DN5—2A 32
Broughton La. S9—3D 88
Broughton Rd. DN4—5B 48
Broughton Rd. S6—2A 86
Broughton Rd. S41—4F 131
Brow Clo. S70—3H 23
Brow Cres. S19—2E 125
Brow Hill Rd. S66—3E 83
Brownell St. S3—2B 4 & 1D 98
Brown Hills La. S10—6A 96
Browning Av. DN4—5B 46
Browning Clo. S6—4B 74
Browning St. S71—2B 14
Browning Clo. S6—4B 74
Browning Dri. S6—4B 74
Browning Rd. DN3—1H 21
Browning Rd. S6—4A 74
Browning Rd. S63—4C 40
Browning Rd. S64—5E 43
Browning Rd. S65—3H 79
Brown La. S1—5E 5 & 3E 99
Brown La. S18—6G 123
Brownroyd Av. S71—3E 9
Brown St. S1—5F 5 & 3F 99
Brown St. S60—2B 78

Brow, The. S65—5A 80
Brow View. S63—1H 41
Broxbourne Gdns. DN5—6B 18
Broxholme La. DN1—5D 32
Broxholme Rd. S8—4D 110
Bruce Av. S70—2H 23
Bruce Cres. DN2—4H 33
Bruce Rd. S11—5B 98
Bruncroft Clo. DN4—5B 48
Brunel Rd. DN5—4H 31
Bruni Way. DN11—6D 62
Brunswick Clo. S71—1H 13
Brunswick Rd. S3—6F 87
Brunswick Rd. S60—5F 79
Brunswick St. S10
— 4A 4 & 2C 98
Brunswick St. S41—1A 138
Brunswick St. S63—1H 29
Brunt Rd. S62—1H 69
Brushfield Gro. S12—3F 113
Brushfield Rd. S40—6B 130
Bryn Lea. S41—3C 138
Bryony Clo. S31—3H 125
Bubwith Rd. S9—1D 88
Buchanan Cres. S5—4C 74
Buchanan Dri. S5—4D 74
Buchanan Rd. S5—4C 74
Buckden Clo. S40—1F 137
Buckden Rd. S70—5F 13
Buckenham Dri. S4—5G 87
Buckenham St. S4—5G 87
Buckingham Clo. S18—1B 128
Buckingham Rd. DN2—5F 33
Buckingham Rd. DN12—2D 58
Buckingham Way. S60—3D 90
Buckingham Way. S66—3G 83
Buckingham Way. S71—1D 8
Buckleigh Rd. S63—1E 55
Buckley Ct. S70—1H 23
Buckley Ho. S70—1H 23
(off Union St.)
Buckthorn Clo. S64—5A 56
Buckwood View. S14—2H 111
Bude Ct. S71—4C 14
Bude Rd. DN4—3B 46
Bullen Rd. S6—4A 74
Bullfinch Clo. S60—3D 90
Bungalow Rd. DN12—3B 60
Bungalows, The. S31—6H 125
(Eckington)
Bungalows, The. S31—3A 126
(Killamarsh)
Bungalows, The. S40—2F 137
(Newbold)
Bungalows, The. S41—4G 131
(Piccadilly)
Bungalows, The. S41—2B 138
(Whittington Moor)
Bungalows, The. S60—1E 103
Bungay Row. S2—1H 99
Bunker's Hill. S31—3C 109
Bunting Clo. S8—5F 111
Bunting Clo. S42—4D 136
Bunting Nook. S8—5F 111
Burbage Clo. S18—1B 128
Burbage Gro. S12—2F 113
Burbage Rd. S43—3B 134
Burcot Rd. S8—2D 110
Burcroft Clo. S74—6F 37
Burcroft Hill. DN12—2F 59
Burden Clo. DN1—1C 46
Burford Av. DN4—6G 45
Burford Cres. S31—6C 104
Burgen Rd. S61—6G 67
Burgess Clo. S41—6D 138
Burgess Rd. S9—5B 88
Burgess St. S1—4E 5 & 2E 99

Burgoyne Clo. S6—5B 86
Burgoyne Rd. S6—5B 86
Burkett Dri. S43—1F 135
Burkinshaw Av. S62—5F 55
Burleigh St. S70—1H 23
Burley Clo. S40—6A 138
Burlington Arc. S70—6H 13
(off Eldon St.)
Burlington Clo. S17—2E 121
Burlington Ct. S6—6C 86
Burlington Glen. S17—2E 121
Burlington Gro. S17—2E 121
Burlington Rd. S17—2E 121
Burlington St. S6—6C 86
Burlington St. S40—2A 138
Burman Rd. S63—6F 41
Burnaby Ct. S6—4B 86
Burnaby Cres. S6—5B 86
Burnaby Grn. S6—4B 86
Burnaby St. DN1—1C 46
Burnaby St. S6—4B 86
Burnaby Wlk. S6—5B 86
Burnaston Clo. S18—2A 128
Burnaston Wlk. DN12—2C 58
Burnbridge Rd. S41—1B 132
Burncross Rd. S30—2C 64
Burnell Rd. S6—2A 86
Burnell St. S43—3F 133
Burngreave Bank. S4—5F 87
Burngreave Rd. S3—4F 87
Burngreave St. S3—5F 87
Burn Gro. S30—3G 65
Burngrove Pl. S3—4F 87
Burnham Av. S75—4F 7
Burnham Clo. DN4—4H 47
Burnham Gro. DN5—1H 31
Burnham Way. S73—4D 26
Burn Pl. S71—6A 8
Burnsall Cres. S60—4C 90
Burnsall Gro. S70—3D 24
Burns Clo. S40—6H 137
Burns Dri. S18—3G 129
Burns Dri. S30—2D 64
Burns Dri. S65—3H 79
Burnside Av. S8—2E 111
Burns Rd. DN3—1H 21
Burns Rd. DN4—5B 46
Burns Rd. S6—1B 98
Burns Rd. S31—5G 107
Burns Rd. S65—3G 79
Burns Rd. S66—5G 83
Burns St. DN5—6B 18
Burns Way. S63—4C 40
Burnt Hill La. S30—4A 72
Burnt Ho. La. S31—1G 103
Burnt Stones Clo. S10—3D 96
Burnt Stones Dri. S10—3D 96
Burnt Stones Gro. S10—3D 96
Burnt Tree La. S30—1B 4 & 1D 98
Burntwood Clo. S63—2D 28
Burntwood Cres. S60—6E 91
Burnt Wood La. S60—1G 103
Burntwood Rd. S72—6H 11
Burrell St. S60—3D 78
Burrowlee Rd. S6—2A 86
Burrows Dri. S5—1E 87
Burrows Gro. S73—6H 25
Bursden Clo. S41—2A 132
Burton Av. DN4—3B 46
Burton Av. S71—3D 14
Burton Bank Rd. S71—4A to
(in two parts) 3B 14
Burton Cres. S12—2E 15
Burton La. S30—3C 72
Burton Rd. S3—5D 86
Burton Rd. S71—4C 14 to 1F 15
Burton St. S6—4B 86
Burton St. S71—4G 13

Burton Ter. DN4—3B 46
Burton Ter. S70—1B 24
Burying La. S62—2A 52
Bushey Wood Rd. S17—3E 121
Bushfield Rd. S63—5D 40
Busk Knoll. S5—1E 87
Busk Meadow. S5—1E 87
Busk Pk. S5—1E 87
Busley Gdns. DN5—1A 32
(in two parts)
Butcher St. S63—1E 29
Butchill Av. S5—1E 75
Bute St. S10—2H 97
Butler Rd. S6—4G 85
Butler Way. S31—2A 126
Butterbusk. DN12—3G 59
Butterfield Ct. S73—3A 40
Butterill Dri. DN3—4H 35
Butterley Dri. S70—3D 24
Buttermere Clo. S31—6E 107
Buttermere Clo. S41—4F 131
Buttermere Clo. S63—2A 42
Buttermere Clo. S64—5G 43
Buttermere Dri. S18—2C 128
Buttermere Rd. S7—3C 110
Buttermere Way. S71—1H 25
Buttermilk La. S44—6H 135
Butterthwaite Cres. S5—2A 76
Butterthwaite La. S30—6H 65
Butterthwaite Rd. S5—1H 75
Butterton Dri. S40—6C 130
Butt Hole Rd. DN12—3G 59
Button Hill. S11—3H 109
Button Row. S30—3D 140
Butts Hill. S17—5D 120
Buxton Rd. S71—6C 8
Byath La. S72—1H 15
Byford Rd. S66—4C 82
Byland Way. S71—5D 14
Byrley Rd. S61—6G 67
Byrne Clo. S75—3A 12
Byron Av. DN4—3A 46
Byron Av. DN5—5H 31
Byron Av. S30—3D 64
Byron Clo. S18—4G 129
Byron Cres. S63—4C 40
Byron Dri. S63—3G 79
Byron Dri. S71—3B 14
Byron Rd. S7—1C 110
Byron Rd. S19—5G 115
Byron Rd. S31—5G 107
(in two parts)
Byron Rd. S40—5A 138
Byron Rd. S64—6F 43
Byron Rd. S66—5G 83
Byron St. S40—4B 138

Cadeby Av. DN12—3C 58
Cadeby Ho. DN1—1C 46
(off St James' St.)
Cadeby Rd. DN5—3C 44
Cadman La. S1—4F 5 & 2E 99
Cadman Rd. S12—1E 113
Cadman St. S4—1G 99
Cadman St. S19—3C 124
Cadman St. S63—5G 41
Cadwell Clo. S72—5C 10
Caernarvon Clo. S40—4E 137
Caernarvon Cres. S63—1H 41
Caernarvon Dri. DN5—1G 43
Caernarvon Rd. S18—3E 129
Caine Gdns. S61—3G 77
Cairns Rd. S10—3G 97
Cairns Rd. S19—3F 115
Caister Av. S30—2D 64
Caistor Av. S70—2E 23

Cait La. S11—4D 108
Calcot Grn. S64—3B 56
Calcot Pk. Av S64—3B 56
Caldbeck Gro. S30—5B 50
Caldbeck Pl. S31—6F 107
Calder Av. S71—2G 9
Calder Ct. S60—1E 91
Calder Cres. S70—2D 24
Calder Rd. S61—5H 67
Calder Rd. S63—2B 42
Calder Ter. DN12—2E 59
Caldervale. S71—1G 9
Calder Way. S5—1G 87
Caldey Rd. S18—3E 129
California Cres. S70—2H 23
California Dri. S30—3E 65
California Gdns. S70—2G 23
California St. S70—2G 23
California Ter. S70—2G 23
Calladine Way. S64—4A 56
Callow Dri. S14—2H 111
Callow Mt. S14—2G 111
Callow Pl. S14—2H 111
Callow Rd. S14—2G 111
Callywhite La. S18—2F 129
Calner Croft. S19—5H 115
Calow Grn. S44—5G 139
Calow La. S41 & S44—6D 138
Calver Clo. S75—4C 22
Calver Cres. S43—3B 134
Calvert Rd. S9—5E 89
Calvert St. S74—6F 37
Camborne Clo. S6—4A 74
Camborne Rd. S6—4A 74
Camborne Way. S71—4B 14
Cambourne Clo. DN6—1D 16
Cambria Dri. DN4—5G 45
Cambrian Clo. DN5—2C 44
Cambrian Clo. S40—5F 131
Cambridge Clo. DN5—1F 43
Cambridge Cres. S65—2G 79
Cambridge Pl. S65—2G 79
Cambridge Rd. S8—1F 111
Cambridge Rd. S30—4H 141
Cambridge Rd. S43—3F 133
Cambridge St. DN11—3C 62
Cambridge St. S1—4D 4 & 2E 99
Cambridge St. S64—6C 42
Cambridge St. S65—2G 79
Cambron Gdns. S66—4H 81
Camdale Rise. S12—6H 113
Camdale View. S12—6A 114
Camden Pl. DN1—1C 46
Camellia Dri. DN3—4D 20
Camilla Clo. DN12—4F 59
Cammell Rd. S5—1H 87
Camms Clo. S31—5D 124
Camm St. S6—5A 86
Campbell Dri. S65—4H 79
Campbell St. S61—3C 68
Camping La. S8—5C 110
Campion Clo. S63—6D 28
Campion Dri. S31—3A 126
Campion Rd. S64—4B 56
Campo La. S1—3D 4 & 1E 99
Campsall Dri. S10—2G 97
Campsall Field Clo. S63—1E 55
Campsall Field Rd. S63—6E 41
Canada St. S4—4H 87
Canada St. S70—2G 23
Canal Bri. S31—3B 108
Canal St. S4—6H 87
Canal St. S71—4H 13
Canal Wharf. S2—2H 5 & 1G 99
Canal Wharf. S41—1B 138
Canberra Rise. S63—1H 41
Canklow Hill Rd. S60—6D 78

Canklow Meadows Ind. Est.
    S60—3D 90
Canklow Rd. S60—1D 90
Canning St. S1—4C 4 & 2D 98
Cannock St. S6—3A 86
Cannon Hall Rd. S5—2G 87
Canon Clo. DN11—4F 63
Canons Way. S71—4C 14
Cantelo Ct. DN11—6C 62
Canterbury Av. S10—5C 96
Canterbury Clo. DN5—3G 31
Canterbury Cres. S10—5C 96
Canterbury Dri. S10—5C 96
Canterbury Rd. DN2—3F 33
Canterbury Rd. S8—2F 111
Cantilupe Cres. S31—5B 104
Cantley La. DN4 & DN3—2A 48
Cantley Mnr. Av. DN4—4E 49
Capel Rise. S43—3D 132
Capel St. S6—4B 86
    (in two parts)
Caperns Rd. S31—2H 119
Capri Ct. S73—3C 26
Capthorne Clo. S40—6B 130
Caraway Gro. S64—5B 56
Carbis Clo. S71—4B 14
Carbrook Hall Business Pk. S9
    —2D 88
Carbrook St. S9—3D 88
Cardew Clo. S62—2G 69
Cardiff St. S9—3C 88
Cardigan Rd. DN2—4A 34
Cardinal Clo. DN11—4F 63
Cardoness Dri. S10—3E 97
Cardoness Rd. S10—3F 97
Carey Av. S71—6A 14
Carfield Av. S8—2F 111
Carfield La. S8—2G 111
Carfield Pl. S8—2F 111
Carisbrooke Rd. DN2—5G 33
Carlby Rd. S6—4G 85
Carley Dri. S19—6F 115
Carlingford Rd. S60—6G 79
Carlin St. S13—1G 113
Carlisle Clo. S41—1G 131
Carlisle Pl. S65—2E 79
    (off Nottingham St.)
Carlisle Rd. DN2—2H 33
Carlisle Rd. S4—3A 88
Carlisle St. S4—6G 87
Carlisle St. S62—4B 56
Carlisle St. S65—2E 79
Carlisle St. E. S4
    —5H 87 to 3B 88
Carlisle Ter. S31—4F 107
Carlthorpe Gro. S30—6A 50
Carlton Av. S65—3F 79
Carlton Clo. S19—3C 124
Carlton Ho. DN1—1C 46
    (off Bond Clo.)
Carlton Rd. S72—6B 10
Carlton Ind. Est. S71—6E 9 &
    (in two parts)   1C 14
Carlton Rd. DN1—4E 33
Carlton Rd. S6—1H 85
Carlton Rd. S40—6A 138
Carlton Rd. S71—2A 14 to 4F 9
Carlton St. S71—3G 13
Carlton St. S71—6B 10
    (Cudworth)
Carlton St. S72—6G 11
    (Grimethorpe)
Carlton Ter. S71—4G 9
Carlyle Rd. S66—5G 83
Carlyle St. S64—6E 43
Carlyon Gdns. S40—5H 137
Carnaby Rd. S6—4A 86

Carnarvon St. S6—6C 86
Carnforth Rd. S71—2D 14
Carnley St. S63—4B 40
Carnoustie Av. S40—5E 137
Carnoustie Clo. S64—3C 56
Carpenter Croft. S12—1E 113
Carpenter Gdns. S12—1E 113
Carpenter M. S12—1E 113
Carr Bank Clo. S11—5F 97
Carr Bank Dri. S11—5E 97
Carr Bank La. S11—5E 97
Carr Clo. S60—3A 90
Carrcroft Ct. S30—4H 141
Carrfield Clo. S75—5B 6
Carrfield Ct. S8—1F 111
Carrfield Dri. S8—1F 111
Carr Field La. S63—6D 28
Carrfield Rd. S8—1F 111
Carrfield St. S8—1F 111
Carr Fold. S30—4H 141
Carr Forge Clo. S12—3A 114
Carr Forge La. S12—3A 114
Carr Forge Mt. S12—3A 114
Carr Forge Pl. S12—3B 114
Carr Forge Rd. S12—3A 114
Carr Forge Ter. S12—3A 114
Carr Forge View. S12—3A 114
Carr Forge Wlk. S12—3B 114
    (off Carter Lodge Dri.)
Carr Grn. S63—6E 29
Carr Grn. La. S75—6G 7
Carr Gro. S30—4G 141
Carr Head La. S63
    —6B 28 to 1A 42
Carr Hill. DN4—3B 46
Carr Ho. Rd. DN1 & DN4—2C 46
Carriage Way, The. DN11
    —4F 63
Carrill Dri. S6—3A 74
Carrill Rd. S6—3A 74
Carrington Av. S75—3G 13
Carrington Rd. S11—5H 97
Carrington St. S65—4F 79
Carrington St. S75—4F 13
Carrington Ter. S31—5H 117
Carr La. DN4—6C 48
    (Bassacarr)
Carr La. DN4—2D 46
    (Hyde Park)
Carr La. DN12—5F 59
Carr La. S1—3C 4 & 2D 98
Carr La. S18—1A 128
Carr La. S30—6F 141
Carr La. S31—3F 95
    (Slade Hooton)
Carr La. S31—2D 104
    (Ulley)
Carr La. S65—1E 71
Carr La. S66—2E 95
    (Carr, Maltby)
Carr La. S66—6D 82
    (Hooton Levitt)
Carr La. S75—1A 50
Carr Rd. DN12—4A 60
Carr Rd. S6—5A 86
Carr Rd. S30—5F 141
Carr Rd. S63—5G 41
Carrs La. S72—2H 15
Carr St. S71—2D 14
Carr View Av. DN4—3B 46
Carr View Rd. S61—1F 77
Carrville Dri. S6—5B 74
Carrville Rd. S6—5B 74
Carrville Rd. W. S6—5A 74
Carrwell La. S6—6A 74
Carrwood Rd. S71—1E 25
Carsick Gro. S10—4D 96
Carsick Hill Cres. S10—4D 96

Carsick Hill Dri. S10—4E 97
Carsick Hill Rd. S10—4D 96
Carsick Hill Way. S10—4D 96
Carsick View Rd. S10—4D 96
Carsington Rd. S40—6D 130
Carson Mt. S12—4D 112
Carson Rd. S10—2H 97
Carterhall La. S12—5E 113
Carterhall Rd. S12—5D 112
Carter Knowle Av. S11—2A 110
Carter Knowle Av. S11—2A 110
Carter Knowle Rd. S11 & S7
    —2H 109
Carter Lodge Av. S12—3A 114
Carter Lodge Dri. S12—3B 114
Carter Lodge Pl. S12—3B 114
Carter Lodge Rise. S12—3B 114
Carter Lodge Wlk. S12—3B 114
    (off Carter Lodge Dri.)
Carter Pl. S8—1F 111
Carter Rd. S8—1E 111
Cartmel Clo. S18—2C 128
Cartmel Clo. S66—3G 83
Cartmel Ct. S71—6F 9
Cartmel Cres. S41—3F 131
Cartmell Cres. S8—4D 110
Cartmell Rd. S8—3C 110
Cartmell Wlk. S31—6F 107
Car Vale Dri. S13—5E 101
Car Vale View. S13—5E 101
Carver Clo. S31—4H 127
Carver Dri. S31—5E 107
Carver La. S1—3D 4 & 2E 99
Carver St. S1—4D 4 & 2E 99
Carver Way. S31—3H 127
Carwood Clo. S4—4H 87
Carwood Grn. S4—4H 87
Carwood Gro. S4—4H 87
Carwood La. S4—4H 87
Carwood Rd. S4—4H 87
Carwood Way. S4—4H 87
Cary Rd. S2—5B 100
Cary Rd. S31—6B 124
Cascades Shopping Centre.
    S60—2D 78
Castell Cres. DN4—2C 48
Castle Av. DN12—3E 59
Castle Av. S60—6D 78
Castlebeck Av. S2—4D 100
Castlebeck Ct. S2—4E 101
    (off Castlebeck Av.)
Castlebeck Croft. S2—4E 101
Castlebeck Dri. S2—5D 100
Castle Clo. DN5—1G 45
Castle Clo. S71—4B 14
Castle Clo. S75—3C 22
Castle Cres. DN12—2E 59
Castledine Croft. S9—6D 76
Castledine Gdns. S9—6D 76
Castle Dri. S75—6A 22
Castlegate. S3—2G 5 & 1F 99
Castle Grn. S3—2F 5 & 1F 99
Castle Grn. S31—1D 106
Castle Gro. DN5—2D 44
Castle Gro. Ter. DN12—2F 59
Castle Hill. DN12—3E 59
Castle Hill. S31—5D 124
Castle Hill Av. S64—1H 57
Castle Hill Clo. S31—5D 124
Castle Hills Rd. DN5—6G 17
Castle Mkt. S1—2G 5 & 1F 99
Castlereagh St. S70—6G 13
Castlerigg Way. S18—2C 128
Castle Row. S17—3H 121
Castlerow Clo. S17—3H 121
Castlerow Dri. S17—3H 121
Castle Sq. S1—2F 5 & 1F 99
Castle St. DN12—3E 59

Castle St. S3—2F 5 & 1F 99
Castle St. S70—1G 23
Castle Ter. DN12—3E 59
Castleton Gro. S43—6H 133
Castle View. DN12—4B 60
Castle View. S31—6D 124
Castle View. S70—3C 36
Castle View. S75—1C 22
    (Dodworth)
Castle View. S75—6A 22
    (Hood Green)
Castlewood Cres. S10—5B 96
Castlewood Dri. S10—5C 96
Castlewood Rd. S10—5B 96
Castle Yd. S40—3A 138
Castor Rd. S9—4B 88
Catania Rise. S73—3C 26
Catch Bar La. S6—1A 86
Catchford View. S41—4D 130
Catcliffe Rd. S9—1E 101
Catherine Av. S31—6B 104
Catherine Ct. S40—2G 137
Catherine Rd. S4—5G 87
Catherine St. DN1—1D 46
Catherine St. S3—5F 87
Catherine St. S40—2G 137
Catherine St. S64—6D 42
Catherine St. S65—3E 79
Cathill Rd. S63—5G 27
Cat La. S2 & S8—1G 111
Catley Rd. S9—6E 89
Catling La. DN3—2H 21
Cattal St. S9—6C 88
Catterick Clo. DN12—3A 58
Cauldon Dri. S40—6C 130
Causeway Gdns. S17—1C 120
Causeway Glade. S17—1C 120
Causeway Head Rd. S17
    —1C 120
Causeway, The. S17—2D 120
Cavendish Av. S6—2E 85
Cavendish Av. S17—2F 121
Cavendish Clo. S65—5B 80
Cavendish Ct. S41—6A 132
Cavendish Pl. S66—3G 83
Cavendish Rise. S18—3D 128
Cavendish Rd. DN5—3A 18
Cavendish Rd. S11—6A 98
Cavendish Rd. S61—3A 78
Cavendish Rd. S75—4G 13
Cavendish St. S3—4B 4 & 2D 98
Cavendish St. S40—2A 138
Cavendish St. S43—3B 134
Cavendish St. N. S41—1A 132
Cavendish Ter. DN5—2A 18
Cave St. S9—6B 88
Cavill Rd. S8—4E 111
Cawdor Rd. S2—1A 112
Cawdor St. DN5—6B 18
Cawdron Rise. S60—4C 90
Cawley Pl. S71—3A 14
Cawston Rd. S4—3G 87
Cawthorne Clo. S8—4C 110
Cawthorne Clo. S65—2A 80
Cawthorne Gro. S73—2C 22
Cawthorne Gro. S8—4C 110
Cawthorne La. S75—6A 6
Cawthorne Rd. S65—2A 80
Cawthorne Rd. S75—2A 12
Caxton Clo. S43—1D 132
Caxton La. S10—3H 97
Caxton Rd. DN6—2D 16
Caxton Rd. S10—3A 98
Caxton St. S70—4G 13
Caythorpe Clo. S71—2G 15
Cayton Clo. S71—6A 8
Cecil Av. DN4—6E 45
Cecil Av. S18—1E 129

Cecil Rd. S18—6E 123
Cecil Sq. S2—5D 98
Cedar Av. S40—6F 131
Cedar Av. S64—5D 42
Cedar Av. S66—4G 81
Cedar Clo. DN4—6G 45
Cedar Clo. S30—4D 140
Cedar Clo. S31—6G 125
  (Eckington)
Cedar Clo. S31—4A 126
  (Killamarsh)
Cedar Clo. S71—1C 8
Cedar Cres. S70—2B 24
Cedar Dri. S66—4D 82
Cedar Gro. DN12—5C 58
Cedar Nook. S31—5G 117
Cedar Rd. DN3—2G 35
Cedar Rd. DN4—6G 45
Cedar Rd. S30—4D 140
Cedar St. S43—2G 133
Cedar Way. S30—3D 64
Cedric Av. DN12—4C 58
Cedric Cres. S66—5A 94
Cedric Dri. DN3—5D 20
Celandine Ct. S17—4G 121
Celandine Gdns. S17—4G 121
Celandine Rise. S64—5A 56
Cemetery Av. S11—4B 98
Cemetery La. S43—2C 134
Cemetery Rd. DN6—3C 16
Cemetery Rd. S11—5C 98
Cemetery Rd. S18—3F 129
Cemetery Rd. S41—3C 138
Cemetery Rd. S63—2A 42
  (Bolton-upon-Dearne)
Cemetery Rd. S63—1E 55 to
  (Wath upon Dearne)   5E 41
Cemetery Rd. S64—6E 43
Cemetery Rd. S70—1A 24
Cemetery Rd. S72—6G 11
Cemetery Rd. S73—4D 38
  (Hemingfield)
Cemetery Rd. S73—6B 26
  (Wombwell)
Cemetery Rd. S74—4C 38
Cemetery Ter. S43—4E 133
Centenary Way. S60 & S65
                      —4C 78
Central Av. DN5—1B 32
Central Av. DN6—3C 16
Central Av. S31—5F 107
Central Av. S40—3G 137
Central Av. S64—3H 55
Central Av. S65—2H 79
Central Av. S66—2F 81
Central Av. S72—5G 11
Central Boulevd. DN2—3H 33
Central Dri. DN11—5C 62
Central Dri. S41—4C 138
Central Dri. S44—2F 139
Central Dri. S62—5C 54
Central Dri. S66—5A 94
Central Dri. S71—2E 9
*Central Pavement. S40—2A 138
  (off Market Pl.)*
Central Rd. S60—3D 78
Central St. S41—4C 138
Central St. S63—3G 29
Central St. S74—6F 37
Central Ter. DN12—3B 60
Central Ter. S40—3B 138
Central Wlk. S43—4D 132
Centre Riding. DN11
                —6F & 5G 61
Centre, The. S66—4H 81
Century St. S9—5D 88
Chadbourne Clo. DN3—4E 35
Chaddesden Clo. S18—2A 128

Chaddeson Wlk. DN12—1D 58
Chadwick Dri. S66—3F 83
Chadwick Rd. DN5—6G 31
Chadwick Rd. DN6—3C 16
Chadwick Rd. S13—6E 101
Chaff Clo. S60—2H 91
Chaffinch Av. S60—3D 90
Chaff La. S60—2H 91
Chalfont Ct. S60—3D 90
Challand Way. S41—5C 138
Challenger Dri. DN5—6G 31
Challoner Grn. S19—1E 125
Challoner Way. S19—1E 125
Chalmers Dri. DN2—6B 20
Chamberlain Av. DN5—3H 31
Chamberlain Ct. S30—1D 64
Chambers Av. DN12—3C 58
Chambers La. S4—2B 88
Chambers Rd. S61—6H 67
Chambers Rd. S74—4H 37
Chamossaire. DN11—6C 62
Champion Clo. S5—3H 75
Champion Rd. S5—3H 75
Chancel Row. S2—2G 99
Chancel Way. S71—4C 14
Chancery Pl. DN1—6C 32
Chancet Wood Clo. S8—1D 122
Chancet Wood Dri. S8—1D 122
Chancet Wood Rise. S8—1D 122
Chancet Wood Rd. S8—6D 110
Chancet Wood View. S8
                —1D 122
Chandos Cres. S31—3A 126
Chandos St. S10—3A 98
Chaneyfield Way. S41—4D 130
Channing Gdns. S6—4B 86
Channing St. S6—4B 86
Chantrey Av. S41—5H 131
Chantrey Rd. S8—4D 110
Chantry Bri. S60—2D 78
Chantry Clo. DN4—4E 49
Chantry Pl. S31—4B 118
Chantry View. S60—3C 78
Chapel Av. S73—3A 40
Chapel Clo. S10—4F 97
Chapel Clo. S30—2C 64
Chapel Clo. S61—3A 68
Chapel Clo. S66—4A 94
Chapel Clo. S70—4C 36
Chapel Ct. S63—6E 41
Chapelfield Cres. S61—2B 66
Chapelfield Dri. S61—2B 66
Chapelfield La. S61—2B 66
Chapelfield Mt. S61—2B 66
Chapelfield Pl. S61—2B 66
Chapelfield Rd. S61—1B 66
Chapelfield Way. S61—2B 66
Chapel Hill. S60—2H 91
Chapel Hill S64—2A 56
Chapel Hill. S74—2H 37
Chapel Ho. S62—2F 69
Chapel La. DN3—3H 49
Chapel La. DN12—4E 59
Chapel La. S9—5C 88
Chapel La. S17—5D 120
Chapel La. S30—1G 141
Chapel La. S60—4D 78
Chapel La. S63—1H 29
Chapel La. S71—5E 9
Chapel La. S72—3B 28
  (Billingley)
Chapel La. S72—1G 27
  (Little Houghton)
Chapel La. E. S41—6D 138
Chapel La. W. S40—3E 137
Chapel Pl. S71—1F 25
Chapel Rise. S31—2F 119

Chapel Rd. S30—3C 64
  (Burncross & Chapeltown)
Chapel Rd. S30—5C 50
  (High Green)
Chapel Rd. S75—5A 36
Chapel St. DN5—1B 32
Chapel St. S13—1B 114
Chapel St. S19—3C 124
Chapel St. S41—3A 132
  (in two parts)
Chapel St. S43—3F 133
Chapel St. S61—3B 68
Chapel St. S62—2F 69
Chapel St. S63—1A 42
  (Bolton-upon-Dearne)
Chapel St. S63—1E 29
  (Thurnscoe)
Chapel St. S63—6E 41
  (Wath upon Dearne)
Chapel St. S64—6C 42
Chapel St. S70—4C 36
Chapel St. S71—1F 25
Chapel St. S72—6G 11
  (Grimethorpe)
Chapel St. S72—2C 10
  (Shafton)
Chapel St. S74—6F 37
Chapel Ter. S10—4F 97
Chapeltown Rd. S30—5F 65
Chapel View. DN3—2D 34
Chapel Wlk. S1—3E 5 & 2E 99
Chapel Wlk. S31—2F 119
Chapel Wlk. S60—3C 78
  (in two parts)
Chapel Wlk. S62—6D 54
Chapel Wlk. S64—1E 57
Chapelwood Rd. S9—5D 88
Chapel Yd. S18—1E 129
Chapman St. S9—5D 76
Chapman St. S63—1G 29
Chappell Dri. DN1—4C 32
Chapter Way. S71—4C 14
Charity St. S71—1F 15
Charles Ashmore Rd. S8
                —1D 122
Charles Cres. DN3—2D 34
Charles Cres. Flats. DN3—2D 34
Charles La. S1—4E 5 & 2E &
  (in two parts)   3F 99
Charles Rd. S63—6G 41
Charles Sq. S30—6B 50
Charles St. DN1—4E 33
Charles St. S1—4E 5 & 2E to
  (in two parts)   3F 99
Charles St. S31—3F 107
Charles St. S40—2G 137
Charles St. S62—6C 56
  (Kilnhurst)
Charles St. S62—6H 55
  (Rawmarsh)
Charles St. S63—4F 29
Charles St. S64—3B 56
Charles St. S66—4A 94
Charles St. S70—1G 23
  (Barnsley)
Charles St. S70—5A 24
  (Worsbrough)
Charles St. S72—5C 10
  (Cudworth)
Charles St. S72—2A 28
  (Little Houghton)
Charlotte La. S1—4B 4
Charlotte Rd. S1 & S2—4E 99
Charlton Brook Cres. S30
                —2C 64
Charlton Clough. S30—2B 64
Charlton Dri. S30—1C 64
Charnell Av. S66—4G 83

Charnley Av. S11—2A 110
Charnley Clo. S11—2A 110
Charnley Dri. S11—1A 110
Charnley Rise. S11—2A 110
Charnock Av. S12—5D 112
Charnock Cres. S12—4C 112
Charnock Dale Rd. S12—5C 112
Charnock Dri. S12—4D 112
Charnock Gro. S12—5D 112
Charnock Hall Rd. S12—5C 112
Charnock View Rd. S12
                —5C 112
Charnock Wood Rd. S12
                —5D 112
Charnwood Ct. S19—5G 115
Charnwood Dri. DN4—6H 45
Charnwood Gro. S61—2H 77
Charnwood St. S64—2B 56
Charter Arc. S70—6H 13
Charter Row. S1—6D 4 & 3E 99
Charter Sq. S1—5D 4 & 3E 99
Chasecliff Clo. S40—6F 131
Chase Rd. S6—3D 84
*Chase, The. S10—4B 98
  (off Clarkegrove Rd.)*
Chase, The. S31—1C 116
Chatfield Rd. S8—5C 110
*Chatham Ho. S65—3E 79
  (off Chatham St.)*
Chatham St. S3—6E 87
Chatham St. S65—3E 79
Chatsworth Av. S40—3D 136
Chatsworth Av. S64—5H 43
Chatsworth Clo. S31—6D 104
Chatsworth Ct. S17—3F 109
Chatsworth Ct. S43—3B 134
Chatsworth Cres. DN5—1H 31
Chatsworth Pk. Av. S12
                —2C 112
Chatsworth Pk. Dri. S12
                —2C 112
Chatsworth Pk. Gro. S12
                —2C 112
Chatsworth Pk. Rise. S12
                —2C 112
Chatsworth Pk. Rd. S12
                —2C 112
Chatsworth Pl. S18—1B 128
Chatsworth Rise. S60—3D 90
Chatsworth Rise. S75—3B 22
Chatsworth Rd. S17—3E 121
Chatsworth Rd. S40
                —3B 136 to 2H 137
Chatsworth Rd. S61—3B 68
Chatsworth Rd. S71—1A 14
Chatterton Dri. S65—5H 79
Chaucer Clo. S5—3B 74
Chaucer Dri. S18—4G 129
*Chaucer Ho. S65—4H 79
  (off Browning Rd.)*
Chaucer Rd. S5—4B 74
Chaucer Rd. S41—3H 131
Chaucer Rd. S64—5F 43
Chaucer Rd. S65—5H 79
Cheadle St. S6—3A 86
Cheapside. S70—6H 13
Checkstone Av. DN4—6C 48
Chedworth Clo. S75—6C 6
Cheedale Av. S40—6E 131
Cheedale Clo. S40—6E 131
Cheedale Wlk. S40—6F 131
Cheetham Dri. S66—3G 83
Chelmsford Av. S31—5C 104
Chelmsford Dri. DN2—3F 33
Chelsea Ct. S11—6A 98
Chelsea Rise. S11—6A 98
Chelsea Rd. S11—1A 110
Cheltenham Rise. DN5—3F 31

Cheltenham Rd. DN2—4A 34
Chemical Yd. S17—5F 121
Chemist La. S60—2C 78
Cheney Row. S1—4E 5
Chepstow Clo. S40—5H 137
Chepstow Dri. S64—5F 43
Chepstow Gdns. DN5—4F 31
Chepstow Gdns. S40—6H 137
Chequer Av. DN4—1E 47
Chequer Rd. DN1—6D 32
Chequers Row. S2—1H 99
Cheriton Av. DN6—1C 16
Cherry Bank Rd. S8—4E 111
Cherry Clo. S71—1C 8
Cherry Clo. S72—5B 10
Cherry Garth. DN5—4B 18
Cherry Gro. DN11—5E 63
Cherry Gro. DN12—5B 58
Cherry La. DN5—5B 32
Cherrys Rd. S71—5D 14
Cherry St. S2—5E 99
Cherry St. S. S2—5E 99
Cherry Tree Clo. S11—6B 98
Cherry Tree Clo. S60—3D 90
Cherry Tree Clo. S75—4G 7
Cherry Tree Ct. S11—6B 98
Cherry Tree Cres. S66—4G 81
Cherry Tree Dell. S11—6B 98
Cherry Tree Dri. S11—6B 98
Cherry Tree Dri. S31—4B 126
Cherry Tree Rd. S63—6F 41
Cherry Tree Rd. DN3—3F 35
Cherry Tree Rd. DN4—1B 46
Cherry Tree Rd. S11—6B 98
Cherry Tree Rd. S31—5E 117
Cherry Tree Rd. S66—4D 82
Cherry Tree St. S74—5B 38
Cherry Wlk. S30—2E 65
Chertsey Clo. S40—5H 137
Cherwell Clo. S43—2E 133
Chesham Rd. S70—6F 13
Cheshire Rd. DN1—4E 33
Chessel Clo. S8—3E 111
Chesterfield Av. S43—1E 133
Chesterfield Inr. Rf. Rd. S41
—1G 131 to 3B 138
(Inner Relief Road)
Chesterfield Rd. S8—5D 110
Chesterfield Rd. S18—1E 129
(Dronfield)
Chesterfield Rd. S31—6G 125
(Eckington)
Chesterfield Rd. S31—2H 115
(in two parts, Swallownest)
Chesterfield Rd. S43—4D 132
(Brimington)
Chesterfield Rd. S43—3G 133 to
(Staveley)   1C 134
Chesterfield Rd. S44—3E 139
(Calow)
Chesterfield Rd. S44—çP 0
(Duckmanton)
Chesterfield Rd. S. S8—4E 123
Chesterhill Av. S65—6C 70
Chester La. S1—5C 4 & 3D 98
Chester Rd. DN2—3F 33
Chester St. S1—4C 4 & 2D 98
Chester St. S40—2G 137
Chesterton Clo. S43—1F 139
Chesterton Rd. DN4—5C 46
Chesterton Rd. S65—1F 79
Chesterton Way. S65—6H 69
Chesterwood Dri. S10—3H 97
Chestnut Av. DN2—2H 33
Chestnut Av. DN3—2F 35
Chestnut Av. DN11—5E 63
Chestnut Av. S9—2G 101
Chestnut Av. S19—2F 115

Chestnut Av. S30—4D 140
Chestnut Av. S31—6G 125
(Eckington)
Chestnut Av. S31—4A 126
(Killamarsh)
Chestnut Av. S31—4G 117
(Kiveton Park)
Chestnut Av. S63—1F 55
Chestnut Av. S65—2H 79
Chestnut Av. S72—3F 11
Chestnut Clo. S18—3G 129
Chestnut Clo. S66—3F 81
Chestnut Cres. S70—2B 24
Chestnut Dri. S30—3C 64
Chestnut Gro. DN5—3D 44
Chestnut Gro. DN12—4C 58
Chestnut Gro. S31—3F 107
Chestnut Gro. S63—2F 29
Chestnut Gro. S64—5D 42
Chestnut Gro. S66—3D 82
Chestnut Rd. S31—5H 103
Chestnut Wlk. S66—5E 83
Chevet Ho. DN1—1C 46
(off Grove Pl.)
Chevet Rise. S71—1D 8
Chevet View. S71—1C 8
Cheviot Dri. DN5—2H 31
Cheviot Wlk. S75—5D 12
Cheviot Way. S40—6E 131
Chevril Ct. S66—5E 81
Chichester Rd. S10—1H 97
Childers St. DN4—2E 47
Chiltern Clo. S40—1E 137
Chiltern Ct. S40—1E 137
Chiltern Cres. DN5—2C 44
Chiltern Rise. S60—4D 90
Chiltern Rd. DN5—2H 31
Chiltern Rd. S6—3H 85
Chiltern Wlk. S75—5D 12
Chilton St. S70—1A 24
Chilwell Rd. S71—4B 8
Chilwell Sq. S71—4B 8
Chinley St. S9—6C 88
Chippingham Pl. S9—5B 88
Chippingham St. S9—5C 88
Chippinghouse Rd. S7 & S8
—6D 98
Chiverton Clo. S18—1E 129
Chorley Av. S10—5C 96
Chorley Dri. S10—5C 96
Chorley Pl. S10—6C 96
Chorley Rd. S10—6C 96
Christchurch Av. S31—5C 104
Christ Chu. Rd. DN1—5D 32
Christ Chu. Rd. S3—4F 87
Christchurch Rd. S63—4C 40
Christ Chu. Ter. DN1—6E 33
Church Av. S62—3E 69
Church Balk. DN3—4C 20
Church Balk Gdns. DN3—4D 20
Church Clo. S30—2D 72
Church Clo. S31—5F 117
Church Clo. S43—4A 134
Church Clo. S64—2A 56
Church Clo. S65—4G 71
Church Clo. S66—5F 83
Church Corner. S31—6F 95
Church Cottage M. DN4—4G 45
Church Ct. DN4—4D 48
Church Ct. S31—3G 119
Church Croft. DN4—4C 20
Churchdale Rd. S12—3F 113
Church Dri. S72—3F 11
Churchfield. S70—5G 13
Churchfield Av. S72—1H 15
Churchfield Av. S75—5A 6
Churchfield Clo. DN5—1A 32
Churchfield Clo. S75—5A 6

Churchfield Ct. S70—5G 13
Churchfield Ct. S75—5B 6
Churchfield Cres. S72—1H 15
Church Field Dri. S66—5F 81
Church Field La. S62—5C 52
Churchfield La. S75—5A 6
Churchfield Rd. DN11—4F 63
Church Fields. S61—2G 77
Church Fields Rd. DN11—3E 63
Churchfield Ter. S72—1H 15
Church Grn. S63—5E 41
Church Gro. S71—3C 14
Church Hill. S60—2A 92
Church Hill. S71—2F 9
Churchill Av. DN5—3A 32
Churchill Av. S66—3G 83
Churchill Rd. DN1—3E 33
Churchill Rd. S10—2A 98
Churchill Rd. S30—2B 140
Church La. DN3—1G 21
Church La. DN4—5C 48
(Bessacarr)
Church La. DN4—4F 45
(Warmsworth)
Church La. DN5—1G 43
Church La. DN6—1E 17
Church La. DN11—6H 61
(in two parts)
Church La. S9—5B 88
Church La. S12—4C 114
Church La. S13—1B 114
Church La. S17—3D 120
Church La. S19—4G 115
Church La. S31—1D 116
(Aston)
Church La. S31—4D 106
(Dinnington)
Church La. S31—3C 126
(Killamarsh)
Church La. S40—2A 138
Church La. S44—2F 139
Church La. S60—5C 90
(Catcliffe)
Church La. S60—1E 103
(Treeton)
Church La. S63—5E 41
Church La. S65—4H 71
Church La. S66—4H 81
(Bramley)
Church La. S66—5F 83
(Maltby)
Church La. S66—5F 81
(Wickersley)
Church La. S70—5G 13
(Barnsley)
Church La. S70—1E 37
(Worsbrough)
Church La. S75—2C 50
Church La. M. S66—3H 81
Church Meadows. S44—2F 139
Church M. DN5—1A 32
Church M. S19—2D 124
Church M. S31—2C 126
Church Rd. DN3—1G 21
(Barnby Dun)
Church Rd. DN3—3D 20
(Kirk Sandall)
Church Rd. DN11—6H 61
Church Rd. DN12—1C 58
(Denaby Main)
Church Rd. DN12—2B 60
(Edlington)
Churchside. S41—6D 138
Churchside. S44—2F 139
Churchside La. S41—6D 138
Church St. DN1—5C 32
Church St. DN3—3E 35
Church St. DN5—1A 32

Church St. DN12—3E 59
Church St. S1—3E 5 & 2E 99
Church St. S6—6C 84
Church St. S18—2E 129
Church St. S30—6E 65
(Ecclesfield)
Church St. S30—2C 72
(Oughtibridge)
Church St. S31—5E 125
(Eckington)
Church St. S31—5F 117
(Wales)
Church St. S43—3E 133
(Brimington)
Church St. S43—1C 134
(Staveley)
Church St. S44—2F 139
Church St. S60—3D 78
Church St. S61—3A 68
(Greasbrough)
Church St. S61—2G 77
(Kimberworth)
Church St. S62—3E 69
Church St. S63—1A 42
(Bolton-upon-Dearne)
Church St. S63—1E 29
(Thurnscoe)
Church St. S63—5E 41
(Wath upon Dearne)
Church St. S64—1F 57
(Mexborough)
Church St. S64—2H 55
(Swinton)
Church St. S66—5B 94
Church St. S70—5G 13
Church St. S71—4F 9
(Carlton)
Church St. S71—2E 9
(Royston)
Church St. S72—2F 11
(Brierley)
Church St. S72—1H 15
(Cudworth)
Church St. S73—4F 27
(Darfield)
Church St. S73—1F 39
(Wombwell)
Church St. S74—6C 38
(Elsecar)
Church St. S74—4B 38
(Jump)
Church St. S75—5C 6
(Darton)
Church St. S75—4C 12
(Gawber)
Church St. S75—4G 7
(Mapplewell)
Church St. Clo. S63—1E 29
Church St. N. S41—1A 132
Church St. S. S40—6A 138
(in two parts)
Church St. W. S40—3E 137
Church Ter. S75—2A 22
Church View. DN1—5C 32
Church View. DN5—1H 43
Church View. DN11—6H 61
Church View. S13—1C 114
Church View. S31—6D 104
(Aston)
Church View. S31—2C 126
(Killamarsh)
Church View. S31—2B 118
(Todwick)
Church View. S40—3E 137
Church View. S64—2A 56
Church View. S65—4D 70
Church View. S66—5F 81

Church View. S72—1H 15
Church View. S73—4G 27
Church View. S74—6F 37
Church View. S75—4E 13
Church Wlk. DN12—1C 58
Church Wlk. S40—2A 138
(off Stephenson Pl.)
Church Wlk. S63—1E 29
(off Church St.)
Church Way. DN1—5C 32
Church Way. S40—2A 138
Churston Rd. S40—2F 137
Cinder Bri. Rd. S61—3C 68
Cinderhill La. S8—1F 123
Cinder Hill La. S30—1B 74
Cinderhill Rd. S61—5G 67
Cinder La. S31—2D 126
Circle, The. DN11—4C 62
Circle, The. S2—4D 100
Circle, The. S30—6C 50
Circuit, The. DN6—1B 16
Circular Rd. S41—5B 138
Circular Rd. S43—3B 134
City Plaza. S1—3D 4
City Rd. S2 & S12—3H 99
Clanricarde St. S71—3G 13
Clara St. S61—3H 77
Clare Ct. S60—2D 78
Clarehurst Rd. S73—3E 27
Clarell Gdns. DN4—2C 48
Claremont Cres. S10—2B 98
Claremont Pl. S10—2B 98
Claremont St. S61—3H 77
Clarence Av. DN4—3B 46
Clarence La. S3—4D 98
Clarence Pl. S66—3G 83
Clarence Rd. S6—3H 85
Clarence Rd. S40—2H 137
Clarence Rd. S71—3B 14
Clarence Sq. S31—4G 107
Clarence St. S31—4G 107
Clarence St. S40—2H 137
Clarence St. S63—4D 40
Clarence Ter. S63—1G 29
(off Clarke St.)
Clarendon Ct. S11—5E 97
Clarendon Dri. S10—5E 97
Clarendon Rd. S10—6E 97
Clarendon Rd. S43—5A 134
Clarendon Rd. S65—2F 79
Clarendon St. S70—6F 13
Clark Av. DN4—1E 47
Clark Av. DN12—5B 60
Clarke Av. S66—5C 94
Clarke Dell. S10—4B 98
Clarke Dri. S10—4B 98
Clarkegrove Rd. S10—4B 98
Clarkehouse Rd. S10—4A 98
Clarke Sq. S2—5D 98
Clarke St. S10—6A 4 & 3C 98
Clarke St. S63—1G 29
Clarke St. S75—4F 13
Clark Gro. S6—5D 84
Clarks Ct. DN6—1D 16
Clarkson Av. S40—5H 137
Clarkson St. S10—4B 98
Clarkson St. S70—4C 24
Clark St. S74—4H 37
Clarney Av. S73—3D 26
Clarney Pl. S73—3E 27
Claycliffe Av. S75—3B 12
Claycliffe Rd. S75—1B 12
Claycliffe Rd. Ind. Est. S75
—2C 12
Claycliffe Ter. S63—4G 29
Claycliffe Ter. S70—1F 23
Clayfield Av. S64—6H 43
Clayfield Clo. S64—6H 43

Clayfield Ct. S64—6H 43
Clayfield La. S62—4D 52
Clayfield Rd. S64—6H 43
Clayfield Rd. S74—3H 37
Clayfields. DN4—6A 46
Clayfield View. S64—5H 43
Clay Flat La. DN11—5D 62
Clay La. DN2—5A 20
Clay La. S1—5E 5
Clay La. W. DN2—6A 20
Clay Pit La. S62—2G 69
Clay Pits La. DN2—3A 140
Clayroyd. S70—5B 24
Clay St. S9—4B & 4C 88
(in two parts)
Clayton Av. S63—1D 28
Clayton Cres. S19—5E 115
Clayton Dri. S63—1D 28
Clayton Hollow. S19—5E 115
Clayton La. S63—1D 28
Clayton St. S41—3B 138
Clay Wheels La. S6—5H 73
Claywood Dri. S2—5H 5 & 3G 99
Claywood Rd. S2—5H 5 & 3G &
(in two parts) 4G 99
Clayworth Dri. DN4—4A 48
Clear View. S72—5G 11
Clearwell Croft. DN5—4H 31
Cleeve Hill Gdns. S19—5D 114
Clematis Rd. S5—6B 76
Clementson Rd. S10—1A 98
Clement St. S9—5D 88
Clement St. S61—3G 77
Clevedon Cres. DN5—6H 17
Clevedon Way. S66—2H 83
Clevedon Way. S71—1D 8
Cleveland Rd. DN3—3G 35
Cleveland St. DN1—1C 46
Cleveland St. S6—6C 86
Cleveland Way. S42—1D 136
Cliff Clo. S72—2F 11
Cliff Ct. DN12—2B 58
Cliff Cres. DN4—2C 48
Cliff. Dri. S73—4G 27
Cliffe Av. S70—4B 24
Cliffe Bank. S64—2B 56
Cliffe Ct. S71—4C 14
Cliffe Cres. S75—2A 22
Cliffedale Cres. S70—3B 24
Cliffe Farm Dri. S11—6G 97
Cliffe Field Rd. S8—2D 110
Cliffefield Rd. S64—2B 56
Cliffe Ho. Rd. S5—5F 75
Cliffe La. S71—4C 14
Cliffe Rd. S6—5G 85
Cliffe Rd. S73—3A 40
Cliffe View Rd. S8—2E 111
Cliff Hill. S66—4D 82
Cliff La. DN12—6H 57
Cliff La. S72—3E 11
Clifford Av. S65—5E 71
Clifford Clo. S40—3D 136
Clifford Rd. S11—6B 98
Clifford Rd. S61—6G 67
Clifford Rd. S66—5A 82
Clifford St. S72—4C 10
Clifford Wlk. DN12—2A 58
Cliff Rd. S6—5D 84
Cliff Rd. S73—4G 27
Cliff St. S11—4D 98
Cliff St. S64—1E 57
Cliff Ter. S71—6A 14
Cliff View. DN12—1B 58
Clifton Av. S9—2G 101
Clifton Av. S65—3G 79
Clifton Bank. S60—3E 79
Clifton Cres. DN2—3H 33
Clifton Cres. S9—2G 101

Clifton Cres. S71—5A 8
Clifton Cres. N. S65—3F 79
Clifton Cres. S. S65—3F 79
Clifton Dri. DN5—1G 45
Clifton Gdns. S72—2E 11
Clifton Gro. S65—3F 79
Clifton Hill. DN12—4E 59
Clifton La. S9—3G 101
Clifton La. S65—3E 79
Clifton Mt. S65—3E 79
Clifton Rise. S66—3E 83
Clifton Rd. S72—6G 11
Clifton St. S40—2G 137
Clifton St. S70—1A 24
Clifton Ter. DN12—3F 59
Clifton Ter. S65—3E 79
Clinton La. S10—6A 4 & 3C 98
Clinton Pl. S10—6A 4 & 3C 98
Clipstone Av. S71—5C 8
Clipstone Gdns. S9—5E 89
Clipstone Rd. S9—5E 89
Clixby Rd. S9—4B 88
Cloisters, The. DN4—4E 49
Cloisters, The. S70—1D 36
Cloisters Way. S71—4D 14
Cloonmore Croft. S8—6G 111
Cloonmore Dri. S8—6G 111
Close, The. DN3—3H 49
Close, The. S71—4E 9
Cloudberry Way. S75—5H 7
Clough Bank. S2—5F 99
Clough Bank. S61—2B 78
(in two parts)
Clough Field Rd. S74—6G 37
Clough Fields. S10—1F 97
Clough Grn. S61—2C 78
Clough La. S10—2A 108
Clough La. S1 & S2—4E 99
Clough Rd. S61—2B 78
(in two parts)
Clough Rd. S74—6H 37
Clough St. S61—2B 78
(in two parts)
Clough, The. S41—4E 139
Clough Wood View. S30—3D 72
Clovelly Rd. DN3—5D 20
Clover Ct. S8—5H 111
Clover Gdns. S5—6A 76
Clover Grn. S61—5G 67
Cloverlands Dri. S75—5H 7
Clover Wlk. S63—6D 28
Club Garden Rd. S11—5D to
4D 98
Club Garden Wlk. S11—4D 98
(off Club Garden Rd.)
Club Mill Rd. S6—2C to 5C 86
Clubmill Ter. S40—1G 137
Club St. S11—5D 98
Club St. S71—3C 14
Club St. S74—6F 37
Clumber Mt. S65—1H 79
Clumber Pl. S43—5A 134
Clumber Rise. S31—1C 116
Clumber Rd. DN4—2F 47
Clumber Rd. S10—4E 97
Clumber St. S75—5E 13
Clun Rd. S4—5G 87
Clun St. S4—5G 87
Clyde Rd. S8—1D 110
Clyde St. S71—6A 14
Coach Dri. S62—4C 52
Coach Ho. Dri. DN5—5F 31
Coach Ho. La. S70—3H 23
Coach Rd. S61—3B 68
Coach Rd. S62—5H 51
Coalbrook Av. S13—5D 102
Coalbrook Cres. S13—5E 103

Coalbrook Gro. S13—5D 102
Coalbrook Rd. S13—5D 102
Coalby Wlk. S70—5G 13
(off Prospect St.)
Coal Pit La. S30—5D 140
(Stocksbridge)
Coal Pit La. S30—4A 72
(Worrall)
Coalpit La. S31—6F 117
Coal Pit La. S72—3D 10
(Shafton)
Coalpit Rd. DN12—2A 58
Coal Riding La. S65—3D 80
Coates St. S2—3G 99
Cobb Dri. S64—4A 56
(in two parts)
Cobcar Av. S74—6D 38
Cobcar Clo. S74—5C 38
Cobcar La. S74—5C 38
Cobcar St. S74—6C 38
Cobden Av. S64—6F 43
Cobden Pl. S10—1A 98
Cobden Rd. S40—1H 137
Cobden Ter. S10—1A 98
Cobden View Rd. S10—1H 97
Cobnar Av. S8—5E 111
Cobnar Dri. S8—5E 111
Cobnar Dri. S41—3F 131
Cobnar Gdns. S8—5D 110
Cobnar Rd. S8—5D 110
Cockayne Pl. S8—2D 110
Cockerham Av. S75—4G 13
Cockerham La. S75—4G 13
Cockshot La. S30—5E 141
Cockshot Pit La. S75—5E 7
Cockshutt Av. S8—1B 122
Cockshutt Dri. S8—1B 122
Cockshutt Rd. S8—1B 122
Cockshutts La. S30—1C 72
Coisley Hill. S13—1H 113
Coisley Rd. S13—2A 114
Coke Hill. S60—4D 78
Coke La. S60—4D 78
Colbeck Clo. DN3—3E 35
Colby Pl. S6—6F 85
Colchester Ct. DN5—3G 31
Colchester Rd. S10—1H 97
Coldstream Av. DN4—5F 45
Coldwell Hill. S30—2B 72
Coldwell La. S10—2E 97
Coleford Rd. S9—6F 89
Coleman St. S62—4F 69
Coleridge Av. S71—3B 14
Coleridge Gdns. S9—5E 89
Coleridge Rd. DN3—1H 21
Coleridge Rd. S9—4C 88
Coleridge Rd. S65—2F 79
Coleridge St. S66—5G 83
Coley La. S62—4F 53
Colister Dri. S9—1E 101
Colister Gdns. S9—1E 101
College Av. S43—2B 134
College Clo. S4—3G 87
College Ct. S4—3G 87
College La. S65—3D 78
(off College St.)
College Pk. Clo. S60—6E 79
College Rd. DN1—1C 46
(in two parts)
College Rd. S60—3B 78
(in two parts)
College Rd. S64—6F 43
College St. S10—3B 98
College St. S65—3D 78
College Ter. S73—4E 27
Collegiate Cres. S10—4B 98
Colleridge Rd. S63—4C 40
Colley Av. S5—3E 75

Sheffield 159

Colley Av. S70—3C 24
Colley Clo. S5—3E 75
Colley Cres. S5—3F 75
Colley Cres. S70—2C 24
Colley Dri. S5—3F 75
Colley Rd. S5—3F 75
Colliers Clo. S13—1B 114
Colliery Rd. S4—2C 88
Colliery Rd. S31—5H 117
Colliery Yd. S75—6B 36
Collin Av. S6—2G 85
Collindridge Rd. S73—1F 39
Collingbourne Av. S19—6G 115
Collingbourne Dri. S19—6G 115
Collingham Rd. S31—1A 116
Collingwood. S65—1H 79
Collins Clo. S75—2A 22
Collinson Rd. S5—5E 75
Collishaw Clo. S41—5C 138
Colne Ct. S60—1E 91
Colonel Ward Dri. S64—2C 56
Colonnades, The. DN1—6C 32
(off Cleveland St.)
Colster Clo. S75—4C 12
Coltfield. S70—2D 36
Coltishall Av. S66—3H 81
Colton Clo. S41—2G 131
Columbia St. S70—2G 23
Columbus Way. S66—3E 83
Colver Rd. S2—5E 99
(in two parts)
Colvin Clo. DN5—6E 19
Colwall St. S9—5B 88
Commerce St. S30—1F 65
Commercial Rd. S63—5E 29
Commercial St. S1
—3G 5 & 2F 99
Commercial St. S70—1B 24
Common Farm Clo. S65—1H 81
Common La. DN4—6F 45
Common La. DN5—2G 19
Common La. DN11—6F 63
Common La. DN12—5F 59
Common La. S11—1D 108
Common La. S30—5G 141
Common La. S42—3A 130
Common La. S63—2C 42
(Bolton-upon-Dearne)
Common La. S63—5H 41
(Wath upon Dearne)
Common La. S65—1A 83
Common La. S66—1H 105
(Brampton en le Morthen)
Common La. S66—1B 106
(Thurcroft)
Common La. S71—1E 9
Common Rd. DN12—4G 59
Common Rd. S31—4A 106
(Anston)
Common Rd. S31—3D 106
(Dinnington)
Common Rd. S63—1D 28
Common Rd. S72—3G 11
Commonside. S10—1A 98
Common, The. S30—5F 65
Commonwealth View. S63
—1H 41
Compton St. S6—5H 85
Compton St. S40—2H 137
Conalan Av. S17—4H 121
Conan Rd. DN12—3D 58
Concord St. S5—3A 76
Concord View Rd. S61—4E 77
Conduit La. S10—1A 98
Conduit Rd. S10—1A 98
Conery Clo. S65—5E 71
Coney Rd. DN5—3A 18

Congress St. S1—3C 4 & 2D 98
Coningsburgh Rd. DN3—5D 20
Coningsby Ho. S10—3D 96
Coningsby Rd. S5—2G 87
Coniston Av. S75—3E 7
Coniston Clo. S31—1H 119
Coniston Ct. S64—5H 43
Coniston Dri. S63—2A 42
Coniston Pl. DN5—1H 31
Coniston Rd. DN2—5A 34
Coniston Rd. DN3—3D 20
Coniston Rd. S8—2C 110
Coniston Rd. S18—3B 128
Coniston Rd. S41—3F 131
Coniston Rd. S64—5G 43
Coniston Rd. S71—6A 14
Coniston Ter. S8—2C 110
Coniston Way. S41—3F 131
Connaught Dri. DN3—3D 20
Connelly Ct. S40—2G 137
Constable Clo. S14—5H 111
Constable Clo. S18—2C 128
Constable Clo. S66—3F 81
Constable Dri. S14—5H 111
Constable La. S31—4F 107
Constable Pl. S14—5A 112
Constable Pl. S63—5E 41
Constable Rd. S14—5H 111
Constable Way. S14—5H 111
Convent Gro. DN4—3B 48
Convent Pl. S3—4B 4 & 2D 98
Convent Wlk. S3—4B 4 & 2D 98
Conway Cres. S65—1H 81
Conway Dri. DN3—3H 49
Conway Dri. DN5—1G 43
Conway Pl. S73—2H 39
Conway St. S3—4A 4 & 2C 98
Conway St. S70—1D 24
Conway Ter. S64—5E 43
Conyers Dri. S31—5B 104
Conyers Rd. DN5—4B 32
Coo Hill. S13—1C 114
Cook Av. S66—3E 83
Cooke St. DN5—1A 32
Cookson Clo. S5—5B 74
Cookson Rd. S5—6B 74
Cookson St. DN4—3B 46
Cooks Rd. S19—5G 115
Cooks Wood Rd. S3—4E 87
Coombe Pl. S10—2A 98
Coombe Rd. S10—2A 98
Co-operative Cotts. S43
—4E 135
Co-operative Cotts. S72—2F 11
(Goldthorpe)
Co-operative St. S63—4G 29
(Goldthorpe)
Co-operative St. S63—4D 40
(Wath upon Dearne)
Co-operative St. S72—1G 15
Cooper Rd. S75—5A 6
Cooper Row. S75—3B 22
(off Stainborough Row)
Coopers Ter. DN1—6D 32
Cooper St. DN4—2E 47
Copeland Rd. S73—6A 26
Cope St. S70—2H 23
Copley Av. DN12—3C 58
Copley Clo. DN5—3E 31
Copley Pl. S61—2A 78
Copley Rd. DN1—5D 32
Copley St. S8—1E 111
Copper Beech Cres. S66—6E 83
Copper Clo. S70—1H 23
Copper St. S3—1D 4 & 1E 99
Coppice Clo. S30—2B 140
Coppice Clo. S41—6D 138
Coppice Gdns. S61—5B 68
Coppice La. S6—1B 96

Coppice Rd. DN6—5D 16
Coppice Rd. S10—2B 96
Coppice, The. S61—5E 67
Coppice View. S10—2F 97
Coppins Clo. S66—3H 81
Coppin Sq. S5—2D 74
Copse, The. S66—3H 81
Coquet Av. S66—5H 81
Coral Clo. S31—3A 104
Coral Dri. S31—3A 104
Coral Pl. S31—3A 104
Coral Way. S31—3A 104
Corby Rd. S4—2B 88
Corby St. S4—5H 87
Cordwell Av. S41—3E 131
Cordwell Clo. S43—3B 134
Corker Bottoms La. S2—2B 100
Corker Rd. S12—1C 112
Cork La. S70—4E 25
Cornfield Clo. S42—6C 130
Corn Hill. DN12—4F 59
Cornish St. S6—6D 86
Cornish Way. S62—5E 69
Cornwall Av. S43—3F 133
Cornwall Clo. S43—3F 133
Cornwall Clo. S71—3B 14
Cornwall Dri. S43—3F 133
Cornwall Rd. DN2—4H 33
Cornwall Clo. S62—5C 54
Coronach Way. DN11—5C 62
Coronation Av. S31—3F 107
(Dinnington)
Coronation Av. S31—5G 117
(Kiveton Park)
Coronation Av. S71—1G 9
Coronation Av. S72—2B 10
Coronation Bri. S61 & S60
—3B 78
Coronation Cotts. DN3—1G 21
Coronation Ct. S64—5E 43
Coronation Cres. S70—2D 36
Coronation Dri. S63—1H 41
Coronation Dri. S70—2D 36
Coronation Gdns. DN4—5E 45
Coronation Rd. DN4—4B 46
Coronation Rd. S30—3D 140
Coronation Rd. S43—3E 133
Coronation Rd. S62—1A 70
Coronation Rd. S63—5G 41
Coronation Rd. S64—2C 56
Coronation Rd. S74—5H 37
Coronation Rd. S75—3A 12
Coronation St. S63—2G 29
Coronation St. S71—3C 14
Coronation St. S73—3F 27
Coronation Ter. S71—1F 25
Coronation Ter. S73—3E 39
Corporation St. S3
—1E 5 & 1E 99
Corporation St. S41—2B 138
Corporation St. S60—3D 78
Corporation St. S70—1A 24
Cortina Rise. S73—3C 26
Cortonwood Ho. DN1—1C 9
(off Bond Clo.)
Cortworth La. S62—4F 53
Cortworth Rd. S11—3G 109
Corve Way. S40—6B 130
Corwen Pl. S13—1A 114
Cossey Rd. S4—5H 87
Coterel Cres. DN4—2D 48
Cotleigh Av. S12—4A 114
Cotleigh Clo. S12—4A 114
Cotleigh Cres. S12—4A 114
Cotleigh Dri. S12—4A 114
Cotleigh Gdns. S12—4A 114
Cotleigh Pl. S12—4A 114
Cotleigh Rd. S12—4A 114

Cotleigh Way. S12—4A 114
Cotswold Av. S30—2C 64
Cotswold Clo. S40—6E 131
Cotswold Clo. S75—5D 12
Cotswold Cres. S60—2A 92
Cotswold Dri. DN5—2C 44
Cotswold Dri. S31—6C 104
Cotswold Gdns. DN5—2H 31
Cotswold Rd. S6—3H 85
Cottage Clo. S43—4E 133
Cottage La. S11—2C 108
Cottam Clo. S60—2A 92
Cottam Rd. S30—6A 50
Cottenham Rd. S65—2F 79
Cotterhill La. S43—4E 133
Cottesmore Clo. S75—4E 13
Cottingham St. S9—1B 100
Cotton Mill Hill. S42—6A 136
Cotton Mill Row. S3
—1E 5 & 6E 87
Cotton Mill Wlk. S3—6E 87
Cotton St. S3—1E 5 & 6E 87
Coulston Dri. S3—1F 5 & 1F 99
Coultas Av. S30—5F 141
Countess Rd. S1—4E 99
County Way. S70—5H 13
(in two parts)
Coupe Rd. S3—5F 87
Coupland Rd. S65—1A 80
Court Clo. DN5—3F 31
Court Pl. S43—3A 134
Coventry Gro. DN2—2H 33
Coventry Rd. S9—6E 89
Cover Clo. S62—4H 51
Coverdale Rd. S7—2C 110
Cover Dri. S73—3F 27
Coverleigh Rd. S63—1F 55
Coward Dri. S30—2D 72
Cow Ho. La. DN3—3G 35
Cow La. S11—5G 97
(Greystones)
Cow La. S11—4G 109
(Parkhead)
Cow La. S43—2E 133
Cowley Dri. S30—3G 65
Cowley Gdns. S19—1E 125
Cowley Hill. S30—3G 65
Cowley La. S18—4A to 3D 128
Cowley La. S30—2F 65
Cowley Pl. DN3—3D 20
Cowley Rd. S30—3D 72
Cowley View Rd. S30—3F 65
Cowlishaw Rd. S11—5A 98
Cowood St. S64—1D 56
Cowper Av. S6—3B 74
Cowper Cres. S6—3B 74
Cowper Dri. S6—3B 74
Cowper Dri. S65—5H 79
Cowper Rd. S64—6F 43
Cowpingle La. S43—2E 133
Cowrakes Clo. S60—2A 92
Cow Rakes La. S60—2A 92
Cox Pl. S6—2F 85
Cox Rd. S6—2F 85
Crabtree Av. S5—3G 87
Crabtree Clo. S5—2G 87
Crabtree Cres. S5—2F 87
Crabtree Dri. S5—2G 87
Crabtree La. S5—2G 87
Crabtree Pl. S5—2G 87
Crabtree Rd. S5—2G 87
Cradley Dri. S31—6C 104
Cradock Rd. S2—6A 100
Craganour Pl. DN12—2B 58
Cragdale Gro. S19—2D 124
Craglands Gro. S40—6C 130
Crags Rd. DN12—2D 58
Crag View Clo. S30—1D 72

Crag View Cres. S30—1D 72
Craigholme Cres. DN2—2A 34
Craig Wlk. S66—4H 81
Craithie Rd. DN2—5F 33
Crakehall Rd. S30—4F 65
Cramfit Clo. S31—1F 119
Cramfit Rd. S31—6C 106
Cranborne Rd. S41—4G 131
Cranbrook Rd. DN1—4E 33
Cranbrook St. S70—2F 23
Crane Dri. S61—2G 77
Crane Moor Clo. DN5—1G 43
Crane Rd. S61—5G 67
Crane Well La. S63—1C 42
Cranfield Clo. DN3—4F 35
Cranford Ct. S19—5A 114
Cranford Dri. S19—4A 114
Cranford Gdns. S71—1D 8
Cranleigh Gdns. DN6—2C 16
Cranleigh Rd. S43—1F 135
Cranston Clo. S71—3D 14
Cranswick Way. DN12—3G 59
Cranwell Rd. DN4—4F 49
Cranworth Clo. S65—2G 79
Cranworth Pl. S3—5F 87
Cranworth Rd. S3—5F 87
Cranworth Rd. S65—1F 79
Craven Av. DN4—3C 48
Craven Clo. S9—6E 89
Craven Clo. S71—1D 8
Craven Rd. S41—6H 131
Craven St. S3—1B 4 & 1D 98
Craven St. S62—4F 69
Craven Wood Clo. S75—4C 12
Crawford Rd. S8—3D 110
Crawshaw Av. S8—1B 122
Crawshaw Gro. S8—1B 122
Crawshaw Rd. DN4—1A 46
Cream St. S2—4F 99
Crecy Av. DN2—5A 34
Creighton Av. S62—2H 69
Cresacre Av. DN5—1G 43
Crescent E., The. S66—2G 81
Crescent End, The. S66—5B 94
Crescent Rd. S7—6C 98
Crescent, The. DN3—4G 35
(Armthorpe)
Crescent, The. DN3—5E 21
(Edenthorpe)
Crescent, The. DN6—3B 16
Crescent, The. DN12—3C 58
(Conisbrough)
Crescent, The. DN12—2B 60
(Edlington)
Crescent, The. S17—4E 121
Crescent, The. S31—4G 107
Crescent, The. S42—6D 138
Crescent, The. S43—4C 132
Crescent, The. S63—6F 29
Crescent, The. S64—3H 55
Crescent, The. S65—2E 79
Crescent, The. S66—5C 94
Crescent, The. S72—6B 10
Crescent, The. S75—3D 12
Crescent W., The. S66—2F 81
Cresswell Rd. S9—1E 101
Cresswell Rd. S64—1B 56
Cresswell St. S75—5E 13
Crest Rd. S5—5F 75
Crestwood Ct. S5—5G 75
Crestwood Gdns. S5—5G 75
Creswell St. S64—5D 56
Creswick Av. S5—2D 74
Creswick Clo. S40—5D 136
Creswick Clo. S65—1B 80
Creswick Greave. S30—2C 74
Creswick Greave Clo. S5
—2C 74

Creswick La. S30—1C 74
Creswick Rd. S65—1B 80
Creswick St. S6—5B 86
(in two parts)
Creswick Way. S6—5B 86
Crewe Hall. S10—4A 98
Crich Av. S71—6C 8
Crich Rd. S43—4A 134
Cricket Inn Cres. S2—2A 100
Cricket Inn Gdns. S2—1G 99
Cricket Inn Rd. S2—1G 99 &
(in two parts)   1A 100
Cricket La. S30—1G 75
Cricket View Rd. S62—4H 51
Crimicar Av. S10—5B 96
Crimicar Clo. S10—6C 96
Crimicar Dri. S10—5B 96
Crimicar La. S10—4B 96
Crimpsall Rd. DN5—5B 32
Crimpsall Dri. DN4—1B 46
Cripps Av. DN11—4E 63
Cripps Clo. S66—5H 83
Crispin Clo. S12—3C 112
Crispin Dri. S12—3C 112
Crispin Gdns. S12—3C 112
Crispin Rd. S12—3C 112
Crochley Clo. DN4—2D 48
Croft Av. S71—2D 8
Croft Bldgs. S1—2D 4
Croft Clo. S11—4F 109
Croft La. S11—4F 109
Croft Lea. S18—1A 128
Crofton Av. S6—1H 85
Crofton Clo. S18—2D 128
Crofton Dri. S63—6E 29
Crofton Rise. S18—2D 128
Crofton Rise. S30—1B 64
Croft Rd. DN4—6G 45
Croft Rd. S6—5D 84
Croft Rd. S12—2D 112
Croft Rd. S60—2B 90
Croft Rd. S70—2C 24
Croft Rd. S74—4H 37
Crofts Dri. S65—5C 70
Crofts, The. S60—3D 78
Crofts, The. S66—6F 81
Croft St. S61—3B 68
Croft St. S70—4A 24
Croft, The. DN5—4E 19
Croft, The. DN12—4E 59
Croft, The. S60—6C 90
Croft, The. S64—3H 55
Croft, The. S74—1C 52
Croft View. S43—5A 134
Croft Way. S70—2C 24
Cromarty Rise. S18—1B 128
Cromer Av. S71—1B 14
Cromer Clo. S62—1F 69
Cromer Rd. DN2—5A 34
Cromer St. S72—6G 11
Cromford Av. S71—1B 14
Cromford Dri. S43—3H 133
Cromford Rd. DN4—5E 49
Cromford St. S2—4F 99
Crompton Av. DN5—5H 31
Crompton Av. S70—1F 23
Crompton Dri. DN2—1H 33
Crompton Rd. S43—1D 134
Cromwell Dri. DN5—1H 45
Cromwell Ho. DN5—4G 31
Cromwell Mt. S70—3G 23
Cromwell Rd. DN5—4B 32
Cromwell Rd. S40—1H 137
Cromwell Rd. S64—6E 43
Cromwell St. S6—6A 86
Cronkhill La. S71—4F 9
Crooked La. DN12—6H 57
Crooke Ho. La. S71—1D 26
Crookes. S10—1H 97

Crookes La. S71—4E 9
Crookesmoor Rd. S6 & S10
—1B 98
Crookes Rd. DN4—5B 46
Crookes Rd. S10—2A 98
Crookes St. S70—6F 13
Crookes Valley Rd. S10—1B 98
Crookhill Rd. DN12—3F 59
Cropton Rd. S71—2D 8
Crosby Av. S66—4H 81
Crosby Ct. S71—2D 14
Crosby Rd. S8—4D 110
Crosby St. S72—5B 10
Cross Allen Rd. S19—5F 115
Cross Bank. DN4—4B 46
Cross Bedford St. S6—6D 86
Cross Burgess St. S1—4E 5
Cross Butcher St. S63—1E 29
Cross Chantrey Rd. S8—4E 111
Cross Dri. S13—1B 114
Crossfield Dri. S63—6E 41
Crossfield Gdns. S30—5B 50
Cross Gate. DN5—3A 32
Crossgate. S63—2F 29
Cross Ga. S64—1G 57
Crossgate. S75—4F 7
Cross Gilpin St. S6—5C 86
Cross Hill. S30—2G 75
Cross Hill. S72—2F 11
Cross Ho. Rd. S30—1A 74
Cross Keys La. S74—5E 37
Crossland Dri. S12—4C 112
Crossland Pl. S12—3D 112
Cross La. S64—3B 56
Crossland Way. DN5—2G 31
Cross La. S10—1H 97
Cross La. S17—1C 120
Cross La. S18—6G 123
(Coal Aston)
Cross La. S18—2E 129
(Dronfield)
Cross La. S18—4G 123
(Dyche La.)
Cross La. S30—2A 140
Cross La. S71—2G 9
Crossley Clo. S66—3E 83
Cross Love St. S3—1E 5
Cross Myrtle Rd. S2—6F 99
Cross Pk. Rd. S8—2E 111
Cross Rd. S66—4A 94
Cross Smithfield. S3
—1C 4 & 1D 98
Cross S. St. S64—4C 68
Cross St. DN4—4A 46
Cross St. DN5—6B 18
Cross St. DN11—5D 62
Cross St. DN12—3B 60
Cross St. S13—1B 114
Cross St. S31—2D 126
Cross St. S40—1H 137
Cross St. S43—3E 133
Cross St. S61—4C 68
(Greasbrough)
Cross St. S61—3A 78
(Kimberworth)
Cross St. S62—4F 69
Cross St. S63—4G 29
(Goldthorpe)
Cross St. S63—5E 41
(Wath upon Dearne)
Cross St. S65—5C 70
Cross St. S66—4H 81
(Bramley)
Cross St. S66—4G 83
(Maltby)
Cross St. S70—3B 24
Cross St. S71—3C 14
Cross St. S73—1E 39

Cross St. S74—6F 37
Cross St. S75—4F 13
(Barnsley)
Cross St. S75—3A 12
(Barugh Green)
Cross Turner St. S2
—5G 5 & 3F 99
*Cross Wlk. S11—4D 98
(off Club Garden Rd.)*
Crossway. S64—3H 55
Crossways. DN2—2H 33
Crossways. S63—6E 29
Crossways N. DN2—2H 33
Crossways S. DN2—2H 33
Crossways, The. S2—4D 100
Crowden Wlk. S75—6C 12
Crowder Av. S5—5D 74
Crowder Clo. S5—6E 75
Crowder Cres. S5—6E 75
Crowder Rd. S5—5E 75
Crowgate. S31—4E 119
Crowland Rd. S5—5F 75
Crow La. S41—2B 138
Crowley Dri. S63—1E 55
*Crown Av. S70—2A 24
(off Crown Clo.)*
Crown Clo. S61—1G 77
Crown Clo. S70—2A 24
Crownhill Rd. S60—2A 90
Crown Hill Rd. S70—6C 12
Crown Pl. S2—3H 5
Crown Rd. S41—6A 132
Crown St. S64—2B 56
Crown St. S70—2A 24
Crown St. S74—5H 37
Crowther Pl. S7—5D 98
Crow Tree La. S64—3D 42
Croydon St. S11—5D 98
Cruck Clo. S18—1B 128
Cruise Rd. S11—5F 97
Crummock Rd. S7—2C 110
Crummock Way. S71—1H 25
Crumpsall Dri. S5—2D 86
Crumpsall Rd. S5—1D 86
Crumwell Rd. S61—5F 67
Crusader Dri. DN5—6G 31
Crystal Peaks Shopping
Centre. S19—5E 115
Cudworth Grn. S72—2H 15
Cudworth View. S72—6G 11
Cullabine Rd. S2—6C 100
Cull Row. S30—4H 141
Cumberland Av. DN2—5H 33
Cumberland Clo. S70—4H 23
Cumberland Clo. S74—4A 38
Cumberland Cres. S30—3F 65
Cumberland Dri. S71—1F 25
Cumberland Pl. DN12—2B 58
Cumberland Rd. S74—4A 38
Cumberland St. S1
—6D 4 & 3E 99
Cumberland Way. S1
—6D 4 & 3E 99
Cumberland Way. S63—2A 42
Cumbrian Wlk. S75—5D 12
Cumwell La. S66—6A 82
Cundy St. S6—6A 86
Cunliffe St. S18—5G 123
Cunningham Rd. DN1—1D 46
Cupola. S3—1D 4 & 1E 99
Cupola La. S30—6A 64
Cupola Yd. S60—3C 78
Curbar Curve. S43—5H 133
Curlew Av. S31—6B 124
Curlew Ct. DN11—4E 63
Curlew Ridge. S2—3H 99
Curlew Rise. S61—1C 66
Curzen Cres. DN3—3E 21

Curzon Av. S18—3D 128
Curzon Clo. S31—3B 126
Cusworth Ho. DN1—1C 46
  (off Camden Pl.)
Cusworth La. DN5—4F 31
Cusworth Rd. DN5—2A 32
Cuthbert Bank Rd. S6—4B 86
Cuthbert Rd. S6—4B 86
Cutler Clo. S31—2H 125
Cutlers Av. S70—1F 23
Cutlers Wlk. S2—6E 99
Cuttholme Clo. S40—1D 136
Cuttholme Rd. S40—1D 136
Cuttholme Way Flats. S40
  —1E 137
Cuttholme Way Shopping
  Centre. S40—1E 137
Cutthorpe Grange. S41—4C 130
Cutthorpe Rd. S42—3C 130
Cutts Av. S63—6D 40
Cutts Ter. S8—6D 98
Cutty La. S75—4F 13
Cyclops St. S4—3A 88
Cypress Av. S8—6G 111
Cypress Clo. S31—4A 126
Cypress Ga. S30—3D 64
Cypress Gro. DN12—5B 58
Cypress Rd. S70—2B 24
Cyprus Rd. S8—2E 111
Cyprus Ter. S6—5B 86
  (off Burgoyne Rd.)

Dacre Row. S2—2G 99
Dade Av. S43—5H 133
Daffodil Rd. S5—6B 76
Dagnam Clo. S2—1B 112
Dagnam Cres. S2—6B 100
Dagnam Dri. S2—6B 100
Dagnam Pl. S2—1C 112
Dagnam Rd. S2—6B 100
Daisy Bank. S3—1A 4 & 1C 98
Daisy Wlk. S3—2B 4 & 1D 98
Daisy Wlk. S19—4F 115
Dalbury Rd. S18—2A 128
Dalby Gdns. S19—6G 115
Dalby Gro. S19—5G 115
Dale Av. S65—4A 80
Dalebrook Ct. S10—4E 97
Dalebrook M. S10—4E 97
Dale Clo. S43—3A 134
Dale Clo. S71—6C 8
Dale Ct. S62—2F 69
Dale Gro. S63—2H 41
Dale Hill Clo. S66—3F 83
Dale Hill Rd. S66—3D 82
Dale Rd. DN12—3E 59
Dale Rd. S18—3F 129
Dale Rd. S31—3C 126
Dale Rd. S62—2F 69
Dale Rd. S65—5A 80
Dale Rd. S66—5E 81
Dale Side. S10—4H 97
Dale St. S62—1F 69
Daleswood Av. S70—6D 12
Daleswood Dri. S70—4D 24
Dale, The. S8—4D 110
Daleview Rd. S8—5B 110
Dalewood Av. S8—6A 110
Dalewood Clo. S41—4E 139
Dalewood Dri. S8—6A 110
Dalewood Rd. S8—6A 110
Dalmore Rd. S7—2A 110
Dalton Ct. DN12—2B 58
Dalton Ct. S8—5B 62
Dalton Ho. S60—6H 79
Dalton La. S65—6B 70

Dalton Ter. S70—1A 24
Damer St. S10—2B 98
Dam Ings La. S31—6E 105
Damon Dri. S43—3F 133
Danby Av. S41—1B 132
Danby Rd. S31—4B 118
Danebrook Clo. S2—4E 101
Danebrook Ct. S2—4E 101
Danebrook Dri. S2—4E 101
Danesthorpe Clo. DN2—3A 34
Dane St. S63—1G 29
Dane St. N. S63—1G 29
Dane St. S. S63—1G 29
Danesway. DN5—6H 17
Danethorpe Way. DN12—5C 58
Danewood Av. S2—4E 101
Danewood Croft. S2—4E 101
Danewood Gdns. S2—4E 101
Danewood Gro. S2—4E 101
Daniel Hill. S6—6C 86
Daniel Hill St. S6—6B 86
Daniel Hill St. S6—6B 86
Daniel Hill Ter. S6—6C 86
Daniel Hill Wlk. S6—6C 86
Daniel La. S62—1B 68
Daniels Dri. S31—6A 104
Danum Ct. DN12—2B 58
Danum Dri. S65—2F 79
Danum Rd. DN4—1F 47
Dara St. S9—4D 76
Darcliffe Lodge. S10—5G 97
Darcy Clo. S31—5B 104
Darcy Rd. S31—6C 124
Daresbury Clo. S2—1H 111
Daresbury Dri. S2—1H 111
Daresbury Pl. S2—1H 111
Daresbury Rd. S2—1H 111
Daresbury View. S2—1H 111
Darfield Av. S19—5H 113
Darfield Clo. DN11—4F 63
Darfield Clo. S19—5H 113
Darfield Ho. DN1—1C 46
  (off St James St.)
Darfield Rd. S72—2H 15
Dargle Av. DN2—4G 33
Darhaven. S73—3E 27
Dark La. S43—1E 139
Dark La. S44—3F 139
Dark La. S70—2D 22
  (Barnsley)
Dark La. S70—6B 24
  (Worsbrough)
Darley. S70—4C 24
Darley Av. S70—3G 23
Darley Av. S71—1A 14
Darley Cliff Cotts. S70—3B 24
Darley Clo. S31—3H 127
Darley Clo. S43—2C 134
Darley Clo. S71—6C 8
Darley Gro. S6—4D 84
Darley Gro. S70—4C 24
Darley Ter. S75—5F 13
Darley Yd. S70—4B 24
Darnall Dri. S9—6D 88
Darnall Rd. S9—5C 88
Darrington Dri. DN4—6F 45
Darrington Pl. S71—4E 15
Dartmouth Rd. DN4—5F 49
Darton Hall Clo. S75—4D 6
Darton Hall Dri. S75—4D 6
Darton La. S75—5D 6
Darton St. S70—1D 24
Dartree Wlk. S73—3D 26
Dart Sq. S3—1C 98
Darwall Clo. S30—5B 50
Darwent La. S30—5B 50
Darwent Rd. S41—5C 132
Darwin Av. S40—6G 131

Darwin Clo. S10—3F 97
Darwin La. S10—3F 97
Darwin Rd. S6—1H 85
Darwin Rd. S40—1H 137
Darwynn Av. S64—2G 55
Davian Way. S40—5G 137
David Clo. S13—6D 102
David La. S10—6A 96
Davies Dri. S64—4B 56
Davis St. S65—2G 79
Davy Dri. S66—3F 83
Davy Rd. DN12—2A 58
Dawber La. S31—2D 126
Daw Croft Av. S70—4A 24
Dawlands Clo. S2—3D 100
Dawlands Dri. S2—4D 100
Daw La. DN5—5B 18
Dawson Av. S62—5C 54
Dawson Croft. S61—3A 68
Dawson La. S63—1E 55
Dawson Ter. S31—5H 117
Daw Wood. DN5—4C 18
Dayhouse La. S75—2D 12
Daykin Clo. S75—5B 6
Daylands Av. DN12—4C 58
Day St. S70—1G 23
Deacon Clo. DN11—4F 63
Deacon Cres. DN11—4C 62
Deacon Cres. S66—5G 83
Deacons Way. S71—4C 14
Deadman's Hole La. S61—4A 78
Deakins Wlk. S10—4F 97
Dean Clo. DN5—1F 45
Dean Clo. DN11—4F 63
Deane Field View. S19—5D 114
Deanhead Ct. S19—5A 114
Deanhead Dri. S19—5H 113
Dean La. S65—3C 80
Deansfield Clo. DN3—4F 35
Dean St. S70—6F 13
Deans Way. S71—3C 14
Dearden Ct. S30—1F 75
Dearne Clo. DN12—5B 58
Dearne Ct. S9—1C 88
Dearne Hall Rd. S75—1B 12
Dearne Rd. S63—3G & 2H 41
Dearne Rd. S73—3A 40
Dearne Rd. Flatlets. S63—2H 41
Dearne St. DN12—2F 59
Dearne St. S9—1C 88
Dearne St. S75—4C 6
Dearne View. S63—4G 29
Dearneway. S63—5F 41
Dearnley View. S75—3F 13
Deben Clo. S40—5E 137
Decoy Bank N. DN4—2D 46
Decoy Bank S. DN4—3D 46
Deepdale Rd. S61—3G 77
Deep La. S5—2A 76
Deerlands Av. S5—3C 74
Deerlands Clo. S5—3C 74
Deerlands Mt. S5—3C 74
Deerlands Rd. S40—2D 136
Deer Leap Dri. S65—5E 71
Deer Pk. Clo. S6—5E 85
Deer Pk. Pl. S6—5E 85
Deer Pk. Rd. S6—5E 85
Deer Pk. Vlew. S6—5E 85
Deer Pk. Way. S6—5F 85
De Houton Clo. S31—2A 118
Deightonby St. S63—1G 29
De Lacy Dri. S70—4A 24
Delamere Clo. S19—5G 115
Delf Edge. S30—1G 141
Delf St. S2—6F 99
Della Av. S70—1F 23
Dell Av. S72—5G 11

Dell Cres. DN4—2H 45
Dell, The. S40—2D 136
Delmar Way. S66—3F 81
Delph Bank. S40—5G 137
Delph Ho. Rd. S10—2F 97
Delta Pl. S65—2H 79
Delta Way. S66—3H 83
Delves Av. S12—3C 114
Delves Clo. S12—3C 114
Delves Clo. S40—4F 137
Delves Dri. S12—4C 114
Delves La. S31—4B 116
Delves Pl. S12—4B 114
Delves Rd. S12—4B 114
Delves Rd. S31—3B 126
Delves Ter. S12—4C 114
Denaby Av. DN12—4B 58
Denaby La. DN12 & S65
  —5E 57 to 1A 58
Denaby La. Ind. Est. DN12
  —2A 58
Den Bank Av. S10—2E 97
Den Bank Clo. S10—2F 97
Den Bank Cres. S10—2E 97
Den Bank Dri. S10—2E 97
Denby Rd. S71—6B 8
Denby St. DN5—5A 18
Denby St. S2—4D 98
Denby Way. S66—4A 82
Dene Clo. S66—5G 81
Dene Cres. S65—1H 79
Denehall Rd. DN3—4E 21
Dene Rd. S65—1H 79
Denham Rd. S11—4C 98
Denholme Clo. S3—6F 87
Denison Rd. DN4—1B 46
Denman Rd. S63—5D 40
Denman St. S65—1E 79
Denmark Rd. S2—1F 111
Dennison Cres. S40—2H 137
Denson Clo. S2—1F 111
Dent La. S12—5H 113
Dentons Grn. La. DN3—3D 20
Denton St. S71—5H 13
Derby Pl. S2—1G 111
Derby Rd. DN2—1A 34
Derby Rd. S40—6A 138
Derbyshire Ct. S8—4F 111
Derbyshire La. S8—2D 110
Derby St. S2—1F 111
Derby St. S70—6F 13
Derby Ter. S2—1G 111
Derriman Av. S11—3H 109
Derriman Clo. S11—3H 109
Derriman Dri. S11—3H 109
Derriman Glen. S11—3G 109
Derriman Gro. S11—3H 109
Derry Gro. S63—2E 29
Derwent Clo. S18—6F 123
Derwent Clo. S31—6F 107
Derwent Clo. S71—6D 8
Derwent Ct. S17—4G 121
Derwent Ct. S60—1F 91
Derwent Cres. S41—4F 131
Derwent Cres. S60—4B 90
Derwent Cres. S70—1D 8
Derwent Dri. DN3—4D 20
Derwent Dri. S30—2C 64
Derwent Dri. S64—5G 43
Derwent Gdns. S63—5G 29
Derwent Pl. DN5—2D 44
Derwent Pl. S73—2H 39
Derwent Rd. S18—6F 123
Derwent Rd. S61—4A 68
Derwent Rd. S64—5G 43
Derwent Rd. S71—6C 8
Derwent Row. S2—1H 99
Derwent St. S2—1H 99

Derwent Ter. S64—5E 43
Derwent Way. S63—3B 40
De Sutton Pl. S31—4H 127
Deveron Rd. S19—2F 125
Devizes Clo. S40—5H 137
Devon Ct. DN12—3B 58
Devon Dri. S43—3F 133
Devon Pk. View. S43—3F 133
Devon Rd. S4—3G 87
Devonshire Av. E. S41—5C 138
Devonshire Clo. S17—3F 121
Devonshire Clo. S18—3D 58
Devonshire Clo. S41—3H 131
Devonshire Clo. S41—1C 134
Devonshire Ct. S17—3F 121
Devonshire Ct. S43—4D 132
Devonshire Dri. S17—2E 121
Devonshire Dri. S31—5E 107
Devonshire Dri. S75—3F 13
Devonshire Glen. S17—3E 121
Devonshire Gro. S17—3E 121
Devonshire La. S1
—4C 4 & 2D 98
Devonshire Rd. DN2—4H 33
Devonshire Rd. S17—2E 121
Devonshire Rd. S66—3G 83
Devonshire Rd. E. S41—5C 138
Devonshire St. S3—4B 4 & 2D 98
Devonshire St. S43—3E 133
(Brimington)
Devonshire St. S43—1C 134
(Staveley)
Devonshire St. S61—3B 78
Devonshire Ter. Rd. S17
—2D 120
Dewar Dri. S7—3A 110
Dewhill Av. S60—2H 91
Dial Clo. S5—5G 75
Dial Ho. Rd. S6—3G 85
Dial, The. S5—5H 75
Dial Way. S5—5G 75
Diamond St. S73—6B 26
Dickan Gdns. DN3—4H 35
Dickenson Ct. S30—2D 64
Dickenson Rd. S41—4B 138
Dickens Rd. S62—6H 55
Dickey La. S6—4G 73
Dickinson Pl. S70—2H 23
Dickinson Rd. S5—2H 75
Dickinson Rd. S70—2H 23
Didcot Clo. S40—5H 137
Digby Clo. S61—1G 77
Dike Hill. S62—4A 52
Dikelands Mt. S30—1B 64
Dillington Rd. S70—2H 23
Dillington Sq. S70—2H 23
Dillington Ter. S70—2H 23
Dingle Bank. S44—4E 139
Dingle La. S44—4E 139
Dinmore Clo. DN4—1G 61
Dinnington Rd. S8—3D 110
Dinnington Rd. S31
—1B 118 & 5A 106
Dirleton Dri. DN4—5F 45
Disraeli Gro. S66—3E 83
Distillery Side. S74—1D 52
Ditchingham St. S4—5G 87
Division La. S1—4D 4 & 2E 99
Division St. S1—4C 4 & 2D 98
Division St. S43—3A 134
Dixon Cres. DN4—4H 45
Dixon La. S1—2G 5 & 1F 99
Dixon Rd. DN12—4A 60
Dixon Rd. S6—2H 85
Dixon Rd. S41—3B 138
Dixon St. S6—6D 86
Dixon St. S65—2E 79
Dobbin Hill. S11—1G 109

Dobbin La. S18—6A 128
Dobcroft Av. S7—4H 109
Dobcroft Clo. S11—3G 109
Dobcroft Rd. S11 & S7—3G 109
Dobie St. S70—1H 23
Dobroyd Ter. S74—4B 38
Dobson Pl. S43—5H 133
Dobsyke Clo. S70—4D 24
Dockin Hill Rd. DN1—5D 32
Dock Wlk. S40—3G 137
Doctor La. S9—5D 88
Dodd St. S6—4A 86
Dodson Dri. S13—3H 101
Dodsworth St. S64—1D 56
Dodworth Rd. S70—6C 12
Doe La. S70—6G 23
Doe Quarry La. S31—3F 107
Doe Quarry Ter. S31—4G 107
Doe Royd Cres. S5—4C 74
Doe Royd Dri. S5—4C 74
Doe Royd La. S5—4C 74
Dog Croft La. DN5—5G 19
Dog Hill. S72—2B 10
Dog Hill Dri. S72—2C 10
Dog Kennels Hill. S31—5D 118
Dog Kennels La. S31—5D 118
Dog La. S70—6G 13
(off Shambles St.)
Dolcliffe Clo. S64—6D 42
Dolcliffe Rd. S64—6E 43
Doles Av. S71—2D 8
Doles Cres. S71—2D 8
Doles La. S60—3A 92
Doleswood Dri. S31—1E 107
Domine La. S60—3D 78
Dominoe Gro. S12—2F 113
Don Av. S6—6G 73
Donavon Rd. S5—6C 74
Doncaster Ga. S65—3E 79
Doncaster La. DN6—2E 17
Doncaster Pl. S65—2G 79
Doncaster Rd. DN3—3D 34
(Armthorpe)
Doncaster Rd. DN3—3F 49
(Branton)
Doncaster Rd. DN3—5B to 2D 20
(Kirk Sandall)
Doncaster Rd. DN5—3A 16
(Adwick-le-Street)
Doncaster Rd. DN5—1H 43
(Barnburgh)
Doncaster Rd. DN5—1F 43
(Harlington)
Doncaster Rd. DN5—5A 44
(Sprotbrough)
Doncaster Rd. DN5—2H 17
(Toll Bar)
Doncaster Rd. DN12—3F 59
(Conisbrough)
Doncaster Rd. DN12—1A to
(Denaby Main) 2D 58
Doncaster Rd. S63—4G 29
(Goldthorpe)
Doncaster Rd. S63—5G 41
(Wath upon Dearne)
Doncaster Rd. S64—1F 57
Doncaster Rd. S65—6A 70
(Dalton, Thrybergh &
Hooton Roberts)
Doncaster Rd. S65—3E 79
(Rotherham)
Doncaster Rd. S70—1A 24
Doncaster Rd. S71
—1E 25 to 2C 26
Doncaster Rd. S73 & S72—3F 27
Doncaster St. S3—1C 4 & 1D 98
Don Dri. S70—2D 24
Donetsk Way. S12—4A 114

Don Hill Height. S30—1E 141
Donnington Rd. S2—4H 99
Donnington Rd. S64—5H 43
Donovan Clo. S5—6C 74
Donovan Rd. S5—6C 74
Don Rd. S9—4B 88
Don St. DN1—4D 32
Don St. DN12—2F 59
Don St. S60—4D 78
Don View. DN5—3E 31
Don View Row. S64—6H 43
Dorchester Pl. S70—4H 23
Dore Clo. S17—2G 121
Dore Hall Croft. S17—2D 120
Dore Rd. S17—2D 120
Dorking St. S4—6G 87
Dorothy Rd. S6—2H 85
Dorothy Vale. S40—1E 137
Dorset Av. S43—3F 133
Dorset Clo. S43—2F 133
Dorset Cres. DN2—4A 34
Dorset Dri. S43—3F 133
Dorset St. S10—3C 98
Douglas Rd. DN4—4G 45
Douglas Rd. S3—5D 86
Douglas Rd. S41—5C 132
Douglas St. S60—3E 79
Douse Croft La. S10—6A 96
Dovecliffe Rd. S73—6E 25
Dove Clo. S63—1B 42
Dove Clo. S73—2H 39
Dovecote La. S65—4G 71
Dovedale. S70—5B 24
Dovedale Av. S43—6H 133
Dovedale Clo. S41—4G 131
Dovedale Pl. S70—5B 24
Dovedale Rd. S7—2B 110
Dovedale Rd. S65—5A 80
Dove Hill. S71—1F 9
Dove La. S31—1C 116
Dovercourt Rd. S2—4A 100
Dovercourt Rd. S61—2A 78
Dover Gdns. S3—1B 4 & 1D 98
Doveridge Clo. S41—1A 132
Dove Rd. S73—2H 39
Dover Rd. S11—4A 98
Dover St. S3—1B 4 & 1D 98
Doveside Dri. S73—5D 26
Dowcar La. S31—3G 127
Dowdeswell St. S41—1A 138
Dowfin. S30—6B 50
Dowland Av. S30—5B 50
Dowland Clo. S30—5C 50
Dowland Ct. S30—5B 50
Dowland Gdns. S30—5C 50
Downes Cres. S75—4D 12
Downgate Dri. S4—3B 88
Downham Rd. S5—6C 74
Downing La. S3—6D 86
Downing Rd. S8—1C 122
Downland Clo. DN4—1F 61
Downlands. S43—4D 132
Down's Row. S60—3D 78
Drake Clo. S30—2C 64
Drake Head La. DN12—3G 59
Drakehouse Cres. S19—4E 115
Drakehouse La. S19—4F 115
Drake House La. W. S19
—4F 115
Drake Rd. DN2—3E 33
Drake Rd. S66—5H 83
(off Seymour Rd.)
Drake Ter. S43—3C 132
Dransfield Clo. S10—3F 97
Dransfield Rd. S10—3E 97
Draycott Pl. S18—3B 128
Driver St. S13—5D 102
Drive, The. DN3—5E 21

Drive, The. S6—1H 85
Dronfield Rd. S31—6B 124
Droppingwell Rd. S61
—3D 76 to 6E 67
Drover Clo. S30—1C 64
Drummond Av. DN5—2E 31
Drummond Cres. S5—4F 75
Drummond Rd. S5—4F 75
Drummond St. S60 & S65
—2D 78
Drury Farm Ct. S75—6C 12
Drury La. S17—2D 120
Drury La. S18—6G 123
Dryden Av. S5—5C 74
Dryden Av. S40—5A 138
Dryden Dri. S5—5C 74
Dryden Rd. DN4—5C 46
Dryden Rd. S5—5C 74
Dryden Rd. S63—4C 40
Dryden Rd. S64—6F 43
Dryden Rd. S65—5H 79
Dryden Rd. S71—5A 14
Dryden Way. S5—6C 74
Dublin Rd. DN2—4G 33
Duchess Rd. S2—4F 99
Duckmanton Rd. S44—6E 135
Ducksett La. S31—6D 124
Dudley Rd. DN2—6H 33
Dudley Rd. S6—1H 85
Dudley St. S62—4F 69
Dugdale Dri. S5—2D 74
Dugdale Rd. S5—2D 74
Duke Av. DN11—4C 62
Duke Av. S66—5H 83
Duke Cres. S61—6G 67
Duke Cres. S70—1H 23
Duke La. S1—6E 5 & 3E 99
Duke of Norfolk La. S66—6D 80
Dukeries Dri. S31—6E 107
Duke's Cres. DN12—2B 60
Dukes Dri. S41—5G 131
Dukes La. S61—1F 77
Dukes Pl. S65—5H 79
Duke St. DN1—6C 32
Duke St. S2—3H 5 & 2G 99
Duke St. S19—3D 124
Duke St. S31—3F 107
Duke St. S41—3A 132
(in two parts)
Duke St. S43—1C 134
Duke St. S64—1B 56
Duke St. S70—1H 23
(in two parts)
Duke St. S74—5A 38
Duke St. Flats. S2—3H 5
Dumbleton Rd. S31—4C 126
Dumfries Row. S70—2A 24
Duncan Rd. S10—1H 97
Duncan St. S60—2C 90
Duncombe St. S6—6A 86
Dundas Rd. DN2—3F 33
Dundas Rd. S9—6G 77
Dundonald Rd. S40—4A 138
Dunedin Glen. S19—3E 125
Dunedin Gro. S19—3E 125
Dunella Dri. S6—2H 85
Dunella Pl. S6—2G 85
Dunella Rd. S6—2H 85
Dun Fields. S3—6D 86
Dunkeld Rd. S11—2H 109
Dunkerley Rd. S6—2D 84
Dunleary Rd. DN2—5G 33
Dunlin Clo. S61—1B 66
Dunlop St. S9—2D 88
Dunmere Clo. S71—2A 14
Dunmow Rd. S4—2A 88
Dunning Rd. S5—2H 75
Dunning Ter. S5—2H 75

Dunniwood Av. DN4—6C 48
Dunniwood Reach. DN4—5D 48
Dunns Dale. S66—4H 83
Dunscroft Gro. DN11—4F 63
Dunstan Rd. S66—5E 83
Dunston Ind. Est. S41—1H 131
Dunston La. S41—2F 131
Dunston Rd. S41
   —3C 130 to 3A 132
Dun St. S3—6D 86
Dun St. S64—2C 56
Durham Av. S43—1D 132
Durham Clo. S43—1D 132
Durham La. S10—2C 98
Durham Pl. S65—5H 79
Durham Rd. DN2—2F 33
Durham Rd. S10—2B 98
Durham St. S66—5H 83
Durley Chine Dri. S41—5C 138
Durlstone Clo. S12—2C 112
Durlstone Cres. S12—2C 112
Durlstone Dri. S12—2C 112
Durlstone Gro. S12—2C 112
Durmast Gro. S6—5C 84
Durnan Gro. S62—5C 54
Durnford Rd. DN2—4E 33
Durrant Rd. S41—2A 138
Durvale Ct. S17—3E 121
Dutton Rd. S6—2B 86
Dyche Clo. S8—3F 123
Dyche Dri. S8—3F 123
Dyche La. S8 & S18—2E 123
Dyche Pl. S8—3F 123
Dyche Rd. S8—3F 123
Dycott Rd. S61—2H 77
Dyer Rd. S74—4C 38
Dykes Hall Gdns. S6—3H 85
Dykes Hall Pl. S6—2H 85
Dykes Hall Rd. S6—2G 85
Dykes La. S6—3G 85
Dyke Vale Av. S12—3A 114
Dyke Vale Clo. S12—3A 114
Dyke Vale Pl. S12—3A 114
Dyke Vale Rd. S12—2H 113
Dyke Vale Way. S12—3A 114
Dykewood Dri. S6—6F 73
Dyson Pl. S11—5B 98
Dyson St. S70—2F 23

Eaden Cres. S74—5B 38
Eagleton Dri. S30—5C 50
Eagleton Rise. S30—5C 50
Eagle View. S31—1C 116
Ealand Way. DN12—2G 59
Eaming View. S71—4A 14
Earl Av. DN11—4B 62
Earl Av. S66—5G 83
Earldom Clo. S4—5G 87
Earldom Dri. S4—5G 87
Earldom Rd. S4—4G 87
Earldom St. S4—5G 87
Earlesmere Av. DN4—3A 46
Earl Marshal Clo. S4—2H 87
Earl Marshal Dri. S4—2H 87
Earl Marshal Rd. S4—2H 87
Earl Marshal View. S4—3G 87
Earlsmere Dri. S71—1G 25
Earlstone Dri. DN5—3B 32
Earl St. S1—6D 4 & 3E 99
(in two parts)
Earl Way. S1—6D 4 & 3E 99
Earnshaw Hall. S10—4H 97
Earnshaw Ter. S75—4G 13
Earsham St. S4—5G & 5H 87
(in two parts)
Easedale Clo. S40—6B 130
East Av. DN6—3C 16

East Av. S62—1F 69
East Av. S64—3H 55
East Av. S73—6H 25
E. Bank Clo. S2—1H 111
E. Bank Pl. S2—1H 111
E. Bank Rd. S2—4F 99 to 1B 112
E. Bank View. S2—1H 111
E. Bank Way. S2—1H 111
E. Bawtry Rd. S60—2G 91
E. Cliffe Dri. S2—5G 99
E. Coast Rd. S9—5A 88
East Cres. S30—3C 140
East Cres. S44—5E 135
East Cres. S65—2H 79
E. Croft. S63—1A 42
Eastcroft Clo. S19—1F 125
Eastcroft Dri. S19—2E 125
Eastcroft Glen. S19—1F 125
Eastcroft View. S19—2F 125
Eastcroft Way. S19—1F 125
E. End Cres. S71—2G 9
Eastern Av. S2
   —1H 111 to 6B 100
Eastern Av. S31—5G 107
Eastern Clo. S31—5G 107
Eastern Cres. S2—1H 111
Eastern Dri. S2—6H 99
Eastern Wlk. S2—6H 99
Eastfield Clo. S75—5H 7
Eastfield Cres. S31—6G 95
Eastfield Cres. S75—5H 7
E. Field La. S31—6H 95
Eastfield Pl. S62—6A 56
Eastfield Rd. DN3—4F 35
Eastfield Rd. S10—6H 85
Eastfield Rd. S18—3G 129
Eastfields. S70—5B 24
Eastgate. S70—5G 13
E. Glade Av. S12—4G 113
E. Glade Cres. S12—4G 113
E. Glade Grn. S12—3G 113
E. Glade Pl. S12—4G 113
E. Glade Rd. S12—3G 113
E. Glade Sq. S12—4G 113
E. Glade Way. S12—3G 113
Eastgrove Rd. S10—4B 98
Easthill. S65—2G 79
E. Laith Ga. DN1—6D 32
Eastleigh Ct. S41—5D 138
East Mall. S19—4E 115
Eastmoor Gro. S71—4E 9
Eastmoor Rd. S43—1F 139
East Pde. S1—2E 5 & 2E 99
E. Pinfold. S71—2E 9
East Rd. S2—6F 99
East Rd. S65—2H 79
E. Side Clo. S41—3B 132
E. Side Rd. S41—3B 132
East St. DN1—2C 46
East St. S31—4F 107
East St. S63—3H 29
East St. S73—3E 27
East Ter. S31—4D 116
E. Vale Dri. S65—5D 70
East View. S72—6B 10
East View. S74—4B 38
E. View Av. S31—6H 125
E. View Ter. S6—2H 85
Eastwood Av. S31—1G 119
Eastwood Clo. S41—5D 138
Eastwood Ct. S65—1F 79
Eastwood Dri. S44—3H 139
Eastwood La. S65—2E 79
Eastwood Mt. S65—3G 79
Eastwood Pk. Dri. S41—5D 138
Eastwood Rd. S11—5B 98
Eastwood Trading Est. S65
   —6G 69

Eastwood Vale. S65—1G 79
Eaton Pl. S2—2H 99
Eaton Sq. DN5—1H 43
Ebenezer Pl. S3—6E 87
Ebenezer Pl. S74—6C 38
Ebenezer St. S3—6E 87
Eben St. S9—1C 88
Ecclesall Rd. S11
   —6H 97 to 4D 98
Ecclesall Rd. S. S11
   —3E to 1H 109
Eccles Dri. DN12—5B 60
Ecclesfield Rd. S5 & S9
   —1H 75 to 4D 76
Ecclesfield Rd. S30—2F 65
Eccles St. S9—5D 76
Eccleston Rd. DN3—2E 21
Eckington Rd. S18—5G 123
Eckington Rd. S19—1F 125 to
(in two parts) 6F 115
Eckington Rd. S43—1D 134
Eckington Way. S19
   —3D 114 to 2F 125
Edale Ct. S41—4G 131
Edale Rise. S75—2A 22
Edale Rd. S11—1G 109
Edale Rd. S61—3H 77
Edderthorpe La. S73—1E 27
Eden Dri. S6—3E 85
Edenfield Clo. S71—1D 14
Eden Field Rd. DN3—5E 21
Eden Glade. S31—1B 116
Eden Gro. DN4—1A 46
Eden Gro. S31—5B 104
Eden Gro. Rd. DN3—5E 21
Edenhall Rd. S2—6B 100
Edensor Ct. S43—3A 134
Edensor Rd. S5—1F 87
Eden Ter. S64—5E 43
Edgar La. DN11—4B 62
Edge Bank. S7—1C 110
Edgebrook Rd. S7—1B 110
Edgecliffe Pl. S71—2A 14
Edge Clo. S8—3A 74
Edgedale Rd. S7—2C 110
Edgefield Rd. S7—2C 110
Edge Grn. DN3—3D 20
Edgehill Rd. DN2—2A 34
Edge Hill Rd. S7—1B 110
Edgehill Rd. S75—3F 7
Edge La. S6—3A 74
Edgemount Rd. S7—2C 110
Edge Well Clo. S6—3A 74
Edge Well Cres. S6—3A 74
Edge Well Dri. S6—4A 74
Edge Well La. S6—3H 73
Edge Well Pl. S6—3A 74
Edge Well Rise. S6—3A 74
Edge Well Way. S6—3A 74
(off Edge Well Cres.)
Edinburgh Av. S63—1H 41
Edinburgh Clo. S71—3B 14
Edinburgh Dri. S31—6D 106
Edinburgh Rd. S41—6H 131
Edinburgh Rd. S74—4A 38
Edith Ter. DN5—2G 31
Edith Wlk. S6—5C 86
Edlington La. DN12 & DN4
   —6E 45
Edlington Riding. DN12—4C 60
Edmonton Clo. S75—5C 12
Edmund Av. S17—3A 122
Edmund Av. S60—4D 90
Edmund Clo. S17—3B 122
Edmund Dri. S17—3B 122
Edmund Rd. S2—5F 99
Edmunds Rd. S70—5C 24
Edmund St. S41—3H 131

Edmund St. S70—5A 24
Edna St. S63—1A 42
(Bolton-upon-Dearne)
Edna St. S63—5H 41
(Wath upon Dearne)
Edward Rd. S63—5E 29
(Goldthorpe)
Edward Rd. S63—3C 40
(Wath upon Dearne)
Edward St. DN3—2D 34
Edward St. DN5—6B 18
Edward St. DN11—4B 62
Edward St. S3—2B 4 & 1D 98
Edward St. S30—3D 140
Edward St. S31—4F 107
(Dinnington)
Edward St. S31—6D 124
(Eckington)
Edward St. S43—3A 134
Edward St. S63—1E 29
Edward St. S64—1B 56
Edward St. S73—4E 27
(Darfield)
Edward St. S73—6C 26
(Wombwell)
Edward St. S74—5H 37
Edward St. S75—5G 7
Edward St. Flats. S3
   —2B 4 & 1D 98
Edwin Av. S40—5F 137
Edwin Rd. DN6—3C 16
Edwin Rd. S2—1G 111
Effingham La. S4—1H 5 & 1G 99
Effingham Rd. S4 & S9—6H 87
Effingham Sq. S65—2D 78
Effingham St. S4
   —1H 5 & 1G 99 to 6H 87
Effingham St. S65—2E 79
(in two parts)
Egerton La. S1—5B 4 & 3D 98
Egerton Rd. S18—1F 129
Egerton St. S31—6B 104
Egerton St. S1—6B 4 & 3D 98
Eggington Clo. DN4—4F 49
Egmanton Rd. S71—4B 8
Eilam Clo. S61—1G 77
Eilam Rd. S61—1G 77
Ekin St. S60—6H 77
Eland Clo. DN11—3D 62
Elcroft Gdns. S19—5F 115
Elder Av. S31—2H 119
Elder Ct. S31—4A 126
Elder Dri. S66—3F 81
Elder Gro. DN12—4C 58
Eldertree Rd. S61—4B 66
Elder Way. S40—2A 138
Eldon Arc. S70—6H 13
(off Eldon St.)
Eldon Rd. S1—4C 4 & 2D 98
Eldon Rd. S65—1F 79
Eldon Rd. S1—4C 4 & 2D 98
Eldon St. S70—6H 13
Eldon St. N. S71—5H 13
Eleanor St. S9—5D 88
Elgin Clo. S40—6E 137
Elgin St. S10—2H 97
Elgitha Dri. S66—5A 94
Eliot Clo. S43—6F 133
Elizabeth Av. DN3—3E 21
Elizabeth St. S31—1B 116
Elizabeth St. S63—4G 29
Elizabeth St. S72—6G 11
Elizabeth St. S74—5B 38
Elizabeth Way. S60—3C 78
(off Vine Clo.)
Elkstone Rd. S40—6C 130
Elland Clo. S71—6A 8
Ella Rd. S4—4G 87

Ellavale Rd. S74—5C 38
Ellenborough Rd. S6—3H 85
Ellen Tree Clo. S60—3B 90
Ellerker Av. DN4—1B 46
Ellers Av. DN4—3A 48
Ellers Cres. DN4—3A 48
Ellers Dri. DN4—3A 48
Ellershaw La. DN12—4C 58
Ellershaw Rd. DN12—4D 58
Ellers Rd. DN4—3A 48
Ellerton Gdns. DN4—2C 48
Ellerton Rd. S5—1H 87
Ellesmere Rd. S4—5G 87
Ellesmere Rd. N. S4—4G 87
Ellesmere Ter. S65—3F 79
Ellesmere Wlk. S4—4G 87
Ellington Ct. S70—2E 23
Ellin St. S1—6D 4 & 4E 99
Elliot Ct. S65—2E 79
Elliott Av. S73—2F 39
Elliott Clo. S63—4C 40
Elliott Dri. S43—5A 134
Elliott Dri. S61—5H 67
Elliott La. S30—4B 64
Elliott Rd. S6—1B 98
Elliottville St. S6—5A 86
Ellis Av. S63—1D 54
Ellis Cres. DN11—4C 62
Ellis Cres. S73—4A 40
Ellisons Rd. S31—1C 126
Ellison St. S3—1B 4 & 1D 98
  (in two parts)
Ellis St. S3—1C 4 & 1D 98
Ellis St. S60—2C 90
Elliston Av. S75—4G 7
Ellorslie Dri. S30—3E 141
Elm Clo. DN3—2H 21
Elm Clo. S31—4A 126
Elm Clo. S41—4H 131
Elm Ct. S70—5B 24
Elm Cres. DN5—5C 18
Elm Cres. S19—1C 124
Elmdale Clo. S64—5B 56
Elm Dri. S31—4A 126
Elmfield Av. S5—5F 75
Elmfield Rd. DN1—1E 47
Elmfield Rd. DN11—5D 62
Elm Grn. La. DN12—3E 59
Elm Gro. S61—4B 68
Elmham Rd. DN4—2C 48
Elmham S9—1F 101
Elmhirst Dri. S65—5A 80
Elm La. S5—5F 75
Elmore Rd. S10—2A 98
Elm Pl. DN3—2E 35
Elm Pl. S40—3G 137
Elm Pl. S62—2G 69
Elm Pl. S71—2D 14
Elm Rise. S30—3D 64
Elm Rd. DN3—2E 35
Elm Rd. S19—3G 115
Elm Rd. S31—6H 125
Elm Rd. S64—5C 42
Elm Row. S71—6B 14
Elmsdale. S70—5B 24
Elm St. S43—2G 133
Elm St. S74—1F 51
Elm Tree Clo. S31—2H 119
Elm Tree Cres. S18—6E 123
Elm Tree Farm Ct. S62—5D 56
Elmtree Rd. S61—4B 66
Elm Tree Rd. S66—4D 82
Elmview Rd. S9—5D 76
Elmville Av. S64—4A 56
Elm Wlk. S63—1F 29
Elm Way. S63—1G 55
Elmwood Av. DN6—1B 16
Elmwood Cres. DN3—3E 35

Elmwood Dri. S19—3D 124
Elsecar Ho. DN1—1C 46
  (off Bond Clo.)
Elsecar Rd. S63—5A 40
Elsham Clo. S66—2H 81
Elstead Clo. S75—2A 12
Elstree Dri. S12—3D 112
Elstree Rd. S12—3D 112
Elsworth Clo. DN1—2C 46
Elton St. S40—3A 138
Elton View. S43—3B 134
Elvaston Clo. S18—2A 128
Elwis St. DN5—5B 32
Elwood Rd. S17—3A 122
Ely Rd. DN2—2F 33
Ely St. DN11—3C 62
Embankment Rd. S10—2A 98
Embassy Ct. S2—3H 5
Emdale Dri. DN3—6D 20
Emerson Clo. S5—4F 75
Emerson Cres. S5—5F 75
Emerson Dri. S5—5F 75
Emily Clo. S71—5D 14
Emily Rd. S7—1C 110
Emley Dri. DN5—2E 31
Emley Ho. DN1—1C 46
  (off St James St.)
Emmetfield Clo. S40—5H 137
Empire Rd. S7—6D 98
Empire Ter. S71—1F 9
Endcliffe Av. S10—4A 98
Endcliffe Cres. S10—4H 97
Endcliffe Edge. S10—4H 97
Endcliffe Glen Rd. S11—4A 98
Endcliffe Gro. Av. S10—4G 97
Endcliffe Hall Av. S10—4G 97
Endcliffe Rise Rd. S11—4A 98
Endcliffe Ter. Rd. S11—4A 98
Endcliffe Vale Av. S11—5A 98
Endcliffe Vale Rd. S10—4H 97
Endcliffe Way. DN2—2A 34
Endfield Rd. S5—1D 74
Endowood Rd. S7—5H 109
Endowood Rd. S40—5C 136
Enfield Pl. S13—3H 101
Enfield Rd. S41—6H 131
Engine La. S63—5H 29
Engine La. S72—4D 10 to 6F 11
Ennerdale Av. S19—3E 125
Ennerdale Clo. S18—2C 128
Ennerdale Clo. S31—6E 107
Ennerdale Clo. S64—5G 43
Ennerdale Cres. S41—4E 131
Ennerdale Dri. S19—3E 125
Ennerdale Rd. DN2—3A 34
Ennerdale Rd. S71—1H 25
Ennis Cres. DN2—4G 33
Entwistle Rd. S30—6C 50
Epping Gdns. S19—5G 115
Epping Gro. S19—5G 115
Epsom Clo. S64—5F 43
Epsom Rd. DN4—1B 48
Erin Rd. S43—2D 134
Ernest Copley Ho. S30—1D 64
Errington Av. S2—1A 112
Errington Clo. S2—1A 112
Errington Cres. S2—1A 112
Errington Rd. S2—1A 112
Errington Rd. S40—5F 137
Errington Way. S2—6A 100
Erskine Cres. S2—6G 99
Erskine Rd. S2—6G 99
Erskine Rd. S65—1E 79
Erskine View. S2—1G 111
Eshton Ct. S75—3E 7
Eshton Wlk. S70—6F 13
  (off Prospect St.)
Eskdale Clo. S6—1A 86

Eskdale Clo. S18—2C 128
Eskdale Dri. DN5—1H 31
Eskdale La. S6—1A 86
Eskdale Rd. S61—4H 67
Eskdale Rd. S71—1G 25
Eskdale Wlk. DN5—2E 31
Esperanto Pl. S1—3F 5
Essendine Cres. S8—4F 111
Essex Av. DN2—6H 33
Essex Clo. S31—4C 118
Essex Rd. S2—4H 99
Essex Rd. S70—2H 23
Estate Rd. S62—6E 55
Estone Dri. S31—5B 104
Estone Dri. S31—5B 104
Ettrick Clo. S40—6E 131
Etwall Clo. S40—5C 130
Etwall Way. S5—5G 75
Evans St. S3—6B 4
Evanston Gdns. DN4—3A 46
Eva Ratcliffe Ho. S5—1E 75
Eveline St. S72—1H 15
Evelyn Av. DN2—4H 33
Evelyn Ct. DN2—5H 33
Evelyn Rd. S10—2H 97
Evelyn St. S62—1H 69
Evelyn Ter. S70—1B 24
Everard Av. S17—4G 121
Everard Dri. S17—4G 121
Everard Glade. S17—4G 121
Everett Clo. S43—4E 133
Everill Ga. La. S73—1H 39
  (in two parts)
Everingham Clo. S5—6E 75
Everingham Cres. S5—6D 74
Everingham Rd. DN4—1C 48
Everingham Rd. S5—6E 75
Everson Clo. S66—2E 83
Everton Rd. S11—5A 98
Evesham Clo. S9—5D 76
Ewden Rd. S73—2H 39
Ewden Way. S75—6C 12
Ewers Rd. S61—3H 77
Ewood Dri. DN4—3C 48
Exchange Gateway. S1—3E 5
Exchange Pl. S2—2G 5
Exchange St. DN1—2D 46
Exchange St. S2—2G 5 & 1F 99
Exeter Dri. S3—6B 4 & 4D 98
Exeter Pl. S3—4D 98
Exeter Rd. DN2—3G 33
Exeter Way. S3—6A 4 & 3C 98
Exley Av. S6—5B 86
Eyam Clo. S75—2A 22
Eyam Rd. S10—2H 97
Eyncourt Rd. S5—6G 75
Eyre Gdns. S30—1B 64
Eyre Gdns. S41—1H 137
Eyre La. S1—6E 5 & 3E 99
Eyre St. S1—6D 4 & 3E 99
Eyre St. E. S41—6C 138

Fabian Way. S66—5H 81
Factory La. DN1—6C 32
Factory St. S40—3F 137
Fairbank Rd. S5—2F 87
Fairbank View. S60—2A 92
Fairbarn Clo. S6—6E 85
Fairbarn Dri. S6—6E 85
Fairbarn Pl. S6—6E 85
Fairbarn Rd. S6—6E 85
Fairbarn Way. S6—6E 85
Fairburn Gdns. S60—3D 90
Fairburn Gro. S74—5D 38
Faircliff. DN5—2D 44
Fair Clo. S40—1G 137
Fairfax Rd. DN2—5H 33

Fairfax Rd. S2—5D 100
Fairfield. S63—6D 28
Fairfield. S70—2D 36
Fairfield Clo. DN4—5B 48
Fairfield Clo. S43—3D 132
Fairfield Clo. S66—2G 81
Fairfield Ct. DN3—4F 35
Fairfield Ct. S42—1B 136
Fairfield Dri. S42—1B 136
Fairfield Rd. DN5—3H 31
Fairfield Rd. S40—1H 137
Fairford Clo. DN4—5E 49
Fairford Clo. S40—6H 137
Fairleigh. S2—6C 100
Fairleigh Dri. S60—5E 79
Fairmount Gdns. S32—4A 114
Fairthorn Rd. S5—5H 75
Fair View Av. DN6—2B 16
Fairview Clo. S74—6G 37
Fair View Dri. S31—6C 104
Fairview Rd. S18—6E 123
Fairview Ter. DN3—1D 20
Fairview Vs. DN3—1E 21
Fairway. S75—3C 22
Fairway Av. S75—3G 7
Fairways. S66—5F 81
Fairway, The. S10—4A 96
Fair Winds Clo. S18—2E 129
Faith St. S71—1F 15
Falcon Ct. DN11—4E 63
Falcon Dri. S60—2F 103
Falcon Dri. S70—3D 36
Falconer Clo. S75—4B 6
Falconer La. S13—5F 103
Falcon Knowle Ing. S75—4A 6
Falcon Rise. S18—6H 123
Falcon Rd. S18—6G 123
Falcon St. S70—5G 13
Falcon Way. S31—6C 104
Falcon Yd. S40—2A 138
  (off Low Pavement)
Falding St. S30—2F 65
Falding St. S60—3C 78
Falkland Rise. S18—3E 129
Falkland Rd. S11—1G 109
Fall Bank Ind. Est. S75—1B 22
Fallon Rd. S6—5D 84
Falmouth Clo. S71—4B 14
Falmouth Rd. S7—2C 110
Falstaff Cres. S5—5D 74
Falstaff Gdns. S5—5D 74
Falstaff Rd. S5—4D 74
Fane Cres. S31—5B 104
Fanny Av. S31—4C 126
Fan Rd. S43—2D 134
Fanshaw Av. S31—6H 125
Far Cres. S65—2H 79
Fanshaw Bank. S18—2E 129
Fanshaw Clo. S31—6H 125
Fanshaw Dri. S31—6H 125
Fanshaw Rd. S18—1F 129
Fanshaw Rd. S31—6H 125
Fanshaw Way. S31—6H 125
Faraday Rd. S9—5A 88
Faranden Rd. S9—6C 88
Far Croft. S63—1A 42
Farcroft Gro. S4—2B 88
Far Dalton La. S65—1C 80
Far Field La. S63—5H 41
Far Field La. S71—1E 15
Far Field Rd. DN3—4E 21
Farfield Rd. S3—5C 86
Far Field Rd. S65—4A 80
Fargate. S1—3E 5 & 2E 99
Farhouse La. S30—2A 72
Farish Pl. S2—1F 111
Far La. S6—2H 85
Far La. S65—1H 79

Farlow Croft. S30—5A 50
Farm Bank Rd. S2
—6H 5 & 3G 99
Farm Clo. DN3—6E 21
Farm Clo. S12—5D 112
Farm Clo. S18—5F 123
Farm Clo. S40—6H 137
Farm Clo. S60—4C 90
Farm Clo. S71—3C 14
Farm Ct. DN6—1E 17
Farm Cres. S19—3C 124
Farm Fields Clo. S19—6D 114
Farmhill Clo. DN5—4G 31
Farm Ho. La. S75—5C 12
Far Moor Clo. DN5—1G 43
Farmoor Gdns. S19—5H 115
Farm Rd. S2—4F 99
Farm Rd. S70—3B 24
Farmstead Clo. S14—2H 111
Farmsworth Ct. S41—5D 138
Farm View Clo. S61—1F 77
Farm View Rd. S61—1F 77
Farm Wlk. S19—2C 124
Farm Way. S73—3E 27
Farnaby Dri. S30—5B 50
Farnaby Gdns. S30—5B 50
Farnborough Dri. DN4—5E 49
Farndale Av. S42—5D 136
Farndale Rd. DN5—2F 31
Farndale Rd. S6—1A 86
Farnley Av. S6—5B 74
Farnsworth Ct. S41—5D 138
Farnsworth St. S41—5C 138
Farnworth Rd. S65—2A 80
Far Pl. S65—2H 79
Farquhar Rd. S66—4H 83
Farrand St. S70—4C 36
Farrar Rd. S7—6D 98
Farrar St. S70—6F 13
Farrier Ga. S30—1C 64
Farringdon Dri. DN11—6E 63
Far View Rd. S5—5F 75
Far View Ter. S70—2G 23
Farwater Clo. S18—3E 129
Farwater La. S18—2D 128
Favell Rd. S3—3A 4
Favell Rd. S65—2B 80
Fawcett St. S3—1A 4 & 1C 98
Fearnehough St. S9—6C 88
Fearn Ho. Cres. S74—6G 37
Fearnley Rd. S74—6G 37
Fearnville Gro. S71—2E 9
Felkin St. S41—2B 138
Felkirk View. S72—2B 10
Fellbrigg Rd. S2—6H 99
Fellowesfield Way. S61—2G 77
Fellows Wlk. S73—5H 25
Fell Rd. S9—4C 88
Fenland Way. S40—5G 137
Fennel Gdns. S64—5B 56
Fenney La. S11—5E 109
Fenn Rd. S75—6D 36
Fensome Way. S73—3E 27
Fenton Clo. DN3—4F 35
Fenton Croft. S61—1A 78
Fenton Fields. S61—1A 78
Fenton Rd. S61—6A 68
Fenton St. S31—6G 125
Fenton St. S61—2H 77
Fentonville St. S11—5C 98
Fenton Way. S61—5B 68
Feoffees Rd. S30—6F 65
Ferguson St. S9—5B 88
Ferham Clo. S61—3A 78
Ferham Pk. Av. S61—3A 78
Ferham Rd. S61—3A 78
Fern Av. DN5—2A 32
Fern Av. S19—3F 115

Fern Av. S43—3A 134
Fern Bank. DN6—1D 16
Fernbank. S61—2G 77
Fernbank Dri. DN3—1F 35
Fernbank Dri. S31—6B 124
Fern Clo. DN2—3A 34
Fern Clo. S31—6B 124
Ferncroft Av. S19—2C 124
Ferndale Clo. S18—6H 123
Ferndale Dri. S66—3G 81
Ferndale Rise. S18—6H 123
Ferndale Rd. DN12—3D 58
Ferndale Rd. S18—6H 123
Fernhall Clo. DN3—4E 21
Fern Hollow. S66—6G 81
Fernhurst Rd. DN2—3A 34
Fern Lea Gro. S30—1F 75
Fern Lea Gro. S63—1H 41
Fernleigh Dri. S60—1B 90
Fern Rd. S6—5H 85
Fernvale Wlk. S64—5B 56
Fern Way. S31—6B 124
Ferrara Clo. S73—3C 26
Ferrars Clo. S9—1H 89
Ferrars Dri. S9—2H 89
Ferrars Rd. S9—6G 77
Ferrars Way. S9—2H 89
Ferrers Rd. DN2—4F 33
Ferriby Rd. S6—1H 85
Ferry Boat La. DN12 & S64
(in two parts)   —2G 57
Ferry La. DN12—2E 59
Ferry Moor La. S72—6D 10
Ferrymore Ho. DN1—1C 46
(off St James St.)
Ferry Ter. DN12—2E 59
Fersfield St. S4—5H 87
Festival Clo. S31—5G 117
Festival Rd. S63—6F 41
Field Clo. S18—1A 128
Field Clo. S73—3E 27
Field Dri. S72—2H 15
Field Ga. DN11—3E 63
Fieldhead Rd. S8—6E 99
Field Head Rd. S74—6A 38
Fieldhead Way. S41—5E 131
Field Ho. Rd. DN5—3D 44
Fieldhouse Way. S4—4H 87
Fielding Dri. S66—4H 81
Fielding Gro. S62—6F 55
Fielding Rd. S6—1A 86
Field La. S31—3H 125
Field La. S60 & S66—4D 92
Field La. S70—2E 25
Fieldsend Gdns. S30—1F 75
Fieldside. DN3—6D 20
Field View. S40—6A 138
Field View. S60—2C 90
Field Way. S60—1D 78
Fife Clo. S9—5C 76
Fife Gdns. S9—5C 76
Fife St. S9—5C 76
Fife St. S70—1F 23
Fife Way. S9—5C 76
Fifth Av. DN6—4D 16
Fig Tree La. S1—2E 5
Filby Rd. DN5—4G 31
Filey Av. S71—1F 9
Filey La. S3—5A 4 & 3C 98
Filey St. S10—4A 4 & 2C 98
Finch Clo. S65—5E 71
Finch Rise. S31—1C 116
Finch Rd. DN4—5H 45
Finchwell Clo. S13—3H 101
Finchwell Cres. S13—3H 101
Finchwell Rd. S13—3H 101
Findon Cres. S6—3G 85
Findon Pl. S6—3G 85

Findon Rd. S6—3G 85
Findon St. S6—3H 85
Finkle St. DN5—1B 32
Finlay Rd. S65—1G 79
Finlay St. S3—1A 4 & 1C 98
Finningley Lodge. S31—5H 117
Firbeck Av. S31—1E 107
Firbeck Ho. DN1—1C 46
(off Camden Pl.)
Firbeck La. S31—6G 95
Firbeck Rd. DN4—1F 47
Firbeck Rd. S8—4C 110
Firbeck Way. DN11—3F 63
Fir Clo. S63—6F 41
Fircroft Av. S5—4H 75
Fircroft Rd. S5—4A 76
Firham Clo. S71—1C 8
Fir Pl. S6—6A 86
Fir Pl. S31—4A 126
Fir Rd. S31—6H 125
Firsby La. DN12—6A 58
Firshill Av. S4—3F 87
Firshill Clo. S4—3F 87
Firshill Cres. S4—3E 87
Firshill Croft. S4—3E 87
Firshill Glade. S4—3E 87
Firshill Rise. S4—3F 87
Firshill Rd. S4—3F 87
Firshill Wlk. S4—3E 87
First Av. DN6—3E 17
First Av. S65—2G 79
First Av. S71—1F 9
Firs, The. S70—3C 24
Firs, The. S71—1C 8
First La. S31—4G 119
First La. S66—6G 81
Fir St. S6—6A 86
Firth Av. S72—1G 15
Firth Cres. S66—5G 83
Firth Pk. Av. S5—6A 76
Firth Pk. Cres. S5—6H 75
Firth Pk. Rd. S5—2H 87
Firth St. S71—6H 13
Firthwood Av. S18—6H 123
Firthwood Clo. S18—6H 123
Firthwood Rd. S18—6H 123
Fir Tree Dri. S31—5E 117
Firtree Rise. S30—3E 65
Fir Vale Pl. S5—2G 87
Fir Vale Rd. S5—2G 87
Firvale Rd. S42—5D 136
Fir View Gdns. S4—3H 87
Fir Wlk. S66—4C 82
Fish Dam La. S71—2D 14 to 5F 9
Fisher Clo. S40—6H 137
Fisher Clo. S60—3C 78
Fisher La. S9—6E 89
Fisher Rd. S66—4H 83
Fisher St. DN5—5B 18
Fisher Ter. DN5—4A 32
Fish Pond La. S66—1H 83
Fishponds Rd. S13—5E 101
Fishponds Rd. W. S13—6E 101
Fitzalan Rd. S13—4H 101
Fitzalan Sq. S1—3F 5 & 2F 99
Fitzgerald Rd. S10—1H 97
Fitzhubert Rd. S2—5C 100
Fitzmaurice Rd. S9—5D 88
Fitzroy Rd. S2—1F 111
Fitzwalter Rd. S2—3H 99

Fitzwilliam Av. DN12—3C 58
Fitzwilliam Av. S63—6E 41
Fitzwilliam Dri. DN5—2G 43
Fitzwilliam Ga. S1
—6C 4 & 3E 99
Fitzwilliam Rd. S65—2E 79
Fitzwilliam Rd. S73 & S72
—3G 27
Fitzwilliam Sq. S61—3B 68
Fitzwilliam St. S1—4B 4 & 2D 98
Fitzwilliam St. S62—4F 69
Fitzwilliam St. S63—6E 41
Fitzwilliam St. S64—2A 56
Fitzwilliam St. S70—6G 13
Fitzwilliam St. S73—4D 38
Fitzwilliam St. S74—6C 38
(Elsecar)
Fitzwilliam St. S74—6F 37
(Hoyland)
Five Oaks. DN5—4E 19
Five Trees Av. S17—3G 121
Five Trees Clo. S17—3G 121
Five Trees Dri. S17—3G 121
Fixby Ho. DN1—1C 46
(off Grove Pl.)
Flamstead Cres. S41—5A 132
Flanders Ct. S61—2B 66
Flanderwell Av. S66—4G 81
Flanderwell Ct. S66—3G 81
Flanderwell Gdns. S66—3G 81
Flanderwell La. S66—2F 81
Flash La. S66—5H 81
Flask View. S6—4C 84
Flat La. S60—2H 91
Flat La. S72—4A 28
Flat St. S1—3F 5 & 2F 99
Flatts Clo. S60—6E 91
Flatts La. S60—6E 91
Flatts La. S63—6D 42
Flaxby Rd. S9—6D 88
Flax Lea. S70—4A 24
Fleet Clo. S63—4B 40
Fleethill Cres. S71—2A 14
Fleet La. S30—5E 73
Fleet St. S70—1H 23
Fleetwood Av. S71—2C 14
Fleming Pl. S70—1G 23
Fleming Sq. S63—5E 41
Fleming Way. S66—4E 81
Fletcher Av. S18—2E 129
Fletcher Ho. S65—2E 79
Fleury Clo. S14—3A 112
Fleury Cres. S14—3A 112
Fleury Pl. S14—3A 112
Fleury Rise. S14—3A 112
Fleury Way. S14—3A 112
Flint Rd. DN2—3A 34
Flintway. S63—2F 55
Flockton Av. S13—5C 102
Flockton Ct. S1—4C 4 & 2D 98
Flockton Cres. S13—5B 102
Flockton Dri. S13—5C 102
Flockton Rd. S13—5B 102
Flodden St. S10—1H 97
Floodgate Dri. S30—1F 75
Flora St. S6—5C 86
Florence Av. DN4—3A 46
Florence Av. S31—6B 104
Florence Rise. S73—4D 26
Florence Rd. S8—5C 110
Florence Rd. S8—3B 78
Flower St. S63—4H 29
Flowitt St. DN4—6D 42
Flowitt St. S64—6D 42
Folderings La. S30—6E 141
Folder La. DN5—2C 44
Folds Cres. S8—6A 110
Folds Dri. S8—6A 110

Folds La. S8—6A 110
Fold, The. S65—1B 80
Foley Av. S73—1E 39
Foley St. S4—6H 87
Foljambe Av. S40—5F 137
Foljambe Cres. DN11—4B 62
Foljambe Dri. S65—6C 70
Foljambe Rd. S40—2H 137
Foljambe Rd. S43—3E 133
Foljambe Rd. S65—1H 79
Foljambe St. S62—3F 69
Follett Rd. S5—4G 75
Fonteyn Ho. DN2—3F 33
Fontwell Dri. S64—5F 43
Foolow Av. S40—4H 137
Footgate Clo. S30—2D 72
Forbes Rd. S6—4A 86
Ford Clo. S18—2D 128
Ford La. S30—2E 141
Fordoles Head La. S66—1C 82
Ford Rd. S11—1H 109
Fordstead La. DN5 & DN3
—2F 19
Fore Hill Av. DN4—5B 48
Foremark Rd. S5—5H 75
Fore's Rd. DN3—4G 35
Forest Edge. S11—6G 109
Forest Rise. DN4—6G 45
Forest Rd. S71—5A 8
Forge Hill. S30—2D 72
Forge La. S1—6D 4 & 4E 99
Forge La. S30—2D 72
Forge La. S31—2H 125
Forge La. S60—3D 78
Forge La. S74—1D 52
Forge Rd. S31—4F 117
Formby Ct. S71—1D 14
Forncett St. S4—5H 87
Fornham St. S2—6F 5 & 3F 99
Forres Av. S10—2G 97
Forres Rd. S10—2G 97
Forrester Clo. S66—3F 81
Forrester's La. S18—5G 123
Forster Rd. DN4—5B 46
Forth Av. S18—1B 128
Fort Hill Rd. S9—6B 76
Fortway Rd. S60—1C 90
Fossard Clo. DN2—2G 33
Fossdale Rd. S7—2B 110
Foster Rd. S66—4F 81
Foster's Clo. S64—2A 56
Fosters, The. S30—6B 50
Foster St. S70—1D 24
Foster Way. S30—5B 50
Foston Dri. S40—6D 130
Foulstone Row. S73—1G 39
Foundry Ct. S3—4F 87
Foundry Rd. DN4—2B 46
Foundry St. S41—3A 132
Foundry St. S62—4F 69
Foundry St. S70—1G 23 to 6G 13
(in two parts)
Foundry St. S74—6C 38
Fountain Clo. S75—4C 6
Fountain Precinct. S1—3E 5
Fountain Sq. S75—4C 6
Fountains Way. S71—4D 14
Fountside. S7—1B 110
Fourth Av. DN6—3D 16
Fourwells Dri. S12—3A 114
Fowler Bri. Rd. DN5—1C 32
Fowler Cres. DN11—4C 62
Fowler St. S41—1H 131
Foxbrook Clo. S42—6B 130
Fox Clo. S61—5F 67
Foxcote Lea. S65—5E 71
Foxcote Way. S42—5D 136
Fox Ct. S64—4B 56

Foxcroft Chase. S31—3A 126
Foxcroft Dri. S31—3A 126
Foxcroft Gro. S31—3A 126
Foxdale Av. S12—2D 112
Foxfield Wlk. S70—3D 24
Fox Glen Rd. S30—4F 141
Foxglove Clo. S44—2G 139
Foxglove Rd. S5—5A 76
Foxhall La. S10—1A 108
Fox Hill. S3—5F 87
Fox Hill Av. S6—4A 74
Fox Hill Clo. S6—4A 74
Fox Hill Cres. S6—4A 74
Fox Hill Dri. S6—4A 74
Fox Hill Pl. S6—3A 74
Fox Hill Rd. S6—5A to 2A 74
Fox Hill Way. S6—3A 74
Foxland Av. S64—3G 55
Fox La. DN5—1G 43
Fox La. S12—5E 113
Fox La. S17—3B 122
Fox Rd. S6—5C 86
Foxroyd Clo. S71—1F 25
Fox's Pl. S40—3F 137
Fox St. S3—5F 87
Fox St. S61—3G 77
Foxtone Clo. S43—3B 134
Fox Wlk. S6—5B 86
Foxwood Av. S12—1D 112
Foxwood Clo. S41—6D 138
Foxwood Dri. S12—1D 112
Foxwood Gro. S12—2D 112
Foxwood Rd. S12—1D 112
Foxwood Rd. S41—1G 131
Framlingham Pl. S2—6H 99
Framlingham Rd. S2—6H 99
France Rd. S6—2D 84
Frances St. DN1—6D 32
France St. S62—4F 69
Francis Clo. S43—4E 133
Francis Cres. N. S60—5B 80
Francis Cres. S. S60—6B 80
Francis Dri. S60—5B 80
Francis Gro. S30—6B 50
Francis St. S60—4E 79
Frankel Clo. S3—1E 99
Frank Hillock Field. S30
—3G 141
Franklin Cres. DN2—6F 33
Franklyn Rd. S40—1G 137
Frank Pl. S9—4C 88
Fraser Clo. S8—4C 110
Fraser Cres. S8—4C 110
Fraser Dri. S8—4D 110
Fraser Rd. S8—4C 110
Fraser Rd. S60—4F 79
Fraser Wlk. S8—4D 110
Frecheville St. S43—2B 134
Frederick Av. S70—1F 23
Frederick Dri. S30—6A 64
Frederick Rd. S7—6D 98
Frederick St. S9—6D 88
Frederick St. S60—6C 90
(Catcliffe)
Frederick St. S60—2D 78
(Rotherham)
Frederick St. S63—4G 29
(Goldthorpe)
Frederick St. S63—4D 40
(Wath upon Dearne)
Frederick St. S64—6D 42
Frederick St. S73—6A 26
Frederic Pl. S70—2H 23
Freebirch View. S41—4D 130
Freedom Ct. S6—4B 86
Freedom Rd. S6—5A 86
Freeman Gdns. S30—1B 64

Freeman Rd. S66—4F 81
Freeman St. S70—1H 23
Freemans Yd. S70—6H 13
Freesia Clo. S31—3E 119
Freeston Pl. S9—4C 88
French Ga. DN1—5C 32
(in two parts)
Frenchgate Shopping Cen. DN1
(off French Ga.) —6C 32
French St. DN5—5B 18
Fretson Rd. S2—5C 100
Fretwell Clo. S66—2E 83
Fretwell Rd. S65—1A 80
Freydon Way. S44—2G 139
Friar Clo. S6—5D 84
Friar's Rd. S71—4E 15
Frickley Bri. La. S72—1E 11
Frickley Rd. S11—5F 97
Frinton Clo. S40—6H 137
Frithbeck Clo. DN3—3F 35
Frith Clo. S12—2D 112
Frith Rd. S12—2D 112
Frobisher Gro. S66—3E 83
Froggatt Clo. S43—5A 134
Froggatt La. S1—5E 5 & 3E 99
Frogmore Clo. S66—3H 81
Frog Wlk. S11—5C 98
Front St. S60—1E 103
Frostings Clo. S30—6A 64
(in two parts)
Frostings, The. S30—6A 64
Fulford Clo. S9—6E 89
Fulford Rd. S40—5E 137
Fulford Pl. S9—6E 89
Fulford Way. DN12—2G 59
Fuller Gro. S64—4B 56
Fullerton Av. DN12—3C 58
Fullerton Cres. S65—4D 70
Fullerton Dri. S60—3B 90
Fullerton Rd. S60—5E 79
Fulmar Way. S61—1C 66
Fulmer Clo. S71—1B 14
Fulmere Cres. S5—3C 74
Fulmere Rd. S5—3C 74
Fulmer Rd. S11—6A 98
Fulney Rd. S11—5F 97
Fulton Rd. S6—6A 86
Fulwood Dri. DN4—1H 61
Fulwood La. S11—3A 108
Fulwood Rd. S10
—6D 96 to 3A 98
Funival Rd. S4—1H 5 & 1G 99
Furlong Rd. DN5—2E 43
Furlong Rd. S63—1B 42 to 5F 29
Furlong View. DN5—1F 43
(in two parts)
Furnace Hill. S3—1D 4 & 1E 99
Furnace La. S13—6E 103
Furnace La. S18—1B 130
Furnace La. S43—5F 133
Furnace Yd. S70—5A 24
Furness Clo. S6—4D 84
Furness Clo. S31—6F 107
Furness Dene. S71—2D 14
Furness Rd. S30—6A 50
Furniss Av. S17—4D 120
Furnival Clo. S31—2A 118
Furnival Ga. S1—5D 4 & 3E 99
Furnival Rd. DN4—3A 46
Furnival Rd. S4—2G 5 & 1F 99
Furnival Rd. S31—2A 118
Furnival Sq. S1—5E 5 & 3E 99
Furnival St. S1—5E 5 & 3E 99
Furnival Way. S60—2B 92
Fylde Clo. S71—1D 14

Gainsborough Clo. S66—4F 81
Gainsborough Rd. S11—6B 98
Gainsborough Rd. S18—3C 128
Gainsborough Way. S71—3B 14
Gainsford Rd. S9—1E 101
Gaitskell Clo. S63—6F 29
Gaitskell Clo. S66—5H 83
Galley Dri. S19—6D 114
Gallow Tree Rd. S65—5B 80
Galsworthy Av. S5—6D 74
Galsworthy Clo. DN4—6H 45
Galsworthy Rd. S5—1C 86
Galway Clo. S62—1G 69
Gamston Rd. S8—6D 98
Gannow Clo. S31—2D 126
Ganton Pl. S71—6A 8
Ganton Rd. S6—1H 85
Garbroads Cres. S65—5C 70
Garbutt St. S63—2B 42
Garden Cres. S60—1G 91
Garden Dri. S73—3A 40
Garden Gro. S73—3E 39
Garden Ho. Clo. S71—2C 14
Gardenia Rd. DN3—4C 20
Garden La. DN4—2H 45
Garden La. S60—2C 78
(off Amen Corner)
Garden La. S45—4H 71
Gardens La. DN12—3D 58
Gardens, The. DN4—4B 48
Gardens, The. S7—5C 98
Garden St. S1—2C 4 & 1D 98
Garden St. S30—4H 29
Garden St. S61—2B 78
Garden St. S63—1F 29
(Thurnscoe)
Garden St. S63—4D 40
(Wath upon Dearne)
Garden St. S64—6E 43
Garden St. S70—1H 23
Garden St. S73—4E 27
Garden Ter. DN5—1B 32
Garden Wlk. S19—4G 115
Garden Wlk. S60—1G 91
Gardom Clo. S18—2B 128
Garfield Mt. S65—4F 79
Garland Clo. S19—1E 125
Garland Croft. S19—2E 125
Garland Dri. S6—2E 85
Garland Mt. S19—1E 125
Garland Way. S19—2E 125
Garry Rd. S6—2H 85
Garter St. S4—4H 87
Garth Rd. S9—6C 88
Garth Way. S18—2D 128
Garth Way Clo. S18—2D 128
Gashouse La. S19 & S31
—3D 124
Gate Cres. S75—1B 22
Gatefield Clo. S41—5F 131
Gatefield Rd. S7—1C 110
Gateland La. S18—6C 128
Gate, The. S75—1B 22
Gateway Ct. S62—5E 69
Gateway Ind. Est. S62—5E 69
Gateway, The. S62—5E 69
Gattison La. DN11—5D 62
Gatty Rd. S5—2H 75
Gaunt Clo. S14—4H 111
Gaunt Clo. S66—3H 81
Gaunt Dri. S14—4H 111
Gaunt Dri. S66—3H 81
Gaunt Pl. S14—3H 111
Gaunt Rd. S14—4H 111
Gaunt Rd. S66—3H 81
Gaunt Way. S14—4H 111
Gawber Rd. S75—4E 13

Gawtress Row. S63—5E 41
Gayle Ct. S70—5F 13
 (off Buckden Rd.)
Gayton Clo. DN4—6A 46
Gayton Ct. DN4—6A 46
Gayton Rd. S4—3G 87
Gelderd Pl. S18—3E 129
Gell St. S3—3A 4 & 2C 98
Genefax Ho. S10—4G 97
Genn La. S70—3F 23
Genoa Clo. S73—2C 26
Genoa St. S64—6F 43
George Pl. S62—2G 69
George Pl. S64—6G 43
George Sq. S70—6G 13
George St. DN3—2D 34
George St. DN5—5A 18
George St. S1—3F 5 & 2F 99
George St. S41—1H 131
George St. S43—3E 133
George St. S60—2D 78
 (in two parts)
George St. S63—4E 29
 (Goldthorpe)
George St. S63—2H 29
 (Thurnscoe)
George St. S70—6G 13
 (Barnsley)
George St. S70—5A 24
 (Worsbrough Bridge)
George St. S70—5C 24
 (Worsbrough Dale)
George St. S72—5C 10
 (Cudworth)
George St. S72—2H 27
 (Little Houghton)
George St. S73—5D 26
 (Low Valley, Wombwell)
George St. S73—1F 39
 (Wombwell)
George St. S74—6A 38
George St. S75—4F 7
George Woofindin Almshouses.
                S11—5A 98
George Yd. S70—6H 13
Gerald Clo. S70—2C 24
Gerald Cres. S70—1D 24
Gerald Pl. S70—2C 24
Gerald Rd. S70—2C 24
Gerald St. S9—4C 88
Gerald Wlk. S70—2C 24
Gerard Av. S65—5E 71
Gerard Clo. S8—1F 111
Gerard Clo. S40—4E 137
Gerard Rd. S60—4E 79
Gerard St. S8—1F 111
Gertrude St. S6—5C 86
Gervase Av. S8—3C 122
Gervase Dri. S8—3C 122
Gervase Pl. S8—3C 122
Gervase Rd. S8—3C 122
Gervase Wlk. S8—4C 122
Gibbing Greaves Rd. S65
                —5C 80
Gibbons Dri. S14—5A 112
Gibbons Wlk. S14—5A 112
 (off Gibbons Dri.)
Gibraltar St. S3—1D 4 & 1E 99
Gibson La. S30—2E 141
Gibson Wlk. S64—4B 56
 (off Haythorne Way)
Gifford Dri. DN4—5F 45
Gifford Rd. S8—6E 99
Gig La. S74—3F 37
Gilbert Av. S40—5F 137
Gilbert Gro. S70—1D 24
Gilberthorpe Dri. S65—3G 79
Gilberthorpe Rd. DN4—4H 45

Gilberthorpe St. S65—3F 79
Gilbert Row. S2—3H 5 & 2G 99
Gilbert St. S2—3G 5 & 2G 99
Giles Av. S63—5C 40
Gill Clo. S66—6G 81
Gill Croft. S6—5C 84
Gilleyfield Av. S17—2E 121
Gill Meadows. S6—5C 84
Gillott Dell. S66—6F 81
Gillott Ind. Est. S70—5F 13
Gillott La. S66—6F 81
Gillott Rd. S6—5A 74
Gill St. DN1—1D 46
Gill St. S74—6B 38
Gilpin La. S6—5C 86
Gilpin St. S6—5C 86
Gilroyd La. S75—4C 22
Ginhouse La. S61—1C 78
Gipsy Grn. La. S63—1F 55
Gipsy La. S41—2B 132
Girton Rd. S9—3D 88
Gisborne Rd. S11—1H 109
Glade Clo. S40—6G 131
Glade Croft. S12—3C 112
Glade Lea. S12—3C 112
Glade, The. S10—4H 97
Glade, The. S40—2F 137
Glade View. DN3—3D 20
Gladstone M. S10—4E 97
Gladstone Pl. S64—6C 42
Gladstone Rd. DN4—2A 46
Gladstone Rd. S10—4F 97
Gladstone Rd. S40—1H 137
Gladstone Rd. S66—3E 83
Gladwin Gdns. S40—5F 137
Gladys St. S65—3G 79
Glaisdale Clo. S31—2C 106
Glamis Rd. DN2—6G 33
Glasshouse La. S62—6C 56
Glasshouse St. S60—2C 78
Glastonbury Ga. DN5—4F 31
Gleadless Av. S12—3B 112
Gleadless Bank. S12—3B 112
Gleadless Comn. S12—1B 112
Gleadless Ct. S2—1F 111
Gleadless Cres. S12—2B 112
Gleadless Dri. S12—3B 112
Gleadless Mt. S12—4C 112
Gleadless Rd. S2, S14 & S12
                —6E 99
Glebe Clo. S64—4A 56
Glebe Ct. S41—1A 132
Glebe Cres. S65—6C 70
Glebe Farm Clo. DN3—2E 35
Glebelands Clo. S62—6E 55
Glebelands Rd. S30—4E 141
Glebe Rd. S10—1A 98
Glebe Rd. S64—4A 56
Glebe St. DN4—5F 45
Glebe, The. S41—1A 132
 (off Glebe Way, The.)
Glebe Way, The. S41—1A 132
Gledhill Clo. S18—2E 129
Glenalmond Rd. S11—6H 97
Glencoe Dri. S2—3G 99
Glencoe Pl. S2—3G 99
Glencoe Rd. S2—3G 99
Glencoe Way. S40—1D 136
Glencroft. S11—6H 97
Glendale Clo. S75—5D 12
Glendale Rd. DN5—2D 44
Gleneagles Clo. S40—5E 137
Gleneagles Dri. DN4—5F 49
Gleneagles Rise. S64—3B 56
Gleneagles Rd. S31—5F 107
Glen Field Av. DN4—2A 46
Glenfield Cres. S41—4H 131
Glenholme Dri. S13—6G 101

Glenholme Pl. S13—6H 101
Glenholme Rd. S13—6H 101
Glenholme Way. S13—5G 101
Glenmoor Av. S70—1D 22
Glenmore Croft. S12—1E 113
Glenmore Rise. S73—2G 39
Glenorchy Rd. S7—2B 110
Glen Rd. DN3—3H 49
Glen Rd. S7—1C 110
Glen, The. S10—4H 97
Glenthorne Clo. S40—3E 137
Glentilt Rd. S7—2B 110
Glen View. S11—5F 97
Glen View Rd. S8—1C 122
Glenville Clo. S74—6H 37
Glenwood Cres. S30—2F 65
Gliwice Way. DN4—2H 47
Glossop La. S10—2C 98
Glossop Rd. S10—4A 4 & 3A 98
Glossop Row. S30—2D 72
Glossop's Croft. S41—1B 132
Gloucester Av. S11—1H 109
Gloucester Cres. S10—3C 98
Gloucester Rd. DN2—4G 33
Gloucester Rd. S11—6H 131
Gloucester Rd. S61—6H 67
Gloucester St. S10—3C 98
Glover Rd. S8—6E 99
Glover Rd. S17—5F 121
Glumangate. S40—2A 138
Glyn Av. DN1—5E 33
Goathland Clo. S13—6D 102
Goathland Dri. S13—6D 102
Goathland Pl. S13—6D 102
Goathland Rd. S13—6D 102
Goddard Av. S30—2B 140
Goddard Hall Rd. S5—2G 87
Godley Clo. S71—1F 9
Godley St. S71—1F 9
Godric Dri. S60—2B 90
Godric Grn. S60—2B 90
Godric Rd. S5—2G 75
Godstone Rd. S60—4E 79
Goldcrest Wlk. S61—2C 66
Golden Oak Dell. S6—4C 84
Golden Smithies La. S64 & S63
                —2H 55
Goldsborough Rd. DN2—6G 33
Goldsmith Dri. S65—3H 79
Goldsmith Rd. DN4—5C 46
Goldsmith Rd. S65—3H 79
Gold St. S70—1A 24
Goldthorpe Grn. S63—5F 29
Goldthorpe Ind. Est. S63—5E 29
Goldthorpe Rd. S63—5G 29
Gomersal La. S18—2E 129
Gomersall Av. DN12—3B 58
Gooder Av. S71—2E 9
Goodison Boulevd. DN4—3E 49
Goodison Ct. DN4—3C 48
Goodison Cres. S6—5F 85
Goodison Rise. S6—5F 85
Goodwin Av. S62—1F 69
Goodwin Cres. S64—1A 56
Goodwin Rd. S8—1E 111
Goodwin Rd. S61—3A 68
Goodwin Way. S61—3A 68
Goodwood Gdns. DN4—1B 48
Goodyear Cres. S73—1F 39
Goore Av. S9—3D 100
Goore Dri. S9—2D 100
Goore Rd. S9—3D 100
Gooseacre Av. S63—1E 29
Goosebutt St. S62—3F 69
Goose Carr La. S31—6H 105
Goosecroft Av. S65—5C 70
Goose La. S66—5G 81
Gordon Av. S8—5E 111

Gordon Rd. DN12—3B 60
Gordon Rd. S11—5B 98
Gordon St. DN1—6C 32
Gordon St. S70—1E 25
Gorman Clo. S41—3G 131
Gorse Dri. S31—4B 126
Gorseland Ct. S66—5E 81
Gorse La. S10—6A 96
Gorse, The. S65—4A 80
Gorse, The. S66—6F 81
Gorse Valley Rd. S41—6E 139
Gorsey Brigg. S18—2B 128
Gosber Rd. S31—6E 125
Gosber St. S31—6D 124
Gosforth Clo. S18—2D 128
Gosforth Cres. S18—2D 128
Gosforth Dri. S18—2B 128
Gosforth Grn. S18—2D 128
Gosforth La. S18—2D 128
Gosling Gate Rd. S63—4G 29
Gotham Rd. S60—1C 90
Gough Clo. S65—5A 80
Gough St. S60—2D 78
Goulding St. S64—1D 56
Gowdall Grn. DN5—4A 18
Gower Cres. S40—6E 131
Gower St. S4—5G 87
Gower St. S73—1G 39
Goyt Side Rd. S40—3F 137
Grace St. S71—1F 15
Graftdyke Clo. DN11—4F 63
Grafton St. S2—3G 99
Grafton St. S70—6F 13
Graham Av. S60—4D 90
Graham Ct. S10—5F 97
Graham Knoll. S10—5F 97
Graham Rise. S10—5F 97
Graham Rd. DN3—4D 20
Graham Rd. S10—5F 97
Graham's Orchard. S70—6G 13
Grainger Dri. DN12—4A 60
Grainger Ct. S10—4F 97
Grammar St. S6—4B 86
Grampian Clo. DN5—4G 31
Grampian Clo. S75—5D 12
Grampian Cres. S40—1D 136
Granary Clo. S41—4C 130
Granby Cres. DN2—1F 47
Granby La. DN11—3B 62
Granby Rd. DN12—3C 60
Granby Rd. S5—1H 87
Grange Av. DN4—4A 46
Grange Av. S18—2C 128
Grange Av. S31—4A 104
Grange Cliffe Clo. S11—3H 109
Grange Clo. DN4—5D 48
Grange Clo. S66—6H 93
Grange Clo. S72—2F 11
Grange Ct. DN5—3B 32
Grange Ct. S66—6F 81
Grange Cres. S63—1G 29
Grange Cres. S71—5E 15
Grange Cres. Rd. S11—5C 98
Grange Dri. S61—6F 67
Grange Dri. S66—5B 82
Grange Farm Dri. S30—5D 72
Grangefield Av. DN11—4D 62
Grangefield Cres. DN11—4D 62
Grangefield Ter. DN11—4D 62
Grange Ho. S72—2F 11
Grange La. DN5—1H 43
Grange La. DN11—5B 62
 (New Rossington)
Grange La. DN11—1E 61
 (Wadworth, in two parts)
Grange La. S5 & S61—1B 76

Grange La. S13—5A 102
Grange La. S60—6A 78
Grange La. S66—4G 83
Grange La. S71—6E 15
Grange La. Ind. Est. S71—6E 15
Grange Mill La. S5 & S9—1B 76
Grange Pk. DN3—2E 21
Grange Pk. Av. S43—1F 139
Grange Rd. DN4—5D 48
Grange Rd. DN5—3A 18
Grange Rd. DN6—4E 17
Grange Rd. DN11—5C 62
Grange Rd. S11—5C 98
Grange Rd. S19—4F 115
Grange Rd. S60—1H 91
Grange Rd. S62—6G 55
Grange Rd. S63—6D 40
Grange Rd. S64—3H 55
Grange Rd. S72—2C 8
Grange Rd. S72—2F 11
Grange St. S63—1G 29
Grange Ter. S63—1G 29
(off Chapman St.)
Grange, The. S42—1B 136
Grange, The. S61—5E 67
Grange View. S74—2H 37
Grange View Cres. S61—1F 77
Grange View Rd. S61—1F 77
Grange Way. DN12—2B 58
Grangewood Rd. S31—1E 107
Grangewood Rd. S40—6H 137
Gransden Way. S40—5E 137
Grantham St. DN11—4C 62
Grantly Clo. S73—3H 39
Granton Pl. S71—6A 8
Granville Clo. S41—5D 138
Granville Rd. S2—6G 5 & 3F 99
Granville Sq. S2—6G 5 & 3F 99
Granville St. S2—6G 5 & 3F 99
Granville St. S75—4F 13
Granville Ter. S65—3F 79
Grasby Ct. S66—2H 81
Grasmere Av. DN2—5A 34
Grasmere Clo. S31—1H 119
Grasmere Clo. S41—4F 131
Grasmere Clo. S63—2A 42
Grasmere Clo. S64—5H 43
Grasmere Cres. S75—3E 7
Grasmere Rd. DN12—3D 58
Grasmere Rd. S8—2C 110
Grasmere Rd. S18—2B 128
Grasmere Rd. S71—6A 14
Grasscroft Clo. S40—5F 131
Grassdale View. S12—4H 113
Grassington Clo. S12—4B 114
Grassington Dri. S12—4B 114
Grassington Way. S30—1D 64
Grassmoor Clo. S12—2B 112
Grassthorpe Rd. S12—3D 112
Gratton Ct. S43—1D 134
Gratton St. S61—3G 77
Graven Clo. S30—1H 73
Graves Trust Homes. S8
—1E 123
Graves Trust Homes. S12
—2C 112
Gray Av. S31—4B 104
Gray Gdns. DN4—5B 46
Grays Ct. DN12—1C 58
Grayshott Wlk. S40—5H 137
Grayson Clo. S30—4E 141
Grayson Ct. S65—1H 81
Grayson Rd. S61—3A 68
Gray's Rd. S71—4E 9
Gray St. S3—5F 87
Gray St. S19—2C 124
Gray St. S74—6C 38
Greasbro Rd. S9—1F 89

Greasbrough La. S62—2D 68
Greasbrough Rd. S61 & S63
(in two parts)   —5C 68
Greasbrough Rd. S62—4D 68
Greasbrough St. S60—2C 78
Great Bank Rd. S65—5A 80
Gt. Central Av. DN4—3B 46
Gt. Croft. S18—1B 128
Gt. North Rd. DN6 & DN5—1B 16
Gt. North Rd. DN11—2G 63
Gt. Park Rd. S61—1G 77
Greaves Clo. S6—5C 84
Greaves Fold. S75—5D 12
Greaves La. S6—5C 84
Greaves La. S30—3B 50
Greaves Rd. S5—1E 75
Greaves Rd. S61—2A 78
Greaves Sike La. S66—1B 83
Greaves St. S6—4B 86
Greenacre Clo. S18—4G 129
Green Acres. S62—2G 69
Greenacres. S74—6A 38
Green Arbour Rd. S66—5A 94
Greenbank Dri. S40—1E 137
Greenbank Wlk. S72—6F 11
Green Boulevarde. DN4—3C 48
(Armthorpe)
Green Chase. S31—6C 124
Green Clo. S43—5A 134
Green Common. DN3—4F 35
Green Cross. S18—1F 129
Greendale Av. S42—5A 136
Greendale Ct. S18—1F 129
Greendale Shopping Centre.
S18—1F 129
Green Farm Clo. S40—5E 131
Greenfield. S62—2F 69
Greenfield Clo. DN3—4G 35
(Armthorpe)
Greenfield Clo. DN3—1E 21
(Barnby Dun)
Greenfield Clo. S8—2D 122
Greenfield Clo. S65—1B 80
Greenfield Cotts. S71—5E 9
Greenfield Ct. S66—3F 81
Greenfield Dri. S8—2D 122
Greenfield Gdns. DN4—4E 49
Greenfield Gdns. S66—3F 81
Greenfield La. DN4—2A 46
Greenfield Rd. S8—2D 122
Greenfield Rd. S65—1B 80
Greenfield Rd. S74—3A 38
Greenfields. S31—6C 124
Greenfinch Clo. S60—3D 90
Greenfoot Clo. S75—4F 13
Greenfoot La. S75—3F to 4E 13
(in two parts)
Greengate Clo. S13—1D 114
Greengate Clo. S40—3E 137
Green Gate Clo. S63—6F 29
Greengate La. S13—1C 114
Greengate La. S30—1B 64
Greengate Rd. S13—1D 114
Green Glen. S40—3D 136
Greenhall Rd. S31—6C 124
Greenhead Gdns. S30—2E 65
Greenhead La. S30—2E 65
Greenhill Av. S8—1C 122
Greenhill Av. S66—5B 82
Greenhill Av. S71—4H 13
Greenhill Main Rd. S8—2C 122
Greenhill Parkway. S8—4A 122
Greenhill Rd. S8—5D 110
Green Ho. Rd. DN2—3H 33
Greenhow St. S6—6A 86
Green Ings La. S63—4G 41
Greenland. S74—2H 37
Greenland Av. S66—3G & 2G 83
(in two parts)

Greenland Clo. S9—5E 89
Greenland Clo. S31—1F 119
Greenland Ct. S9—5E 89
Greenland Dri. S9—5E 89
Greenland Rd. S9—4E 89
Greenland Rd. Ind. & Business
Pk. S9—4E 89
Greenlands Av. DN11—3E 63
Greenland View. S9—6E 89
Greenland View. S70—5H 23
Greenland Wlk. S9—5E 89
Greenland Way. S9—4E & 5E 89
(in two parts)
Greenland Way. S66—2G 83
Green La. DN3—2F 49
Green La. DN5—5A 16 to 6F 17
Green La. DN6—3C 16
Green La. DN11—6G 61
Green La. S3—6D 86
Green La. S18—2F 129
Green La. S30—1E 75
(Ecclesfield)
Green La. S30—1B 72
(Onesacre)
Green La. S30—2A 140
(Stocksbridge)
Green La. S30—1B 72
(Wharncliffe Side)
Green La. S31—6E 105
(Aston)
Green La. S31—5A 126
(Killamarsh)
Green La. S31—1B 104
(Ulley)
Green La. S41—1D 138
Green La. S42—4A 130
Green La. S60—4B 90
(Brinsworth)
Green La. S60—1G 91
(Rotherham)
Green La. S61—2E 77
Green La. S62—2F 69
Green La. S63—2D 54
Green La. S66—3E 95
(Carr, Maltby)
Green La. S66—2H 93
(Thurcroft)
Green La. S66—4E 81
(Wickersley)
Green La. S70—4E 23
Green La. S74—6E 37
Green La. S75—3C 22
Green Lea. S18—1A 128
Greenleafe Av. DN2—2A 34
Green Moor Rd. S30—1F 141
Green Oak Av. S17—5E 121
Green Oak Cres. S17—5E 121
Green Oak Dri. S17—5E 121
Green Oak Dri. S31—5E 117
Green Oak Gro. S17—5E 121
Green Oak Rd. S17—6E 121
Green Oak View. S17—5E 121
Greenock St. S6—3H 85
Green Rise. S62—6D 54
Green Rd. S75—3A 22
Greenside. S61—4B 68
Greenside. S72—1B 10
Greenside. S75—4G 7
Greenside Av. S31—5G 117
Greenside Av. S41—4H 131
Greenside Av. S75—4G 7
Greenside Ho. S75—4G 7
Greenside La. S74—5A 38
Greenside M. S12—4B 114
Green Spring Av. S70—3D 36
Greens Rd. S65—3H 79
Green St. DN4—5H 45
Green St. S30—3F 141

Green St. S41—1A 132
Green St. S61—3B 68
Green St. S70—4C 24
Green St. S74—5A 38
Green, The. DN12—2G 57
Green, The. S9—1E 101
Green, The. S17—5D 120
Green, The. S31—1F 119
(Anston)
Green, The. S31—4B 116
(Waleswood, Kiveton Park)
Green, The. S41—6D 138
Green, The. S60—6F 79
(Rotherham)
Green, The. S60—3H 91
(Whiston)
Green, The. S63—6E 29
Green, The. S64—3H 55
Green, The. S71—2E 9
Green, The. S72—2C 10
Green, The. S73—4E 39
Green, The. S75—6A 22
Green View, The. S72—1B 10
Greenways. S40—5E 137
Greenway, The. S8—1D 122
Greenway, The. S30—4G 141
Greenwich Ct. S65—1H 79
Greenwood Av. S9—2D 100
Greenwood Av. S70—4B 24
Greenwood Clo. S9—2D 100
Greenwood Cres. S9—2C 100
Greenwood Cres. S66—4G 81
Greenwood Cres. S71—1D 8
Greenwood Dri. S9—2C 100
Greenwood La. S13—6D 102
Greenwood Rd. S9—2D 100
Greenwood Rd. S30—6D 50
Greenwood Rd. S62—6C 56
Greenwood Ter. S70—5G 13
Greenwood Way. S9—2D 100
Greeton Dri. S30—3E 73
Gregg Ho. Cres. S5—4H 75
Gregg Ho. Rd. S5—3H 75
Gregory La. S43—2D 132
Gregory Rd. S8—1E 111
Grenfell Av. S64—6F 43
Grenfolds Rd. S30—1B 74
Grenobank Rd. S30—1B 74
Greno Cres. S30—1B 74
Greno Ho. S30—6A 64
Greno Ho. S30—6A 64
Grenomoor Clo. S30—2A 74
Greno Rd. S64—3B 56
Greno View. S74—6G 37
Greno View. S75—6A 22
Greno View Rd. S30—6C 50
Greno Wood Ct. S30—6A 64
Grenville Pl. S75—4E 13
Grenville Rd. DN4—5G 45
Gresham Av. S60—2C 90
Gresham Rd. S6—5A 86
Gresley Rd. S8—4C 122
Gresley Wlk. S8—4C 122
Greyfriars. S11—6G 97
Grey Friars Rd. DN1—5C 32
Greystock St. S4—6H 87 &
(in two parts)   5A 88
Greystones Av. S11—5H 97
Greystones Av. S70—3H 23
Greystones Clo. S11—6G 97
Greystones Ct. S11—6G 97
Greystones Ct. S31—3H 127
Greystones Cres. S11—6G 97
Greystones Dri. S11—6G 97
Greystones Grange. S11—6G 97
Greystones Grange Cres. S11
—6G 97

Greystones Grange Rd. S11
　—6G 97
Greystones Hall Rd. S11—5G 97
Greystones Rise. S11—6G 97
Greystones Rd. S11—6F 97
Greystones Rd. S60—2B 92
Grice Clo. DN4—1D 48
Griffin Rd. S64—2H 55
Griffiths Clo. S62—3F 69
Griffiths Rd. S30—1C 64
Grimesthorpe Rd. S4—5G 87 to
　(in three parts)　　3A 88
Grimesthorpe Rd. S. S4—5G 87
Grimsell Clo. S6—2B 74
Grimsell Cres. S6—2B 74
Grimsell Dri. S6—2B 74
Grimsell Way. S6—3B 74
Grinders Hill. S1—5F 5
Grinders Wlk. S6—2F 85
Grindlow Av. S40—4H 137
Grindlow Clo. S14—1G 111
Grindlow Dri. S14—1G 111
Grindon Clo. S40—6E 131
Grinton Wlk. S40—5H 137
Grisedale Wlk. S18—2C 128
Grizedale Av. S19—5G 115
Grizedale Clo. S19—5G 115
Grosvenor Cres. DN4—5F 45
Grosvenor Cres. DN5—5D 18
Grosvenor Dri. S70—6E 13
Grosvenor Rd. DN6—2D 16
Grosvenor Rd. S65—1F 79
Grosvenor Sq. S2—5D 98
Grosvenor Ter. DN4—5G 45
Grouse Croft. S6—5B 86
Grouse St. S6—4A 86
Grove Av. DN5—4A 32
Grove Av. S6—1G 85
Grove Av. S17—5D 120
Grove Clo. S63—3C 40
Grove Ct. S64—4D 82
　(off Leslie Av.)
Grove Farm Clo. S43—4E 133
Grove Hall Clo. DN3—5E 21
Grove Hill Rd. DN2—2A 34
Grove Ho. Ct. S17—4E 121
Grove Pl. DN1—1C 46
Grove Rd. S7—4A 110
Grove Rd. S17—4E 121
Grove Rd. S30—4H 141
Grove Rd. S41—4A 132
Grove Rd. S43—6F 133
Grove Rd. S60—4D 78
Grove Rd. S63—3C 40
Grove Rd. S75—4E 7
Grove Sq. S6—4C 86
Grove St. S41—5C 138
Grove St. S70—4C 24
Grove St. S71—6A 14
Grove Ter. S66—4D 82
Grove, The. DN2—4G & 3H 33
　(in two parts)
Grove, The. DN3—1G 21
Grove, The. S6—3E 85
Grove, The. S17—4D 120
Grove, The. S43—3E 135
Grove, The. S62—2G 69
Grove, The. S65—2H 79
Grove, The. S66—5F 81
Grove, The. S72—4B 10
Grove Vale. DN2—2A 34
Grove Wlk. S17—4E 121
　(off Grove Rd.)
Grove Way. S43—6F 133
Guernsey Rd. S2—6E 99
Guest La. DN4—4F 45
Guest Pl. S60—5F 79
Guest Pl. S74—4A 38

Guest Rd. S11—5A 98
Guest Rd. S60—5F 79
Guest Rd. S75—4F 13
Guest St. S74—4A 38
Guilbert Av. S66—6A 94
Guildford Av. S2—5H 99
Guildford Av. S40—5F 137
Guildford Clo. S2—5H 99
Guildford Dr`. S2—5H 99
Guildford Rise. S2—6A 100
Guildford Rd. DN2—2H 33
Guildford Rd. S71—1D 8
Guildford View. S2—6A 100
Guildford Wlk. S2—5G 99
Guildford Way. S2—5H 99
Guildhall Ind. Est. DN3—4C 20
Guild Rd. S65—3H 79
Guildway. S31—2A 118
Guilthwaite Comn. La. S60
　—6A 92
Guilthwaite Cres. S60—2G 91
Guilthwaite Hill. S60—3H 91
Gullane Dri. DN4—5F 45
Gulling Wood Dri. S65—5E 71
Gunhills La. DN3—2G 35
Gun La. S3—1G 5 & 1F 99
Gurney Rd. DN4—5B 46
Gurth Av. DN3—5E 21
Gurth Av. Caravan Site. DN3
　—5E 21
Gurth Dri. S66—6A 94
Gypsy La. S73—2G 39

Habershon Ct. S30—2E 65
Habershon Dri. S30—1D 64
Habershon Rd. S30—6H 67
Hackness La. S60—2B 90
Hackney La. S18—1B 130
Hackthorn Rd. S8—4D 110
Haddon Clo. S18—1F 129
Haddon Clo. S40—3E 137
Haddon Clo. S75—2A 22
Haddon Pl. S43—3B 134
Haddon Rise. S64—5H 43
Haddon Rd. S71—1B 14
Haddon St. S3—5D 86
Haddon Way. S31—6D 104
Haden St. S6—3A 86
Hadfield St. S6—6A 86
Hadfield St. S73—2F 39
Hadrian Rd. S60—1C 90
Hadrians Clo. DN11—6E 63
Hady Cres. S41—3C 138
Hady Hill. S41—3B 138
Hady La. S41—3D 138
Haggard Rd. S6—3B 86
Hagg Hill. S6—6F 85
　(Clough Field)
Hagg Hill. S6—4H 73
　(Wadsley Bridge)
Hagg La. S10—2E 97
Hagg La. Cotts. S10—2D 96
Haggstones Dri. S30—3C 72
Haggstones Rd. S30—3C 72
Hague Av. S62—6E 55
Hague La. S30—6A 50
Hague La. S62—1D 66
Hague Row. S2—4H 5 & 2G 99
Haids Clo. S66—2F 83
Haids La. S66—2F 83
Haids Rd. S66—2E 83
Haig Cres. DN11—5C 62
Haigh Croft. S71—1D 8
Haigh La. S75—1A 6
Haigh Moor Clo. S13—5G 101
Haigh Moor Rd. S13—5H 101
Haigh Moor Wlk. S13—5G 101

Haigh Rd. DN4—4A 46
Hail Mary Dri. S13—5D 102
Hakehill Clo. DN4—5B 48
Halcyon Clo. S12—4H 113
Haldane Clo. S72—2F 11
Haldane Rd. S65—1G 79
Haldene. S70—5A 24
Haldynby Gdns. DN3—3H 35
Hale St. S8—1D 110
Halesworth Clo. S40—5D 136
Halesworth Rd. S13—3G 101
Halfacre La. S18—3H 129
Half Croft. S43—4F 133
Halfway Centre. S19—2E 125
Halfway Dri. S19—2E 125
Halfway Gdns. S19—2E 125
Halifax Av. DN12—3C 58
Halifax Cres. DN5—3H 31
Halifax Hall. S10—4A 98
Halifax Rd. S6 & S30—5B 74
Halifax St. S71—3G 13
Hallam Chase. S10—4H 97
　(Endcliffe Crescent)
Hallam Chase. S10—3D 96
　(Sandygate)
Hallam Clo. DN4—4A 48
Hallam Clo. S31—4A 104
Hallam Ct. S10—4B 98
　(off Clarke Dri.)
Hallam Ct. S18—3E 129
Hallam Ct. S63—2H 41
Hallam Dale Ct. S62—6G 55
Hallamgate Rd. S10—2H 97
Hallam Grange Clo. S10—5C 96
Hallam Grange Cres. S10
　—4C 96
Hallam Grange Croft. S10
　—4C 96
Hallam Grange Rise. S10
　—4C 96
Hallam Grange Rd. S10—4C 96
Hallam La. S1—6E 5 & 3E 99
Hallam Pl. S62—2G 69
Hallam Rd. S60—1F 91
Hallam Rock. S5—2F 87
Hallamshire Clo. S10—5B 96
Hallamshire Ct. S30—2E 65
Hallamshire Dri. S10—5B 96
Hallamshire Rd. S10—5B 96
Hallam Way. S30—1F 75
Hall Av. S64—6F 43
Hall Av. S74—4C 38
Hall Balk La. S75—4F 13
Hall Broome Gdns. S63—6E 29
Hallcar St. S4—6G 87
Hall Clo. S18—1A 128
Hall Clo. S31—1F 119
Hall Clo. S63—4B 40
Hall Clo. S70—1E 37
Hall Clo. Av. S60—2A 92
Hall Ct. S65—3G 71
Hall Cres. S60—1H 91
Hall Croft. S66—5G 81
Hallcroft Dri. DN3—5G 35
Hall Croft Rise. S71—2D 8
Hall Cross Hill. DN1—1E 47
Hall Dri. S63—6D 40
Hall Farm Clo. S31—3B 104
Hall Flat La. DN4—4A 46
Hall Ga. DN1—6D 32
Hallgate. S63—2F 29
Hall Ga. S64—1G 57
Hallgate Rd. S10—2G 97
Hall Gro. S60—4E 79
Hall Gro. S75—4G 7
Halliwell Clo. S5—6B 74
Halliwell Cres. S5—6C 74
Hall M. S65—3G 71

Hallowes Ct. S18—2F 129
Hallowes Dri. S18—3F 129
Hallowes La. S18—2F 129
Hallowes Rise. S18—3G 129
Hallowmoor Rd. S6—2F 85
Hall Pk. Head. S6—6E 85
Hall Pk. Hill. S6—6E 85
Hall Pk. Mt. S6—6E 85
Hall Pl. S71—3C 14
Hall Rd. S9—2G 101
Hall Rd. S13—3H 101
Hall Rd. S31—4B 104
Hall Rd. S43—4E 133
Hall Rd. S60—4E 79
Hall Rd. S66—4C 82
Hall St. S60—3C 78
Hall St. S63—5G 29
Hall St. S73—1G 39
Hall St. S74—5A 38
Hallsworth Av. S73—4D 38
Hall View. S30—1E 65
Hall View Rd. DN11—6E 63
Hall Villa La. DN5—2A 18
Hall Wood Rd. S30—2A 64
Hallyburton Clo. S2—1G 111
Hallyburton Dri. S2—1G 111
Hallyburton Rd. S2—1G 111
Halmshaw Ter. DN5—1A 32
Halsall Av. S9—2E 101
Halsall Dri. S9—2E 101
Halsall Rd. S9—2E 101
Halsbury Rd. S65—1G 79
Halstead Gro. S75—3E 7
Halsteads. S13—4G 101
Halton Clo. S41—2G 131
Halton Ct. S12—4C 114
Hambledon Clo. S40—6E 131
Hambleton Clo. S74—5D 38
Hambleton Clo. S75—5D 12
Hameline Rd. DN12—3D 58
Hamer Wlk. S65—2A 80
Hamilton Clo. DN4—2F 47
Hamilton Clo. S64—5G 43
Hamilton Pk. Rd. DN5—3F 31
Hamilton Rd. DN4—2F 47
Hamilton Rd. S5—1H 87
Hamilton Rd. S66—5H 83
Hammerton Av. S64—4A 86
Hammerton Rd. S6—4A 86
Hammond St. S3—1A 4 & 1C 98
Hampden Rd. S64—6F 43
Hampton Rd. DN2—5F 33
Hampton Rd. S5—2G 87
Hampton St. S41—6D 138
Hamstead Grn. S61—6G 67
Hanbury Clo. DN4—1G 61
Hanbury Clo. S18—2D 128
Hanbury Clo. S40—6C 130
Hanbury Clo. S71—3D 14
Handby St. S41—5D 138
Handley St. S3—6F 87
Hands Rd. S10—1A 98
Handsworth Av. S9—2F 101
Handsworth Cres. S9—2F 101
Handsworth Gdns. DN3—3G 35
Handsworth Grange Clo. S13
　—4A 102
Handsworth Grange Cres. S13
　—4B 102
Handsworth Grange Dri. S13
　—4B 102
Handsworth Grange Rd. S13
　—4A 102
Handsworth Grange Way. S13
　—4B 102
Handsworth Rd. S9 & S13
　—2G 101
Hangingwater Clo. S11—5F 97

Hangingwater Rd. S11—6F 97
Hangram La. S11—3B 108
Hangsman La. S31—2C 106
Hangthwaite La. DN6—4F 17
Hanley Clo. S12—3B 114
Hanmoor Rd. S6—5C 84
Hannah Rd. S13—6D 102
Hanover Ct. S3—6A 4 & 3C 98
Hanover Sq. S3—6B 4 & 3D 98
Hanover Sq. S63—1G 29
Hanover St. S3—6B 4 & 3D 98
(in two parts)
Hanover St. S63—1G 29
Hanover Way. S3—5A 4 & 3D 98
Hanson Rd. S6—3D 84
Hanson St. S70—5H 13
Harbord Rd. S8—5C 110
Harborough Av. S2
—2B to 5D 100
Harborough Clo. S2—3C 100
Harborough Dri. S2—3C 100
Harborough Hill Rd. S71—6H 13
Harborough Rise. S2—3C 100
Harborough Rd. S2—3C 100
Harborough Way. S2—4C 100
Harbury St. S13—5E 103
Harcourt Clo. DN4—4A 48
Harcourt Cres. S10—1B 98
Harcourt Rise. S30—3F 65
Harcourt Rd. S10—2B 98
Harcourt Ter. S65—3F 79
Hardcastle Dri. S13—6A 102
Hardcastle Gdns. S13—6A 102
Hardcastle Rd. S13—1A 114
Harden Clo. S75—5C 12
Hardie Clo. S66—5H 83
Hardie Pl. S43—3B 134
Hardie Pl. S62—1F 69
Hardie St. S31—6D 124
Harding Av. S62—5D 54
Harding Clo. S62—6D 54
Harding Ct. S62—6D 54
Harding St. S9—5D 88
Hard La. S31—6A 118
Hardwick Av. S43—1D 132
Hardwick Clo. S18—1F 129
Hardwick Clo. S31—6D 104
Hardwick Clo. S70—5A 24
Hardwick Cres. S11—5A 98
Hardwick Cres. S71—6D 8
Hardwicke Rd. S65—1E 79
Hardwick Gro. S75—3B 22
Hardwick La. S31—5G 105
Hardwick St. S41—1A 138
Hardwick St. S65—1B 80
Hardwicks Yd. S40—3G 137
Hardy Pl. S6—5B 86
Hardy Rd. DN2—3E 33
Hardy St. S60—2C 78
Haredon Clo. S75—3E 7
Harefield Rd. S11—5B 98
Harehill Rd. S40—6H 137
Harehills Rd. S60—4E 79
Harewood Av. DN3—3D 20
Harewood Av. DN6—2B 16
Harewood Av. S70—6D 12
Harewood Gro. S66—3H 81
Harewood Rd. DN2—6G 33
Harewood Way. S11—5G 109
Hargrave Pl. S65—5D 70
Harland Rd. S11—4C 98
Harlech Clo. S30—1D 64
Harleston St. S4—5H 87
Harley Rd. S11—2F 109
Harley Rd. S62—4H 51
Harlington Ct. DN12—1C 58
Harlington Rd. S64—3D 42
(Adwick upon Dearne)

Harlington Rd. S64—6F 43
(Mexborough)
Harmer La. S1—4F 5 & 2F 99
Harmony Way. S60—5C 90
Harney Clo. S9—6E 89
Harold Av. DN6—2C 16
Harold Av. S71—3E 15
Harold Croft. S61—3C 68
Harold St. S6—5B 86
Harperhill Clo. S40—6H 137
Harriet Clo. S70—2A 24
Harrington Ct. S71—3E 15
Harrington Rd. S2—6E 99
Harrington St. DN1—5D 32
Harrison La. S10—6A 96
Harrison Rd. S6—3H 85
Harrison St. S61—3A 78
Harris Rd. S6—1H 85
Harrogate Dri. DN12—2A 58
Harrogate Rd. S31—1A 116
Harrop Dri. S64—4A 56
Harrowden Ct. S9—1G 89
Harrowden Rd. DN2—3E 33
Harrowden Rd. S9—1G 89
Harrow Rd. DN3—2G 35
Harrow St. S11—4D 98
Harry Firth Clo. S9—6C 88
Harry Rd. S75—4D 12
Hartfield Clo. S41—6B 138
Hartford Clo. S8—4E 111
Hartford Rd. S8—4E 111
Hart Hill. S62—5D 54
Harthill Rd. DN12—4C 58
Harthill Rd. S13—6D 100
Hartington Av. S7—4A 110
Hartington Clo. S61—3A 78
Hartington Ct. S18—1F 129
(off Hartington Rd.)
Hartington Dri. S71—3H 13
Hartington Rd. S7—4A 110
Hartington Rd. S18—1F 129
Hartington Rd. S41—3C 138
Hartington Rd. S61—3A 78
Hartland Av. S19—5G 115
Hartland Ct. S19—5G 115
Hartland Cres. DN3—5D 20
Hartland Dri. S19—5G 115
Hartland Way. S41—2A 132
Hartley Brook Av. S5—3G 75
Hartley Brook Rd. S5—3G 75
Hartley St. S2—6E 99
Hartley St. S64—1D 56
Hartopp Av. S2—1H 111
Hartopp Clo. S2—1H 111
Hartopp Dri. S2—1H 111
Hartopp Rd. S2—1H 111
Harts Head. S1—2F 5 & 1F 99
Hartside Clo. S40—6F 131
Harvest Clo. DN4—1E 21
Harvest La. S3—6E 87
Harvest Rd. S66—4F 81
Harvest Way. S42—6B 130
Harvey Clough Rd. S8—4E 111
Harvey Rd. S30—2E 65
Harvey Rd. S41—3E 139
Harvey St. S30—3F 141
Harvey St. S70—1F 23
Harwell Rd. S8—6D 98
Harwich Rd. S2—4A 100
Harwood Clo. S2—5E 99
Harwood Dri. S19—6D 114
Harwood Gdns. S19—6E 115
Harwood St. S2—5E 99
Harwood Ter. S71—5E 15
Haslam Cres. S8—3B 122
Haslam Pl. S66—3H 83
Haslam Rd. DN11—4D 62

Hasland By Pass. S41
—4B 138 to 6F 139
Hasland La. S44—5G 139
Hasland Rd. S41—4B 138
(in two parts)
Haslehurst Rd. S2—3A 100
Haslemere Gro. DN5—3A 32
Hassocky La. S44—6H 139
Hassop Rd. S43—1D 134
Hastilar Clo. S2—5D 100
Hastilar Rd. S2—5D 100
Hastilar Rd. S. S13—5E 101
Hastings Clo. S41—5F 131
Hastings Mt. S2—3A 110
Hastings Rd. S7—3A 110
Hastings St. S72—6G 11
Hatchell Dri. DN4—6E 49
Hatfield Clo. S71—6A 8
Hatfield Cres. S31—3C 106
Hatfield Gdns. S71—1D 8
Hatfield Ho. DN1—1C 46
(off Grove Pl.)
Hatfield Ho. Ct. S5—4H 75
Hatfield Ho. Croft. S5—4H 75
Hatfield Ho. La. S5—5G 75
Hatfield La. DN3—2G 35 to 5F 21
(Armthorpe)
Hatfield La. DN3—2H 21
(Barnby Dun)
Hatherley Rd. S9—6G 77
Hatherley Rd. S64—6B 42
Hatherley Rd. S65—1E 79
Hathern Clo. S43—1F 139
Hathersage Rd. S17
—1A 120 to 5E 109
Hatter Dri. DN12—5B 60
Hatton Clo. S18—3B 128
Hatton Dri. S40—6D 130
Hatton Rd. S6—4B 86
Haugh La. S11—2F 109
Haugh Rd. S62—5C 54
Haughton Rd. S8—5D 110
Havelock Rd. DN4—2C 46
Havelock St. S10—3C 98
Havelock St. S70—1F 23
Havelock St. S73—4E 27
Havens, The. S40—2F 137
Havercroft Pl. S31—2H 125
Havercroft Rd. S8—3C 110
Havercroft Rd. S60—6A 80
Havercroft Ter. S31—2H 125
Haverdale Rise. S75—5F 13
Haverlands La. S70—5F 23
Haverlands Ridge. S70—5H 23
Hawes Clo. S64—5G 43
Hawfield Clo. DN4—2A 46
Hawke Clo. S62—6C 54
Hawke Rd. DN2—3F 33
Hawke St. S9—3C 88
Hawk Hill La. S66—1H 105
Hawkhurst Ridge. S65—1H 79
Hawking Houses. S40—6F 131
Hawkins Av. S30—2C 64
Hawkshead Av. S18—2B 128
Hawkshead Cres. S31—6F 107
Hawkshead Rd. S4—2B 88
Hawksley Av. S6—3A 86
Hawksley Av. S40—6G 131
Hawksley M. S6—3A 86
Hawksley Rise. S30—3D 72
Hawksley Rd. S6—3A 86
Hawksway. S31—6B 124
Hawksworth Clo. S65—2A 80
Hawksworth Rd. S6—5B 86
Hawksworth Rd. S65—2A 80
Hawley St. S1—2D 4 & 1E 99
Hawley St. S62—2F 69
Haworth Bank. S60—2F 91

Haworth Clo. S71—4B 14
Haworth Cres. S60—2F 91
Haworth La. S60—3E 91
Hawshaw La. S74—5G 39
Hawson St. S73—1G 39
Hawthorn Av. DN3—1F 35
Hawthorn Av. S19—6D 114
Hawthorn Av. S66—4D 82
Hawthorn Clo. S31—4B 126
Hawthorn Ct. S65—2H 79
Hawthorne Av. S18—6E 123
Hawthorne Av. S30—2B 140
Hawthorne Av. S31—4F 119
Hawthorne Av. S62—2G 69
Hawthorne Cres. S64—6C 42
Hawthorne Cres. S75—1A 22
Hawthorne Flats. S63—1F 29
(off Lingamore Leys)
Hawthorne Gro. DN5—5B 18
Hawthorne Rd. S63—6G 41
Hawthorne St. S6—5H 85
Hawthorne St. S40—4A 138
Hawthorne St. S70—1G 23
Hawthorne St. S72—2C 10
Hawthorne Way. S72—2C 10
Hawthorn Gro. DN12—5C 58
Hawthorn Rd. S6—3H 85
Hawthorn Rd. S30—6C 50
Hawthorn Rd. S31—6G 125
Hawthorn Ter. S10—2A 98
(off Parker's La.)
Hawthorn Way. S42—6B 130
Haxby Clo. S13—1G 113
Haxby Pl. S13—1G 113
Haxby St. S13—1G 113
Haybrook Ct. S17—4E 121
Haydn Rd. S66—5H 83
Haydock Clo. S64—5F 43
Haydon Gro. S66—3F 81
Hayes Ct. S19—3E 125
Hayes Croft. S70—6H 13
Hayes Dri. S19—3E 125
Hayfield Clo. DN3—1E 21
Hayfield Clo. S18—2B 128
Hayfield Clo. S43—1D 134
Hayfield Clo. S75—2A 22
Hayfield Cres. S12—4F 113
Hayfield Dri. S12—4F 113
Hayfield La. DN9—2G 63
Hayfield Pl. S12—4F 113
Hayfield View. S31—6B 124
Hayfield Wlk. S61—6G 67
(off Byrley Rd.)
Hayford Way. S43—2C 134
Hay Grn. La. S70—4D 13
Hayhurst Cres. S66—5G 83
Hayland St. S9—1D 88
Haylock Clo. S75—4A 12
Haymarket. S1—2F 5 & 1F 99
Haythorne Way. S64—4B 56
Haywood Av. S30—3F 141
Haywood Clo. S65—2A 80
Haywood La. S30—3F 141
Hazel Av. S31—4A 126
Hazelbadge Cres. S12—4G 113
Hazel Clo. S18—3F 129
Hazel Dri. S40—5F 137
Hazel Gro. DN3—2G 35
Hazel Gro. DN12—4D 58
Hazel Gro. S30—3E 65
Hazel Gro. S66—4G 81
Hazelhurst. S8—3F 123
(off Jordanthorpe Centre)
Hazel Rd. DN12—3B 60
Hazel Rd. S31—6H 125
Hazel Rd. S66—4D 82
Hazelshaw. S75—3C 22

Hazelshaw Gdns. S30—6B 50
Hazelwood Clo. S18—2A 128
Hazelwood Dri. S64—5B 56
Hazlebarrow Clo. S8—3F 123
Hazlebarrow Ct. S8—2F 123
Hazlebarrow Cres. S8—3F 123
Hazlebarrow Dri. S8—2F 123
Hazlebarrow Gro. S8—2E 123
Hazlebarrow Rd. S8—3F 123
Hazledene Cres. S72—4D 10
Hazledene Rd. S72—4D 10
Hazlehurst Av. S41—5B 132
Hazlehurst La. S41—6A 132
Headford St. S3—5B 4 & 3D 98
Headland Dri. S10—2G 97
Headland Rd. S10—2G 97
Headlands Rd. S74—5H 37
Healaugh Way. S40—5B 138
Heath Av. S31—4B 126
Heath Bank Rd. DN2—2A 34
Heathcote Dri. S41—5E 139
Heathcote St. S4—2H 87
Heatherbank Rd. DN4—4C 48
Heatherdale Rd. S66—4H 83
Heather Clo. S44—2G 139
Heather Clo. S60—5E 79
Heather Ct. S66—5H 81
Heather Lea Av. S17—2C 120
Heather Lea Pl. S17—2C 120
Heather Rd. S5—6A 76
Heather Vale Rd. S41—6D 138
Heather Wlk. S63—6D 28
Heatherwood Clo. DN2—3A 34
Heathfield Av. S40—2F 137
Heathfield Clo. DN3—1E 21
Heathfield Clo. S18—3D 128
Heathfield Dri. S12—3F 113
Heath Gro. S63—2H 41
Heath Ho. DN1—1C 46
(off Grove Pl.)
Heath Rd. S6—5B 74
Heath Rd. S30—4F 141
Heaton Clo. S18—2B 128
Heatons Bank. S62—1G 69
Heaton St. S40—3E 137
Heavygate Av. S10—5H 85
Heavygate Rd. S10—5A 86
Hedge La. S75—6B 6
Heeley Bank Rd. S2—6F 99
Heeley Grn. S2—1F 111
Heelis St. S70—1H 23
Heighton View. S31—4B 104
Helena Clo. S70—1F 23
Helena St. S64—6E 43
Helensburgh Clo. S75—5E 13
Hellaby Euroway Ind. Est. S66
                        —4A 82
Hellaby Hall Rd. S66—5B 82
Hellaby La. S66—4B 82
Hellaby View. S65—2H 81
Helliwell Ct. S30—5G 141
Helliwell La. S30—5G 141
Helmsley Av. S19—2D 124
Helmsley Clo. S31—1A 116
Helmton Dri. S8—5E 111
Helmton Rd. S8—5D 110
Helston Clo. S41—5B 138
Helston Cres. S71—4B 14
Helston Rise. S7—3A 110
Hemingfield Rd. S73—2D 38
Hemper Gro. S8—2B 122
Hemper La. S8—3B 122
Hemp Pits Rd. DN5—6D 18
Hemsworth Rd. S8—5E 111
Henderson Glen. S71—2C 8
Hendon St. S13—4H 101
Hengist Rd. DN5—1H 45

Henley Av. S8—1F 123
Henley Gro. Rd. S61—2B 78
    (in two parts)
Henley La. S61—1A 78
Henley Rise. S61—2B 78
Henley Rd. DN2—4A 34
Henley Rd. S61—2B 78
Henley Way. S61—2A 78
Hennings Clo. DN4—4H 47
Hennings La. DN4—3H 47
Hennings Rd. DN4—6A 48
Henry Clo. S72—2C 10
Henry La. DN11—3B 62
Henry Pl. S64—6G 43
Henry Rd. S63—5G 41
Henry St. S3—6D 86
Henry St. S30—6A 50
Henry St. S31—6D 124
Henry St. S41—3B 132
Henry St. S62—4F 69
Henry St. S65—2E 79
Henry St. S70—4A 24
Henry St. S73—5D 26
Henshall St. S70—1A 24
Heppenstall La. S9—5B 88
Heptinstall St. S70—4B 24
Hepworth Dri. S31—6B 104
Hepworth Rd. DN4—4H 45
Herbert Clo. DN5—4A 32
Herbert Rd. DN5—4A 32
Herbert Rd. S7—1C 110
Herbert St. S61—2G 77
Herbert St. S64—6F 43
Herdings Ct. S12—4C 112
Herdings Rd. S12—4C 112
Herdings View. S12—4C 112
Hereford Dri. S43—3F 133
Hereford Rd. DN2—2H 33
Hereford St. S1—6D 4 & 4E 99
    (in two parts)
Hereward Rd. S5—5F 75
Hereward's Rd. S8—6H 111
Hermitage St. S2—4D 98
Hermit La. S75—5A 12
Heron Hill. S31—1C 116
Heron Mt. S2—3A 100
Herons Way. S70—3D 36
Herrick Gdns. DN4—5C 46
Herrick Rd. DN3—1H 21
Herries Av. S5—1E 87
Herries Dri. S5—1E 87
Herries Pl. S5—1E 87
Herries Rd. S5 & S6
                —1B 86 to 2G 87
Herries Rd. S. S6—1B 86
Herringthorpe Av. S65—5H 79
Herringthorpe Clo. S65—4H 79
Herringthorpe Gro. S65—5A 80
Herringthorpe La. S65—4A 80
Herringthorpe Valley Rd. S65 &
                S60—6A 70
Herriot Dri. S40—4B 138
Herschell Rd. S7—6D 98
    (in two parts)
Hesketh Dri. DN3—3E 21
Hesley Bar. S61—3A 66
Hesley Ct. DN12—2B 58
Hesley Grange. S61—5E 67
Hesley Gro. S30—3G 65
Hesley La. S61—3A 66
Hesley Rd. DN11—5D 62
Hesley Rd. S5—2H 75
Hesley Ter. S5—2H 75
Heslow Gro. S61—2A 66
Hessey St. S13—1H 113
Hessle Rd. S6—1H 85
Hethersett Way. DN11—6C 62
Hewitt St. S64—6G 43

Hexthorpe Rd. DN4—1B 46
Heyhouse Dri. S30—6E 51
Heyhouse Way. S30—6D 50
Heysham Grn. S71—1D 14
Heywood St. S43—3E 133
Hibberd Pl. S6—3G 85
Hibberd Rd. S6—3G & 3H 85
    (in two parts)
Hibbert Ter. S70—2H 23
Hickleton Ct. S63—2E 29
Hickleton Dri. DN12—2B 58
Hickleton Ter. S63—2G 29
Hickmott Rd. S11—5B 98
Hicks La. S3—1E 5 & 1E 99
Hickson Dri. S71—3E 15
Hicks St. S3—5E 87
Hides St. S9—3D 88
Higgitt Rd. S9—3D 88
Higham Comn. Rd. S75—3A 12
Higham La. S75—5A 12
Higham View. S75—6B 6
High Ash Dri. S31—4F 119
Highbury Av. DN4—3C 48
Highbury Cres. DN4—3C 48
Highbury Rd. S41—6H 131
Highbury Vale. DN12—4A 60
Highcliffe Ct. S11—6G 97
Highcliffe Ct. S64—2B 56
Highcliffe Dri. S11—6F 97
Highcliffe Dri. S30—3C 72
Highcliffe Dri. S64—2B 56
Highcliffe Pl. S11—1F 109
Highcliffe Rd. S11—6F 97
Highcliffe Ter. S70—1A 24
(off Gold St.)
High Clo. S75—4B 6
High Ct. S1—2F 5 & 1F 99
High Croft. S74—6A 38
Higher Albert St. S41—1A 138
Highfield. S63—5F 41
Highfield Av. S31—4A 118
Highfield Av. S41—6G 131
Highfield Av. S63—4F 29
Highfield Av. S70—3H 23
Highfield Av. S71—1A 14
Highfield Clo. DN3—1E 21
Highfield Ct. S64—2A 56
Highfield Gro. S63—4A 40
Highfield La. S13 & S60—3B 102
Highfield La. S41—5G 131
Highfield Pk. S66—3H 83
Highfield Pl. S2—5E 99
Highfield Range. S73—2E 27
Highfield Rise. S6—5B 84
Highfield Rd. DN1—5E 33
Highfield Rd. DN12—3F 59
Highfield Rd. S41—6H 131
Highfield Rd. S61—5C 68
Highfield Rd. S64—2H 55
Highfield Rd. S73—3E 27
Highfields Cres. S18—3E 129
Highfields Rd. S18—3E 129
Highfields Rd. S75—5A 6
Highfield Ter. S41—6H 131
Highfield View. S60—5C 90
Highfield View Rd. S41—6H 131
    (in two parts)
High Fisher Ga. DN1—5D 32
Highgate. S9—5G 77
    (in two parts)
Highgate Clo. DN11—6E 63
Highgate Dri. S18—4G 129
Highgate La. S18—4F 129
Highgate La. S63—6E 29
Highgreave. S5—2G 75
High Greave Av. S5—2F 75
High Greave Pl. S65—2A 80
High Greave Rd. S65—1A 80

High Hazel Cres. S60—5C 90
High Hazels Clo. S9—1F 101
High Hazels Mead. S9—1F 101
High Hazels Pk. S9—1F 101
High Hooton Rd. S31 & S66
                —3G 95
High Ho. Farm Ct. S31—5F 117
High Ho. Rd. S6—4B 86
High Ho. Ter. S6—4B 86
High La. S12—6E 113
High La. S8—3F 105
Highlightley La. S18—6A 128
Highlow Clo. S40—6E 131
Highlow View. S60—2C 90
High Matlock Av. S6—5D 84
High Matlock Rd. S6—4D 84
Highmill Av. S64—2G 55
Highmoor Av. S31—5G 117
Highnam Cres. Rd. S10—2A 98
High Nook Rd. S31—5G 107
High Pavement Row. S2—3H 5
High Ridge. S70—4H 23
High Rd. DN4—4A 46
    (Balby)
High Rd. DN4—5E 45
    (Warmsworth)
High Rd. DN12—4B 60
High Royd Av. S72—1H 15
Highroyds. S70—3H 23
Highstone Av. S70—2G 23
    (Barnsley)
Highstone Av. S70—3H 23
    (Worsbrough)
Highstone Cres. S70—2G 23
Highstone La. S70—3H 23
Highstone Rd. S70—2H 23
Highstone Vale. S70—2G 23
High Storrs Clo. S11—1G 109
High Storrs Cres. S11—6G 97
High Storrs Dri. S11—1F 109
High Storrs Rise. S11—6G 97
High Storrs Rd. S11—1F 109
High St. Anston. S31—3F 119
High St. Arksey. DN5—4D 18
High St. Barnby Dun. DN3
                —2G 21
High St. Beighton. S19—3G 115
High St. Bentley. DN5—2A 32
High St. Billingley. S72—2B 28
High St. Bolton-u-Dearne. S63
                —1A 42
High St. Brimington. S43
                —3F 133
High St. Chesterfield. S40
                —2A 138
High St. Conisbrough. DN12
                —3E 59
High St. Darton. S75—3E 7
High St. Dodworth. S75—2B 22
High St. Doncaster. DN1—6C 32
High St. Dore. S17—2D 120
High St. Dronfield. S18—2E 129
High St. Dunsville. DN7—4G 21
High St. Ecclesfield. S30—1F 75
High St. Eckington. S31
                —6C 124
High St. Goldthorpe. S63
                —4G 29
High St. Grimethorpe. S72
                —6F 11
High St. Hoyland. S74—5A 38
High St. Killamarsh. S31
                —3B 126
High St. Kimberworth. S61
                —2G 77
High St. Laughton. S31—6F 95
High St. Maltby. S66—4G 83

High St. Meadowhall Shopping Mall. S9—1E 89
High St. Mexborough, S64 —1E 57
High St. Monk Bretton, S71 —3C 14
High St. Mosborough, S19 —2C 124
High St. Old Whittington, S41 —1A 132
High St. Rawmarsh, S62—3F 69
High St. Rotherham, S60 —3D78
High St. Royston, S71—2C 8
High St. Shafton, S72—2C 10
High St. Sheffield, S1 —3E 5 & 2F 99
High St. Staveley, S43—1C 134
High St. Swallownest, S31 —6A 104
High St. Thurnscoe, S63—1E 29
High St. Wadworth, DN11 —6H 61
High St. Wath upon Dearne S63 —5F 41
High St. Whiston, S60—2H 91
High St. Wombwell, S73—6B 26
High St. Worsbrough, S70 —4B 24
High St. La. S2—3H 5 & 2G 99
Highthorn Rd. S62—4B 56
Highton St. S6—5A 86
High Trees. S17—2D 120
High Trees. S60—6H 79
High View. S71—2D 8
High View Clo. S41—3D 138
High View Clo. S73—3F 27
Highwood Clo. S75—5A 6
Highwood Pl. S31—6C 124
Highwoods Cres. S64—6C 42
Highwoods Rd. S64—6C 42
High Wray Clo. S11—3H 109
Hilary Way. S31—6B 104
Hilda Ter. S72—6F 12
Hillary Ho. DN2—3G 33
Hill Clo. S6—5C 84
Hill Clo. S65—5C 80
Hillcote Clo. S10—4D 96
Hillcote Dri. S10—4D 96
Hillcote M. S10—4D 96
Hillcote Rise. S10—4D 96
Hillcrest. S63—2E 29
Hill Crest. S74—6G 37
Hillcrest Dri. S30—3C 72
Hillcrest Dri. S31—4F 119
Hillcrest Rise. S30—4H 141
Hillcrest Rd. DN2—3G 33
Hill Crest Rd. S30—2D 64
(Chapeltown)
Hillcrest Rd. S30—4H 141
(Deepcar)
Hillcrest Rd. S41—6D 138
Hill Crest Rd. S65—2H 79
Hill End Rd. S75—6G 7
Hill Farm Clo. S63—2D 28
Hillfoot Rd. S3—5C 86
Hillfoot Rd. S17—4C 120
Hillman Dri. S43—5A 134
Hillsborough Arc., The. S6 —3A 86
Hillsborough Pl. S6—3A 86
Hillsborough Rd. DN4—3C 48
Hillsborough Rd. S6—3A 86
Hills Clo. DN5—1G 45
Hillside. S19—2C 124
Hillside. S31—1F 119
Hill Side. S60—2H 91
Hillside. S71—1G 25

Hillside Av. S5—3F 75
Hillside Av. S18—3E 129
Hillside Ct. S61—6D 68
Hillside Cres. S72—3G 11
Hillside Dri. DN12—4A 60
Hillside Dri. S40—3F 137
Hillside Dri. S74—6B 38
Hillside Gro. S72—3G 11
Hillside Mt. S72—3G 11
Hillside Rd. DN12—2A 34
Hills Rd. S30—3F 141
Hill St. S2—4D 98
Hill St. S71—1E 25
Hill St. S73—4E 27
Hill St. S74—6C 38
Hilltop. S72—2F 11
Hill Top Clo. S60—2B 90
Hill Top Clo. S61—3F 77
Hill Top Clo. S66—3D 82
Hill Top Cres. DN2—2A 34
Hill Top Cres. DN12—5B 60
Hill Top Cres. S19—6D 114
Hilltop Dri. S30—1B 72
Hill Top La. S30—1E 141
Hill Top La. S61—3F 77
Hill Top La. S66—2D 80
Hill Top La. S75—4D 12
Hill Top Rise. S30—1B 74
Hill Top Rd. DN12—2A 58
Hilltop Rd. S18—3E 129
Hill Top Rd. S30—1B 74
Hilltop Rd. S41—1A 132
Hill Top Rd. S70—3D 36
Hill Top Smithies. S71—1H 13
Hilltop View. S18—4F 129
Hill Turrets Clo. S11—3F 109
Hill View E. S61—1F 77
Hill View Rd. S43—3E 133
Hill View Rd. S61—1F 77
Hilton Dri. S30—1F 75
Hilton St. S75—5F 13
Hindburn Clo. DN4—4A 48
Hinde Ho. Cres. S4—1A 88
Hinde Ho. Croft. S4—1A 88
Hinde Ho. La. S4—2H 87
Hinde St. S4—2A 88
Hindewood Clo. S4—1A 88
Hindle St. S70—6F 13
Hind Rd. S60—1A 92
Hipley Clo. S40—5D 130
Hipper St. S40—3A 138
Hipper St. S. S40—3A 138
Hipper St. W. S40—3G 137
Hirst Comn. La. S6—3H 73
Hirst Dri. S65—2B 80
Hirst Ga. S64—1G 57
Hobart St. S11—5D 98
Hobner La. S43—3A 134
Hobson Av. S6—4C 86
Hobson Pl. S6—4C 86
Hodder Ct. S30—1D 64
Hodgson St. S3—6C 4 & 3D 98
Hodroyd Clo. S72—4D 10
Hodroyd Cotts. S72—3F 11
Hogarth Rise. S18—3D 128
Holbeach Dri. S40—5G 137
Holbeck Clo. S41—1B 138
Holbein Clo. S18—3D 128
Holberry Clo. S10—5A 4 & 3C 98
Holberry Gdns. S10—3C 98
Holborn Av. S18—1E 129
Holbourne Dri. S18—1E 129
Holbrook Av. S19—1F 125
Holbrook Clo. S40—5E 137
Holbrook Dri. S13—1D 112
Holbrook Grn. S19—1G 125
Holbrook Rise. S19—6F 115
Holbrook Rd. S13—6D 100

Holbrook Trading Est. S19 —1G 125
Holderness Dri. S31—5B 104
Holdings Rd. S2—4H 99
Holdroyds Yd. S75—3B 22
Holdworth La. S6—6A 72
Hole Ho. La. S30—3D 140
Holgate. S73—4H 25
Holgate Av. S5—3D 74
Holgate Clo. S5—3D 74
Holgate Cres. S5—3E 75
Holgate Dri. S5—3E 75
Holgate Mt. S70—3H 23
Holgate Rd. S5—3E 75
Holgate View. S72—2H 11
Holiwell Clo. S66—3H 83
Holkham Rise. S11—5F 109
Holland Clo. S62—6F 55
Holland Pl. S2—5E 99
Holland Rd. S2—5E 99
Holland Rd. S30—6B 50
Holland Rd. S41—1H 131
Holland St. S1—3C 4 & 2D 98
Hollens Way. S40—5B 130
Hollies Clo. S18—3G 129
Hollinberry La. S30—4A 50
Hollin Busk La. S30—5E 141
Hollin Busk Rd. S30—4E 141
Hollin Clo. DN11—3F 63
Hollin Clo. S41—3E 131
Hollindale Dri. S12—2E 113
Hollin Edge La. S30—6H 141
Holling Croft. S30—3G 141
Holling Moor La. S66—6E 81
Holling's La. S65 —5D 70 to 1H 81
Hollingwood Cres. S43—1G 133
Hollingworth Clo. S64—5H 43
Hollin Hill La. S66—5D 80
Hollin Ho. La. S6—1A 84
Hollin Rd. S30—3C 72
Hollins Clo. S6—6F 85
Hollins Ct. S6—5F 85
Hollins Dri. S6—6G 85
Hollinsend Av. S12—2E 113
Hollinsend Pl. S12—2E 113
Hollinsend Rd. S12—3C 112
Hollins La. S6—5F 85
Hollins Spring Av. S18—3E 129
Hollins Spring Rd. S18—3E 129
Hollins, The. S75—3C 22
Hollis Clo. S62—5D 54
Hollis Croft. S1—2C 4 & 1D 98
Hollis Croft. S13—1A 114
Hollis La. S41—3B 138
(in two parts)
Hollowdene. S75—4D 12
Hollowgate. DN5—1F 43
Hollow Ga. S30—2B 64
Hollowgate. S60—4E 79
(Rotherham)
Hollow Ga. S60—2H 91
(Whiston)
Hollowgate Av. S63—3C 40
Hollow La. S19—3D 124
Hollows, The. DN4—5C 48
Holly Av. DN5—2A 32
Hollybank Av. S12—1E 113
Hollybank Clo. S12—1F 113
Hollybank Cres. S12—1E 113
Hollybank Dri. S12—1F 113
Hollybank Rd. S12—1E 113
Hollybank Way. S12—1F 113
Holly Barn Fold. S65—1G 71
Holly Bush La. DN3—4C 20
Hollybush St. S62—4F 69
Holly Clo. S30—3D 64
Holly Clo. S31—4A 126

Holly Clo. S41—1A 132
Holly Cres. S66—3G 81
Hollycroft Av. S71—2D 8
Holly Dene. DN3—1F 35
Holly Dri. DN5—5B 18
Holly Gdns. S12—1E 113
Holly Ga. S70—4C 24
Holly Gro. S63—1F 55
Holly Gro. S72—2G 11
Holly Hall La. S30—1H 141
Holly Ho. La. S30—1H 73
Holly La. S1—3D 4
Holly Mt. S66—5G 81
Holly St. DN1—2C 46
Holly St. S1—3D 4 & 2E 99
(in two parts)
Holly Ter. DN4—4H 45
Holly Ter. S31—5A 104
Hollythorpe Clo. S41—5D 138
Hollythorpe Cres. S8—3E 111
Hollythorpe Rise. S8—3F 111
Hollythorpe St. S8—3F 111
Hollytree Av. S66—3D 82
Hollywell Clo. S62—6H 55
Holm Clo. S18—1B 128
Holmebank Clo. S40—1G 137
Holmebank E. S40—1G 137
Holmebank View. S40—1G 137
Holmebank W. S40—1G 137
Holme Clo. S6—3A 86
Holme Ct. S60—1E 91
Holme Hall Cres. S40—5B 130
Holme La. S6—4H 85
Holme La. S30—2B 74
Holme Pk. Av. S41—4D 130
Holme Rd. S41—5A 132
Holmes Carr Cres. DN11—4B 62
Holmes Carr Rd. DN4—5B 48
Holmes Carr Rd. DN11—4B 62
Holmes Cres. S60—1E 103
Holmesdale Clo. S18—6G 123
Holmesdale Rd. S18—6F 123
Holmesfield. S61—3A 78
(off Rosebery St.)
Holmesfield Rd. S18—2A 128
Holmesfield Rd. S30—3D 72
Holmes La. S61—3A 78
Holmes La. S65—6G 57
Holmes Rd. S66—5H 81
Holme View Rd. S75—5A 6
Holme Wood Gdns. DN4—4C 48
Holme Wood La. DN3—3H 35
Holmfield Clo. DN3—4G 35
Holm Flatt St. S62—4E 69
Holmhirst Clo. S8—5C 110
Holmhirst Dri. S8—4C 110
Holmhirst Rd. S8—4C 110
Holmhirst Way. S8—4C 110
Holmley Bank. S18—6E 123
Holmley La. S18—6E 123
Holmoak Clo. S64—4B 56
Holm Oak Way. S6—4C 84
Holmshaw Dri. S13—5G 101
Holmshaw Gro. S13—5G 101
Holtwood Rd. S4—4F 87
Holwick Ct. S70—6G 13
Holy Grn. S1—6D 4 & 3E 99
Holyoake Av. S13—5G 101
Holymoor Rd. S42—5A 136
Holyrood Rise. S66—3H 81
Holyrood Rd. DN2—6G 33
Holywell La. DN12—4E 59
Holywell La. S66—1G 83
Holywell Pl. S65—2E 79
(off Nottingham St.)

Holywell Rd. S4 & S9—2B 88
Holywell Rd. S62—4B 56
Holywell St. S41—2A 138
Homecroft Rd. S63—4F 29
Homefield Cres. DN5—1G 31
Homestead Clo. S5—4H 75
Homestead Dri. S60—2B 90
Homestead Rd. S62—6F 55
Homestead Rd. S5—4G 75
Homestead, The. DN5—6B 18
Honeysuckle Rd. S5—6B 76
Honeywell Clo. S71—4H 13
Honeywell Gro. S71—3H 13
Honeywell La. S75 & S71
     —4G 13
Honeywell Pl. S71—4G 13
Honeywell St. S71—4H 13
Honister Clo. S63—4A 40
Hoober Av. S11—2G 109
Hoober Ct. S62—5D 54
Hoober Field Rd. S62—4A 54
Hoober Hall La. S62 & S63
     —2G 53
Hoober La. S62—4A 54
Hoober Rd. S11—2G 109
Hoober St. S63—4B 40
Hoober View. S62—5D 54
Hoober View. S73—2H 39
Hood Grn. Rd. S75—6A 22
Hoole La. S10—3A 98
Hoole Rd. S10—2A 98
Hoole St. S6—5A 86
Hoole St. S41—5D 138
Hooley Rd. S13—1D 114
Hooton Clo. S31—6G 95
Hooton La. S31—6G 95
Hooton La. S65—4G 71
Hooton La. S66—5E 83
Hooton Rd. S62—6C 56
Hope Av. S63—4F 29
Hopedale Rd. S12—3F 113
Hopefield Av. S12—3F 113
Hope Rd. S30—3E 73
Hope Sq. S9—3B 88
Hope St. S3—2A 4 & 1C 98
Hope St. S30—3E 141
Hope St. S40—2G 137
Hope St. S60—2C 78
Hope St. S64—1E 57
Hope St. S71—1F 15
Hope St. S73—5D 26
  (Low Valley, Wombwell)
Hope St. S73—1G 39
  (Wombwell)
Hope St. S75—5F 13
  (Barnsley)
Hope St. S75—5G 7
  (Mapplewell)
Hope St. Ind. Est. S60—1C 78
Hopewell St. S70—1D 24
Hopwood La. S6—1B 96
Hopwood St. S70—5G 13
Horace St. S60—4E 79
Horbiry End. S31—2A 118
Horbury La. S30—3C 64
Horbury Rd. S72—5B 10
Hornbeam Clo. S30—3D 64
Hornbeam Rd. S66—3F 81
Hornby Ct. S11—6G 97
Hornby St. S70—2A 24
Horndean Rd. S6—2H 87
Horner Clo. S30—3D 140
Horner Rd. S7—6E 99
Hornes La. S75—4G 7
Horninglow Clo. DN4—4E 49
Horninglow Clo. S5—6G 75
Horninglow Mt. S5—1G 87
Horninglow Rd. S5—6G 75

Hornsby Rd. DN3—4G 35
Hornthorpe Rd. S31—6G 125
Horse Carr View. S71—1G 25
Horse Croft La. S30—1B 72
Horsehills La. DN3—4E 35
Horsemoor Rd. S63—1D 28
Horseshoe Clo. S31—4G 117
Horsewood Clo. S70—1D 22
Horsewood Rd. S13—5D 102
Horsewood Rd. S42—5D 136
Horsley Clo. S40—6C 130
Horton Clo. S19—2C 124
Horton Dri. S19—2C 124
Hough La. S73—1E 39
Houghton Rd. S31—5B 106
Houghton Rd. S63—1C 28
Houldsworth Dri. S41—3D 138
Hound Hill La. S64—4B 42
Hound Hill La. S70—5F 23
Houndkirk Rd. S11—4A 108
Hounsfield Cres. S65—2B 80
Hounsfield La. S3—4A 4
Hounsfield Rd. S3
    —3A 4 & 2C 98
Hounsfield Rd. S65—2B 80
Housley La. S30—2D 64
Housley Pk. S30—1D 64
Houstead Rd. S9—2F 101
Hoveringham Ct. S31—1A 116
Howard Dri. S41—1A 132
Howard La. S1—5F 5 & 3F 99
  (in two parts)
Howard Rd. S6—6A 86
Howard Rd. S66—4H 81
  (Bramley)
Howard Rd. S66—4H 83
  (Maltby)
Howards Clo. S66—5C 94
Howard St. S1—4F 5 & 3F 99
Howard St. S60 & S65—2D 78
Howard St. S70—2H 23
Howard St. S73—2F 27
Howarth Rd. S60—3D 90
Howbeck Dri. DN12—4A 60
Howbrook Clo. S30—5A 50
Howden Clo. DN4—5A 48
Howden Clo. S43—1D 134
Howden Clo. S75—4D 6
Howden Rd. S9—4C 88
Howdike La. S65—6F 57
Howe La. S31—3G 95
Howlett Clo. S60—2B 92
Howlett Dri. S60—4C 90
Howse St. S74—5D 38
Howson Rd. S30—3F 141
Hoylake Av. S40—6E 137
Hoylake Dri. S64—4B 56
Hoyland Rd. S3—4C 86
Hoyland Rd. S74—6F 37
Hoyland St. S66—5H 83
Hoyland St. S73—1F 39
Hoy La. S64—4C 42
Hoyle Croft La. S66—1E 83
Hoyle Mill Rd. S70—1D 24
Hoyle St. S3—1C 4 & 1D 98
Hucklow Av. S40—5H 137
Hucklow Av. S43—4A 134
Hucklow Dri. S5—6H 75
Hucklow Rd. S5—1H 87
Hucknall Av. S40—1E 137
Huddersfield Rd. S75 & S70
  (Barnsley)   —3E 13
Huddersfield Rd. S75—4A 6
  (Darton)
Hudson Haven. S73—6H 25
Hudson Rd. S13—5E 103
Hudson Rd. S61—5G 67

Hudson's M. DN1—6C 32
Humphrey Rd. S8—1C 122
Humphries Av. S62—6D 54
Hungerhill Clo. S61—1F 77
Hungerhill La. DN3—5B 20
Hunger Hill La. S60—2A 92
Hunger Hill Rd. S60—1H 91
Hungerhill Rd. S61—6F 67
Hunloke Av. S40—4F 137
Hunloke Cres. S40—4G 137
Hunningley Clo. S70—2E 25
Hunningley La. S70—4D 24
Hunsdon Rd. S31—6C 124
Hunshelf Pk. S30—2E 141
Hunshelf Rd. S30—2D 64
  (Chapeltown)
Hunshelf Rd. S30—1C to 2D 140
  (in two parts, Stocksbridge)
Hunsley St. S4—3A 88
Hunster Clo. DN4—4D 48
Hunster Flat La. DN11—6D 62
Hunstone Av. S8—2E 123
Hunt Clo. S71—3C 14
Hunter Ct. S11—6H 97
Hunter Hill Rd. S11—5A 98
Hunter Ho. Rd. S11—5A 98
Hunter Rd. S6—3H 85
Hunter's Av. S70—1C 22
Hunters Bar. S11—5A 98
Hunters Chase. S31—2F 107
Hunters Clo. S31—2F 107
Hunters Ct. S31—2F 107
Hunters Dri. S31—2F 107
Hunters Gdns. S6—2D 84
Hunters Gdns. S31—2F 107
Hunters Grn. S31—2F 107
Hunters La. S13—1E 113
Hunters Pk. S31—2F 107
Hunters Rise. S75—6D 12
Hunters Way. S31—2F 107
Huntingdon Cres. S11—5C 98
Huntingdon Rd. DN2—4A 34
Huntington St. DN5—5A 18
Huntingtower Rd. S11—6H 97
Hunt La. DN5—4B 32
Huntley Clo. S43—3H 133
Huntley Gro. S11—1F 109
Huntley Rd. S11—1G 109
Huntsman Rd. S9—1F 101
Huntsman Rd. S43—1C 134
Hunt St. S74—4F 37
Hurl Dri. S12—2B 112
Hurley Croft. S63—4A 40
Hurlfield Av. S12—2B 112
Hurlfield Ct. S12—1C 112
Hurlfield Dri. S12—1B 112
Hurlfield Rd. S65—2H 81
Hurlfield Rd. S12—2A to 1C 112
Hurlfield View. S12—1B 112
Hurlingham Clo. S11—2A 110
Hursley Clo. S19—6G 115
Hursley Dri. S19—6G 115
Hurst Grn. S30—6B 50
Hurst La. DN9—4H 63
Hutchinson Ct. S60—4E 79
Hutchinson La. S7—4B 110
Hutchinson Rd. S7—4B 110
Hutchinson Rd. S62—1G 69
Hutcliffe Dri. S8—5B 110
Hutcliffe Wood Rd. S8—5B 110
Hut La. S31—5C 126
Hutton Croft. S12—4B 114
Hutton Rd. S61—6H 67
Hyacinth Clo. S5—6B 76
Hyacinth Rd. S5—6B 76
Hyde Pk. Ind. Est. DN4—3E 47
Hyde Pk. Ter. S2—2G 99

Hyde Pk. Wlk. S2—2G 99
Hyman Clo. DN4—4F 45
Hyperion Way. DN11—5C 62

Ians Way. S40—1E 137
Ibberson Av. S75—5F 7
Ibbotson Rd. S6—5A 86
Ibsen Cres. DN3—1H 21
Icknield Way. S60—3C 90
Ida's Rd. S31—5D 124
Idsworth Rd. S5—1H 87
Ilam Clo. S43—5A 134
Ilkley Cres. S31—1A 116
Ilkley Rd. S5—5H 75
Illsley Rd. S73—3E 27
Immingham Gro. S43—2B 134
Imperial Cres. DN2—5F 33
Imperial St. S70—2H 23
Industry Rd. S9—6D 88
Industry Rd. S71—6E 9
Industry St. S6—5A 86
  (in two parts)
Infield La. S9—1F 101
Infirmary Rd. S6—5C 86
Infirmary Rd. S41—1B 138
Infirmary Rd. S62—4G 69
Ingelow Av. S5—4F 75
Ingfield Av. S9—1G 89
Ingleborough Croft. S30—1D 64
Ingleborough Dri. DN5—1G 45
Ingleby Clo. S18—2A 128
Ingle Gro. DN5—1G 45
Ingleton Rd. S41—6B 138
Ingleton Wlk. S70—5F 13
Inglewood Av. S19—6G 115
Inglewood Ct. S19—6G 115
Inglewood Dell. S19—6G 115
Ingram Ct. S2—3H 99
Ingram Rd. S2—3H 99
Ingsfield La. S63—1G 41
Ingshead Av. S62—2F 69
Ingshead Ho. S62—2F 69
Ings La. DN5—5E 19
  (Arksey)
Ings La. DN5—5F 19
  (Arksey Common)
Ings La. S72—2F 27
Ings Rd. DN5—3C 32
Ings Rd. S73—5D 26
Ings Way. DN5—5D 18
Inkerman St. S73—4E 27
Inkersall Dri. S19—1E 125
Inkersall Grn. Rd. S43—3H 133
Inkersall Rd. S43—5B 134
Innovation Way. S75—3E 13
Insley Gdns. DN4—4C 48
Intake Cres. S75—3B 22
Intake La. S72—5C 10
Intake La. S75—4D 12
Ireland St. S43—1D 134
Irongate. S40—2A 138
  (off High St.)
Ironside St. S14—5H 111
Ironside Pl. S14—4A 112
Ironside Rd. S14—5H 111
Ironside Wlk. S14—5H 111
Irving St. S9—1E 101
Irwell Gdns. DN4—1B 48
Islay St. S10—2H 97
Issott St. S71—4H 13
Ivanbrook Clo. S18—2A 128
Ivanhoe Av. S31—4A 118
Ivanhoe Clo. DN5—5H 31
Ivanhoe M. S31—5A 104
Ivanhoe Rd. DN3—6D 20
Ivanhoe Rd. DN4—5G 45

Ivanhoe Rd. DN12—3D 58 (Conisbrough)
Ivanhoe Rd. DN12—4B 60 (Edlington)
Ivanhoe Rd. S6—5G 85
Ivanhoe Rd. S66—5A 94
Ivanhoe Way. DN5—5H 31
Ivor Gro. DN4—3A 46
Ivy Clo. DN11—3E 63
Ivy. Clo. S41—1A 132
Ivy Cottage La. S11—1C 108
Ivy Cotts. S71—1F 9
Ivy Farm Clo. S71—4F 9
Ivy Farm Croft. S65—6B 70
Ivy Gro. S10—1B 98
Ivy Hall Rd. S5—3A 76
Ivy La. S19—3G 115
Ivy Pk. Clo. S10—1E 97
Ivy Pk. Rd. S10—3E 97
Ivy Side Clo. S31—3B 126
Ivy Side Gdns. S31—3B 126
Ivy Ter. S70—1A 24

Jack Close Orchard. S71—1E 9
Jackey La. S30—2B 72
Jackson Cres. S62—6E 55
Jackson St. S63—4G 29
Jackson St. S72—1G 15
Jacobs Clo. S5—5A 76
Jacobs Dri. S5—5A 76
Jacobs Hall Ct. S75—5A 6
Jamaica St. S4—4H 87
James Andrew Clo. S8—2D 122
James Andrew Cres. S8 —2C 122
James Andrew Croft. S8 —2D 122
James St. S9—2E 101
James St. S41—5A 132
James St. S60—2C 78 (in two parts)
James St. S64—6H 43
James St. S70—4C 24
James St. S71—5H 13
Janet's Wlk. S73—5G 25
Janson St. S9—3C 88
Jaques Pl. S71—5D 14
Jardine Clo. S9—5C 76
Jardine St. S9—5D 76
Jardine St. S73—1F 39
Jarratt St. DN1—1D 46
Jarrow Rd. S11—5B 98
Jasmine Av. S19—4F 115
Jaunty Av. S12—4D 112
Jaunty Clo. S12—4D 112
Jaunty Cres. S12—3D 112
Jaunty Dri. S12—4D 112
Jaunty La. S12—2D 112
Jaunty Mt. S12—4E 113
Jaunty Pl. S12—4D 112
Jaunty Rd. S12—4E 113
Jaunty View. S12—4E 113
Jaunty Way. S12—3D 112
Jaw Bones Hill. S40—5A 138
Jay La. S31—1C 116
Jedburgh Dri. S9—5C 76
Jedburgh St. S9—5C 76
Jeffcock Pl. S30—6C 50
Jeffcock Rd. S9—1E 101
Jeffcock Rd. S30—6C 50
Jefferson Av. DN2—6B 20
Jeffery Cres. S30—4F 141
Jeffrey Grn. S10—6A 96
Jeffrey St. S2—1F 111
Jenkin Av. S9—1C 88
Jenkin Clo. S9—6C 76
Jenkin Dri. S9—1C 88

Jenkin Rd. S9—6C 76
Jenny La. S72—1H 15
Jepson Rd. S5—5B 76
Jericho St. S3—1B 4 & 1C 98
Jermyn Av. S12—3G 113
Jermyn Clo. S12—4H 113
Jermyn Cres. S12—4H 113
Jermyn Croft. S75—2B 22
Jermyn Dri. S12—4H 113
Jermyn Sq. S12—4H 113
Jermyn Way. S12—4G 113
Jersey Rd. S2—6E 99
Jervis Pl. S43—5H 133
Jesmond Av. S71—2D 8
Jessamine Rd. S5—5A 76
Jessell St. S9—6B 88
Jessop St. S1—6D 4 & 3E 99
Jewitt Rd. S61—5G 67
Jew La. S1—3G 5 & 2F 99
Joan La. S66—5E 83
Joan's Wlk. S74—4B 38
Jobson Pl. S3—6D 86
Jobson Rd. S3—6D 86
Jockel Dri. S62—2F 69
John Calvert Rd. S13—1D 114
John Eaton's Almshouses. S8 —5F 111
John La. DN11—4C 62
Johnson Ct. S65—4F 79
Johnson La. S3—1F 5 & 1F 99
Johnson La. S30—6F 65
Johnson St. S3—6F 87
Johnson St. S30—3D 140
Johnson St. S75—5F 13
Johnstone Clo. S40—4H 137
John St. DN6—1E 17
John St. S2—4D 98
John St. S31—6D 124
John St. S40—2G 137
John St. S43—3E 133
John St. S60—3C 78
John St. S63—1F 29
John St. S64—1E 57
John St. S66—4A 94
John St. S70—1H 23 (Barnsley)
John St. S70—5A 24 (Worsbrough)
John St. S72—1B 28 (Great Houghton)
John St. S72—2A 28 (Little Houghton)
John St. S73—6A 26
John Trickett Ho. S30—2D 64 (off Lansbury Av.)
John Ward St. S13—6D 102
John West St. S30—4D 140
Joiner St. S3—1F 5
Jones Av. S73—6H 25
Jordan Cres. S61—4G 77
Jordanthorpe Centre. S8 —3F 123
Jordanthorpe Parkway. S8 —1F to 4E 123
Josephine Rd. S61—3A 78
Joseph Rd. S6—6A 86
Joseph St. S31—6D 124
Joseph St. S60—2C 78
Joseph St. S70—1H 23
Joseph St. S72—6G 11
Joshua Rd. S7—1C 110
Josselin Ct. S30—2D 64
Jossey La. DN5—1F 31 to 1A 32
Jowitt Clo. S66—6H 83
Jowitt Rd. S11—1A 110
Jubb Clo. S65—5B 80
Jubilee Cotts. S44—4G 139
Jubilee Cotts. S60—2B 90

Jubilee Ct. DN2—3A 34
Jubilee Cres. S31—2C 126
Jubilee Rd. DN1—4E 33
Jubilee Rd. S9—5D 88
Jubilee St. S60—5D 78
Jubilee Ter. S70—1B 24
Judith Rd. S31—1B 116
Judy Row. S71—3C 14
Julian Rd. S9—6D 76
Julian Way. S9—6D 76
Jumble La. S30—6H 65
Jumble Rd. S11—6A 108
Junction 34 Ind. Est. S9—2G 89
Junction Clo. S73—2A 40
Junction Rd. DN11—5C 62
Junction Rd. S11—5A 98
Junction Rd. S13—6D 102
Junction St. S70—1B 24
Junction St. S73—2H 39
Junction Ter. S70—1B 24
June Rd. S13—6D 102
Juniper Rise. S31—4A 126

Kashmir Gdns. S9—6D 88
Katherine Rd. S66—4A 94
Katherine St. S66—5B 94
Kathleen Gro. S63—3H 29
Kathleen St. S63—3H 29
Kay Cres. S62—5C 54
Kaye Pl. S10—1B 98
Kaye St. S71—5H 13
Kay's Ter. S70—2E 25
Kay St. S74—6F 37
Kearsley La. DN12—5D 58
Kearsley Rd. S2—5E 99
Keats Dri. S31—5H 107
Keats Rd. DN4—5B 46
Keats Rd. S6—3B 74
Keats Rd. S41—3H 131
Keble Martin Way. S63—5D 40
Keeper La. WF4—1H 7
Keepers Clo. DN11—3F 63
Keeton Hall Rd. S31—4B 118
Keeton's Hill. S2—5D 98
Keighley Wlk. DN12—4B 58
Keilder Ct. S40—4F 137
Keir Clo. S40—4E 137
Keir Dri. DN1—2C 46
Keir Pl. S62—1H 69
Keir St. S70—5F 13
Keir Ter. S70—5F 13
Kelburn Av. S40—4E 137
Kelham Ct. DN1—2C 46
Kelham Island. S3—6E 87
Kelham St. DN1—2C 46
Kelly St. S63—4G 29
Kelsey Gdns. DN4—6C 48
Kelsey Ter. S70—2H 23
Kelso Dri. DN4—4F 45
Kelvin Gro. S73—1G 39
Kelvin St. S64—6E 43
Kelvin St. S65—6B 70
Kelvin Wlk. S6—6C 86
Kempton Gdns. S64—5G 43
Kempton Pk. Rd. DN5—3F 31
Kempton St. DN4—1B 48
Kempwell Dri. S62—5F 55
Kenbourne Gro. S7—6C 98
Kenbourne Rd. S7—6C 98
Kendal Av. S31—1H 119
Kendal Clo. DN5—2C 44
Kendal Cres. DN12—3F 59
Kendal Cres. S70—5A 24
Kendal Dri. S18—2C 128
Kendal Dri. S63—2A 42
Kendal Grn. S70—5G 23
Kendal Grn. Rd. S70—5G 23
Kendal Gro. S71—1G 25
Kendal Pl. S6—3H 85

Kendal Rd. DN5—2A 32
Kendal Rd. S6—3H 85
Kendal Rd. S41—3G 131
Kendray St. S70—6H 13
Kenilworth Clo. DN5—3F 31
Kenilworth Ct. S11—3F 109
Kenilworth Pl. S11—5A 98
Kenilworth Rd. DN4—4G 45
Kenmare Cres. DN2—4G 33
Kennedy Ct. S10—2H 97
Kennedy Dri. S63—6F 29
Kennedy Rd. S8—5C 110
Kenneth St. S65—2E 79
Kennet Vale. S40—6F 131
Kenninghall Clo. S2—6H 99
Kenninghall Dri. S2—6H 99
Kenninghall Mt. S2—6H 99
Kenninghall Pl. S2—6H 99
Kenninghall Rd. S2—6H 99
Kennington Av. DN6—2B 16
Kenrock Clo. DN5—6E 19
Kensington Rd. S75—4F 13
Kent Av. S62—6E 55
Kent Clo. S41—6H 131
Kentmere Clo. S18—2C 128
Kent Rd. DN4—4B 46
Kent Rd. S8—2F 111
Kent Rd. S61—6G 67
Kent St. S41—5C 138
Kenwell Dri. S17—4H 121
Kenwood Av. S7—6C 98
Kenwood Bank. S7—5C 98
Kenwood Chase. S7—5D 98 (off Wostenholm Rd.)
Kenwood Clo. S70—1D 24
Kenwood Pk. Rd. S7—6C 98
Kenwood Rise. S66—3G 81
Kenwood Rd. S7—6B 98
Kenworthy Rd. S30—4D 140
Kenworthy Rd. S70—2H 23
Kenyon All. S3—2B 4
Kenyon Rd. S44—4E 139
Kenyon St. S1—2C 4 & 1D 98
Keppel Dri. S61—5D 66
Keppel Heights. S61—5D 66
Keppel Pl. S5—3B 76
Keppel Rd. S5—3B 76
Keppel Rd. S61—5D 66
Keppels View. S61—6H 67
Keppel View Rd. S61—1F 77
Kepple Clo. DN11—6D 62
Keresforth Clo. S70—2E 23
Keresforth Hall Dri. S70—2E 23
Keresforth Hall Rd. S70—2F 23
Keresforth Hill Rd. S70—3D 22
Keresforth Rd. S75—3B 22
Kerwin Clo. S17—1C 120
Kerwin Dri. S17—1C 120
Kerwin Rd. S17—1C 120
Kestrel Av. S61—2C 66
Kestrel Dri. DN11—4E 63
Kestrel Dri. S31—6B 124
Kestrel Grn. S2—3A 100
Kestrel Rise. S70—3D 36
Keswick Clo. DN5—1A 32
Keswick Clo. S6—3B 85
Keswick Cres. S60—4B 90
Keswick Dri. S41—4E 131
Keswick Pl. S18—2B 128
Keswick Rd. S7—3C 110
Keswick Rd. S75—2E 7
Keswick Wlk. S71—3B 22
Keswick Way. S31—1H 119
Ket Hill La. S72—2F 11
Kettlebridge Rd. S9—2C 100
Ketton Av. S8—4F 111
Ketton Wlk. S75—4E 13
Kevin Gro. S66—5B 82

Kew Cres. S12—5B 112
Kexbrough Dri. S75—5B 6
Key Av. S74—5B 38
Keyworth Pl. S13—1A 114
Keyworth Rd. S6—2A 86
Kibroyd Dri. S75—6A 6
Kidsley Clo. S40—6A 130
Kier Hardie Av. DN11—5E 63
Kilburn Rd. S18—2A 128
Kildale Gdns. S19—2D 124
Kildonan Gro. S12—4E 113
Killamarsh La. S31—4E 127
Kilner Way. S6—6B 74
Kiln Hill. S18—6G 123
Kilnhurst Rd. S62—6G 55
Kilnhurst Rd. S65—6D 56
Kiln Rd. S61—1H 77
Kilnsea Wlk. S70—6G 13
  (off Fitzwilliam St.)
Kilton Hill. S3—5F 87
Kilton Pl. S3—5F 87
Kilvington Av. S13—6D 100
Kilvington Cres. S13—6D 100
Kilvington Rd. S13—1D 112
Kimberley St. S9—5B 88
Kimberworth Pk. Rd. S61
  (in two parts)—5F 67 & 2H 77
Kimberworth Rd. S61—2H 77
Kinder Rd. S43—5H 133
King Av. DN11—4C 62
King Av. S66—5H 83
King Ecgbert Rd. S17—4E 121
King Edward Rd. DN4—3B 46
King Edwards Gdns. S70
  —1G 23
King Edward St. S71—1D 14
Kingfield Ct. S11—6B 98
Kingfield Rd. S11—6B 98
Kingfisher Ct. DN11—4E 63
Kingfisher Rise. S61—1B 66
King George Sq. DN3—2D 20
King George's Rd. DN11—3B 62
King George Ter. S70—1B 24
King James St. S6—5B 86
Kingsclere Wlk. S40—6H 137
King's Cres. DN12—2B 60
Kingscroft Clo. S17—1E 121
Kingsforth La. S66—3A 94
Kingsforth Rd. S66—4A 94
Kingsgate. DN1—6D 32
Kingsland Ct. S71—1F 9
Kingsley Av. DN5—5H 31
Kingsley Av. S40—5H 137
Kingsley Clo. S71—1A 14
Kingsley Cres. DN3—3G 35
Kingsley Pk. Av. S7—3H 109
Kingsley Pk. Gro. S11—3H 109
Kingsley Rd. DN6—2C 16
Kingsmead Dri. DN3—3H 49
Kingsmede Av S40—4F 137
King s Rd. DN1—5E 33
Kings Rd. S31—6E 125
King's Rd. S64—6F 43
King's Rd. S72—4C 10
Kings Rd. S73—1G 39
King's Stocks. S72—3A 28
King's St. S72—6G 11
Kingstone Pl. S70—2F 23
Kingston Rd. DN2—5H 33
Kingston St. S4—4H 87
King St. DN1—6D 32
King St. DN3—2D 34
King St. S3—2F 5 & 1F 99
King St. S30—1E 65
King St. S31—5A 104
King St. S43—2F 133

King St. S63—4G 29
  (Goldthorpe)
King St. S63—2G 29
  (Thurnscoe)
King St. S64—2B 56
King St. S70—1H 23
King St. S74—5A 38
King St. N. S41—4A 132
King St. S. S40—6A 138
Kings Way. S60—1G 91
Kingsway. S63—1E 29
Kingsway. S73—1F 39
Kingsway. S75—4E 7
Kingsway Clo. DN11—6E 63
Kingsway Gro. S63—1E 29
Kingswood Av. S19—5A 114
Kingswood Av. S31—1E 107
Kingswood Clo. S19—5A 114
Kingswood Clo. S41—3F 131
Kingswood Cres. S74—4A 38
Kingswood Croft. S19—5A 114
Kingswood Gro. S19—5A 114
Kingwell Cres. S70—3H 23
Kingwell Croft. S70—4A 24
Kingwell Rd. S70—4H 23
Kinharvie Rd. S5—6D 74
Kinnaird Av. S5—4G 75
Kinnaird Pl. S5—4G 75
Kinnaird Rd. S5—4G 75
Kinsey Rd. S30—6A 50
Kipling Av. DN4—5H 45
Kipling Clo. S18—4G 129
Kipling Rd. DN3—1H 21
Kipling Rd. S6—3A 86
Kipling Rd. S41—3H 131
Kirby Clo. S9—1E 101
Kirby La. S30—5H 51
Kirby St. S64—6E 43
Kirkby Av. DN5—3B 32
Kirkby Av. S12—3C 112
Kirkby Av. S71—5C 8
Kirkby Dri. S12—3C 112
Kirkby Rd. S12—3C 112
Kirkby View. S12—3C 112
Kirkby Way. S12—4C 112
Kirkcroft Av. S31—2B 126
Kirkcroft Av. S61—2C 66
Kirkcroft Clo. S61—2B 66
Kirkcroft Dri. S31—3B 126
Kirkcroft La. S31—3B 126
Kirk Croft Rd. S31—1E 107
Kirk Cross Cres. S71—3E 9
Kirkdale Clo. S40—5B 138
Kirkdale Cres. S13—4B 102
Kirkdale Dri. S13—4B 102
Kirk Edge Av. S30—5D 72
Kirk Edge Dri. S30—5C 72
Kirk Edge Rd. S30—4A 72
Kirkfield Way. S71—3E 9
Kirkham Clo. S31—4C 14
Kirkham Pl. S71—6F 9
Kirkhill Clo. DN3—4G 35
Kirklands Dri. S62—1E 69
Kirk Sandall Ind. Est. DN3
  —3B to 4B 20
Kirkstall Clo. DN5—4F 31
Kirkstall Clo. S31—4F 119
Kirkstall Clo. S60—2A 90
Kirkstall Rd. S11—5A 98
Kirkstall Rd. S71—6A 8
Kirkstead Abbey M. S61—5C 66
Kirkstead Rd. S61—2C 76
Kirkstone Clo. DN5—2A 32
Kirkstone Rd. S6—4A 86
Kirkstone Rd. S41—3E 131
Kirk St. DN4—1B 46
Kirk St. S4—5G 87

Kirk View. S74—5H 37
Kirk Way. S71—4D 14
Kirton Rd. S4—4G 87
Kitchen Rd. S73—6H 25
Kitson Dri. S71—4D 14
Kiveton La. S31—2B 118
Knab Clo. S7—2A 110
Knab Croft. S7—2A 110
Knab Rise. S7—2A 110
Knab Rd. S7—2A 110
Knapton Av. S62—1E 69
Knaresborough Clo. S31
  —6A 104
Knaresborough Rd. DN12
  —4B 58
Knaresborough Rd. S7—4A 110
Knavesmire Gdns. DN4—1B 48
Knifesmithgate. S40—2A 138
Knightwood Pl. S65—1H 79
Knollbeck Av. S73—3A 40
Knollbeck Cres. S73—3A 40
Knollbeck La. S73—2A 40
Knoll Clo. S30—3E 141
Knoll, The. S18—6H 123
Knoll, The. S40—3B 136
Knowle Clo. S6—5C 84
Knowle Ct. S11—2H 109
Knowle Croft. S11—2G 109
Knowle La. S11—2F 109
Knowle Rd. S5—3F 75
Knowle Rd. S70—3B 24
Knowles Av. S30—4F 141
Knowle Top. S19—2E 125
Knowsley St. S70—6F 13
Knutton Cres. S5—3C 74
Knutton Rise. S5—2C 74
Knutton Rd. S5—3C 74
Kyle Clo. S5—5C 74
Kyle Cres. S5—5C 74
Kynance Cres. S60—4B 90

Laburnham Gro. S70—5C 24
Laburnum Av. S66—3F 81
Laburnum Clo. S30—3E 65
Laburnum Clo. S31—3F 119
Laburnum Ct. S44—2G 139
Laburnum Dri. DN3—2G 35
Laburnum Gro. S30—4D 140
Laburnum Gro. S31—4A 126
Laburnum Pde. S66—4D 82
Laburnum Pl. DN5—5B 18
Laburnum Rd. DN4—5H 45
Laburnum Rd. S64—5D 42
Laburnum Rd. S66—4D 82
Laburnum St. S43—2H 133
Laceby Clo. S66—2H 81
Laceby Ct. S70—2E 23
Lack Hill Rd. S65—5B 80
Ladies Spring Dri. S17—2G 121
Ladies Spring Gro. S17—2G 121
Ladock Clo. S71—4B 14
Ladybank Rd. S19—3D 124
Ladybank View. S31—5D 124
Ladybower Ct. S17—4G 121
Ladybower La. S43—3B 134
Ladycroft. S63—1A 42
  (Bolton-upon-Dearne)
Lady Croft. S63—5E 41
  (Wath upon Dearne)
Ladycroft Rd. DN3—5F 35
Lady Field Rd. S31—6D 118
Lady Ida's Dri. S31—3A 124
Lady Oak Rd. S65—1A 80
Lady's Bri. S3—1F 5 & 1F 99
Ladysmith Av. S7—1B 110
Ladywood Rd. S72—6H 11

Laird Av. S6—2G 85
Laird Dri. S6—2G 85
Laird Rd. S6—2G 85
Laithes Clo. S71—6D 8
Laithes Cres. S71—6B 8
Laithes La. S71—6B 8
Lakeen Rd. DN2—5G 33
Lakeland Clo. S72—2H 15
Lakeland Dri. S31—1G 119
Lake Rd. DN6—4E 17
Lake View Av. S40—4E 137
Lambcote Way. S66—3H 83
Lambcroft La. S13—1C 114
Lambcroft View. S13—1C 114
Lamb Dri. S5—6B 74
Lambe Flatt. S75—5A 6
Lambert Rd. S70—2C 24
Lamberts La. S65—4D 70
Lambert St. S3—1D 4 & 1E 99
Lambert Wlk. S70—1C 24
Lambeth Rd. DN4—4B 46
Lamb Hill Clo. S13—6F 101
Lamb La. S71—2C 14
Lambra Rd. S70—6H 13
Lambrell Av. S31—5G 117
Lambrell Grn. S31—5G 117
Lamb Rd. S5—6B 74
Lanark Dri. S64—4G 43
Lanark Gdns. DN2—4A 34
Lancaster Av. DN2—5A 34
Lancaster Av. DN3—3D 20
Lancaster Ga. S70—5G 13
  (off St Mary's Pl.)
Lancaster Rd. S30—3D 140
Lancaster Rd. S41—3G 131
Lancaster St. S3—6D 86
Lancaster St. S63—1G 29
Lancaster St. S70—6F 13
Lancelot Clo. S40—5F 137
Lancing Rd. S2—5E 99
  (in two parts)
Landon Clo. S42—6D 136
Landseer Clo. S14—5H 111
Landseer Clo. S18—2C 128
Landseer Ct. S66—3F 81
Landseer Dri. S14—5A 112
Landseer Pl. S14—5A 112
Landseer Wlk. S14—5A 112
Lane Cotts. S71—2E 9
Lane End. S30—6D 50
Lane End Rd. S60—6G 79
Laneham Clo. DN4—5B 48
Lane Head. S30—1H 73
Lane Head Clo. S62—1G 69
Lane Head Clo. S75—3E 7
Lane Head Rise. S75—3E 7
Lane Head Rd. S17—5C 120
Laneside Clo. DN4—2A 46
Lanes, The. S65—2H 79
Langar Clo. DN5—3A 18
Lang Av. S71—5E 15
Langcliff Clo. S75—3E 7
Lang Cres. S71—5E 15
Langdale Clo. S40—6C 130
Langdale Dri. DN5—1H 31
Langdale Dri. S18—6G 123
Langdale Rd. S8—2C 110
Langdale Rd. S71—6A 14
Langdale Rd. S75—2A 12
Langdale Sq. S43—3D 132
Langdale Way. S31—6F 107
Langdon Rd. S61—1G 77
Langdon St. S11—5D 98
Langdon Wlk. S61—1G 77
Langdon Wlk. S70—5F 13
  (off Summer St.)
Langer Field Av. S40—6A 138
Langer La. S40—6H 137

Langer St. DN4—2A 46
Langhurst Rd. S40—1F 137
Langley Clo. S40—6C 130
Langley Clo. S65—2B 80
Langsett Av. S6—1G 85
Langsett Clo. S6—4B 86
Langsett Ct. S71—6A 8
Langsett Cres. S6—4B 86
Langsett Gro. S6—5B 86
Langsett Rise. S6—4B 86
Langsett Rd. S6—3A 86
Langsett Rd. S71—6A 8
Langsett Rd. N. S30—1C 72
Langsett Rd. S. S30—2D 72
Langsett Wlk. S6—4B 86
Langthwaite La. DN5—5F 17
Langthwaite Rd. DN5—6F 17
Langtree Av. S41—2A 132
Lansbury Av. DN11—4E 63
Lansbury Av. S30—2D 64
Lansbury Av. S66—5H 83
Lansbury Pl. S62—1A 70
Lansbury Rd. S31—6D 124
Lansdowne Av. S41—4G 131
Lansdowne Clo. S63—1E 29
Lansdowne Cres. S64—3B 56
Lansdowne Cres. S75—6B 6
Lansdowne Rd. DN2—4A 34
Lansdowne Rd. S11—4D 98
Lansdowne Rd. S43—4D 132
Lanyon Way. S71—4B 14
Lapwater Rd. S61—4H 67
Lapwater Wlk. S61—4H 67
Lapwing Vale. S61—1C 66
Larch Av. S31—4A 126
Larch Av. S66—4F 81
Larch Dri. DN3—3F 35
Larches, The. S64—2A 56
Larchfield Pl. S71—2D 14
Larchfield Rd. DN4—4H 45
Larch Gro. DN12—5C 58
Larch Hill. S9—2G 101
Larch Pl. S70—2C 24
Larch Rd. S31—6G 125
Larch Rd. S66—3D 82
Larch Way. S40—6F 131
Lark Av. S60—3D 90
Larkspur Clo. DN3—6D 20
Larkspur Clo. S64—5A 56
Lark St. S6—5H 85
Latham Sq. DN3—2E 21
Latham Sq. S11—2E 109
Lathe Rd. S60—1A 92
Lathkill Av. S43—5A 134
Lathkill Clo. S13—6E 101
Lathkill Rd. S13—6E 101
Latimer Clo. S31—5B 118
Latin Gdns. DN5—2E 31
Lauder Rd. DN5—3A 32
Lauder St. S4—1A 88
Laudsdale Clo. S65—2B 80
Laudsdale Rd. S65—1A 80
Laughton Comn. Rd. S66
—1A 106
Laughton Rd. DN4—1B 46
Laughton Rd. S9—1D 88
Laughton Rd. S31—5F 107
Laughton Rd. S66—5B 94
Launce Rd. S5—5D 74
Laurel Av. DN5—4G 31
Laurel Av. S66—4H 81
Laurel Av. S70—2D 24
Laurel Clo. S31—4F 119
Laurel Cres. S43—2G 133
Laurel Dri. S31—4A 126
Laurel Garth Clo. S41—1B 132
Laurel Rd. DN3—2F 35

Laurel Ter. DN4—4A 46
Laverack Clo. S13—4H 101
Laverack St. S13—4H 101
Laverdene Av. S17—5F 121
Laverdene Clo. S17—5F 121
Laverdene Dri. S17—5F 121
Laverdene Rd. S17—5F 121
Laverdene Way. S17—5F 121
Laverock Way. S5—4H 75
Lavinia Rd. S30—1C 74
Lawn Av. DN1—6E 33
Lawn Av. DN6—1B 16
Lawn Garth. DN5—2A 32
Lawn Rd. DN1—6E 33
Lawns, The. S11—1H 109
Lawn, The. S18—1F 129
Lawn Vs. S44—2G 139
Lawrence Clo. S41—1A 132
Lawrence Clo. S66—4F 81
Lawrence Clo. S75—3A 12
Lawrence Ct. S64—4A 56
Lawrence Dri. S64—4A 56
Lawrence St. S9—5B 88
Lawson Rd. S10—3H 97
Lawton La. S60—6E 79
Lawton Ter. S6—3H 85
Laxey Rd. S6—6E 85
Laxfield Clo. S40—5E 137
Laxton Rd. S71—5B 8
Laycock Av. S31—6C 104
Layton Dri. S41—2B 132
Lea Brook La. S62—2G 53
Leabrook Rd. S18—2A 128
Leadbeater Dri. S12—2C 112
Leadbeater Rd. S12—3B 112
Leader Ct. S6—2H 85
Leader Rd. S6—2H 85
Leadley St. S63—4G 29
Leadmill Rd. S1 & S2
—6F 5 & 3F 99
Leadmill St. S1—6F 5 & 3F 99
Leaf Clo. S66—3H 83
Leake Rd. S6—1A 86
Leamington Gdns. DN2—4A 34
Leamington St. S10—1A 98
Leander Ct. S43—1D 134
Lea Rd. S18—2E 129
Lea Rd. S71—6D 8
Lease Gate Rd. S60—2H 91
Lea, The. S11—5D 114
Lea, The. S64—3H 55
Leaton Clo. S6—2D 84
Leavy Greave. S3—4A 4
Leavy Greave Rd. S3—4A 4 &
(in two parts) 2C 98
Leawood Pl. S6—5D 84
Ledbury Gdns. DN5—4F 31
Ledbury Rd. S71—1H 13
Ledger Clo. S31—5G 117
Ledsham Ct. S74—4D 38
Ledsham Rd. S60—5G 79
Ledstone Rd. S8—3C 110
Lee Av. S30—3F 141
Lee Croft. S1—2E 5 & 1E 99
Lee Croft. S66—6H 83
Leedham Clo. S5—5B 76
Leedham Rd. S5—5B 76
Leedham Rd. S65—5A 80
Leeds Av. S31—6E 107
Leeds Dri. S31—4C 118
Leeds Rd. S9—5C 88
Lee House La. S30—4B 140
Lee La. S71—3H 7 to 2C 8
Lee Moor La. S6—4A 84
Lee Rd. S6—2D 84
Lee Rd. S43—3E 139
Lees Hall Av. S8—2F 111
Lees Hall Pl. S8—2F 111

Lees Hall Rd. S8—2F 111
Lees Ho. Ct. S8—3E 111
Lees Nook. S8—3E 111
Lees, The. S8—4E 111
Lees, The. S71—1H 25
Leeswood Clo. S41—3F 131
Leger Ct. DN2—1E 47
Leger Way. DN2—1G 47 to 2B 34
Legion Dri. S31—6C 104
Leicester Av. DN2—5G 33
Leicester Rd. S31—4G 107
Leicester Wlk. S3—2B 4 & 1D 98
Leigh St. S9—4C 88
Leighton Clo. S71—4H 13
Leighton Dri. S14—4B 112
Leighton Pl. S14—4B 112
Leighton Rd. S14—2A 112
Leinster Av. DN2—4G 33
Lemont Rd. S17—5E 121
Lennox Dri. DN2—4H 33
Lennox Rd. S6—2H 85
Lenthall's Bk. Row. S40
—2F 137
Lenton St. S2—4F 99
Leonard Clo. S2—6C 100
Leopold Av. S31—5F 107
Leopold St. S1—3E 5 & 2E 99
Leopold St. S31—4F 107
Leopold St. S70—1F 23
Leppings La. S6—1A 86
Lepton Gdns. S70—3D 24
Lescar La. S11—5A 98
Lesley Rd. S63—4G 29
Leslie Av. DN12—3C 58
Leslie Av. S66—4D 82
Leslie Rd. S6—2H 85
Leslie Rd. S70—1D 24
Lesmond Cres. S72—3A 28
Lestermoor Av. S31—5G 117
Letard Dri. S62—2C 90
Levens Way. S41—3G 131
Leverick Dri. S62—6A 56
Leverton Dri. S11—4D 98
Leverton Gdns. S11—4D 98
Leverton Way. S65—6C 70
Leveson St. S4—6H 87
Levet Rd. DN4—2D 48
Lewdendale. S70—5A 24
Lewes Rd. DN12—4D 58
Lewis Rd. S13—6E 101
Lewis Rd. S71—3E 15
Lewyns Dri. DN4—2D 48
Leybourne Rd. S61—6G 67
Leyburn Clo. DN4—4D 48
Leyburn Clo. S40—6G 131
Leyburn Dri. S31—5A 104
Leyburn Gro. S30—1E 65
Leyburn Rd. S8—1D 110
(in two parts)
Ley End. S70—5H 23
Leyfield Ct. DN3—4G 35
Leyfield Rd. S17—2D 120
Leys Clo. DN4—6H 45
Leys La. S31—4H 107
Liberty Clo. S6—6E 85
Liberty Dri. S6—6E 85
Liberty Hill. S6—6E 85
Liberty Pl. S6—6E 85
Liberty Rd. S6—6E 85
Library Clo. S61—4A 68
Lichen Clo. DN3—6D 20
Lichfield Gdns. DN12—4A 60
Lichfield Rd. DN2—3F 33
Lichfield Rd. S40—5E 137
Lichfield Way. S60—3D 90
Lichford Rd. S2—1G 111
Lidgate La. S72—2B 10
Lidget Clo. DN4—4C 48

Lidget La. S63—1G 29
Lidget La. S65—3H 81 & 1A 82
Lidget La. Ind. Est. S63—1H 29
Lidgett La. S31—5F 107
Lidgett La. S75—6B 36
Liffey Av. DN2—4G 33
Lifford Pl. S74—6D 38
Lifford Rd. DN2—4F 33
Lifford St. S9—6G 77
Lightwood La. S8—6A 112
Lilac Av. S30—4D 140
Lilac Clo. S31—3F 119
Lilac Cres. DN12—4B 60
Lilac Cres. S74—4A 38
Lilac Gro. DN4—3D 48
Lilac Gro. DN12—4C 58
Lilac Gro. S66—4G 81
(Bramley)
Lilac Gro. S66—4D 82
(Maltby)
Lilac Rd. DN3—2G 35
Lilac Rd. S5—6A 76
Lilac Rd. S19—4F 115
Lilacs, The. S71—1G 9
Lilac St. S43—2H 133
Lilian St. S60—4E 79
Lilian St. S. S60—4E 79
Lillford Rd. DN3—3H 49
Lilly Hall Rd. S66—3D 82
Lilydene Av. S72—6G 11
Lily Ter. S74—4B 38
Limb La. S17—1D 120
Limbrick Clo. S6—4A 86
Limbrick Rd. S6—4A 86
Lime Av. S43—2C 134
Lime Clo. S44—2G 139
Lime Clo. S65—5H 71
Limedale View. DN3—1E 21
Lime Gro. S30—3E 65
(Chapeltown)
Lime Gro. S30—4D 140
(Stocksbridge)
Lime Gro. S60—5G 79
Lime Gro. S64—3B 56
Lime Gro. S66—4H 83
Lime Gro. S71—4E 9
Limekilns. S31—1F 119
Lime Rd. S31—6G 125
Limes Av. S75—4D 12
(Barnsley)
Limes Av. S75—3G 7
(Mapplewell)
Limes Clo. S75—3G 7
Limestone Cottage La. S6
—5H 73
Lime St. S6—5C 86
Lime St. S19—3F 115
Limesway. S66—4F 83
Limesway. S75—4D 12
Lime Tree Av. DN3—2F 35
Lime Tree Av. DN4—1E 47
Lime Tree Av. S31—4A 126
(Killamarsh)
Limetree Av. S31—4G 117
(Kiveton Park)
Limetree Av. S66—5B 94
Lime Tree Clo. S72—6B 10
Lime Tree Ct. DN4—2F 47
Lime Tree Cres. DN11—5E 63
Lime Tree Cres. S62—1H 69
Lime Tree Wlk. DN12—1B 58
Limpool Clo. DN4—4D 48
Limpsfield Rd. S9—1C 88
Linacre Rd. S40—1C 136
Linaker Rd. S6—5G 85
Linburn Clo. S71—1C 8
Linburn Rd. S8—5D 110
Linby Rd. S71—5B 8

Lincoln Clo. DN12—3B 58
Lincoln Gdns. S63—4F 29
Lincoln Rd. DN2—3F 33
Lincoln St. DN11—3C 62
Lincoln St. S9—1D 88
Lincoln St. S40—5A 138
Lincoln St. S60—1D 78
Lincoln St. S66—5G 83
Lindale Clo. S31—2H 119
Lindale Gdns. S63—5H 29
Lindale Rd. S41—2F 131
Lindales, The. S75—5E 13
Linden Av. S8—5C 110
Linden Av. S18—6F 123
Linden Av. S40—4D 136
Linden Av. S66—3G 81
Linden Ct. S10—4H 97
Linden Ct. S30—6F 65
Linden Cres. S30—3D 140
Linden Dri. S41—6D 138
Linden Gro. DN12—4B 60
Linden Gro. S66—4D 82
Linden Rd. S30—6F 65
Linden Rd. S63—5B 40
Linden Wlk. DN5—3A 18
Lindholme Dri. DN11—3F 63
Lindholme Gdns. S19—5C 114
Lindhurst Lodge. S71—5B 8
Lindhurst Rd. S71—5A 8
Lindisfarne Ct. S40—4E 137
Lindisfarne Rd. S18—3F 129
Lindley Cres. S63—2F 29
Lindley Rd. S5—1H 87
Lindley's Croft. S31—2B 118
Lindley St. S65—1E 79
Lindrick Av. S64—3C 56
Lindrick Clo. DN4—5A 48
Lindrick Clo. DN12—2G 59
Lindrick Clo. S72—4C 10
Lindrick Dri. DN3—4F 35
Lindrick Gdns. S40—5E 137
Lindsay Av. S5—5F 75
Lindsay Clo. S5—4F 75
Lindsay Cres. S5—4F 75
Lindsay Dri. S5—4F 75
Lindsay Pl. S31—6B 104
Lindsay Rd. S5—4F 75
Lindsey Clo. DN4—6B 48
Lindum Dri. S66—5G 81
Lindum St. DN4—1B 46
Lindum Ter. S65—3E 79
(off Walker La.)
Lingamore Leys. S63—1F 29
Lingard Ct. S75—4F 13
(off Lingard St.)
Lingard La. S30—4D 72
Lingard St. S75—4F 13
Lingfield Dri. DN5—4F 31
Lingfield Wlk. S64—5G 43
Lingfoot Av. S8—3F 123
Lingfoot Clo. S8—3F 123
Lingfoot Cres. S8—3F 123
Lingfoot Dri. S8—3F 123
Lingfoot Pl. S8—3F 123
Lingfoot Wlk. S8—3G 123
Lingmoor Clo. DN4—5G 45
Lingodell Clo. S31—1F 107
Ling Rd. S40—5F 137
Lings La. S66—5G 81
Lings, The. DN4—4H 35
Lings, The. S66—5H 81
Link Rd. S65—5E 71
Link Row. S2—2H 5
Links Rd. S18—3F 129
Links View. S75—3F 7
Linkswood Av. DN2—2A 34
Link, The. S75—3C 22
Linkway DN2—3H 33

Linley La. S12 & S13—2F 113
Linnet Mt. S61—2B 66
Linsay Cres. S5—4E 75
Linscott Clo. S41—4F 131
Linscott Rd. S8—5C 110
Linthwaite La. S74 & S62
—1E 53
Linton Clo. S70—1D 22
Linton Rd. S40—5E 137
Lipp Av. S31—2A 126
Liskeard Pl. DN6—2C 16
Lisle Rd. S60—5G 79
Lismore Rd. S8—2F 111
Lister Av. DN4—3B 46
Lister Av. S12—3D 112
Lister Av. S62—6E 55
Lister Clo. S12—4D 112
Lister Ct. DN2—4G 33
Lister Cres. S12—4D 112
Listerdale Shopping Centre.
S65—5C 80
Lister Dri. S12—4D 112
Lister La. S3—6D 86
Lister Pl. S12—4D 112
Lister Rd. S6—4A 86
Lister St. S9—1E 101
Lister St. S65—3F 79
Lister Way. S12—4D 112
Lit. Cockhill La. DN12—6B 60
Lit. Common La. S11—4F 109
Lit. Common La. S60—2C 92
Lit. Common La. S61—2F 77
Littledale Rd. S9—3E 101
Lit. Field La. S73—6B 26
(in two parts)
Littlefield Rd. S31—5E 107
Lit. Haynooking La. S66—4F 83
Lit. Houghton La. S73—3F 27
Lit. John Copse. S6—4C 84
Little La. DN2—6A 20
Little La. DN5—5C 30
Little La. S4—2B 88
Little La. S12—1D 112
Little La. S61—3D 66
(Scholes)
Little La. S61—1A 66
(Thorpe Hesley)
Lit. Leeds. S74—5A 38
Lit. London Pl. S8—1D 110
Lit. London Rd. S8—3C 110
Lit. Matlock Gdns. S6—5D 84
Lit. Matlock Way. S6—5D 84
Littlemoor. S31—6E 125
Littlemoor. S41—5F 131
Littlemoor Av. S31—5G 117
Littlemoor Centre. S41—4G 131
Littlemoor Cres. S41—4F 131
Littlemoor La. DN4—2B 46
Littlemoor St. DN4—2B 46
Lit. Norton Av. S8—2E 123
Lit. Norton Dri. S8—1E 123
Lit. Norton La. S8—1E 123
Lit. Norton Way. S8—2E 123
Littlewood Dri. S12—4C 112
Littlewood La. S12—4B 112
Littlewood Rd. S12—4C 112
Littlewood St. DN4—1B 46
Littlewood Way. S66—3H 83
Littleworth Clo. DN11—4F 63
Littleworth La. DN11—3F 63
Littleworth La. S71—3D 14
Littleworth M. DN11—3F 63
Litton Clo. S43—3A 134
Litton Clo. S72—2C 10
Litton Wlk. S70—5F 13
Litton Wlk. S72—2C 10
Liverpool Av. DN2—3F 33
Liverpool Pl. S9—4B 88

Liverpool St. S9—4B 88
Livesey St. S6—3B 86
Livingstone Av. DN2—6B 20
Livingstone Cres. S71—2B 14
Livingstone Rd. S9—5A 88
Livingstone Rd. S30—2C 64
Livingstone Ter. S70—1G 23
Lloyd St. S4—2H 87
Lloyd St. S62—4F 69
Loakfield Dri. S5—2D 74
Lobelia Ct. S31—3F 119
Lobelia Cres. DN3—4D 20
Lobwood. S70—4A 24
Lobwood La. S70—4B 24
Lockeaflash Cres. S70—2D 24
Locke Av. S70—2G 23
(Barnsley)
Locke Av. S70—3H 23
(Worsbrough)
Locke Rd. S75—3C 22
Lockesley Av. DN12—3C 58
Locke St. S70—2F 23
Lockhouse Rd. S9—2E 89
Locking Dri. DN3—4G 35
Lock La. S9—6G 77
Lockoford La. S41—5A to
(in two parts)   5B 132
Locksley Av. DN3—5D 20
Locksley Dri. S66—5A 94
Lock St. S6—5C 86
Lockton Clo. S30—5A 50
Lockton Way. DN12—2F 59
Lockwood Av. S31—4F 119
Lockwood Clo. S65—2A 80
Lockwood La. S63—2G 29
Lockwood La. S70—2H 23
Lockwood Rd. DN1—4E 33
Lockwood Rd. S63—4G 29
Lockwood Rd. S65—2A 80
Lodge Clo. S43—1G 139
Lodge Dri. S62—4H 51
Lodge Farm Clo. S31—1F 119
Lodge Farm M. S31—1F 119
Lodge Hill Dri. S31—5F 117
Lodge La. S6 & S10—2A 96
Lodge La. S31—1B 116
(Aston)
Lodge La. S31—4H 107
(Dinnington)
Lodge La. S61—4B 66
Lodge Moor Rd. S10—5A 96
Lodge Pl. S43—5A 134
Lodge, The. S11—2G 109
Lodge Wlk. S43—5A 134
Lodge Way. S60—2C 90
Logan Rd. S9—1F 101
Loicher La. S30—6G 65
Lomas Clo. S6—4C 84
Lomas Lea. S6—5B 84
Lombard Clo. S75—4G 13
Lombard Cres. S73—4C 26
London Rd. S2—4D 98 to 1E 111
London Way. S61—3A 66
Londside Way. S75—5C 12
Longacre Clo. S19—2G 125
Longacre Rd. S18—4E 129
Longacre Way. S19—1G 125
Long Balk. S75—2A 12
Longcar La. S70—1F 23
Long Causeway. S71—5C 14
Long Clo. DN4—5C 48
Longcroft Av. S18—1A 128
Longcroft Ct. S40—6H 137
Longcroft Cres. S18—1A 128
Longcroft Rd. S18—1A 128
Long Edge La. DN5—6G 17
Longfellow Dri. S65—4H 79
Longfellow Rd. DN4—5C 46

Longfield Dri. DN4—5B 48
Longfield Dri. S65—1H 81
Longfield Dri. S75—4F 7
Longfield Rd. DN3—4E 21
Longfield Rd. S10—6H 85
Longfields Cres. S74—5H 37
Long Fold. S63—5C 40
Longford Clo. S17—4G 121
Longford Cres. S17—4G 121
Longford Dri. S17—5F 121
Longford Rd. S17—5F 121
Longford Spinney. S17—5F 121
Long Henry Row. S2
—4H 5 & 2G 99
Longlands Av. S31—5G 117
Longlands Dri. S65—4E 71
Longlands Dri. S75—5F 7
Long Lands La. DN5—3A 16
Long La. DN5—5D 30
Long La. S6—2C 84
(Loxley)
Long La. S6—6D 84
(Stannington)
Long La. S10—2C 96
Long La. S30—2B 72
(Onesacre)
Long La. S30—4A 140
(Stocksbridge)
Long La. S30—6D 72
(Worrall)
Long La. S31—3C 126
Long La. S60—3F 91
Longley Av. W. S5—1C 86
Longley Clo. S5—1F 87
Longley Cres. S5—6F 75
Longley Dri. S5—1F 87
Longley Est. S5—6F 75
Longley Hall Gro. S5—1F 87
Longley Hall Rise. S5—6F 75
Longley Hall Rd. S5—1F 87
Longley Hall Way. S5—1G 87
Longley La. S5—1F 87
Longley St. S75—3A 12
Long Line. S11—5A 108
Longman Rd. S70—4G 13
Longodell Clo. S31—1F 107
Long Plantation. DN3—5E 21
Longridge Rd. S71—1D 14
Long Rd. S66—2H 105
Longshaw Clo. S43—3B 134
Longside Way. S75—5C 12
Longsight Rd. S75—4E 7
Long Steps. S2—2H 5
Longstone Cres. S12—3F 113
Longthwaite Clo. S31—1E 107
Longton Rd. DN3—3E 21
Long Wlk. S10—1G 97
Lonsdale Av. DN2
—6H 33 to 4B 34
Lonsdale Av. S71—1H 25
Lonsdale Clo. S31—1H 119
Lonsdale Ho. DN2—4A 34
Lonsdale Rd. S6—4A 86
Loosemore Dri. S12—2B 112
Lopham St. S3—5F & 6F 87
(in two parts)
Lorcher La. S30—6H 65
Lordens Hill. S31—4G 107
Lord Roberts Rd. S40—4A 138
Lord Row. S2—2G 99
Lord's Head La. DN4 & DN12
—6E 45
Lordsmill St. S41—3B 138
Lord St. S65—2G 79
Lord St. S71—5C 14
Loretta Cotts. S74—5H 37
Lorna Rd. S64—6E 43

Lorne Clo. S18—1B 128
Lorne Rd. S63—1D 28
Lothian Rd. DN2—4A 34
Louden Clo. S61—5D 66
Louden Rd. S61—5D 66
Lounde Clo. DN5—2E 45
Loundes Wood Av. S41—3E 131
Lound Rd. S9—2F 101
Lound Side. S30—1E 65
Loundsley Ct. S42—1B 136
Loundsley Grn. Rd. S40
—1D 136 to 5F 131
Lousy Busk La. S64—5C 42
Louth Rd. S11—6H 97
Love La. S3—1E 5 & 1E 99
Lovell St. S4—6H 87
Loversall Clo. DN4—6B 46
Love St. S3—1E 5 & 1E 99
Lovetot Av. S31—5B 104
Lovetot Rd. S61—5G 67
Lovetot St. S9—6A 88
 (in two parts)
Lowburn Rd. S13—6E 101
Low Cronkhill La. S71—3G 9
Lowedges Cres. S8—3D 122
Lowedges Dri. S8—3D 122
Lowedges Pl. S8—3E 123
Lowedges Rd. S8—4B 122
Lowe La. S75—6A 22
Lowell Av. DN4—5B 46
Lwr. Dolcliffe Rd. S64—6D 42
Lwr. Grove Rd. S40—2H 137
Lwr. Malton Rd. DN5—2G 31
Lwr. Thomas St. S70—1G 23
Lwr. York St. S73—6B 26
Lowfield Av. S12—6G 113
Lowfield Av. S61—4C 68
Lowfield Clo. DN3—1F 21
Lowfield Rd. DN2—2A 34
Lowfield Rd. S63—1B 42
Lowfields. S43—1E 135
Lowfield Wlk. DN12—1B 58
 (off Lime Tree Wlk.)
Low Fisher Ga. DN1—5D 32
Lowgate. DN5—2G 31
Lowgates. S43—1D 134
Low Grange Rd. S63—1E 29
Low Grange Sq. S63—1E 29
Lowgreave. S65—1A 80
Lowhouse Rd. S5—2A 76
Lowlands Clo. S71—2D 14
Low La. DN4—5A 48
Low La. S61—1A 78
Low La. S66—1E 95
Low Matlock La. S6—4D 84
Low Pavement. S40—2A 138
Low Rd. DN4—4A 46
Low Rd. DN12—2E 59
Low Rd. S6—5G 85
Low Rd. S30—2D 72
Low Rd. E. DN4—5F 45
 (in two parts)
Low Rd. W. DN4—6E 45
Low Row. S75—2C 6
Lowry Dri. S18—2D 128
Low St. DN11—6H 61
Low St. S75—3D 22
Lowther Rd. DN1—4E 33
Lowther Rd. S6—2B 86
Lowton Way. S66—4A 82
Low Valley Ind. Est. S73—5D 26
Low View. S75—2B 22
Loxley Av. S73—1E 39
Loxley Clo. S40—2D 136
Loxley Ct. S6—4H 85
Loxley Ct. S60—1F 91
Loxley New Rd. S6—4H 85
Loxley Rd. S6—1A 84 to 4H 85

Loxley Rd. S71—4F 15
Loxley View Rd. S10—6H 85
Loy Clo. S61—4A 68
Lucas Rd. S41—5G 131
Lucas St. S4—4G 87
Lucknow Ct. S7—1C 110
Ludgate Clo. DN11—6E 63
Ludham Clo. S41—4H 131
Ludham Gdns. S41—4H 131
Ludwell Hill. DN5—1H 43
Lugano Rd. S73—3C 26
Luke La. S6—2F 85
Lulworth Clo. S70—1B 24
Lumb La. S30—1A 72
Lumley Clo. S66—4H 83
Lumley Cres. S66—5H 83
Lumley Dri. S31—3C 106
Lumley Dri. S66—5H 83
Lumley St. S4—1H 99
Lumley St. S9—1B 100
Lump La. S30—6A 64
Lumsdale Rd. S43—3A 134
Luna Croft. S12—5B 112
Lunbreck Rd. DN4—6E 45
Lund Av. S71—4F 15
Lund Clo. S71—4F 15
Lund Cres. S71—4F 15
Lundhill Clo. S73—2G 39
Lundhill Gro. S73—2G 39
Lund Hill La. S71—1H 9
Lundhill Rd. S73—3G 39
Lund La. S71—4E 15
Lund Rd. S30—4D 72
Lundwood Clo. S19—5C 114
Lundwood Dri. S19—5C 114
Lundwood Gro. S19—5C 114
Lundwood Ho. DN1—1C 46
 (off Bond Clo.)
Lundy Rd. S18—3F 129
Lunn Rd. S72—1H 15
Lupin Way. S44—2G 139
Lupton Cres. S8—3D 122
Lupton Dri. S8—3D 122
Lupton Rd. S8—3D 122
Lupton Wlk. S8—3E 123
Luterel Dri. S31—5B 104
Lutterworth Dri. DN6—1C 16
Lych Gate Clo. DN4—4E 49
Lydden Clo. S43—3E 133
Lydford Av. S41—2B 132
Lydgate Hall Cres. S10—2G 97
Lydgate La. S10—2G 97
Lyme St. S60—3C 78
Lyminster Av. S6—4A 74
Lymister Av. S60—1H 89
Lyncroft Clo. S60—3D 90
Lyndale Av. DN3—6C 20
Lyndhurst Clo. S11—1A 110
Lyndhurst Cres. DN3—4C 20
Lyndhurst Rd. S11—1A 110
Lyndon Av. DN6—2C 16
Lynmouth Rd. S7—2C 110
Lynn Pl. S9—3D 88
Lynton Av. S60—6G 79
Lynton Dri. DN3—5C 20
Lynton Pl. S75—5B 6
Lynton Rd. S11—5B 98
Lynwood Clo. S18—2B 128
Lynwood Dri. S71—4E 9
Lyons Clo. S4—4G 87
Lyons Rd. S4—4G 87
Lyons St. S4—4G 87
Lytham Av. S31—6F 107
Lytham Av. S71—1D 14
Lytham Clo. DN4—5F 49
Lytton Av. S5—4C 74
Lytton Clo. DN4—5B 46
Lytton Cres. S5—4C 74

Lytton Dri. S5—4C 74
Lytton Rd. S5—4C 74

Mabel St. S60—4F 79
Macaulay Cres. DN3—3G 35
McConnel Cres. DN11—4B 62
McCulloch Cres. DN11—4B 62
Machin Ct. S18—1E 129
Machin Dri. S62—5D 54
Machin La. S30—3A 140
Machon Bank. S7—1C 110
Machon Bank Rd. S7—1B 110
McIntyre Rd. S30—3D 140
Mackenzie Cres. S10—3C 98
Mackenzie Cres. S30—3C 64
Mackenzie St. S11—5C 98
Mackey Cres. S72—2E 11
Mackey La. S72—2E 11
McLaren Cres. S66—5G 83
McMahon Av. S43—5H 133
McManus Av. S62—5F 55
Macnaughton Rd. S75—6D 36
Macro Rd. S73—1G 39
Madam La. DN3—1G 21
Madehurst Gdns. S2—6F 99
Madehurst Rise. S2—6F 99
Madehurst Rd. S2—6F 99
Madehurst View. S2—6F 99
Madin Dri. S43—5H 133
Madingley Clo. DN4—6A 46
Madin St. S41—1A 138
Mafeking Pl. S30—1E 65
Magellan Rd. S66—3E 83
Magna Clo. S66—3F 81
Magna Cres. S66—3E 81
Magna La. S65—6B 70
Magnolia Clo. DN3—4D 20
Magnolia Clo. S31—4F 119
Magnolia Clo. S72—3D 10
Magnolia Ct. S10—5E 97
Magpie Gro. S2—3A 100
Mahon Av. S62—1F 69
Maidstone Rd. S6—5B 74
Main Av. DN12—2B 60
Main Av. S17—5E 121
Main Rd. S9—6E 89 to 1F 101
Main Rd. S12—6G 113
Main Rd. S31—6A 124
Main Rd. S42—4A 130
Main St. DN3—2F 49
Main St. DN5—3D 44
Main St. DN11—6H 61
Main St. S12—3B 114
Main St. S30—6A 64
Main St. S31—2F 119
 (Anston)
Main St. S31—4A 104
 (Aughton)
Main St. S31—6A 104
 (Swallownest)
Main St. S31—1C 104
 (Ulley)
Main St. S60—6D 90
 (Catcliffe)
Main St. S60—3C 78
 (Rotherham)
Main St. S61—3C 68
Main St. S62—1G 69
 (Rawmarsh)
Main St. S62—4D 52
 (Wentworth)
Main St. S63—4G 29
Main St. S64—6D 42
Main St. S65—4H 71
Main St. S66—4H 81
Main St. S73—6A 26
Majuba St. S6—5B 86
Makin St. S64—1G 57

Malcolm Clo. S70—1D 24
Malham Clo. S40—6F 131
Malham Clo. S72—2C 10
Malham Ct. S70—5F 13
 (off Summer St.)
Malham Pl. S30—1D 64
Malia Rd. S41—5C 132
Malinda St. S3—6D 86
Malin Rd. S6—4G 85
Malin Rd. S65—1B 80
Malkin St. S41—2B 138
Mallard Av. DN3—1E 21
Mallard Clo. S61—1C 66
Mallard Ct. S43—1D 134
Mallard Dri. S31—2H 125
Mallin Dri. DN12—5B 60
Mallory Av. S62—1E 69
Mallory Dri. S64—5H 43
Mallory Rd. S65—1A 80
Mallory Way. S72—6C 10
Malson Way. S41—5H 131
Maltas Ct. S70—4C 24
Maltby Ho. DN1—1C 46
 (off Burden Clo.)
Maltby St. S9—4C 88
Malthouse Cotts. S31—6D 118
Malthouse La. S71—6H 13
Malting La. S4—1H 5 & 1G 99
Maltings, The. S60—4D 78
Maltkiln St. S60—4D 78
Malton Dri. S31—6C 104
Malton Pl. S71—6A 8
Malton Rd. DN2—4H 33
Malton Rd. DN5—2F 31
Malton St. S4—4G 87
Malton Wlk. S40—6H 137
Maltravers Clo. S2—3A 100
Maltravers Cres. S2—2H 99
Maltravers Pl. S2—2A 100
Maltravers Rd. S2—1H 99
Maltravers St. S4—1H 5 & 1G 99
Maltravers Ter. S2—3A 100
 (in two parts)
Maltravers Way. S2—2A 100
Malvern Av. DN5—4G 31
Malvern Clo. S75—5D 12
Malvern Rd. DN2—5A 34
Malvern Rd. S9—6D 88
Malvern Rd. S40—1G 137
Malwood Way. S66—3H 83
Manchester Rd. S10 & S6
—2A 96
Manchester Rd. S30—1B 140
Mandale St. DN3—1H 21
Mandeville St. S9—6E 89
Manell Ter. S3—6D 86
Mangham Rd. S61 & S62—6D 68
Mangham Way. S61—6D 68
Manifold Av. S43—3B 134
Manknell Rd. S41—3A 132
Mannering Rd. DN4—5G 45
Manners St. S3—5D 86
Manning St. DN1—6D 32
Manor App. S61—2H 77
Manor Av. S43—4F 133
Manor Av. S63—4G 29
Manor Clo. DN3—2G 21
Manor Clo. S31—2B 118
Manor Clo. S62—5C 54
Manor Clo. S63—4B 40
Manor Clo. S66—4F 83
Manor Ct. DN12—2B 58
Manor Ct. S71—2C 8
Manor Cres. S18—2D 128
Manor Cres. S40—2F 137
Manor Cres. S60—3B 90
Manor Cres. S72—5G 11
Manor Dri. DN2—6F 33

Manor Dri. S31—2B 118
Manor Dri. S40—2F 137
Manor Dri. S43—4F 133
Manor Dri. S60—2A 92
Manor Dri. S71—2D 8
Manor End. S70—4H 23
Manor Est. DN5—3H 17
Manor Farm Clo. DN6—1D 16
Manor Farm Clo. S31—3B 104
Manor Farm Clo. S71—5F 9
Manor Farm Ct. S65—3D 70
Manor Farm Dri. S64—3A 56
Manor Farm Gdns. S31—3F 119
Manor Fields. S61—1G 77
Manor Gdns. DN5—2D 44
Manor Gdns. S71—1H 25
Manor Gro. S71—2D 8
Manor Gro. S72—5F 11
Manor Ho. S6—5C 84
Manor Ho. Clo. S73—5A 38
Manor Ho. Rd. S61—1G 77
Manor Laith Rd. S2—3H 99
Manor La. S2—2B to 4A 100
Manor La. S31—2G 107
Manor La. S64—3E 43
Manor Oaks Clo. S2—2A 100
Manor Oaks Pl. S2—3A 100
Manor Oaks Rd. S2
        —2G 99 to 3B 100
Manor Occupation Rd. S71
        —1D 8
Manor Pk. Av. S2—4B 100
Manor Pk. Centre. S2—3B 100
Manor Pk. Clo. S2—4B 100
Manor Pk. Ct. S2—4B 100
Manor Pk. Cres. S2—4B 100
Manor Pk. Dri. S2—4B 100
Manor Pk. Pl. S2—3B 100
Manor Pk. Rise. S2—4B 100
Manor Pk. Rd. S2—3B 100
Manor Pk. Way. S2—4B 100
Manor Pl. S62—2G 69
Manor Pl. S74—5B 38
Manor Rd. DN3—1G 21
Manor Rd. DN5—2G 43
(Harlington)
Manor Rd. DN5—3A 18
(Toll Bar)
Manor Rd. S31—2F 107
(Dinnington)
Manor Rd. S31—4B 126
(Killamarsh)
Manor Rd. S31—6C 118
(Kiveton Park Station)
Manor Rd. S31—5F 117
(Wales)
Manor Rd. S42—2F & 2E 137
(in two parts)
Manor Rd. S43
        —4F 133 to 1F 139
Manor Rd. S60—3B 90
Manor Rd. S61—3G 77
Manor Rd. S63—4A 40
(Brampton Bierlow)
Manor Rd. S63—1E 29
(Thurnscoe)
Manor Rd. S64—3B 56
Manor Rd. S66—4G 83
Manor Rd. S72—1G 15
Manor Sq. S63—1E 29
Manor St. S71—5F 9
Manor View. S19—2E 125
Manor View. S72—3C 10
Manor Wlk. DN11—6H 61
Manor Way. S2—1A 100
Manor Way. S31—2B 118
Manor Way. S74—5A 38
Manse Clo. DN4—3E 49

Mansel Av. S5—3C 74
Mansel Ct. S5—3C 74
Mansel Cres. S5—3C 74
Mansel Rd. S5—3C 74
Mansfeldt Cres. S41—5G 131
Mansfeldt Rd. S41—5G 131
Mansfield Clo. DN3—2D 34
Mansfield Dri. S12—1D 112
Mansfield Rd. DN4—2B 46
Mansfield Rd. S12—1C 112
Mansfield Rd. S31—2D 126
(Killamarsh)
Mansfield Rd. S31—6D 116
(Kiveton Park)
Mansfield Rd. S31—6A 104 to
(Swallownest & Aston)2C 116
Mansfield Rd. S41—6D 138
Mansfield Rd. S60—3E 79
Mansfield Rd. S71—5B 8
Manton Ho. DN1—1C 46
(off St James St.)
Manton St. S2—4F 99
Manvers Clo. S31—6E 107
(Anston)
Manvers Clo. S31—6B 104
(Swallownest)
Manvers Rd. S6—4A 86
Manvers Rd. S19—3F 115
Manvers Rd. S31—6A 104
Manvers Rd. S44—1G 139
Manvers Rd. S64—6C 42
Maori Av. S63—1G 41
Maple Av. DN4—3D 48
Maple Av. S66—4D 82
Maplebeck Dri. S9—1H 89
Maplebeck Rd. S9—1H 89
Maple Clo. S70—2P 24
Maple Croft Cres. S9—6B 76
Maple Croft Rd. S9—6B 76
Maple Dri. S31—4A 126
Maple Dri. S66—3F 81
Maple Gro. DN3—2F 35
Maple Gro. S9—2G 101
Maple Gro. S30—4D 140
Maple Gro. S31—5D 104
Maple Leaf Ct. S64—6D 42
Maple Pl. S30—3E 65
Maple Rd. S31—4G 117
Maple Rd. S64—6D 42
Maple Rd. S75—4E 7
(Mapplewell)
Maple Rd. S75—2B 50
(Tankersley)
Maple St. S43—3H 133
Mapperley Rd. S18—2A 128
Mappin's Rd. S60—6C 90
Mappin St. S1—3B 4 & 2D 98
Mapplebeck Rd. S30—6C 50
Maran Av. S73—4G 27
Marcham Dri. S19—3G 115
March Bank. S65—4E 71
March Flatts Rd. S65—5E 71
March Ga. DN12—4E 59
March St. DN12—3E 59
March St. S9—4D 88
March Vale Rise. DN12—4E 59
Marchwood Av. S6—5E 85
Marchwood Clo. S40—1G 137
Marchwood Dri. S6—4E 85
Marchwood Rd. S6—5E 85
Marcliff Clo. S66—5D 80
Marcliff Cres. S66—5D 80
Marcliff La. S66—5D 80
Marcus Dri. S3—6F 87
Mardale Clo. S41—2G 131
Mardale Wlk. DN2—3A 34
Marden Rd. S7—1C 110

Margaret Clo. S31—1B 116
Margaret Clo. S73—4D 26
Margaret Rd. S73—4D 26
(Darfield)
Margaret Rd. S73—1G 39
(Wombwell)
Margaret St. S1—4E 99
Margaret St. S66—6H 83
Margate Dri. S4—3H 87
Margate St. S4—3A 88
Margate St. S72—6G 11
Margerison St. S8—6E 99
Margetson Cres. S5—3D 74
Margetson Dri. S5—3D 74
Margetson Rd. S5—3D 74
Marian Rd. DN3—4C 20
Marigold Clo. S5—6A 76
Marina Rise. S73—4C 26
Marion Rd. S6—1H 85
Markbrook Dri. S30—5A 50
Market Hill. S70—6G 13
Market Pde. S70—6H 13
Market Pl. DN1—6D 32
Market Pl. S1—2F 5 & 1F 99
Market Pl. S30—2F 65
Market Pl. S40—2A 138
Market Pl. S60—3D 78
Market Pl. S72—6B 10
Market Pl. S73—1G 39
Market Pl. S74—6C 38
Market Rd. DN1—5D 32
Market Sq. S13—1C 114
Market Sq. S63—4G 29
Market St. DN6—5D 16
Market St. S9—1E 89
Market St. S13—1C 114
Market St. S30—2F 65
Market St. S31—6D 124
Market St. S43—1C 134
Market St. S60—3D 78
Market St. S63—4G 29
(Goldthorpe)
Market St. S63—1E 29
(Thurnscoe)
Market St. S64—1E & 1F 57
(in two parts, Mexborough)
Market St. S64—2C 56
(Swinton)
Market St. S70—6G 13
Market St. S72—6B 10
Market St. S74—4A 38
Markfield Dri. S66—3F 81
Mark Gro. S66—4F 81
Markham Av. DN3—2E 35
Markham Av. DN12—3C 58
Markham Ct. S44—6E 135
Markham Cres. S43—1D 134
Markham Ho. DN1—1C 46
(off Burden Clo.)
Markham La. S43 & S44
(in two parts)   —4F 135
Markham Rd. DN12—3B 60
Markham Rd. S40—3H 137
Markham Rd. S44—6E 135
Markham Sq. DN12—3C 60
Markham Ter. DN12—3B 60
Mark La. S10—1A 108
Mark St. S70—6G 13
Marlborough Av. DN5—5H 31
Marlborough Clo. S31—6D 106
Marlborough Clo. S63—1E 29
Marlborough Rise. S31—1C 116
Marlborough Rd. DN2—5F 33
Marlborough Rd. S10—2A 98
Marlborough Ter. S70—1G 23
Marlcliffe Rd. S6—1G 85
Marlfield Croft. S30—1F 75

Marlow Clo. DN2—4A 34
Marlowe Dri. S65—4H 79
Marlowe Rd. DN3—1H 21
Marlowe Rd. S65—4H 79
Marlow Rd. DN2—4A 34
Marmion Rd. S11—6H 97
Marples Clo. S8—6D 98
Marples Dri. S8—6D 98
Marquis Gdns. DN3—2H 21
Marr Grange La. DN5—2A 30
Marrick Ct. S30—2D 64
Marrion Rd. S62—1G 69
Marriott La. S7—4B 110
Marriott Pl. S62—6D 54
Marriott Rd. S7—4B 110
Marriott Rd. S64—1C 56
Marrison Dri. S31—3A 126
Marr Ter. S10—4F 97
Marsala Wlk. S73—3D 26
Marsden Ind. Est. S13—3H 101
Marsden La. S3—2B 4 & 1D 98
Marsden Pl. S40—1A 138
(Newbold Rd.)
Marsden Pl. S40—3F 137
(Old Rd.)
Marsden Rd. S30—3E 141
Marsden St. S40—2A 138
Marshall Av. DN4—4A 46
Marshall Clo. S62—4F 69
Marshall Gro. S63—6F 41
Marshall Hall. S10—4B 98
Marshall Rd. S8—5C 110
Marsh Av. S18—6F 123
Marsh Clo. S19—3C 124
Marshfield. S70—2D 36
Marshfield Gro. S43—1E 135
Marsh Ga. DN5—5B 32
Marsh Hill. S66—1C 83
Marsh Ho. Rd. S11—2F 109
Marsh La. DN3—1A 20
Marsh La. DN5—4D & 3C 18
(in two parts)
Marsh La. S10—2F 97
Marsh Rd. DN5—4B 32
Marsh St. S30—3F 141
Marsh St. S60—4C 78
Marsh St. S73—2D 26
Marsh View. S31—6G 125
Marson Av. DN6—2B 16
Marston Clo. S18—3B 128
Marston Cres. S71—5B 8
Marstone Cres. S17—4E 121
Marston Rd. S10—1H 97
Martin Clo. S31—5A 104
Martin Ct. S31—6C 124
Martin Cres. S5—3F 75
Martindale Ter. S30—2E 65
(off Greenland Gdns.)
Martin La. S74—2H 37
Martin Rise. S31—6C 124
Martin Rise. S61—1C 66
Martin's Rd. S71—4E 15
Martin Well's Rd. DN12—4C 60
Marton Rd. DN5—2H 17
Marvell Rd. DN5—3F 31
Mary Ann Clo. S71—5D 14
Mary La. S73—4F 27
Mary's Pl. S75—1C 83
Mary's Rd. S73—4F 27
Mary St. S1—4E 99
Mary St. S31—6D 124
Mary St. S60—2C 78
Mary St. S72—2A 28
Mary St. S75—3A 12
Masbrough St. S60—3B 78
(in two parts)
Masefield Clo. S31—5G 107
Masefield Rd. DN2—2A 34

Masefield Rd. S13—6E 101
Masefield Rd. S63—4C 40
Masham Rd. DN4—4C 48
Mason Av. S31—4B 104
Mason Cres. S13—6F 101
Mason Dri. S31—4B 104
Mason Gro. S13—6F 101
Mason Lathe Rd. S5—4A 76
Mason St. S63—4G 29
Masons Way. S70—2C 24
Massey Rd. S13—2D 114
Masson Clo. S40—6F 131
Mastall La. DN5—5F 19
Masters Cres. S5—4F 75
Masters Rd. S5—4F 75
Mather Av. S9—2D 100
Mather Cres. S9—2D 100
Mather Dri. S9—2D 100
Mather Rd. S9—2D 100
Mather Wlk. S9—2D 100
Matilda La. S1—6F 5 & 3F 99
Matilda St. S1—5D 4 & 3E 99
  (in two parts)
Matilda Way. S1—5E 5 & 3E 99
Matlock Dri. S43—6A 134
Matlock Rd. S6—6A 86
Matlock Rd. S42 & S40—6D 136
Matlock Rd. S71—1B 14
Mattersey Clo. DN4—6C 48
Matthews Dri. S66—6F 81
Matthews La. S8—6G 111
Matthew St. S3—6D 86
Mauds Ter. S71—2C 14
Maugerhay. S8—6G 111
Mauncer Cres. S13—6B 102
Mauncer Dri. S13—6B 102
Mauncer La. S13—1B 114
Maun Way. S5—6G 75
Maurice St. S62—4F 69
Mawfa Av. S14—5H 111
Mawfa Cres. S14—5H 111
Mawfa Dri. S14—5H 111
Mawfa La. S14—4H & 5H 111
  (in two parts)
Mawfa Rd. S14—6H 111
Mawfa Wlk. S14—5H 111
Mawfield Rd. S75—3B 12
Maxey Pl. S8—1E 111
Maxfield Av. S10—2A 98
Maxwell St. S4—5G 87
Maxwell Way. S4—5G 87
May Av. DN4—5H 45
May Av. S41—1C 132
Maycock Av. S61—5F 67
May Day Grn. S70—6H 13
May Day Grn. Arc. S70—6H 13
Mayfield. S71—3B 14
Mayfield Cres. DN11—5D 62
Mayfield Cres. S70—3G 23
Mayfield Rd. DN5—4A 32
Mayfield Rd. S10
  —6A 96 to 1B 108
Mayfield Rd. S40—3E 137
Mayfields. S5—6F 17
Mayflower Cres. DN4—6E 45
Mayflower Rd. DN4—6E 45
Maynard Rd. S40—4H 137
Maynard Rd. S60—1A 92
May Rd. S6—3H 85
May Ter. S70—6E 13
Maythorn Clo. S75—5G 7
May Tree Clo. S19—6E 115
May Tree Croft. S19—6E 115
May Tree La. S19—6E 115
Meaburn Clo. DN4—4D 48
Meadowland Rise. S72—3H 15
Meadow Av. S62—6D 54

Meadow Bank Av. S7—6B 98
Meadow Bank Ind. Est. S61
  —4H 77
Meadow Bank Rd. S11—6B 98
Meadow Bank Rd. S61—4F 77
Meadow Clo. S18—5G 123
Meadow Clo. S31—4A 118
Meadow Clo. S43—1D 132
Meadow Clo. S65—6C 70
Meadow Cres. S19—2B 124
Meadow Cres. S71—1F 9
Meadow Cres. S72—6F 11
Meadow Croft. DN3—5E 21
Meadow Croft. S64—5A 56
Meadow Croft. S72—2C 10
Meadowcroft Clo. S60—3H 91
Meadowcroft Gdns. S19
  —1E 125
Meadowcroft Glade. S19
  —1E 125
Meadowcroft Rise. S19—1E 125
Meadow Dri. S30—2C 64
Meadow Dri. S64—3A 56
Meadow Dri. S71—3D 14
Meadow Dri. S73—4F 27
Meadow Field Rd. DN3—1E 21
Meadow Ga. Av. S19—5H 115
Meadow Ga. Clo. S19—5H 115
Meadow Gro. S17—5E 121
Meadow Gro. Rd. S17—5D 120
Meadowhall Dri. S9—2D 88
Meadow Hall Rd. S9—1D 88
Meadowhall Rd. S61—4F 77
Meadowhall Shopping Mall. S9
  —1E 89
Meadowhall Way. S9—1D 88 to
  6E 77
Meadowhead. S8—6D 110
Meadow Head Av. S8—2C 122
Meadow Head Clo. S8—2C 122
Meadow Head Dri. S8—1D 122
Meadowhill Rd. S41—5D 138
Meadow Ho. Dri. S10—4D 96
Meadowland Rise. S72—2H 15
Meadow La. DN12—2E 57
Meadow La. S62—5D 54
Meadow La. S66—5G 83
Meadow La. S75—6C 6
Meadow Rise. DN3—1E 21
Meadow Rise. DN11—6H 61
Meadow Rise. S42—1B 136
Meadow Rd. S71—2F 9
Meadow Spur. S65—6D 70
Meadows, The. S31—2A 118
Meadows, The. S42—6C 130
Meadow St. S3—1B 4 & 6D 86
Meadow St. S31—3C 106
  (in two parts)
Meadow St. S61—3A 78
Meadow St. S71—5H 13
Meadow Ter. S11—5A 98
Meadow View. S40—5C 136
Meadow View. S70—4A 24
Meadow View Clo. S74—6H 37
Meadow View Rd. S8—1D 122
Meadow View Rd. S62—5B 56
Meadow Wlk. DN3—4E 21
Meadow Way. S64—2D 56
Meadstead Dri. S71—2D 8
Meads, The. S8—1F 123
Mead, The. S41—5C 138
Meadway Dri. S17—2C 120
Meadway, The. S17—2C 120
Meakin St. S41—5D 138
Mede, The. DN6—2B 16
Medley View. DN12—4F 59
Medlock Clo. S13—4A 102
Medlock Clo. S42—6D 136

Medlock Cres. S13—3A 102
Medlock Croft. S13—3A 102
Medlock Dri. S13—4A 102
Medlock Rd. S13—4A 102
Medlock Rd. S40—5E 137
Medlock Way. S13—3A 102
Medway Pl. S73—2H 39
Meersbrook Av. S8—2D 110
Meersbrook Pk. Rd. S8—1E 111
Meersbrook Rd. S8—2F 111
Meetinghouse Croft. S13
  —1C 114
Meetinghouse La. S1
  —2F 5 & 1F 99
Meetinghouse La. S13—1C 114
Mekyll Clo. S66—3F 81
Melbeck Ct. S30—2C 64
Melbourne Av. S10—3A 98
Melbourne Av. S18—2A 128
Melbourne Av. S31—5C 104
Melbourne Av. S63—1H 41
Melbourne Rd. DN4—5G 45
Melbourne Rd. S30—3C 140
Melbourn Rd. S10—1A 98
Melciss Rd. S66—5E 81
Meld Clo. DN11—6D 62
Melford Clo. S75—4F 7
Melford Dri. DN4—1G 61
Melfort Glen. S10—2F 97
Mell Av. S74—5A 38
Melling Av. DN5—6H 31
Melling Clo. S40—5H 137
Mellington Clo. S8—5G 111
Mellor La. S18—2A 130
Mellor Rd. S73—1F 39
Mellor Way. S40—6A 138
Mellow Fields Rd. S31—1D 106
Mellwood Gro. S73—3E 39
Melrose Clo. DN4—4G 45
Melrose Clo. S40—2E 137
Melrose Clo. S66—5H 93
Melrose Gro. S60—1G 91
Melrose Rd. S3—4F 87
Melrose Way. S71—5D 14
Meltham La. S41—5B 132
Melton Av. S63—4G 29
Melton Av. S73—3B 40
Melton Ct. DN12—1B 58
Meltonfield Clo. DN3—4G 35
Melton Gdns. DN5—2D 44
Melton Grn. S63—5C 40
Melton Gro. S19—5A 114
Melton High St. S63—5C 40
Melton Rd. DN5—2A 44 to 6H 31
Melton St. S64—1G 57
Melton St. S73—3B 40
Melton Ter. S70—4C 24
Melton Wood Gro. DN5—2C 44
Melville Av. DN4—4A 46
Melville Cres. S43—1F 139
Melville St. S73—6B 26
Melvinia Cres. S75—3F 13
Melwood Ct. DN3—5G 35
Memesia Clo. S31—3E 119
Memoir Gro. DN11—6C 62
Mendip Clo. DN5—4G 31
Mendip Clo. S75—5D 12
Mendip Cres. S40—1D 136
Mendip Rise. S60—4D 90
Merbeck Dri. S30—4B 50
Merbeck Gro. S30—5C 50
Mercaston Clo. S40—6C 130
Mercel Av. DN3—1G 35
Mercia Dri. S17—3E 121
Meredith Cres. DN4—5B 46
Meredith Rd. S6—3H 85
Mere Gro. DN3—2E 35
Mere La. DN3—6E 21 to 2E 35

Merlin Clo. S70—3D 36
Merlin Way. S5—6G 75
Merlin Way. S61—1C 66
Merrick Clo. S40—6F 131
Merrill Rd. S63—1E 29
Merton La. S9—5D 76
Merton Rise. S9—5D 76
Merton Rd. S9—5C 76
Metcalfe Av. S31—3A 126
Methley Clo. S12—1B 112
Methley Ho. DN1—1C 46
  (off Grove Pl.)
Methley St. S72—1H 15
Metro Trading Centre. S75
  —2A 12
Mews Ct. S19—5A 114
Mews Ct. S63—2A 42
Mexborough Rd. S63—2B 42
Meynell Clo. S40—3E 137
Meynell Cres. S5—5B 74
Meynell Rd. S5—5B 74
Meynell Way. S31—3A 126
Meyrick Dri. S75—6B 6
Michael Croft. S63—5D 40
Michael Rd. S71—5E 15
Michael's Est. S72—6G 14
Micklebring Gro. DN12—5C 58
Micklebring Way. S66—2B 82
Mickleden Way. S75—6C 12
Mickley La. S17 & S18—5E 121
Middcliff Ct. S19—6E 115
Middle Av. S62—2F 69
Middle Bank. DN4—3E 47
Middleburn Clo. S70—2A 24
Middlecliff Clo. S19—6E 115
Middlecliff Cotts. S72—2A 28
Middlecliff Ct. S19—6E 115
Middlecliff La. S72
  —1G 27 to 2A 28
Middlecliff Rise. S19—6E 115
Middle Clo. S75—4A 6
Middlecroft Rd. S43—4A 134
Middle Dri. S60—2F 91
Middlefield Clo. S17—2C 120
Middlefield Croft. S17—2C 120
Middlefield Rd. DN4—4B 48
Middlefield Rd. S60—1G 91
Middlefields Dri. S60—2A 92
Middlegate. DN5—5G 17
  (in two parts)
Middleham Rd. DN4—4C 48
Middle Hay Clo. S14—2A 112
Middle Hay Pl. S14—3A 112
Middle Hay Rise. S14—3A 112
Middle Hay View. S14—3A 112
Middle La. S6—5G 85
Middle La. S30—1H 73
Middle La. S65—2F 79
Middle La. S. S65—3G 79
Middle Pavement. S40—2A 138
  (off Low Pavement)
Middle Pl. S65—2H 79
Middlesex St. S70—1H 23
Middleton Av. S31—5E 107
Middleton Dri. S43—6H 133
Middleton La. S30—1B 74
Middleton Rd. S65—3F 79
Middlewood Rd. S6
  —5G 73 to 3A 86
Middlewood Rd. N. S30—4F 73
Midfield Rd. S10—1G 97
Midhill Rd. S2—6F 99
Midhope Way. S75—6C 12
Midhurst Gro. S75—2A 12
Midhurst Rd. S6—3H 73
Midland Rd. S61—3A 78
Midland Rd. S64—2C 56
Midland Rd. S71—1E 9

Midland St. S1—4E 99
Midland St. S70—6H 13
Midland Ter. S41—6B 138
Milano Rise. S73—4D 26
Milbanke St. DN1—5D 32
Milburn Ct. S19—6G 115
Milburn Gro. S19—6G 115
Milden Pl. S70—2A 24
Milden Rd. S6—1G 85
Milefield View. S72—6F 11
Mile Oak Rd. S60—6G 79
Miles Clo. S5—2E 87
Miles Rd. S5—2D 86
Miles Rd. S30—6C 50
Mile Thorn La. DN1—4D 32
Milford Av. S74—5D 38
Milford Rd. S43—6A 134
Milford St. S9—3D 88
Milgate St. S71—1F 9
Milgrove Cres. S30—5B 50
Milking La. S73—4A 40
Millais Rise. S66—2F 81
Millard La. S66—4G 83
Millbank Clo. S30—1B 64
Mill Clo. S31—5F 95
(Brookhouse, Laughton)
Mill Clo. S31—3B 118
(Todwick)
Millcross La. S18—1A 130
Milldale Clo. S40—6E 131
Milldale Rd. S17—4F 121
Milldyke Clo. S60—2B 92
Miller Croft. S13—1A 114
Miller Dale Dri. S60—4D 90
Miller Rd. S7—6D 98
Miller St. S30—3H 141
Millfield Ct. DN3—1E 21
Millfield Ind. Est. DN5—6C 18
Millfield Rd. DN5—1C 32
Mill Fields. S31—3A 118
Mill Ga. DN5—1B 32
Mill Grn. S43—1C 134
Mill Hill. S60—2A 92
Mill Hill. S73—5H 25
Millhill Clo. DN3—5G 35
Mill Hills. S31—2B 118
Millhouses Ct. S11—3H 109
Millhouses Glen. S11—3H 109
Millhouses La. S11 & S7
—2H 109
Millhouses St. S74—6A 38
Millicent Sq. S66—5G 83
Millindale. S66—4G 83
Mill La. DN3—3G 49
Mill La. DN4—3D 44
Mill La. DN5—2G 43
Mill La. DN6—1D 16
Mill La. S3—1F 5 & 1B 98
Mill La. S17—4F 121
Mill La. S18—2F 129
Mill La. S30—3H 141
Mill La. S31—2F 119
Mill La. S40—3F 137
Mill La. S60—1D 102
Mill La. S62—4B 52
Mill La. S63—6C 40
Mill La. S75—4C 6
Mill Meadow Clo. S19—6H 115
Mill Meadow Gdns. S19
—6H 115
Millmoor La. S60—3C 78
Millmoor Rd. DN4—3C 48
Millmoor Rd. S73—5D 26
Millmount Rd. S8—2D 110
Millmount Rd. S74—6B 38
Mill Rd. S30—6F 65
Mill Rd. S31—5D 124
Mill Rd. S60—1D 102

Millsands. S3—1F 5 & 1F 99
Millside. S72—2C 10
Millside Wlk. S72—2C 10
Millstone Clo. S18—1B 128
Millstone Dri. S31—5B 104
Mill Stream Clo. S40—4E 137
Mill St. DN3—3F 35
Mill St. S41—2B 138
Mill St. S60—4D 78
Mill St. S61—3B 68
Mill St. S71—6B 14
Millthorpe Rd. S5—5H 75
Mill View. S63—2H 41
Mill Wlk. S3—1F 5 & 1F 99
Millwood Rd. DN4—6H 45
Millwood View. S6—4C 84
Milner Clo. S66—3H 81
Milner Ga. DN12—2G 59
Milner Ga. La. DN12—3F 59
Milner Rd. DN4—4H 45
Milnes St. S70—1A 24
Milne St. S75—3A 12
Milnrow Cres. S5—3D 74
Milnrow Dri. S5—3D 74
Milnrow Rd. S5—3D 74
Milnrow View. S5—3D 74
Milton Av. DN5—5H 31
Milton Clo. S63—3C 40
Milton Clo. S74—4B 38
Milton Ct. DN1—1C 46
Milton Ct. S64—2A 56
Milton Cres. S40—5A 138
Milton Cres. S74—6A 38
Milton Gdns. DN3—3F 35
Milton Gro. DN3—5D 20
Milton Gro. S73—1G 39
Milton La. S3—6C 4 & 3D 98
Milton Pl. S43—1D 134
Milton Rd. S7—6D 98
Milton Rd. S30—2B 64
Milton Rd. S31—5G 107
Milton Rd. S63—3H 29
Milton Rd. S64—6E 43
Milton Rd. S65—1F 79
Milton Rd. S74—6A 38 to 1A 52
Milton St. S1 & S3—6B 4 & 3D 98
Milton St. S60—1D 78
Milton St. S64—2A 56
Milton St. S66—5F 83
Milton Wlk. DN1—1C 46
Minimum Ter. S40—3G 137
Minna Rd. S3—4F 87
Minneymoor Hill. DN12—2F 59
Minneymoor La. DN12—3F 59
Minster Clo. DN4—4E 49
Minster Clo. S30—1G 75
Minster Rd. S30—1F 75
Minster Way. S71—4D 14
Minto Rd. S6—3H 85
Miriam Av. S40—5C 136
Mission Field. S73—3A 40
Mitchell Clo. S70—4D 24
Mitchell Rd. S8—5D 110
Mitchell Rd. S73—4A 26
Mitchell St. S3—2A 4 & 1C 98
Mitchell St. S70—4E 25
Mitchelson Av. S75—2A 22
Moat Hill Ct. DN5—6B 18
Moat La. S66—2G 93
Modena Ct. S73—3C 26
Moffat Gdns. DN2—6B 20
Moffatt Rd. S2—6F 99
Molineaux Clo. S5—5H 75
Molineaux Rd. S5—3G 75
Molineux Av. S43—2B 134
Molloy Pl. S8—1E 111
Molloy St. S8—1E 111
Mona Rd. S10—1A 98

Mona Rd. DN4—3B 46
Mona Rd. S10—6A 86
Mona St. S75—5F 13
Monckton Rd. S5—6B 76
Moncrieffe Rd. S7—1C 106
Monk's Bri. Rd. S31—3C 106
Monks Clo. S61—5E 67
Monkspring. S70—4C 24
Monks Way. S71—4D 14
Monk Ter. S71—2E 15
Monkwood Rd. S41—3F 131
Monkwood Rd. S62—6D 54
Monmouth Rd. DN2—3G 33
Monmouth St. S3—5A 4 & 3C 98
Monsal Cres. S43—5H 133
Monsal Cres. S71—6C 8
Monsal St. S63—1E 29
Montague Av. DN12—3C 58
Montague St. DN1—5D 32
Montague St. S6—4B 86
Montague St. S11—4C 98
Montague St. S72—5C 10
Montagu Rd. DN5—1G 45
Montagu St. S64—1G 57
Monteney Cres. S5—1E 75
Monteney Rd. S5—2E 75
Montfort Dri. S3—5F 87
Montgomery Av. S7—6C 98
Montgomery Ct. S11—2G 109
Montgomery Dri. S7—6C 98
Montgomery Gdns. DN2—3A 34
Montgomery Rd. S7—6C 98
Montgomery Rd. S63—5E 41
Montgomery Sq. S63—5F 41
Montgomery Ter. Rd. S6—6D 86
Montrose Av. DN2—4H 33
Montrose Av. S75—4D 6
Montrose Ct. S11—3F 109
Montrose Pl. S18—1B 128
Montrose Rd. S7—2A 110
Moonpenny Way. S18—2E 129
Moonshine La. S5—6D 74
Moorbank Clo. S10—3D 96
Moorbank Clo. S73—5H 25
Moorbank Clo. S75—3E 13
Moorbank Ct. S10—2D 96
Moorbank Dri. S10—2E 97
Moorbank Rd. S10—2E 96
Moorbank Rd. S73—4H 25
Moorbank View. S73—4H 25
Moorbridge Cres. S73—2B 40
Moor Cres. S19—2C 124
Moorcrest Rise. S75—3F 7
Moorcroft Av. S10—6B 96
Moorcroft Clo. S10—6B 96
Moorcroft Dri. S10—6B 96
Moorcroft Rd. S10—6B 96
Moordale View. S62—6A 56
Moor End Rd. S10—1A 98
Moore St. S3—1C 4 & 4D 98
Moorfield Av. S65—2H 81
Moorfield Clo. S65—2H 81
Moorfield Dri. DN3—4F 35
Moorfield Gro. S65—2H 81
Moorfields. S3—1D 4 & 1E 99
Moorfoot. S1—6D 4
Moor Gap. DN3—3H 49
Moorgate. S60—4E 79
Moorgate Av. S10—1B 98
Moorgate Av. S60—5E 79
(in two parts)
Moorgate Business Centre. S60
(off Moorgate Rd.)   —3E 79
Moorgate Chase. S60—4E 79
Moorgate Ct. S60—4E 79
Moorgate Cres. S18—3F 129
Moorgate Gro. S60—5E 79
Moorgate La. S60—5E 79

Moorgate St. S60—3D 78
Moor Grn. Clo. S75—6C 12
Moorhay Clo. S41—4D 130
Moorhead. S1—5D 4
Moorhouse Clo. S60—2B 92
Moorhouse La. S60—2A 92
Moorhouse La. S75—1B 6
Moorland Av. S70—6D 12
Moorland Av. S75—3F 7
Moorland Cres. S75—3F 7
Moorland Dri. DN1—6E 33
Moorland Gro. DN4—2A 48
Moorland Pl. S6—5C 84
Moorlands. S66—5D 80
Moorlands Cres. S60—2A 92
Moorland View. S12—5C 112
Moorland View. S31—6C 104
Moorland View Rd. S40—5E 137
Moor La. DN3—2B 20
Moor La. S44—6A 139
Moor La. S66—1B 83
Moor La. S70—6D 36
Moor La. N. S65—5H 71
Moor La. S. S65—1H 81
Moorlawn Av. S42—6A 136
Moor Ley. S70—2C 36
Moor Oaks Rd. S10—3A 98
Moor Pk. Av. S40—5E 137
Moor Rd. S63—4F 41
Moor Rd. S65—3H 79
Moorside. S10—5A 96
Moorside Clo. S19—1C 124
Moorside Clo. S75—5F 7
Moorsyde Av. S10—6H 85
Moorsyde Cres. S10—6H 85
Moor, The. S1—6D 4 & 3E 99
Moorthorpe Gdns. S19—5H 113
Moorthorpe Grn. S19—5H 113
Moorthorpe Way. S19—5H 113
(in two parts)   & 5C 114
Moortown Av. S31—6G 107
Moor Valley. S19—5H 113
Moor View. DN3—3H 49
Moorview. S61—3F 77
Moorview Clo. S43—4D 132
Moorview Ct. S17—4H 121
Moor View Dri. S8—4C 110
Moor View Rd. S8—5C 110
Moor View Rd. S43—1E 135
Moor View Ter. S11—2E 109
Moorwoods Av. S30—2E 65
Moorwoods La. S30—2E 65
Moray Pl. S18—1B 128
Mordaunt Rd. S2—1B 112
Morgan Av. S5—1D 86
Morgan Clo. S5—6D 74
Morgan Rd. DN2—5A 34
Morgan Rd. S5—1D 86
Morland Clo. S14—4B 112
Morland Dri. S14—4B 112
Morland Pl. S14—4B 112
Morland Rd. S14—4A 112
Morley Av. S40—1E 137
Morley Clo. S18—2A 128
Morley Pl. DN12—4D 58
Morley Rd. DN1—4E 33
Morley Rd. S61—6G 67
Morley St. S6—4H 85
Morley St. S62—3F 69
Morpeth Gdns. S3—1B 4
Morpeth St. S3—1B 4 & 1D 98
Morpeth St. S65—3E 79
Morrall Rd. S5—2E 75
Morrell St. S66—5G 83
Morris Av. S41—6G 131
Morris Av. S62—5F 55
Morris Cres. DN4—5G 45

Morris Dri. S41—6G 131
Morrison Av. S66—3G 83
Morrison Dri. DN11—5E 63
Morrison Pl. S73—3E 27
Morrison Rd. S73—3D 26
Morris Rd. DN4—5G 45
Mortain Rd. S60—1F 91
Mortains. S31—1B 118
Morthen Hall La. S66—4F 93
Morthen La. S60—5C 92
Morthen La. S66—3E 93
Morthen Rd. S66
—5F 81 to 4A 94
Mortimer Rd. S66—5H 83
Mortimer St. S1—6F 5 & 3F 99
Mortlake Rd. S5—1H 87
Mortomley Clo. S30—6C 50
Mortomley Hall Gdns. S30
—6C 50
Mortomley La. S30—6C 50
Morton Clo. S71—2D 14
Morton Pl. S30—1A 74
Morton Rd. S64—6F 43
Mosborough Hall Dri. S19
—4E 125
Mosborough Moor. S19
—6A 114
Mosborough Parkway. S12
—2H 113
Mosborough Rd. S13—6D 100
Moscar Cotts. S7—3B 110
Moss Beck Ct. S31—6C 124
Moss Clo. S66—5F 81
Mossdale Av. S19—2D 124
Mossdale Clo. DN5—2G 31
Moss Dri. S31—4B 126
Moss Gro. S12—4D 114
Moss Rise. Pl. S31—6C 124
Moss Rd. S17—5A 120
Moss View. S19—3B 124
Moss Way. S19
—2D 124 to 3D 114
Moston Wlk. S66—6G 137
Motehall Dri. S2—4C 100
Motehall Pl. S2—4D 100
Motehall Rd. S2—4C 100
Motehall Way. S2—4C 100
Motte, The. S61—1H 77
Mottram St. S71—5H 13
Mound Rd. S40—4A 138
Mount Av. S72—5G 11
Mountbatten Dri. S30—2B 64
Mountcastle St. S41—3H 131
Mountcastle Wlk. S41—3H 131
Mount Clo. S70—2H 23
Mount Cres. S74—4H 37
Mountenoy Rd. S60—4D 78
Mountford Croft. S17—4E 121
Mt. Pleasant. DN4—4A 46
Mt. Pleasant. S30—1E 65
Mt. Pleasant. S70—5B 24
Mt. Pleasant. S72—5G 11
Mt. Pleasant Clo. S30—1E 65
Mt. Pleasant Rd. S61—2B 78
Mt. Pleasant Rd. S63—1F 55
Mount Rd. S30—2C 64
Mount Rd. S72—5G 11
Mount St. S11—4D 98
Mount St. S61—2B 78
Mount St. S70—1G 23
Mount St. S71—1F 25
Mount Ter. S73—6A 26
Mount, The. DN3—6E 21
Mt. Vernon Av. S70—2H 23
Mt. Vernon Cres. S70—3A 24
Mt. Vernon Rd. S70
—4H 23 to 2A 24
Mount View. DN12—4B 60

Mt. View Av. S8—4E 111
Mt. View Gdns. S8—4E 111
Mt. View Rd. S8—5E 111
Mount Wlk. S73—5G 25
Mousehole La. S65—6C 70
Mouse Pk. Ga. S30—1F 73
Mowbray Gdns. S65—1A 80
Mowbray Pl. S65—1A 80
Mowbray St. S3—6E 87
Mowbray St. S65—1A 80
Mowson Cres. S30—4D 72
Mowson Dri. S30—4D 72
Mowson La. S30—4D 72
Moxon Clo. S30—4G 141
Mucky La. S30—1C 140
(Smithy Moor)
Mucky La. S30—5B 140
(Whitwell Moor)
Mucky La. S71—6G 15
Muglet La. S66—6H 83
Muirfield Av. DN4—5F 49
Muirfield Av. S64—3C 56
Muirfield Clo. S41—5B 132
Muirfield Clo. S72—4C 10
Mulberry Clo. DN5—4F 31
Mulberry Rd. S31—1G 119
(Anston)
Mulberry Rd. S31—6G 125
(Eckington)
Mulberry St. S1—3F 5 & 2F 99
Mulberry Way. S31—4H 125
Mulehouse Rd. S10—1G 97
Mundella Pl. S8—4E 111
Mungy La. S65—5B 70
Munro Clo. S31—3B 126
Munsbrough La. S61—5B 68
Munsbrough Rise. S61—4B 68
Munsdale. S61—4B 68
Murdoch Pl. S71—6A 8
Murdock Rd. S5—5D 74
Murrayfield Dri. S19—3E 125
Murray Rd. S11—6H 97
Murray Rd. S31—2C 126
Murray Rd. S62—1G 69
Musard Pl. S43—2B 134
Musard Way. S31—3A 126
Musgrave Cres. S5—2E 87
Musgrave Dri. S5—2E 87
Musgrave Pl. S5—2E 87
Musgrave Rd. S5—2D 86
Musgrove Av. S65—5E 71
Muskoka Av. S11—2E 109
Muskoka Dri. S11—1E 109
Mutual St. DN4—1B 46
Myers Av. S30—1D 72
Myers Gro. La. S6—5E 85
Myers La. S6—6A 72
Mylnhurst Rd. S11—2H 109
Mylor Ct. S71—4C 14
Mylor Rd. S11—1G 109
Myndon Wlk. DN12—2C 58
Myrtle Cres. S66—4G 81
Myrtle Gro. S31—5G 117
Myrtle Gro. S43—2G 133
Myrtle Rd. S2—6E 99
Myrtle Rd. S73—6A 26
Myrtle Springs. S12—2B 112
Myrtle St. S75—5E 13
Myton Rd. S9—1C 100

Nairn Dri. S18—2B 128
Nairn St. S10—2H 97
Nancy Rd. S72—6H 11
Nanny Hill. S30—3E 141
Nanny Marr Rd. S73—4E 27
Napier Mt. S70—4H 23
Napier St. S11—4C 98

Narrow La. S31—2G 119
Narrow Twitchell. S60—3E 79
(off Hollowgate)
Narrow Wlk. S10—2A 98
Naseby Av. DN5—3F 31
Naseby St. S9—1C 88
Nathan Ct. S19—6F 115
Nathan Dri. S19—5F 115
Nathan Gro. S19—5E 115
Navan Rd. S2—6C 100
Naylor Gro. S30—3C 72
Naylor Gro. S75—2B 22
Naylor Rd. S30—2C 72
Naylor St. S62—4F 69
Neale Bank. S43—4D 132
Neale Rd. DN2—1H 33
Nearcroft Rd. S61—1H 77
Nearfield Rd. DN4—4B 48
Needham Way. S7—2A 110
Needlewood. S75—3B 22
Neepsend La. S3—5D 86
Neild Rd. S74—5B 38
Neill Rd. S11—5A 98
Nelson Av. S71—3B 14
Nelson Clo. S60—3D 90
Nelson Mandela Wlk. S2
(off Saxonlea Av.) —4D 100
Nelson Pl. S30—2B 64
Nelson Rd. DN11—4B 62
Nelson Rd. DN12—3B 60
Nelson Rd. S6—5F 85
Nelson Rd. S66—4H 83
(in three parts)
Nelson St. S41—5A 132
Nelson St. S65—2E 79
Nelson St. S70—6G 13
Nemesia Clo. S31—3E 119
Nesfield Clo. S41—3F 131
Nesfield Way. S5—5H 75
Nether Av. S30—6B 64
Nether Av. S31—3A 126
Nether Cantley La. DN3—1F 49
Nether Cres. S30—6B 64
Netherdene Rd. S18—2E 129
(in two parts)
Nether Edge Rd. S7—1C 110
Netherfield. S65—1H 79
Netherfield Clo. S30—3H 141
Netherfield Clo. S43—1E 135
Netherfield Ct. S65—1F 79
Netherfield La. S62—1F 69
Netherfield Rd. S10—1H 97
Netherfield Rd. S40—5C 136
Netherfields Cres. S18—3E 129
Nethergate. S6—6C 84
Nethergreen Av. S31—2B 126
Nethergreen Gdns. S31—2B 126
Nethergreen Rd. S11—5F 97
Nether Hall Rd. DN1—5D 32
Nether La. S30—5F 65
Netherleigh Ct. S40—2D 136
Netherleigh Rd. S40—2D 136
Nether Ley Av. S30—2E 65
Nether Ley Ct. S30—2E 65
Nether Ley Croft. S30—2E 65
Nether Ley Gdns. S30—2E 65
Nethermoor Av. S31—2B 126
Nethermoor Clo. S31—2B 126
Nethermoor Dri. S31—2B 126
Nethermoor Dri. S66—1G 93
Nethermoor La. S31—2B 126
Nether Oak Clo. S19—5H 115
Nether Oak Dri. S19—5H 115
Nether Oak View. S19—5H 115
Nether Rd. S30—6F 65
Nether Shire La. S5—2G 75
Netherthorpe. S43—1E 135
Netherthorpe Clo. S31—2A 126

Netherthorpe Clo. S43—2D 134
Netherthorpe La. S31—3A 126
Netherthorpe Pl. S3
—1B 4 & 6D 86
Netherthorpe Rd. S3
—3A 4 & 1C 98
Netherthorpe Rd. S43—1D 134
Netherthorpe St. S3
—1B 4 & 1D 98
Netherthorpe Wlk. S3
—1B 4 & 1D 98
Netherthorpe Way. S31
—6E 107
Nether Wheel Row. S13
—2G 113
Netherwood Rd. S73—4B 26
Nettleham Rd. S8—4D 110
Neville Av. S70—2D 24
Neville Clo. S3—5F 87
Neville Clo. S70—2D 24
Neville Clo. S73—5H 25
Neville Ct. S73—5H 25
Neville Cres. S70—2D 24
Neville Dri. S3—5F 87
Neville Rd. S61—6H 67
Neville St. S60—2D 78
Nevis Clo. S40—1F 137
Newark Clo. S75—3F 7
Newark Rd. S64—6C 42
Newark St. S9—4C 88
New Beetwell St. S40—2A 138
Newbold Av. S41—5G 131
Newbold Back La. S40—5F to
(in two parts) 6F 131
Newbold Dri. S41—5G 131
Newbold Rd. S41
—3C 130 to 1A 138
Newbold Ter. DN5—4H 31
Newbolt Rd. DN4—5B 46
Newbould Cres. S19—4G 115
Newbould La. S10—3A 98
Newbridge Dri. S43—3D 132
Newbridge La. S41 & S43
—1A 132
Newbridge St. S41—2A 132
Newburn Dri. S9—1G 89
Newburn Rd. S9—1F 89
(off Town St.)
Newbury Rd. S10—1H 97
Newbury Way. DN5—3F 31
Newby Cres. DN4—6A 46
Newby Rd. S41—3E 131
Newcastle Clo. S31—6E 107
Newcastle St. S1—3C 4 & 2D 98
Newcomen Rd. DN5—4A 32
New Cross Dri. S13—1A 114
New Cross Wlk. S13—6A 102
New Cross Way. S13—1A 114
Newdale Av. S72—2G 15
New Droppingwell Rd. S61
—3D 76
Newent La. S10—1H 97
Newfield Clo. DN3—1F 21
Newfield Ct. S10—5H 97
Newfield Cres. S17—2C 120
Newfield Cres. S63—6D 40
Newfield Croft. S17—1C 120
Newfield Farm Clo. S14
—2A 112
Newfield Grn. Rd. S2—1H 111
Newfield La. S17—2C 120
Newfields Av. S71—3D 14
Newgate Clo. S30—6C 50
Newhall Av. S66—1G 93
New Hall Cres. S30—2B 140
New Hall La. S30—3A 140

Newhall La. S66—6A 82
New Hall La. S71—2H 25
Newhall Rd. DN3—4E 21
Newhall Rd. S9—4B 88
New Hall Rd. S40—3F 137
New Haven Clo. S40—4D 136
New Hill. DN12—3E 59
Newhill Rd. S63—6D 40
Newhill Rd. S71—2A 14
New Ings. DN3—3E 35
Newington Av. S72—5B 10
Newington Clo. DN4—4D 48
Newington Dri. S31—6C 104
Newington Rd. S11—5A 98
Newland Av. S66—3F 83
Newland Av. S72—2G 15
Newland Dale. S41—1A 138
Newland Gdns. S41—6G 131
Newland Rd. S71—6A 8
Newlands Av. S12—1C 112
Newlands Av. S40—2E 137
Newlands Clo. DN4—4D 48
Newlands Dri. DN5—4H 31
Newlands Dri. S12—1C 112
Newlands Gro. S12—1D 112
Newlands Rd. S12—1C 112
New La. DN5—2C 44
New La. DN11—4E 63
New La. S63—5H 27
New Lodge Cres. S71—6A 8
Newlyn Dri. S71—4B 14
Newlyn Pl. S8—4D 110
Newlyn Rd. S8—4D 110
Newman Av. S71—4E 9
Newman Clo. S9—5D 76
Newman Ct. S9—5D 76
Newman Ct. S60—1G 91
Newman Dri. S9—5C 76
Newman Rd. S9—6C 76
Newman Rd. S60—1G 91
Newmarch St. S9—6G 77
Newmarket Rd. DN4—1B 48
New Mill Bank. S30—6E 141
New Orchard La. S66—4A 94
New Orchard Rd. S66—4A 94
New Queen St. S41—1A 138
New Rd. S30—3F 141
New Rd. S31—1E 119
 (Anston)
New Rd. S31—5F 107
 (Dinnington)
New Rd. S31—3D 116
 (Wales)
New Rd. S42—5A 136
New Rd. S61—4D 76
New Rd. S63—5F 41
New Rd. S73—4F 39
New Rd. S75—3E 7
 (Mapplewell)
New Rd. S75—6B 36
 (Tankersley)
Newsam Rd. S62—4B 56
Newsham Rd. S8—3D 110
Newsome Av. S73—6H 25
New Sq. S40—2A 138
New Station Rd. S64—2C 56
Newstead Av. S12—5G 113
Newstead Av. S30—1D 72
Newstead Clo. S12—4G 113
Newstead Clo. S18—2A 128
Newstead Clo. S65—1H 79
Newstead Dri. S12—5G 113
Newstead Gro. S12—4G 113
Newstead Pl. S12—5G 113
Newstead Rise. S12—5H 113
Newstead Rd. DN5—1H 31
Newstead Rd. S12—4G 113
Newstead Rd. S71—5A 8

Newstead Way. S12—5G 113
New St. DN1—2C 46
New St. DN5—1A 32
New St. S1—2E 5 & 1E 99
New St. S19—2G 125
New St. S30—3G 141
 (Deepcar)
New St. S30—5B 50
 (High Green)
New St. S31—4F 107
 (Dinnington)
New St. S31—1E 107
 (Laughton)
New St. S40—3A 138
New St. S60—5D 90
New St. S61—3B 68
 (Greasbrough)
New St. S61—3B 66
 (Thorpe Hesley)
New St. S62—2F 69
New St. S63—2B 42
New St. S64—6H 43
New St. S70—1G 23 to 6H 13
 (in two parts, Barnsley)
New St. S70—5A 24
 (Worsbrough Bridge)
New St. S70—5C 24
 (Worsbrough Dale)
New St. S71—2E 9
 (Royston)
New St. S71—1E 25
 (Stairfoot)
New St. S72—1A 28
 (Great Houghton)
New St. S72—6G 11
 (Grimethorpe)
New St. S73—4E 27
 (Darfield)
New St. S73—4D 38
 (Hemingfield)
New St. S73—6C 26
 (Wombwell)
New St. S75—3B 22
 (Dodworth)
New St. S75—4F 7
 (Mapplewell)
Newton Av. S30—2B 140
Newton Dri. DN5—6H 31
Newton Dri. S65—3G 79
Newton La. DN5—6H 31
Newton La. S1—6E 5 & 3E 99
Newton La. S30—2B 140
Newton Pl. S61—4B 66
Newton Rd. S30—6C 50
Newton St. S65—3G 79
Newton St. S70—5F 13
Newtown Av. S71—1D 8
Newtown Av. S72—2H 15
Newtown Grn. S72—2H 15
New Tree Dri. DN11—6H 61
New Winterwell. S63—4D 40
New World Centre. S61—1G 77
New Wortley Rd. S61 & S60
 —2A 78
Niagara Rd. S6—6A 74
Nicholas La. S63—4E 29
Nicholas St. S41—6D 138
Nicholas St. S70—6F 13
Nicholson Av. S63—6D 40
Nicholson Av. S75—3A 12
Nicholson Pl. S8—1F 111
Nicholson Rd. DN4—2A 46
Nicholson Rd. S8—1E 111
Nichols Rd. S6—6G 85
Nickerwood Dri. S31—1B 116
Nidderdale Pl. S66—3G 81
Nidderdale Rd. S61—4H 67
Nidd Rd. S9—6C 88

Nidd Rd. E. S9—6D 88
Nightingale Clo. S60—4D 78
Nightingale Croft. S61—1C 66
Nightingale Rd. S30—1B 74
Nightingale St. S9—6D 88
Nile St. S10—3A 98
Nine Trees Ind. Est. S66—3H 93
Ninian Gro. DN4—3C 48
Noble St. S74—6B 38
Noblethorpe Rd. S62—6D 56
Nodder Rd. S13—5E 101
Noehill Pl. S2—4D 100
Noehill Rd. S2—4D 100
Nook End. S6—5D 84
Nookery Clo. S66—3H 83
Nooking Clo. DN3—2G 35
Nook La. S6—5C 84
Nook, The. S10—1B 98
Nora St. S63—3H 29
Norborough Rd. DN2—4F 33
Norborough Rd. S9—1G 89
Norbreck Cres. DN4—6E 45
Norbreck Rd. DN4—6E 45
Norbriggs Rd. S43—1F 135
Norbrook Way. S60—2B 92
Norburn Dri. S31—3B 126
Norbury Clo. S18—2B 128
Norbury Clo. S40—5D 130
Norcroft. S70—3H 23
Norfolk Clo. S42—5D 136
Norfolk Clo. S71—3B 14
Norfolk Ct. S65—2E 79
Norfolk Dri. S31—1G 119
Norfolk Hill. S30—6A 64
Norfolk Hill Croft. S30—6A 64
Norfolk La. S1—5E 5
Norfolk Pk. Av. S2—4H 99
Norfolk Pk. Dri. S2—4G 99
Norfolk Pk. Rd. S2—4G 99
Norfolk Pl. S66—4G 83
Norfolk Rd. DN4—5B 46
Norfolk Rd. S2—5H 5 & 3G 99
Norfolk Rd. S72—1A 28
Norfolk Row. S1—3E 5 & 2E 99
Norfolk St. S1—4E 5 & 2E 99
 (in two parts)
Norfolk St. S65—2E 79
Norfolk Way. S60—1G 91
Norgreave Way. S19—2E 125
Norman Clo. S70—4A 24
Norman Clo. S71—3C 14
Norman Cres. DN5—2G 31
Norman Cres. S66—4H 81
Normancroft Ct. S2—4D 100
Normancroft Cres. S2—4E 101
Normancroft Dri. S2—4D 100
Normancroft Way. S2—4E 101
Normandale Av. S6—3E 85
Normandale Rd. S6—4B 86
Norman St. S9—4C 88
Norman St. S63—1G 29
Normanton Gdns. S4—4G 87
Normanton Gro. S13—1H 113
Normanton Hill. S13—1E 113
Normanton Spring Ct. S13
 —1H 113
Normanton Spring Rd. S13
 —2G 113
Normanville Av. S60—2B 90
Norrel's Croft. S60—5F 79
Norris Rd. S6—3H 85
Norroy St. S4—5H 87
Norstead Cres. S66—4H 81
Northampton Rd. DN2—4A 34
N. Anston Trading Est. S31
 —5B 106
N. Bridge Rd. DN5—5B 32
N. Carr La. S73—1E 27

N. Church St. S1—2E 5 & 1E 99
N. Cliff Rd. DN12—2D 58
North Clo. S71—2E 9
Northcote Av. S2—1F 111
Northcote Ho. S8—4D 110
 (off Chantrey Rd.)
Northcote Rd. S2—1F 111
Northcote Ter. S75—5E 13
North Cres. S31—1C 126
North Cres. S44—5E 135
North Cres. S65—2G 79
North Dri. S60—1D 78
N. End Dri. DN5—1F 43
Northern Av. S2—6A 100
Northern Comn. S18—6H 121
Northfield Av. S10—6H 85
Northfield Av. S62—6F 55
Northfield Clo. S10—6H 85
Northfield Ind. Est. S60—1D 78
Northfield La. DN3—1G 21
Northfield La. S66—4E 81
Northfield Rd. DN5—4A 32
Northfield Rd. S10—1H 97
Northfield Rd. S60—2D 78
North Ga. S31—6D 124
North Ga. S64—1G 57
Northgate. S75—3E 13
North Gro. S44—5E 135
N. Hill Rd. S5—5D 74
Northlands. DN6—1C 16
Northlands. S71—1E 9
Northlands Rd. S5—5D 74
North Mall. DN1—6C 32
 (off French Ga.)
Northmoor Clo. S43—4F 133
N. Pitt St. S61—3H 77
North Pl. S65—2G 79
North Pl. S75—4D 12
N. Quadrant. S5—5H 75
North Rd. S44—2F 139
North Rd. S65—1H 79
North Rd. S71—1F 9
Northside Rd. S63—5F 41
North Sq. DN12—3C 60
North St. DN4—2E 47
North St. DN12—3C 60
North St. S6—6D 86
North St. S60—2C 78
North St. S62—6G 55
North St. S64—2C 56
North St. S73—3E 27
North Ter. S4—1B 138
Norththorpe. S75—3D 22
Northumberland Av. DN2
 —4H 33
Northumberland Av. S74
 —4A 38
Northumberland La. DN12
 —2A 58
Northumberland Rd. S10
 —2B 98
Northumberland Way. S71
 —1G 25
North View. S31—6B 104
North View. S72—6F 11
Norton Av. S8, S14 & S12
 —6H 111
Norton Av. S40—5C 136
Norton Church Rd. S8—6F 111
Norton Grn. Clo. S8—6G 111
Norton Hammer La. S8—3C 110
Norton La. S8—2E 123 to 5H 111
Norton Lees Clo. S8—4E 111
Norton Lees Cres. S8—3E 111
Norton Lees La. S8—3D 110
Norton Lees Rd. S8—2D 110
Norton Lees Sq. S8—3E 111
Norton Pk. Av. S8—1F 123

Norton Pk. Cres. S8—1E 123
Norton Pk. Dri. S8—1E 123
Norton Pk. Rd. S8—2E 123
Norton Pk. View. S8—1E 123
Norton Rd. DN2—4H 33
Norville Cres. S73—3F 27
Norwich Rd. DN2—2G 33
Norwich Row. S2—5H 5 & 2G 99
Norwith Rd. DN4—5B 48
Norwood Av. S5—1F 87
Norwood Av. S41—6D 138
Norwood Av. S66—3F 83
Norwood Clo. S5—2F 87
Norwood Clo. S41—6E 139
Norwood Clo. S66—3F 83
Norwood Cres. S31—2D 126
(Killamarsh)
Norwood Cres. S31—5G 117
(Kiveton Park)
Norwood Dri. DN5—4B 18
Norwood Dri. S5—2F 87
Norwood Dri. S72—2G 11
Norwood Dri. S75—2A 12
Norwood Grange Dri. S5—1F 87
Norwood Pl. S31—2D 126
Norwood Rd. DN12—3D 58
Norwood Rd. S5—2F 87
Norwood St. S65—6B 70
Nostel Ho. DN1—1C 46
(off Grove Pl.)
Nostell Fold. S75—3B 22
Nostell Pl. DN4—5B 48
Nottingham Cliff. S3—5F 87
Nottingham Clo. DN5—3F 31
Nottingham Clo. S31—3F 119
Nottingham Clo. S71—2G 25
Nottingham St. S3—5F 87
Nottingham St. S65—2E 79
Novello St. S66—5H 83
Nowill Ct. S8—1E 111
Nowill Pl. S8—1E 111
Nunnery Cres. S60—5C 90
Nunnery Dri. S2—1B 100
Nunnery Ter. S2—2B 100
Nursery Cres. S31—1F 119
Nursery Dri. S30—1F 75
Nursery Dri. S60—5C 90
Nursery Gdns. S70—2E 25
Nursery Gro. S30—1G 75
Nursery La. DN5—4C 44
Nursery La. S3—1F 5 & 6F 87
Nursery Rd. S31—1G 119
(Anston & Dinnington)
Nursery Rd. S31—5A 104
(Swallownest)
Nursery St. S3—1F 5 & 6F 87
Nursery St. S70—1G 23
Nuttall Pl. S2—2H 99
Nutwell Clo. DN4—5C 48
Nutwell La. DN3—2F 49 to 3G 35

Oakamoor Clo. S40—6D 130
Oak Apple Clo. S6—4C 84
Oak Av. S63—6G 41
Oak Bank Av. S41—1B 132
Oakbank Clo. S64—5B 56
Oakbank Ct. S17—4E 121
Oakbrook Ct. S10—5F 97
Oakbrook Rd. S11—5F 97
Oakbrook View. S10—4G 97
Oak Clo. S31—4A 126
Oak Clo. S64—6C 42
Oak Clo. S66—3F 81
Oak Clo. S74—6H 37
Oakdale. S70—4B 24
Oakdale Clo. DN3—6D 20
Oakdale Clo. S70—5B 24
Oakdale Pl. S61—4H 77
Oak Dale Rd. DN4—1C 60
Oak Dale Rd. S7—1B 110
Oakdale Rd. S31—2H 119
Oakdale Rd. S61—4H 77
Oakdell. S18—6H 123
Oakdene. DN11—5D 62
Oaken Wood Clo. S61—2C 66
Oaken Wood Rd. S61—2B 66
Oakes Grn. S9—5A 88
Oakes Pk. View. S14—6H 111
Oakes St. S9—5D 76
Oakfern Gro. S30—5B 50
Oakfield Av. S40—4D 136
Oakfield Ct. S75—4E 7
Oakfield Wlk. S75—5D 12
Oak Gro. DN3—1E 35
Oak Gro. DN12—4C 58
Oakham Dri. S3—5D 86
Oakham Pl. S75—4E 13
Oak Hill. S65—1G 79
Oakhill Rd. DN2—3H 33
Oak Hill Rd. S7—1B 110
Oakhill Rd. S18—1G 129
Oakholme M. S10—4A 98
Oakholme Rd. S10—3A 98
Oakland Rd. S6—3H 85
Oaklands Av. S71—3G 17
Oaklands Dri. DN4—3B 48
Oaklands Gdns. DN4—4B 48
Oaklands Pl. S63—6E 41
Oakland Ter. DN12—3B 60
Oak Lea. S61—4B 68
Oak Lea. S70—5C 24
Oak Lea Av. S63—4C 40
Oaklea Clo. S75—3F 7
Oakley Av. S40—1G 137
Oakley Rd. S13—3G 101
Oak Lodge Rd. S30—6A 50
Oak Pk. S10—3H 97
Oak Pk. Rise. S70—2A 24
Oak Pl. S10—3H 97
Oak Rd. DN3—1E 35
Oak Rd. S12—5C 112
Oak Rd. S19—3F 115
Oak Rd. S63—1F 29
(Thurnscoe)
Oak Rd. S63—6G 41
(Wath upon Dearne)
Oak Rd. S64—6C 42
Oak Rd. S66—4D 82
Oak Rd. S72—3D 10
Oaks Av. S30—3C 140
Oaks Clo. S63—1G 55
Oaks Cres. S70—1C 24
Oaks Farm Clo. S75—4D 6
Oaks Farm Dri. S75—4D 6
Oaks Farm La. S44—3G 139
Oaks Fold. S5—3A 76
Oaks Fold Av. S5—4A 76
Oaks Fold Rd. S5—4A 76
Oaks La. S5—4A 76
Oaks La. S30—2A 140
Oaks La. S61—6E 67
Oaks La. S71 & S70—6C 14
(in two parts)
Oak St. S8—6E 99
Oak St. S19—1C 124
Oak St. S43—2G 133
Oak St. S70—6F 13
Oak Ter. DN1—2C 46
Oak Ter. S31—5H 103
Oak Tree Av. S72—6B 10
Oak Tree Clo. S75—5B 6
Oak Tree Cotts. S44—4G 139
Oak Tree Rd. DN3—2H 49
Oakwell Clo. S66—3G 83
Oakwell La. S71—6A 14
Oakwell Ter. S71—6A 14
Oakwood Av. S5—2D 74
Oakwood Av. S71—1E 9
Oakwood Clo. S70—5C 24
Oakwood Cres. S30—4D 72
Oakwood Cres. S62—6E 55
Oakwood Cres. S71—1D 8
Oakwood Dri. DN3—4E 35
(Armthorpe)
Oakwood Dri. DN3—3H 49
(Branton)
Oakwood Dri. S60—5G 79
Oakwood Gro. S60—5G 79
Oakwood Hall Dri. S60—1F 91
Oakwood Rd. DN4—4H 45
Oakwood Rd. S71—1D 8
Oakwood Rd. E. S60—6G 79
Oakwood Rd. W. S60—6F 79
Oakwood Sq. S75—5A 6
Oakworth Clo. S19—3E 125
Oakworth Clo. S75—4D 12
Oakworth Dri. S19—3D 124
Oakworth Gro. S19—3D 124
Oakworth View. S19—3D 124
Oasis, The. S9—1E 89
Oates Av. S62—2F 69
Oates Clo. S61—2A 78
Oates Orchard. S19—3D 124
Oates St. S61—2A 78
Oberon Cres. S73—3D 26
Occupation La. S6—2D 84
Occupation La. S12—4G 113
Occupation Rd. S41—3H 131
Occupation Rd. S62—4H 51
(Harley)
Occupation Rd. S62—3E 69
(Parkgate)
Ochre Dike Clo. S19—5E 115
Ochre Dike La. S19—5D 114
Ochre Dike Wlk. S61
—3H 67 to 3A 68
Octavia Clo. S60—1C 90
Odom Ct. S2—1F 111
Ogden Pl. S8—1E 123
Ogden Rd. DN2—1B 34
Oil Mill Rd. S60—3D 78
Oldale Clo. S13—2C 114
Oldale Ct. S13—1C 114
Oldale Gro. S13—1C 114
Old Bakery Clo. S41—1A 132
Oldcotes Rd. S31—2F 107
Old Cotts. S41—2C 138
Old Cross La. S63—5F 41
Old Ecclesall Rd. S11—4D 98
Old Farm Ct. S64—5C 42
Oldfield Av. DN12—3B 58
Oldfield Av. S6—5D 84
Oldfield Clo. IF 21
Oldfield Clo. S6—5D 84
Oldfield Gro. S6—5D 84
Oldfield Rd. S6—6C 84
Oldfield Rd. S65—2B 80
Old Field Shutt La. S65—1D 80
Oldfield Ter. S6—6D 84
Old Fulwood Rd. S10—6D 96
Old Garden Dri. S65—2G 79
Old Gate La. S65—6C 70
Old Hall Clo. DN5—2E 45
Old Hall Clo. S31—1D 106
(Laughton)
Old Hall Clo. S31—3A 118
(Todwick)
Old Hall Clo. S66—4H 81
Old Hall Cres. DN5—1B 32
Old Hall Dri. S66—4H 81
Old Hall Pl. DN5—1B 32
Old Hall Rd. DN5—1B 32
Old Hall Rd. S9—4C 88
Old Hall Rd. S40—3F 137
Old Hall Rd. S70—1B 36
Old Hay Clo. S17—3D 120
Old Hay Gdns. S17—3C 120
Old Hay La. S17—4C 120
Old Hexthorpe. DN4—2H 45
Old Hill. DN12—3E 59
Old Hill La. S65—2D 80
Old La. S19—2G 125
Old La. S30—3A 72
Old Mkt. Pl. S73—1F 39
Old Mill Dri. S41—4C 130
Old Mill La. S70 & S71—4G 13
Old Mill Rd. DN12—4F 59
Old Pk. Av. S8—2B 122
Old Pk. Rd. S8—2B 122
Old Peverel Rd. S44—6E 135
Old Quarry Av. S31—4F 117
Old Retford Rd. S13—5C 102
Oldridge Clo. S40—5D 130
Old Rd. DN12—5B 58 to 3E 59
Old Rd. S40—2C 136 to 3F 137
Old Rd. S71—2A 14
Old Row. S74—6D 38
Oldroyd Row. S75—3B 22
(off Stainborough Rd.)
Old School La. S60—5D 90
Old Sheffield Rd. S40—6D 78
Old St. S2—1G 99
Old Warren Vale. S62—6G 55
Oldwell Clo. S17—5D 120
Old Wortley Rd. S61—1G 77
Old Yew Ga. S30—1E 73
Olive Clo. S31—6B 104
Olive Cres. S12—5C 112
Olive Gro. Rd. S2—6F 99
Olive Rd. S19—2D 124
Olive Rd. S30—3D 140
Oliver Rd. DN4—4A 46
Oliver Rd. S7—3A 110
Olivers Dri. S9—1F 101
Olivers Mt. S9—1F 101
Oliver St. S64—6D 42
Olive Ter. S6—4D 84
Olivet Rd. S8—4D 110
Ollerton Rd. S71—4A 8
Onchan Rd. S6—6E 85
Onesmoor Bottom. S30—3A 72
Onslow Rd. S11—6H 97
Orange St. S1—3C 4 & 2D 98
Orchard Av. S31—6E 107
Orchard Clo. S5—2F 75
Orchard Clo. S31—1E 107
Orchard Clo. S60—5D 90
Orchard Clo. S71—2C 14
Orchard Clo. S75—4F 7
Orchard Cres. S5—2F 75
Orchard Flatts Cres. S61
—5A 68
Orchard Gdns. S31—3F 119
Orchard La. S1—3E 5 & 2E 99
Orchard La. S19—4F 115
Orchard La. S31—5F 117
Orchard Lea Dri. S31—6B 104
Orchard Pl. S1—3E 5
Orchard Pl. S31—3B 126
Orchard Pl. S60—3C 78
Orchard Pl. S63—5D 40
Orchard Rd. S6—5A 86
Orchard Sq. S18—1B 128
Orchard Sq. Shopping Centre.
S1—3E 5 & 2E 99
Orchard St. DN4—2B 46
Orchard St. S1—3E 5 & 2E 99
Orchard St. S30—4H 141
(Deepcar)

Orchard St. S30—2D 72
(Oughtibridge)
Orchard St. S63—5G 29
(Goldthorpe)
Orchard St. S63—1E 29
(Thurnscoe)
Orchard St. S73—6B 26
Orchards Way. S40—4F 137
Orchard, The. S31—1G 119
Orchard View Rd. S40—1E 137
Orchard Wlk. S71—4H 13
Orchid Clo. S44—2G 139
Orchid Way. S31—3E 119
Ordnance Ter. S61—3H 77
(off Up. Clara St.)
Orgreave Clo. S13—4C 102
Orgreave Cres. S13—4C 102
Orgreave Dri. S13—4C 102
Orgreave Ho. DN1—1C 46
(off Burden Clo.)
Orgreave La. S13—3B 102
Orgreave Pl. S13—3B 102
Orgreave Rise. S13—5D 102
Orgreave Rd. S13—4B 102
Orgreave Rd. S60—1C 102
Orgreave Way. S13—5C 102
Oriel Mt. S10—6C 96
Oriel Rd. S10—6D 96
Oriel Way. S71—4D 14
Ormesby Clo. S18—2A 128
Ormesby Cres. DN5—4G 31
Ormesby Way. S66—4H 81
Ormes Meadow. S19—5C 114
Ormond Clo. S8—3F 123
Ormond Clo. S42—6D 136
Ormond Dri. S8—3F 123
Ormonde Way. DN11—5C 62
Ormond Rd. S8—3F 123
Ormond Way. S8—2F 123
Ormsby Clo. DN4—1G 61
Ormsby Rd. S41—4H 131
Orpen Dri. S14—5A 112
Orpen Way. S14—5A 112
Orphanage Rd. S3—3F 87
Orwell Clo. S73—2H 39
Orwins Clo. S41—4F 131
Osbert Dri. S66—4A 94
Osberton Pl. S11—5B 98
Osberton St. DN11—6H 61
Osberton St. S62—1H 69
Osberton St. S65—6A 70
Osbert Rd. S60—1H 91
Osborne Av. DN6—2B 16
Osborne Av. S31—5C 104
Osborne Clo. S11—6A 98
Osborne Ct. S11—6A 98
Osborne Ct. S71—3D 14
Osborne Dri. S31—2B 118
Osborne Rd. DN2—5F 33
Osborne Rd. S11—6A 98
Osborne Rd. S31—5B 118
(Kiveton Park)
Osborne Rd. S31—2B 118
(Todwick)
Osborne St. S70—1A 24
Osgathorpe Cres. S4—3G 87
Osgathorpe Dri. S4—3G 87
Osgathorpe Rd. S4—3G 87
Osmaston Rd. S8—5D 110
Osmond Dri. S70—4A 24
Osmond Pl. S70—4A 24
Osmund Rd. S31—6B 124
Osprey Av. S70—3D 36
Osprey Gdns. S2—3A 100
Osprey Rd. S31—1C 116
Oswestry Rd. S5—5G 75
Oswin Av. DN4—4A 46
Otley La. DN12—3F 59

Otley Wlk. S6—5B 86
Otter St. S9—5B 88
Oughtibridge Clo. S30—2D 72
Oughtibridge La. S30—2E 73
Oulton Av. S66—3H 81
Oulton Dri. S72—6C 10
Oulton Rise. S64—5H 43
Ouseburn Croft. S9—6C 88
Ouseburn Rd. S9—6C 88
Ouseburn St. S9—6C 88
Ouse Rd. S9—6C 88
Ouse Ter. DN12—2E 59
Outgang La. S31—2C 106
Outgang La. S66—6H 83
Outram Rd. S2—3A 100
Outram Rd. S41—5H 131
Oval Rd. S65—2H 79
Oval, The. DN4—2A 48
Oval, The. DN6—1B 16
Oval, The. DN12—2E 59
Oval, The. S5—6H 75
Oval, The. S31—1G 119
Overcroft Rise. S17—5D 120
Overdale Av. S70—3B 24
Overdale Gdns. S17—3C 120
Overdale Rise. S17—3C 120
Overdale Rd. S73—2G 39
Overend Clo. S14—3H 111
Overend Dri. S14—3H 111
Overend Rd. S14—3H 111
Overend Way. S14—3H 111
Oversley Rd. DN2—3F 33
Oversley St. S9—6G 77
Overton Clo. S43—1D 134
Overton Rd. S6—1H 85
Owen Clo. S6—3B 74
Owen Clo. S65—1E 79
Owen Pl. S6—3B 74
Owen Wlk. S6—3B 74
Owler Ga. S30—1A 72
Owler La. S4—2H 87 to 2A 88
(in three parts)
Owlerton Grn. S6—3B 86
Owlet La. S4—2A 88
Owlings Pl. S6—3G 85
Owlings Rd. S6—2G 85
Owlthorpe Greenway. S19
—6D 114 to 6H 115
Owlthorpe La. S19—1B 124
Owlthorpe Rise. S19—1B 124
Owram St. S73—4E 27
Ox Carr. DN3—3E 35
Ox Close Av. S17—4G 121
Ox Close Av. S61—6G 67
Oxclose Dri. S18—2A 128
Oxclose La. S18—2A 128
Oxford Clo. S43—3F 133
Oxford Clo. S61—4C 68
Oxford Pl. DN1—1C 46
Oxford Pl. S71—1E 25
Oxford Rd. S43—3F 133
Oxford St. DN11—4C 62
Oxford St. S6—1B 98
Oxford St. S64—6C 42
Oxford St. S65—2G 79
Oxford St. S70—2A 24
Oxford St. S71—1E 25
Oxley Clo. S30—3C 140
Oxley Gro. S60—5F 79
Oxspring Bank. S5—1B 86
Oxted Rd. S9—1C 88
Oxton Dri. DN4—5F 45
Oxton Rd. S71—5C 8

Packer's Row. S40—2A 138
Packhorse La. S30—5C 50
Packington Rd. DN4—4F 49

Packman La. S31—6D 118
Packman Rd. S62—4C 54
Packman Rd. S63—4B 40
Packmans Clo. S30—6A 64
Packmans Way. S30—6A 64
Packwood Clo. S66—3H 83
Paddock Clo. DN5—4G 31
Paddock Clo. S75—4G 7
Paddock Cres. S2—2A 112
Paddock Rd. S75—4G 7
Paddocks, The. S31—6C 104
Paddocks, The. S43—1G 135
Paddocks, The. S65—5E 71
Paddock, The. S61—3D 66
Paddock, The. S73—3E 27
Paddock Way. S18—1F 129
(in two parts)
Padley Clo. S75—2A 22
Padley Wlk. S5—5H 75
Padley Way. S5—5G 75
Padua Rise. S73—4D 26
Page Hall Rd. S4—2H 87
Pagenall Dri. S31—5B 104
Paget St. S9—4B 88
Pagnell Av. S63—2D 28
Paisley Clo. S43—3A 134
Palermo Fold. S73—3D 26
Palgrave Cres. S5—5C 74
Palgrave Rd. S5—5B 74
Palington Gro. DN4—2C 48
Palm Av. DN3—2G 35
Palmer Cres. S18—3F 129
Palmer Rd. S9—5E 89
Palmerston Av. S66—3E 83
Palmerston Rd. S10—2B 98
Palmer St. DN4—2E 47
Palmer St. S9—6B 88
Palmers Way. S66—5H 93
Palm Gro. DN12—4C 58
Palm Hollow Clo. S66—5D 80
Palm La. S6—5A 86
Palm St. S6—5A 86
Palm St. S75—4F 13
Pamela Dri. DN4—5E 45
Pangbourne Rd. S63—1E 29
Pantry Grn. S70—5C 24
Pantry Well. S70—5C 24
Paper Mill Rd. S5—2A 76
Parade, The. S12—1C 112
Parade, The. S62—6E 55
Parade, The. S74—6H 37
Paradise La. S1—2E 5
Paradise Sq. S1—2E 5 & 1E 99
Paradise St. S1—2E 5 & 1E 99
Parish Way. S71—4D 14
Park Av. DN3—2D 34
Park Av. DN5—2E 45
Park Av. DN12—4E 59
Park Av. S10—5H 97
Park Av. S18—1F 129
Park Av. S30—3E 65
Park Av. S31—6E 107
Park Av. S60—1A 92
Park Av. S64—6E 43
Park Av. S70—6G 13
Park Av. S71—6B 8
(Athersley)
Park Av. S71—2F 9
(Royston)
Park Av. S72—2H 11
(Brierley)
Park Av. S72—5B 10
(Cudworth)
Park Av. S72—5G 11
(Grimethorpe)
Park Clo. DN3—3F 35
Park Clo. DN5—2E 45
Park Clo. S40—6A 138

Park Clo. S64—2A 56
Park Clo. S65—5D 70
Park Clo. S75—5G 7
Park Cotts. S70—6A 24
Park Ct. S30—1A 74
Park Cres. DN4—6E 45
Park Cres. S10—3B 98
Park Cres. S30—1F 75
Park Cres. S71—2F 9
Park Dri. DN5—2D 44
Park Dri. S30—3D 140
Park Dri. S31—6H 103
Park Dri. S41—4B 138
Park Dri. S75—5D 22
Park Dri. Way. S30—2D 140
Park End Rd. S63—5F 29
Parker Av. S44—1F 139
Parker's La. S10—2A 98
Parkers La. S17—1D 120
Parker's Rd. S10—2A 98
Parker's Ter. S70—4C 36
Parker St. S70—6F 13
Parkers Yd. S41—2B 138
Parkfield Pl. S2—5E 99
Parkfield Rd. S65—3F 79
Parkgate Av. DN12—3C 58
Parkgate Clo. S19—2A 124
Parkgate Croft. S19—6A 114
Parkgate Dri. S19—6A 114
Park Grange Clo. S2—5H 99
Park Grange Croft. S2—4G 99
Park Grange Dri. S2—5G 99
Park Grange Mt. S2—5G 99
Park Grange Rd. S2
—4G 99 to 5A 100
Park Grange View. S2—5H 99
Park Gro. S30—2D 140
Park Gro. S62—6F 55
Park Gro. S66—4H 81
Park Gro. S70—1G 23
Park Hall Av. S42—5D 136
Park Hall Clo. S42—6D 136
Park Hall Gdns. S42—6D 136
Parkhead Clo. S71—1C 8
Parkhead Ct. S11—3F 109
Parkhead Cres. S11—3F 109
Parkhead Rd. S11—4E 109
Park Hill. S31—6E 125
(Eckington)
Park Hill. S31—6H 103
(Swallownest)
Park Hill. S73—3F 27
Parkhill Cres. DN3—2H 21
Parkhill Rd. DN3—2H 21
Park Hill Rd. S73—6C 26
Park Hollow. S73—1H 39
Park Ho. La. S9—1H 89
Parkinson St. DN1—4D 32
Parkland Clo. DN11—4E 63
Parkland Dri. DN11—4F 63
Parklands. DN3—6D 20
Park La. DN4—1A 48
Park La. DN12—6C 58
Park La. S9—6E 77
Park La. S10—3B 98
Park La. S30—2E 141
(Deepcar)
Park La. S30—4E 51
(High Green)
Park La. S31—3C 106
Park La. S41—4H 131
Park La. S65—1A 83
(Braithwell Common)
Park La. S65—4D 70
(Thrybergh)
Park La. Ct. S65—4D 70
Parkman Rd. S62 & S63
—4C 54 to 6C 40

Park Nook. S65—5C 70
Park Pl. S65—2H 79
Park Rd. DN1—6D 32
Park Rd. DN5—6A 18
Park Rd. DN12—4D 58
Park Rd. S6—5F 85
Park Rd. S40—4H 137
Park Rd. S63—1E 29
(Thurnscoe)
Park Rd. S63—6E 41
(Wath upon Dearne)
Park Rd. S64—6E 43
(Mexborough)
Park Rd. S64—3H 55
(Swinton)
Park Rd. S65—2H 79
Park Rd. S70—2E 23
(Barnsley)
Park Rd. S70—6A 24
(Worsbrough)
Park Rd. S72—2H 11
(Brierley)
Park Rd. S72—6G 11
(Grimethorpe)
Parkside La. S6—6D 84
Parkside Rd. S6—2A 86
Parkside Rd. S74—1F 51
Parkside Shopping Centre. S31
—2B 126
Parkson Rd. S60—1H 91
Park Spring Clo. S2—5G 99
Park Spring Dri. S2—5G 99
Park Spring Gro. S2—5G 99
Park Spring Pl. S2—5G 99
Park Spring Way. S2—5G 99
Park Sq. S2—3H 5 & 2F 99
Parkstone Cres. S66—5B 82
Parkstone Delph. S12—5C 112
Parkstone Way. DN2—2A 34
Park St. S31—6A 104
Park St. S40—6A 138
Park St. S61—2B 78
Park St. S62—1F 69
Park St. S70—1G 23
Park St. S73—1G 39
Park Ter. DN1—6D 32
Park Ter. S30—3F 65
Park Ter. S31—5B 118
Park Ter. S65—5C 70
Park, The. DN6—4C 16
Park Vale Dri. S65—5D 70
Park View. DN6—2E 17
Park View. S31—4A 118
Park View. S41—6D 138
Park View. S61—3A 66
Park View. S64—6C 42
Park View. S66—3H 83
(in two parts)
Park View. S70—2F 23
(Barnsley)
Park View. S70—4B 24
(Worsbrough)
Park View. S71—1F 9
Park View. S72—2H 11
(Brierley)
Park View. S72—3C 10
(Shafton)
Park View. S75—2B 22
Park View Av. S19—2E 125
Parkview Ct. S8—5E 111
Park View Rd. S6—2A 86
Park View Rd. S30—3E 65
Park View Rd. S61—4E 77
Park View Rd. S75—3D 24
Park View Ter. S9—6E 89
Parkway. DN3—4F 35
Park Way. DN6—1D 16
Parkway Av. S9—1B 100

Parkway Clo. S9—1B 100
Parkway Dri. S9—2C 100
Parkway Mkt. S9—1D 100
Parkway N. DN2—3F 33
Parkway S. DN2—3F 33
Parkwood Ind. Est. S3—5E 87
Parkwood Rise. DN3—2E 21
Parkwood Rd. S3—4C 86
Parkwood Rd. N. S5—1D 86
Parma Rise. S73—4C 26
Parsley Hay Clo. S13—4H 101
Parsley Hay Dri. S13—4H 101
Parsley Hay Gdns. S13—4H 101
Parsley Hay Rd. S13—4H 101
Parsonage Clo. S19—3D 124
Parsonage Cres. S6—5A 86
Parsonage St. S6—5A 86
Parson Cross Rd. S6—5A 74
Parson La. S75—3A 22
Partridge Clo. S31—6B 124
Partridge Flatt Rd. DN4—5D 48
Partridge Pl. S31—1C 116
Partridge Rise. DN4—5D 48
Partridge Rd. DN3—2H 21
Partridge View. S2—3A 100
Parwich Clo. S40—6C 130
Passfield Rd. DN11—5E 63
Passhouses Rd. S4—3F 87
Pasture Dri. DN3—4E 35
(in two parts)
Pasture Gro. S31—6C 124
Pasture La. S63—5H 27
Pastures Rd. S64—6H 43
Pastures, The. S31—2A 118
Paternoster Row. S1
—5F 5 & 3F 99
Paterson Clo. S30—2C 140
Paterson Ct. S30—2D 140
Paterson Croft. S30—2C 140
Paterson Gdns. S30—2D 140
Paterson Rd. S31—4G 107
Patmore Rd. S5—5H 75
Paton Gro. S43—3D 132
Patterdale Clo. S18—2C 128
Patterdale Way. S31—1H 119
Pavement, The. S2—3H 5
Pavilion La. S60—1B 90
Paxton Ct. S14—3B 112
Paxton Cres. DN3—2D 34
Paxton La. S10—3B 98
Paxton Rd. S41—6C 132
Payler Clo. S2—5C 100
Payne Dri. S60—3D 78
Paynes Cres. S62—6E 55
Peacehaven. DN3—2H 21
Peacock Clo. S61—1B 66
Peakdale Cres. S12—2G 113
Peake Av. DN12—3C 58
Peak La. S66—6E 83
Peak Pl. S43—4B 134
Peak Rd. S71—6C 8
Peaks Mt. S19—4E 115
Peaks Sq. S19—5E 115
Peak View Rd. S40—1F 137
Pearce Rd. S9—2E 101
Pearce Wlk. S9—1E 101
Pea Royd La. S30—2E 141
Pearson Cres. S73—4H 25
Pearson Pl. S8—2D 110
Pearson's Clo. S65—5A 80
Pearson's Field. S73—8B 26
Pearson St. S30—2D 140
Pear St. S11—4C 98
Peartree Av. S63—1E 29
Pear Tree Av. S66—4G 81
Pear Tree Clo. S4—4A 126
Pear Tree Clo. S43—3G 133

Pear Tree Clo. S60—3D 90
Pear Tree Ct. S63—1E 29
Pear Tree Rd. S5—3H 75
Pearwood Cres. DN4—6H 45
Peashill St. S62—2F 69
Peatfield Rd. S31—2D 126
Peckham Rd. S30—1D 64
Pedley Av. S19—1E 125
Pedley Clo. S19—6E 115
Pedley Dri. S19—1E 125
Pedley Gro. S19—6E 115
Peel Clo. S66—3E 83
Peel Pde. S70—6G 13
Peel Pl. S71—4A 14
Peel Sq. S70—6G 13
Peel St. S10—3A 98
Peel St. S70—6G 13
(Barnsley)
Peel St. S70—2H 23
(Worsborough Common)
Peel St. Arc. S70—6G 13
Peel Ter. S10—2C 98
Peet Wlk. S74—4B 38
Peg Folly. S30—3A 140
Peggy La. S30—6A 66
Pell's Clo. DN1—6C 32
Pembrey Ct. S19—5G 115
Pembridge Ct. S71—1E 9
Pembroke Av. DN4—5A 46
Pembroke Clo. S40—4E 137
Pembroke Cres. S30—1C 64
Pembroke Rise. DN5—3F 31
Pembroke Rise. S31—3F 119
Pembroke Rd. S18—3E 129
Pembroke Rd. S11—4C 98
Pembroke St. S61—3H 77
Pendeen Rd. S11—5F 97
Pendlebury Gro. S74—6G 37
Pendle Croft. S19—6H 115
Penistone Rd. S6—2A to 6D 86
Penistone Rd. S30—1A 64
(Chapeltown)
Penistone Rd. S30—1B 74 to
(Grenoside)   5B 64
Penistone Rd. N. S6
—1A 86 & 6A 74
Penistone St. DN1—5D 32
Penley St. S71—5D 98
Penmore Clo. S41—4C 138
Penmore Gdns. S41—5C 138
Penmore La. S41—5C 138
Penmore St. S41—5C 138
Pennine Centre, The. S1—2D 4
Pennine Clo. S75—3E 7
Pennine View. S30—5D 140
Pennine View. S75—3E 7
Pennine Way. S40—6E 131
Pennine Way. S75—5D 12
Pen Nook Clo. S30—5G 141
Pen Nook Ct. S30—5G 141
Pen Nook Dri. S30—5G 141
Pen Nook Gdns. S30—5G 141
Penns Rd. S2—1G 111
Penny Hill La. S31 & S66
—1D 104
Pennyholme Clo. S31—5B 118
Penny La. S17—5C 120
Penny Piece La. S31—1F 119
Penny Piece Pl. S31—1F 119
Penrhyn Rd. S11—6A 98
Penrhyn Wlk. S71—1G 25
Penrith Clo. S5—1C 86
Penrith Cres. S5—1C 86
Penrith Gro. S71—1G 25
Penrith Rd. DN2—5A 34
Penrith Rd. S5—1C 86
Penrose Pl. S13—1A 114
Penshurst Clo. S65—1H 79

Penthorpe Clo. S12—1D 112
Pentland Clo. S40—6E 131
Pentland Gdns. S19—5D 114
Pentland Rd. S18—2B 128
Penton St. S1—3D 4
Penyghent Clo. S30—1D 64
Pepper Clo. S61—5F 67
Pepper St. S74—3A 38
Percy St. S3—6D 86
Percy St. S65—3E 79
Peregrine Dri. S70—3D 36
Peregrine Way. S31—4H 127
(in two parts)
Perigree Rd. S8—4C 110
Periwood La. S8—4C 110
Perkyn Rd. S5—2H 75
Perkyn Ter. S5—2H 75
Perran Gro. DN5—4H 31
Perseverance St. S70—6F 13
Persimman Clo. DN11—6D 62
Perth Clo. S64—5G 43
Petal Clo. S66—3H 83
Peter Av. S30—4H 141
Peterborough Clo. S10—5A 96
Peterborough Dri. S10—4A 96
Peterborough Rd. S10—4A 96
Peterdale Clo. S43—3E 133
Peterdale Rd. S43—3E 133
Petersgate. DN5
—1G 31 to 6H 17
Peter's Rd. DN12—4B 60
Peter St. S61—2G 77
Peter St. S66—4A 94
Petre Dri. S4—3A 88
Petre St. S4—4H 87
Pettyclose La. S41—6D 132
Petunia Rd. DN3—4D 20
Petworth Croft. S71—1D 8
Petworth Dri. S11—5F 109
Pevensey Av. S41—5G 131
Pevensey Ct. S41—4G 131
Peveril Clo. S31—4A 118
Peveril Cres. S71—6C 8
Peveril Rd. DN4—5G 45
Peveril Rd. S11—6H 97
Peveril Rd. S31—5E 125
Peveril Rd. S41—4H 131
Pexton Rd. S4—3G 87
Pheasant Bank. DN11—4E 63
Philip La. S30—5A 50
Philip Rd. S70—2D 24
Phillimore Rd. S9—5D 88
Phillips Rd. S6—2D 84
Phoenix Gro. S60—1B 90
Phoenix Rd. S12—6E 113
Phoenix Rd. S60—5G 77
Piccadilly. DN5—1A 32
Piccadilly Rd. S41—3B 138
Piccadilly Rd. S64—4A 56
Pickering Cres. S31—6A 104
Pickering Rd. DN5—4A 18
Pickering Rd. S3—4D 86
Pickering St. S9—3D 88
Pickhill's Av. S30—4H 29
Picking La. S30—1F 75
Pickmere Rd. S10—1H 97
Pickton Clo. S40—3F 137
Pickup Cres. S73—1F 39
Piece End. S30—5B 50
(in two parts)
Piece End Clo. S30—5B 50
Pieces N., The. S60—3H 91
Pieces S., The. S60—3H 91
Pighills La. S18—5F 123
Pike Clo. S40—6D 130
Pike Low Gro. S75—5H 7
Pike Rd. S60—2C 90
Pilgrim St. S3—4F 87

Pilley Grn. S75—6B 36
Pilley La. S75—5A 36
Pilley La. End. S75—4A 36
Pinchfield Ct. S66—6F 81
Pinchfield Holt. S66—6F 81
Pinchfield La. S66—6F 81
Pinch Mill La. S60—2C 92
Pindale Av. S43—4A 134
Pindar Oaks Cotts. S70—1B 24
Pindar Oaks St. S70—1A 24
Pindar St. S70—1B 24
Pine Av. S31—4F 119
Pine Clo. S31—4A 126
Pine Clo. S66—3G 81
Pine Clo. S70—3C 24
Pine Clo. S74—6A 38
Pine Croft. S30—3E 65
Pinecroft Way. S30—3E 65
Pinefield Av. DN3—1E 21
Pinefield Rd. DN3—1E 21
Pine Gro. DN12—5C 58
Pinehall Dri. S71—3D 14
Pine Hall Rd. DN3—1E 21
Pinehurst Rise. S64—3B 56
Pine Rd. DN4—3D 48
Pines, The. S10—5A 96
Pine St. S43—3G 133
Pine View. S40—2D 136
Pine Wlk. S64—5B 56
Pinewood Av. DN3—1F 35
Pinewood Av. DN4—6G 45
Pinfold. S63—5E 41
Pinfold Clo. S42—5A 136
Pinfold Clo. S64—3A 56
Pinfold Clo. S71—1E 25
Pinfold Cotts. S72—1H 15
Pinfold Hill. S70—3A 24
Pinfold Lands. S64—1F 57
Pinfold La. S3—4F 87
Pinfold La. S60—3E 79
Pinfold La. S71—2E 9
Pinfold La. S73—4F 27
Pinfold St. S1—3D 4 & 2E 99
Pinfold St. S31—6D 124
Pingle Av. S7—4A 110
Pingle La. S65—5G 71
Pingle Rd. S7—4H 109
Pingle Rd. S31—2C 126
Pingles Cres. S65—5C 70
Pinner Rd. S11—5A 98
Pinstone St. S1—5E 5 & 3E 99
Pipe Ho. La. S62—6F 55
(in two parts)
Piper Clo. S5—6E 75
Piper Cres. S5—5E 75
Pipering La. DN5—2G to 2H 31
(in two parts)
Piper La. S31—6D 104
Piper La. S42—2A 136
Piper Rd. S5—6F 75
Pipeyard La. S31—6C 124
Pipworth Gro. S2—4E 101
Pipworth La. S31—5F 125
Pisgah Ho. Rd. S10—2A 98
Pitchard Clo. S12—4B 114
Pitchford La. S10—4D 96
Pit La. S12—1C 112
Pit La. S60—1F 103
Pit La. S61—3B 66
Pit La. S73—1C 38
Pitman Rd. DN12—2A 58
Pit Row. S73—5E 39
Pitsmoor Rd. S3—5E 87
Pittam Clo. DN3—3F 35
Pitt Clo. S1—4B 4
Pitt La. S1—4B 4
Pitt La. S75—4E 7

Pitt St. S1—4B 4 & 2D 98
Pitt St. S31—6H 125
Pitt St. S61—3H 77
Pitt St. S64—1G 57
Pitt St. S70—6G 13
Pitt St. S73—4C 26
Pitt St. W. S70—6F 13
Plane Clo. DN4—3D 48
Plane Dri. S66—4G 81
Planet Rd. DN6—1E 17
Plank Ga. S31—1E 73
Plantation Av. DN4—1F 63
Plantation Av. S31—1G 119
(Anston)
Plantation Av. S31—4F 107
(Dinnington)
Plantation Av. S71—2F 9
Plantation Clo. S66—3F 83
Plantation Rd. S8—1E 111
Plantin Rise. S19—2E 125
Plantin, The. S19—2E 125
Plaster Pits La. DN5—5D 30
Platt St S3—5E 87
Platts Comn. Ind. Est. S74
—4H 37
Platts Dri. S19—3G 115
Platts La. S30—2E 73
Playford Yd. S74—3H 37
Pleasant Clo. S12—1D 112
Pleasant Pl. S40—2F 137
Pleasant Rd. S12—1D 112
Pleasant View St. S71—3G 13
Pleasley Rd. S60 & S31—2H 91
Plover Ct. DN11—4E 63
Plover Ct. S2—3A 100
Plover Croft. S61—1C 66
Plover Dri. S70—3D 36
Plover Way. S44—2F 139
Plowmans Way. S61—4H 67
Plowright Clo. S14—2H 111
Plowright Dri. S14—2H 111
Plowright Mt. S14—2H 111
Plowright Way. S14—2H 111
Plumber St. S70—6F 13
Plumbley Hall M. S19—3C 124
Plumbley Hall Rd. S19—2C 124
Plumbley La. S19—3B 124
Plumbleywood La. S19—3A 124
Plum La. S3—1E 5 & 1E 99
Plumpers Rd. S9—1F 89
Plumpton Av. S64—5G 43
Plumpton Gdns. DN4—5E 49
Plumpton Pk. Rd. DN4—6E 49
Plum St. S3—1E 5 & 1E 99
Plunket Rd. DN2—5F 33
Plymouth St. S7—2C 110
Pocknedge La. S42—4A 136
Pogmoor La. S75—5C 12
Pogmoor Rd. S75 & S70—5D 12
Pog Well La. S75—4A 12
Polka Ct. S3—4E 87
Pollard Av. S5—6C 74
Pollard Cres. S5—6C 74
Pollard Rd. S5—6C 74
Pollard St. S61—3G 77
Pollitt St. S75—4G 13
Pollyfox Way. S75—2B 22
Pomona St. S11—4C 98
Pond Clo. S6—5D 84
Pond Hill. S1—3G 5 & 2F 99
Pond Rd. S6—5D 84
Pond St. S1—3F 5 & 2F 99
Pond St. S40—3A 138
Pond St. S70—1G 23
(in two parts)
Pondwell Dri. S43—4F 133
Pontefract Rd. S70 & S71
—6H 13 to 1F 15

Pontefract Rd. S72—5B 10
Pontefract Rd. S73—3B to 1B 40
Pool Dri. DN4—6F 49
Poole Pl. S9—1E 101
Poole Rd. S9—1D 100
Poolsbrook Av. S43—3E 135
Poolsbrook Cres. S43—3E 135
Poolsbrook Rd. S44—5E 135
Poolsbrook Sq. S43—3E 135
Poolsbrook View. S43—3E 135
Pools La. S71—2G 9
Pool Sq. S1—4E 5 & 2E 99
Pope Av. DN12—3B 58
Pop La. DN12—3E 59
Poplar Av. S19—2F 115
Poplar Av. S30—4D 140
Poplar Av. S40—3D 136
Poplar Av. S63—4G 29
Poplar Av. S65—5C 70
Poplar Av. S72—3C 10
Poplar Clo. DN3—2H 49
Poplar Clo. S18—4G 129
Poplar Clo. S30—2C 72
Poplar Clo. S31—4A 126
Poplar Clo. S64—5D 42
Poplar Dri. DN2—3A 34
Poplar Dri. S60—3B 90
Poplar Dri. S63—1F 55
Poplar Glade. S66—5F 81
Poplar Gro. DN4—1C 60
Poplar Gro. DN12—5D 58
Poplar Gro. S64—2B 56
Poplar Gro. S65—1H 81
Poplar Nook. S31—4G 117
Poplar Pl. DN3—3F 35
Poplar Rise. S66—3D 82
Poplar Rd. S30—2C 72
Poplar Rd. S31—6H 125
Poplar Rd. S73—1G 39
Poplars Rd. S70—2B 24
Poplar Ter. DN5—1B 32
Poplar Ter. S71—1F 9
Poplar Way. S60—6B 90
Popple St. S4—2H 87
Porter Av. S75—5E 13
Porter Brook View. S11—5B 98
Porter St. S43—1C 134
Porter Ter. S11—5A 98
Porter Ter. S75—5D 12
Portland Av. S31—6C 104
Portland Bldgs. S6—6C 86
(off Portland St.)
Portland Clo. S31—5E 107
Portland La. S1—4B 4 & 2D 98
Portland Pl. S66—4G 83
Portland Rd. DN11—6D 62
Portland Rd. S19—5G 115
Portland St. S6—6C 86
(in two parts)
Portland St. S64—2B 56
Portland St. S70—1B 24
Portland Wlk. S6—5C 86
Portobello. S1—3B 4 & 2D 98
Portobello La. S1—3B 4 & 2D 98
Portobello St. S1—3C 4 & 2D 98
Portsea Rd. S6—3H 85
Pot Ho. La. S30—3D 140
Potterdyke Av. S62—5F 55
Potter Hill. S61—4C 68
Potter Hill La. S30—6A 50
Potters Ga. S30—6A 50
(in two parts)
Pottery Clo. S62—2F 69
Pottery La. E. S41—4B 132
Pottery La. W. S41—4A 132
Pottery Row. S61—4A 78
Poucher St. S61—4H 77
Poulton St. S71—1D 14

Powder Mill La. S70—6C 24
Powell Dri. S31—3A 126
Powell St. S3—2A 4 & 1C 98
Powell St. S70—5B 24
Powley Rd. S6—4B 74
Poynton Av. S31—2C 104
Poynton Way. S31—2C 104
Poynton Wood Cres. S17
—3G 121
Poynton Wood Glade. S17
—3G 121
Prescott Rd. S6—1G 85
Preston Av. S74—4C 38
Preston St. S8—6E 99
Preston Way. S71—1D 14
Prestwich St. S70—5D 76
Prestwood Gdns. S30—2C 64
Priest Croft La. S73—1D 26
Priestfield Gdns. S41—4D 130
Priestley Av S62—6H 55
Priestley Av. S75—5A 6
Priestley Clo. DN4—6H 45
Priestley St. S2—4F 99
Primrose Av. S5—5A 76
Primrose Av. S60—4D 90
Primrose Av. S73—4D 26
Primrose Circ. DN11—5E 63
Primrose Clo. S31—2C 126
Primrose Clo. S63—6D 28
Primrose Ct. S41—1H 137
Primrose Cres. S19—4F 115
Primrose Dri. S30—1F 75
Primrose Hill. S6—5B & 5C 86
(in two parts)
Primrose Hill. S60—1C 78
Primrose Hill. S74—6A 38
Primrose La. S31—1C 126
Primrose Way. S74—1A 52
Primulas Clo. S31—3E 119
Prince Arthur St. S75—5F 13
Princegate. DN1—6D 32
Prince of Wales Rd. S2 & S9
—6C 100
Prince's Cres. DN12—2B 60
Prince's Rd. DN4—2H 47
Princess Clo. S63—1H 41
Princess Ct. S2—5D 100
Princess Dri. S30—4E 141
Princess Gdns. S73—1F 39
Princess Gro. S75—6A 36
Prince's Sq. DN3—3D 20
Princess Rd. S18—1E 129
Princess Rd. S63—4G 29
Princess Rd. S64—6F 43
Princess St. DN6—3D 16
Princess St. S4—6H 87
Princess St. S31—3C 106
Princess St. S41—1H 137
Princess St. S43—2F 133
Princess St. S63—4D 40
Princess St. S70—6G 13
Princess St. S72—4C 10
Princess St. S73—6A 26
Princess St. S74—6F 37
Princess St. S75—4E 7
Prince's St. DN1—6D 32
Princes St. S60—3B 78
Prince St. S64—1B 56
Pringle Rd. S60—2B 90
Printing Office St. DN1—6C 32
Prior Rd. DN12—4D 58
Priory Av. S7—5D 98
Priory Clo. DN12—2E 59
Priory Clo. S30—6E 65
Priory Clo. S70—1D 36
Priory Cres. S71—4E 15
Priory Pl. DN1—6C 32
Priory Pl. S7—5D 98

Priory Pl. S71—3E 15
Priory Rd. S7—6C 98
Priory Rd. S30—6E 65
Priory Rd. S63—1A 42
Priory Rd. S71—3E 15
Priory Ter. S7—5D 98
Priory Way. S31—6C 104
Pritchard Clo. S12—4B 114
Private Dri. S43—3G 133
Probert Av. S63—4F 29
Proctor Pl. S6—3A 86
Progress Dri. S66—5H 81
Prospect Clo. S66—5H 81
Prospect Cotts. S70—2H 23
Prospect Ct. S17—4H 121
Prospect Dri. S17—4F 121
Prospect Pl. DN1—1C 46
Prospect Pl. S17—3G 121
Prospect Rd. DN5—3A 18
Prospect Rd. S2—6E 99
Prospect Rd. S4—6D 136
Prospect Rd. S12—4B 121
Prospect Rd. S18—6G 123
Prospect Rd. S41—1H 131
Prospect Rd. S63—6E 29
Prospect Rd. S72—1H 15
Prospect St. S70—6F 13
Prospect St. S72—6B 10
Prospect Ter. S40—1G 137
Providence Ct. S70—1H 23
Providence Rd. S6—5H 85
Providence St. S60—3C 78
Providence St. S61—4C 68
Providence St. S73—5D 26
Psalter Ct. S11—6A 98
Psalter La. S11—6H 97 to 5C 98
Psalters La. S61—3H 77 & 3A 78
Pullman Clo. S43—1D 134
Pump Riding. DN12—4D 60
Purbeck Av. S40—1F 137
Purbeck Ct. S19—5D 114
Purbeck Gro. S19—5D 114
Purbeck Rd. S19—5D 114
Purcell Clo. S66—5H 83
Pye Av. S75—5E 7
Pye Bank Clo. S3—5E 87
Pye Bank Dri. S3—5E 87
Pye Bank Rd. S3—5E 87
Pym Rd. S64—6E 43
Pynot Rd. S41—1B 132

Quadrant, The. S17—4E 121
Quail Rise. S2—3A 100
Quaker Clo. S63—6D 40
Quaker La. DN4—5F 45
Quaker La. S71—1G 25
Quantock Way. S40—6D 130
Quarry Bank Rd. S41—3C 138
Quarry Clo. S60—3A 90
Quarry Clo. S75—5B 6
Quarryfield La. S66—3F 83
   (Maltby)
Quarry Field La. S66—6F 81
   (Wickersley)
Quarry Hill. S19—1A 124
Quarry Hill. S60—3D 78
Quarry Hill Rd. S63—1E 55
Quarry La. S11—1A 110
Quarry La. S31—1F 119
Quarry La. S40—3E 137
Quarry La. S61—1C 78
Quarry La. S64—4D 42
Quarry La. S73—4G 27
Quarry Rd. S13—3H 101
Quarry Rd. S17—4E 121
Quarry Rd. S31—2A 126
Quarry Rd. S74—2H 37

Quarry St. S62—1F 69
Quarry St. S64—1F 57
Quarry St. S70—1H 23
Quarry St. S71—2A 14
Quarry St. S72—6B 10
Quarry Vale. S72—2H 15
Quarry Vale Gro. S12—3E 113
Quarry Vale Rd. S12—3E 113
Queen Av. DN11—4C 62
Queen Av. S66—5G 83
Queen Mary Clo. S2—6C 100
Queen Mary Cres. DN3—3D 20
Queen Mary Cres. S2—5C 100
Queen Mary Rd. S2—5B 100
Queen Mary Rd. S40—4D 136
Queen Mary's Dri. DN11—4C 62
Queen Mary St. S66—6H 83
Queen's Av. S31—5G 117
Queen's Av. S64—1B 56
Queen's Av. S72—2H 27
Queen's Av. S75—5F 13
Queensberry Rd. DN2—5A 34
Queen's Ct. DN5—3A 32
Queen's Cres. DN12—2B 60
Queens Cres. S74—6E 37
Queen's Dri. S72—4C 10
   (Cudworth)
Queen's Dri. S72—2B 10
   (Shafton)
Queen's Dri. S75—4E 13
   (Barnsley)
Queen's Dri. S75—2B 22
   (Dodsworth)
Queens Gdns. S73—1F 39
Queens Gdns. S74—6F 37
Queens Gdns. S75—4E 13
Queensgate. DN1—1D 46
Queensgate. S30—1B 74
Queen's Rd. DN1—5E 33
Queens Rd. S2—6E 99
Queens Rd. S3—9F 115
Queen's Rd. S31—6A 104
Queen's Rd. S71—6H 13
Queen's Rd. S72—4C 10
Queens Row. S3—1C 4 & 1D 98
Queen's Ter. S64—6E 43
Queen St. DN4—3B 46
   (in two parts)
Queen St. S1—2E 5 & 1E 99
Queen St. S19—2C 124
Queen St. S30—2E 65
Queen St. S31—3F 107
   (Dinnington)
Queen St. S31—6E 125
   (Eckington)
Queen St. S40—1H 137
Queen St. S43—2F 133
   (Brimington)
Queen St. S43—3B 134
   (Staveley)
Queen St. S62—6G 55
Queen St. S63—4G 29
   (Goldthorpe)
Queen St. S63—2G 29
   (Thurnscoe)
Queen St. S64—2B 56
Queen St. S65—2G 79
Queen St. S70—6H 13
Queen St. S72—6G 11
Queen St. S73—3F 27
Queen St. S74—6E 37
Queen St. N. S41—3A 132
Queen St. S. S70—6H 13
Queensway. S60—1F 91
Queensway. S70—4B 24
Queensway. S71—1E 9
Queensway. S74—5B 38
Queensway. S75—4E 13

Queen Victoria Rd. S17—5F 121
Quern Way. S73—3E 27
Quest Av. S73—3E 39
Quiet La. S10—1B 108
Quilter Rd. S66—5H 83
Quintec Ct. S61—6E 69
Quoit Grn. S18—2F 129
Quorn Dri. S40—6C 130

Raby Rd. DN2—4F 33
Raby St. S9—6G 77
Racecommon La. S70—2F 23
Racecommon Rd. S70—2F 23
Racecourse Mt. S41—3H 131
Racecourse Rd. S41—3H 131
Racecourse Rd. S64—2G 55
Race St. S70—6G 13
Racker Way. S6—4H 85
Rackford La. S31—3H 119
Rackford Rd. S31—2G 119
Radbourne Comn. S18—2B 128
Radburn Rd. DN11—5C 62
Radcliffe Mt. DN5—5A 18
Radcliffe Rd. DN5—5A 18
Radcliffe Rd. S71—5B 8
Radford St. S3—2B 4 & 1D 98
Radiance Rd. DN1—4E 33
Radley Av. S66—4F 81
Radnor Clo. S19—5G 115
Radnor Way. DN2—3A 34
Raeburn Clo. S14—3A 112
Raeburn Pl. S14—4A 112
Raeburn Rd. S14—5A 112
Raeburn Way. S14—5A 112
Ragusa Dri. DN11—6D 62
Raikes St. S64—1D 56
Rails Rd. S6—1A 96
Railway Av. S60—6C 90
Railway Cotts. S60—5C 90
Railway Cotts. S75—2A 22
Railway Ter. S41—6B 138
Railway Ter. S60—3C 78
Railway Ter. S63—4F 29
Railway View. S63—4G 29
Rainborough Rd. S63—5B 40
Rainboro View. S73—4E 39
Rainbow Av. S12—3B 114
Rainbow Clo. S12—3C 114
Rainbow Cres. S12—3C 114
Rainbow Dri. S12—3C 114
Rainbow Gro. S12—3C 114
Rainbow Pl. S12—5C 114
Rainbow Wlk. S12—3B 114
   (off Carter Lodge Dri.)
Rainbow Way. S12—3B 114
Rainford Dri. S71—1D 14
Rainford Sq. DN3—2D 20
Rainton Gro. S75—3D 12
Rainton Rd. DN1—1E 47
Raisen Hall Pl. S5—1E 87
Raisen Hall Rd. S5—6D 74
Rakes La. DN12—6D 60
Raleigh Dri. S30—2B 64
Raleigh Rd. S2—1F 111
Raleigh Ter. DN4—5G 45
Raley St. S70—2F 23
   (in two parts)
Ralph Ellis Dri. S30—4D 140
Ralph Rd. S43—1E 135
Ralston Ct. S19—3D 124
Ralston Croft. S19—3E 125
Ralston Gro. S19—3D 124
Ralston Pl. S19—3D 124
Ramper La. DN3—2G 21
Ramper Rd. S66—2D 94
Rampton Rd. S7—6D 98

Ramsay Cres. DN5—3H 31
Ramsden Rd. DN4—1A 46
Ramsden Rd. S60—4E 79
Ramsey Av. S40—4F 137
Ramsey Rd. S10—1A 98
Ramsker Dri. DN3—4F 35
Ramsworth Clo. DN5—4G 31
Ranby Rd. S11—6H 97
Randall Pl. S2—5D 98
Randall St. S2—4E 99
Randall St. S31—6G 125
Randerson Dri. S62—4C 56
Rands La. DN3—2G 35
Ranelagh Dri. S11—2H 109
Raneld Mt. S40—5E 137
Ranfield Ct. S65—1H 81
Rangeley Rd. S6—6G 85
Range Rd. S4—2B 88
Ranmoor Chase. S10—4H 97
Ranmoor Cliffe Rd. S10—4E 97
Ranmoor Clo. S41—4C 138
Ranmoor Ct. S10—5G 97
Ranmoor Cres. S10—4F 97
Ranmoor Ho. S10—3C 98
Ranmoor Pk. Rd. S10—4F 97
Ranmoor Rise. S10—4F 97
Ranmoor Rd. S10—4F 97
Ranmoor View. S10—4F 97
Ranskill Ct. S9—4E 89
Ranworth Rd. S66—4H 81
Ranyard Rd. DN4—4H 45
Raseby Av. S19—5E 115
Raseby Clo. S19—5E 115
Raseby Pl. S19—5E 115
Rasen Clo. S64—5G 43
Ratcliffe Rd. S11—5B 98
Ratten Row. DN11—6H 61
Ratten Row. S75—3A 22
Ravencar Rd. S31—6B 124
Ravencarr Pl. S2—4C 100
Ravencarr Rd. S2—4C 100
Raven Dri. S61—1C 66
Ravenfield Clo. S5—3A 114
Ravenfield Dri. S71—2A 14
Ravenfield La. S65—1G 71
Ravenfield Rd. DN3—4G 35
Ravenholt. S70—5A 24
Raven Meadows. S64—4A 56
Raven Rd. S7—1B 110
Ravenscar Clo. DN12—2A 58
Ravens Clo. S75—5F 7
Ravens Ct. S70—5B 24
Ravenscroft Av. S13—5G 101
Ravenscroft Clo. S13—5G 101
Ravenscroft Ct. S13—5G 101
Ravenscroft Cres. S13—5G 101
Ravenscroft Dri. S13—5G 101
Ravenscroft Oval. S13—5G 101
Ravenscroft Pl. S13—5G 101
Ravenscroft Rd. S13—6G 101
Ravenscroft Way. S13—5G 101
Ravensdale Clo. S43—5A 134
Ravensdale Rd. S18—2A 128
Ravensfield. DN12—1B 58
Ravenshaw Clo. S75—4D 12
Ravensmead Ct. S63—2A 42
Ravenswood Rd. S40—6C 130
Ravensworth Rd. DN1—1E 47
Ravine, The. S5—2A 76
Rawlins Ct. S18—5G 123
Rawmarsh Hill. S62—3F 69
Rawmarsh Rd. S60—2D 78
Rawmarsh Shopping Centre.
   S62—2F 69
Rawson Clo. DN4—2D 48
Rawson Rd. S65—2E 79
Rawsons Bank. S30—1F 75
Rawson Spring Av. S6—1B 86

Rawson Spring Rd. S6—1B 86
Rawson Spring Way. S6—1B 86
Rawson St. S6—4C 86
Raybould Rd. S61—6H 67
Rayleigh Av. S43—3D 132
Rayls Rise. S31—2B 118
Rayls Rd. S31—2B 118
Raymond Rd. DN5—3H 31
Raymond Rd. S70—1D 24
Raynald Rd. S2—4C 100
Raynor Sike La. S30—1A 72
Reader Cres. S64—1B 56
Reaper Cres. S30—1C 64
Reasbeck Ter. S71—2H 13
Reasby Av S65—1H 81
Rebecca Row. S70—1H 23
Recreation Av. S66—5B 94
Recreation La. DN11—4C 62
Recreation Rd. DN6—3D 16
Recreation Rd. S43—6F 133
Recreation Rd. S63—4F 41
Rectory Clo. S30—3E 141
Rectory Clo. S31—5E 125
Rectory Clo. S63—1D 28
Rectory Clo. S71—4F 9
Rectory Clo. S73—1F 39
Rectory Dri. S60—3A 92
Rectory Gdns. DN1—5E 33
Rectory Gdns. DN12—6A 60
Rectory Gdns. S31—3B 126
 (Killamarsh)
Rectory Gdns. S31—3B 118
 (Todwick)
Rectory La. S63—2D 28
Rectory M. DN5—3D 44
Rectory Rd. S31—4B 126
Rectory Rd. S43—1C 134
Rectory Rd. S44—6E 135
Rectory St. S62—3F 69
Rectory Way. S71—4D 14
Redbourne Rd. DN5—6B 18
Redbrook Av. S41—5B 138
Redbrook Business Pk. S75
 —3D 12
Redbrook Croft. S19—4A 114
Redbrook Gro. S19—4A 114
Redbrook Rd. S75—3C 12
Redcar Clo. DN12—3A 58
Redcar Rd. S10—2A 98
Redcliffe Clo. S75—3D 12
Redfearn St. S71—5H 13
Redfern Av. S19—6D 114
Redfern Ct. S19—6D 114
Redfern Dri. S19—6D 114
Redfern Gro. S19—6D 114
Red Fern Gro. S30—4D 140
Redgrave Pl. S66—3F 81
Redgrove Way. S40—5E 137
Redhall Clo. DN3—3E 21
Red Hill. S1—2B 4 & 1D 98
Red Hill. S31—5B 118
Redhill Av. S70—2C 24
Redhill Ct. DN11—6H 61
Redholme. S10—3E 97
Red Ho. La. DN6—1A & 1C 16
 (in two parts)
Red House Wlk. S40—6F 131
Redland Gro. S75—3E 7
Redland La. S7—4B 110
Redland Way. S66—3E 83
Red La. S10—4A 98
Red La. S41—2C 132
Red Lion Yd. S60—3D 78
 (off Effingham St.)
Redmarsh Av. S62—6E 55
Redmires Rd. S10—4A 96
Rednall Clo. S40—6C 130
Red Oak La. S6—4C 84

Redrock Rd. S60—1G 91
Redscope Cres. S61—5F 67
Redscope Rd. S61—6F 67
Redthorne Way. S72—2B 10
Redthorn Rd. S13—5H 101
Redthorpe Crest. S75—3C 12
Redvers Buller Rd. S40—4A 138
Redwood Av. S31—4A 126
Redwood Av. S71—2E 9
Redwood Clo. S74—6H 37
Redwood Dri. S66—4C 82
Redwood Glen. S30—3D 64
Reedham St. S66—4H 81
Regency Ter. S30—2E 65
 (off Greenhead Gdns.)
Regent Av. DN3—4G 35
Regent Ct. DN1—6E 33
Regent St. S6—3B 86
Regent Cres. S71—6B 8
Regent Gdns. S70—4G 13
Regent Gro. DN5—4H 31
Regent Ho. S70—6H 13
Regent Sq. DN1—6E 33
Regent St. S1—3B 4 & 2D 98
Regent St. S61—3H 77
Regent St. S70—5H 13
Regent St. S74—6E 37
Regent St. S. S70—5H 13
Regents Way. S31—6C 104
Regent Ter. DN1—6E 33
Regent Ter. S3—4B 4 & 2D 98
Regina Cres. S72—3E 11
Reginald Rd. S70—2D 24
Reginald Rd. S73—1H 39
Rembrandt Dri. S18—2C 128
Remington Av. S5—2D 74
Remington Dri. S5—2D 74
Remington Rd. S5—2D 74
Remount Rd. S61—5F 67
Remount Way. S61—5F 67
Renathorpe Rd. S5—3H 75
Rencliffe Av. S60—6F 79
Reneville Clo. S5—1E 75
Reneville Clo. S60—5E 79
Reneville Ct. S60—5D 78
Reneville Cres. S5—1E 75
Reneville Dri. S5—1E 75
Reneville Rd. S60—5D 78
Reney Av. S8—3B 122
Reney Cres. S8—3B 122
Reney Dri. S8—3B 122
Reney Rd. S8—2C 122
Reney Wlk. S8—3B 122
Renishaw Av. S60—1H 91
Renshaw Clo. S30—5A 50
Renshaw Rd. S11—1G 109
Renton St. S11—4D 98
Renville Clo. S62—6E 55
Renway Rd. S60—6G 79
Repton Clo. S40—6C 130
Repton Pl. S18—2A 128
Reresby Cres. S60—1A 92
Reresby Dri. S60—1A 92
Reresby Rd. S60—1H 91
Reresby Rd. S65—5E 71
Reresby Wlk. DN12—1B 58
Reservoir Rd. S10—2A 98
Reservoir Rd. S31—1A 104
Reservoir Ter. S40—1G 137
Retail World. S60—5F 69
Retford Rd. S13—4B 102
Retford Wlk. DN11—4F 63
Revell Clo. S65—2B 80
Revill Clo. S66—3F 83
Revill La. S13—1C 114
Rex Av. S7—3H 109

Reynard La. S6—6B 84
Reynolds Clo. S18—3C 128
Reynolds Clo. S66—3F 81
Rhodes Av. S41—6G 131
Rhodes Av. S61—5F 67
Rhodes Dri. S60—1A 92
Rhodesia Ct. DN4—3B 48
Rhodesia Rd. S40—3E 137
Rhodes St. S2—4H 5 & 2G 99
Rhodes Ter. S70—1A 24
Ribble Croft. S30—1E 65
Ribblesdale Dri. S12—6H 113
Ribble Way. S5—6G 75
Riber Av. S71—6C 8
Riber Clo. S6—5D 84
Riber Clo. S43—6A 134
Riber Ter. S40—3G 137
Ribston Ct. S9—6C 88
Ribston Rd. S9—1C 100
Richard Av. S71—1A 14
Richard La. DN11—4C 62
Richard Rd. S60—4E 79
Richard Rd. S71—1A 14
Richard Rd. S75—5B 6
Richards Ct. S2—1F 111
Richardson Wlk. S75—5H 25
Richards Rd. S2—6E to 6F 99
 (in two parts)
Richard St. S70—6F 13
Richards Way. S62—1G 69
Rich Farm Clo. DN5—4D 18
Richmond Av. S13—5G 101
Richmond Av. S75—6B 6
Richmond Clo. S40—5G 137
Richmond Gro. S13—5G 101
Richmond Hall Av. S13—5F 101
Richmond Hall Cres. S13
 —6F 101
Richmond Hall Dri. S13—5F 101
Richmond Hall Rd. S13—5F 101
Richmond Hall Way. S13
 —6F 101
Richmond Hill Rd. DN5—1G 45
Richmond Hill Rd. S13—6G 101
Richmond Pk. Av. S13—3G 101
Richmond Pk. Av. S61—3F 77
Richmond Pk. Clo. S13—4G 101
Richmond Pk. Cres. S13
 —3G 101
Richmond Pk. Croft. S13
 —3G 101
Richmond Pk. Dri. S13—4G 101
Richmond Pk. Gro. S13—4G 101
Richmond Pk. Rise. S13
 —3F 101
Richmond Pk. Rd. S13—4G 101
Richmond Pk. View. S13
 —4G 101
Richmond Pk. Way. S13
 —4G 101
Richmond Pl. S13—6F 101
Richmond Rd. DN5—2F 31
Richmond Rd. S13
 —1E 113 to 4H 101
Richmond Rd. S61—3G 77
Richmond Rd. S63—1E 29
Richmond St. S3—5F 87
Richmond St. S70—6F 13
Richworth Rd. S13—5H 101
Ricknald Clo. S31—4B 104
Ridal Av. S30—2C 140
Ridal Clo. S30—2C 140
Ridal Croft. S30—2C 140
Riddings Clo. S2—6C 100
Riddings Clo. S66—5B 94
Rider Rd. S6—3A 86
Ridge Balk La. DN6—2B 16
Ridgehill Av. S12—2C 112

Ridgehill Gro. S12—2D 112
Ridge Rd. DN6—5D 16
Ridge Rd. S65—2E 79
Ridge, The. DN6—3B 16
Ridge, The. S10—4C 96
Ridge View Clo. S9—6C 76
Ridge View Dri. S9—6C 76
Ridgewalk Way. S70—3H 23
Ridgeway. S65—2A 80
Ridgeway Clo. S65—2B 80
Ridgeway Clo. S66—5A 82
Ridgeway Cres. S12—2C 112
Ridgeway Cres. S71—4E 9
Ridgeway Dri. S12—1C 112
Ridgeway Rd. S12—1C 112
Ridgeway Rd. S60—3C 90
Ridgeway, The. S18—6H 123
Ridgewood Av. DN3—6D 20
Ridgway Av. S37—3E 27
Riding Clo. S66—4E 81
Ridings Av. S71—2B 14
Ridings Clo. DN4—5F 49
Ridings, The. S71—2C 14
Rig Clo. S61—6H 67
Rig Dri. S64—2G 55
Riggotts La. S40—6F 137
Riggotts Way. S42—3A 130
Riggs High Rd. S6—6A 84
Riggs Low Rd. S6—6A 84
Riley Av. DN4—5H 45
Riley Rd. S63—6F 41
Rimington Rd. S73—6B 26
Rimini Rise. S73—4C 26
Ringinglow Rd. S11
 —3A 108 to 1H 109
Ringstead Av. S10—3E 97
Ringstead Cres. S10—3E 97
Ringstone Gro. S72—2H 11
Ringway. S63—6D 28
Ringwood Av. S41—4G 131
Ringwood Av. S43—3A 134
Ringwood Cres. S19—5G 115
Ringwood Dri. S19—5G 115
Ringwood Gro. S19—5G 115
Ringwood Rd. S19—5G 115
Ringwood View. S43—4F 133
Ripley Gro. S75—3D 12
Ripley St. S6—4A 86
Ripon Av. DN2—3F 33
Ripon St. S9—6B 88
 (in two parts)
Ripon Way. S31—6A 104
Rippon Ct. S62—6F 55
Rippon Cres. S3—3H 85
Rippon Rd. S6—3H 85
Risedale Rd. S63—5H 29
Rise, The. S31—2G 119
Rise, The. S64—3H 55
Rising St. S3—5F 87
Rivelin Bank. S6—4H 85
Rivelin Ct. S60—1E 91
Rivelin Glen Cotts. S6—1E 97
Rivelin Pk. Ct. S6—5G 85
Rivelin Pk. Cres. S6—5G 85
Rivelin Pk. Dri. S6—5G 85
Rivelin Pk. Rd. S6—6G 85
Rivelin Rd. S6—5G 85
Rivelin St. S6—5H 85
Rivelin Ter. S6—5G 85
Rivelin Valley Rd. S6
 —2A 96 to 4H 85
Riverdale Av. S10—5G 97
Riverdale Pk. Caravan Pk. S43
 —1E 135
Riverdale Rd. DN5—1G 31
Riverdale Rd. S10—4G 97
Riverhead. DN5—2D 44

River La. S1—4G 5 & 2F 99
Riverside Clo. S6—3F 85
Riverside Clo. S73—4G 27
Riverside Ct. S64—1G 57
Riverside Cres. S42—6A 136
Riverside Dri. DN5—2E 45
Riverside Precinct. S60—3D 78
(off Corporation St.)
River Ter. S6—3A 86
River View Rd. S30—2D 72
Riviera Mt. DN5—4B 32
Riviera Pde. DN5—4B 32
Rix Rd. S62—5B 56
Roache Dri. S63—5E 29
Roach Rd. S11—6A 98
Robert Av. S71—5D 14
Robert Rd. S8—2D 122
Robert's Av. DN12—4F 59
Robertshaw Cres. S30—3F 141
Robertson Dri. S6—5H 85
Robertson Rd. S6—5G 85
Roberts Rd. DN4—2B 46
Roberts Rd. DN12—4C 60
Roberts St. S72—6B 10
Roberts St. S73—1E 39
Robert St. S60—3B 78
Robert St. S70—5A 24
Robey St. S4—2H 87
Robinbrook La. S12—6E 113
Robincroft. S40—6H 137
Robinets Rd. S61—4A 68
Robin Hood Av. S71—1F 9
Robin Hood Chase. S6—4C 84
Robin Hood Cres. DN3—6E 21
Robin Hood Rd. DN3—6E 21
Robin Hood Rd. S9—5C 76
Robin La. S19—2F 115
Robin Pl. S31—1C 116
Robins Clo. S31—6C 104
Robinson Rd. S2—3G 99
Robinson's Sq. S70—4C 36
Robinson St. S60—5D 78
Robinson Way. S31—3A 126
Rob Royd. S70—4E 23
Rob Royd. S75—3B 22
Rob Royd La. S75—4F 23
Roche. S19—1E 125
(off Shortbrook Dri.)
Roche Clo. S71—4B 14
Roche End. S31—2A 118
Rocher Av. S30—2C 74
Rocher Clo. S30—2C 74
Rocher Gro. S30—2C 74
Rochester Clo. S10—4A 96
Rochester Dri. S10—4A 96
Rochester Rd. S10—4A 96
Rochester Rd. S31—4F 119
Rochester Rd. S71—3B 14
Rochester Row. DN5—4F 31
Rockcliffe Dri. DN11—6H 61
Rockcliffe Rd. S62—3F 69
Rockingham. S19—1E 125
(off Shortbrook Dri.)
Rockingham Clo. S1—5D 4
Rockingham Clo. S18—2A 128
Rockingham Clo. S40—2E 137
Rockingham Ga. S1
—5D 4 & 3E 99
Rockingham Ho. DN1—1C 46
(off Elsworth Clo.)
Rockingham Ho. S62—1G 69
Rockingham La. S1
—4D 4 & 2E 99
Rockingham Rd. DN2—4E 33
Rockingham Rd. S62—1G 69
Rockingham Rd. S64—3G 55
Rockingham Rd. S75—3C 22
Rockingham Row. S70—5D 36

Rockingham St. S1
—3C 4 & 2D 98
Rockingham St. S70—5D 36
Rockingham St. S71—3G 13
Rockingham St. S72—6G 11
Rockingham St. S74—5F 37
Rockingham Way. S1
—5D 4 & 3E 99
Rockingham Way. S61—4H 67
Rockland Vs. S65—5C 70
Rocklea Clo. S64—3A 56
Rockley Av. S70—3C 36
Rockley Clo. S40—6H 137
Rockley Cres. S70—4C 36
Rockley La. S75 & S70—6E 23
Rockley Nook. DN2—2H 33
Rockley Rd. S6—1H 85
Rockleys. S75—3C 22
Rockley View. S75—5B 36
Rock Mt. S74—5B 38
Rockmount Rd. S9—5D 76
Rock Pl. S30—3F 141
Rock St. S3—6E 87
Rock St. S70—5F 13
Rockwood Clo. S30—2C 64
Rockwood Clo. S75—4D 6
Roden Way. S62—5C 54
Rodger Rd. S13—6D 102
Rodger St. S61—2B 78
Rodley La. S2—6F 5
Rodman Dri. S13—5D 102
Rodman St. S13—5D 102
Rod Moor Rd. S18—5H 121
Rodney Hill. S6—3D 84
Rodsley Clo. S40—6D 130
Roebuck Hill. S74—3B 38
Roebuck Rd. S6—1B 98
Roebuck St. S73—2F 39
Roeburn Clo. S75—3E 7
Roecar Clo. S41—1B 132
Roe Croft Clo. DN5—1D 44
Roehampton Rise. DN5—4F 31
Roehampton Rise. S60—2A 90
Roehampton Rise. S71—1F 25
Roe La. S3—3F 87
Roewood Ct. S3—3F 87
(off Orphanage Rd.)
Roger Rd. S71—5E 15
Rojean Rd. S30—1B 74
Rokeby Dri. S5—3E 75
Rokeby Rd. S5—3E 75
Roland Row. S2—2G 99
Rolleston Av. S66—5E 83
Rolleston Rd. S5—5G 75
Rollet Clo. S2—5C 100
Rollin Dri. S6—2H 85
Rolling Dales Clo. S66—3E 83
Rolls Cres. S62—5C 54
Roman Ct. S61—3G 77
Roman Cres. S60—1C 90
Roman Cres. S62—1E 69
Romandale Gdns. S2—4E 101
Roman Ridge. DN5—2G 31
Roman Ridge Rd. S9—6D 76
Roman Rd. DN4—1E 47
Roman Rd. S75—6B 6
Roman St. S63—1G 29
Romney Clo. S66—3F 81
Romney Dri. S18—2C 128
Romney Gdns. S2—1F 111
Romsdal Rd. S10—1A 98
Romwood Av. S64—2G 55
Ronald Rd. DN4—3A 46
Ronald Rd. S9—1E 101
Ronksley Cres. S5—3H 75
Ronksley Rd. S5—3H 75
Rookdale Clo. S75—3D 12
Rookery Clo. S31—4G 117

Rookery Rd. S64—3H 55
Rookhill. S70—4C 24
Ropery Row. S2—1G 99
Rosamond Av. S17—3G 121
Rosamond Clo. S17—3G 121
Rosamond Ct. S17—3G 121
Rosamond Dri. S17—4G 121
Rosamond Glade. S17—3G 121
Rosamond Pl. S17—3G 121
Rosa Rd. S10—1A 98
Roscoe Bank. S6—1D 96
Roscoe Ct. S6—5F 85
Roscoe Dri. S6—6F 85
Roscoe Mt. S6—6F 85
Roscoe Rd. S3—6D 86
Rose Av. DN4—3B 46
Rose Av. S19—4F 115
Rose Av. S44—2G 139
Rose Av. S73—2D 26
Roseberry Clo. S74—1A 52
Rosebery St. S61—3A 78
Rosebery St. S70—1D 24
Rosebery Ter. S70—1A 24
Rose Clo. S60—4D 90
Rose Cottage. DN3—1H 21
Rose Ct. S66—5E 81
Rose Cres. DN5—2G 31
Rose Cres. S62—1H 69
Rosedale Av. S40—5B 138
Rosedale Av. S62—1G 69
Rosedale Clo. S31—5C 104
Rosedale Gdns. S11—5B 98
Rosedale Gdns. S70—6E 13
Rosedale Rd. DN5—5A 18
(Bentley)
Rosedale Rd. DN5—2F 31
(Doncaster)
Rosedale Rd. S11—5B 98
Rosedale Rd. S31—5B 104
Rosedale Way. S66—3G 81
Rose Dri. S66—4G 81
Rose Garth Av. S31—5B 104
Rosegarth Clo. DN5—2H 31
Rose Gro. DN3—3E 35
Rose Gro. S73—5H 25
Rose Hill. DN4—2A 48
Rose Hill. S40—2H 137
Rosehill Av. S62—6G 55
Rose Hill Ct. DN4—1A 48
Rosehill Ct. S70—5G 13
Rose Hill E. S40—2A 138
Rose Hill Rise. DN4—2A 48
Rosehill Rd. S62—1F 69
Rose Hill W. S40—2H 137
Rose Ho. DN3—3E 35
Rose La. S31—5D 94
Roselle St. S6—3A 86
Rosemary Ct. S10—6A 86
(off Heavygate Rd.)
Rosemary Rd. S19—3F 115
Rosemary Rd. S66—4E 81
Rosene Cotts. S42—4A 130
Rose Pl. S73—5A 26
Rose Tree Av. S72—6B 10
Rose Tree Ct. S72—6B 10
Roseville. S73—3E 27
Rose Way. S31—4B 126
Rose Wood Clo. S41—3F 131
Rosewood Dri. DN3—2G 21
Roslin Rd. S10—2A 98
Rossendale Clo. S40—5G 137
Rosser Av. S12—5B 112
Rossetti Mt. S66—3F 81
Rossington Ho. DN1—2C 46
(off Elsworth Clo.)
Rossington Rd. S11—5A 98
Rossington St. DN12—1B 58
Rossiter Rd. S61—3C 68

Rosslyn Av. S31—5C 104
Rosslyn Cres. DN5—5B 18
Ross St. S9—1F 101
Rosston Rd. S66—4H 83
Rostholme Sq. DN5—5B 18
Roston Clo. S18—2B 128
Rothay Clo. S18—3C 128
Rothay Rd. S4—2B 88
Rothbury Clo. S19—5G 115
Rothbury Ct. S19—5G 115
Rothbury Way. S60—2D 90
Rother Av. S43—3D 132
Rother Clo. S40—5G 137
Rother Ct. S60—1F 91
Rother Cres. S60—1E 103
Rotherham Clo. S31—1D 126
Rotherham La. S31—6E 95
Rotherham Rd. S13—3B 102
Rotherham Rd. S19—3G 115
(Beighton)
Rotherham Rd. S19—2F 125
(Halfway)
Rotherham Rd. S31—4F 125
(Eckington)
Rotherham Rd. S31—2D 126
(Killamarsh)
Rotherham Rd. S31—3C 106
(Laughton Common)
Rotherham Rd. S31—6A 104
(Swallownest)
Rotherham Rd. S31 & S43
(Woodall) —5E 127
Rotherham Rd. S60—5D 90
(Catcliffe)
Rotherham Rd. S60 & S62
(Parkgate) —6E 69
Rotherham Rd. S63—5B 40
Rotherham Rd. S66—4C 82
Rotherham Rd. S71
—1H 13 to 5D 14
Rotherham Rd. S72
—3H 27 to 1A 28
Rotherham Rd. Nth. S19
—2F 125
Rotherham St. S9—4C 88
Rotherhill Clo. S65—2G 79
Rothermoor Av. S31—5G 117
Rother Rd. S60—6D 78
Rotherside Rd. S31—5F 125
Rotherstoke Clo. S60—5E 79
Rother St. S73—3A 40
Rother Ter. S60—6D 78
Rothervale Clo. S19—3G 115
Rothervale Rd. S40—5A &
(in two parts) 6A 138
Rother Valley Way. S19
—2H 125
Rother View Rd. S60—6D 78
Rother Way. S41—5B 132
Rotherway. S60—3E 91
Rother Way. S66—3A 82
Rotherwood Av. S13—5D 102
Rotherwood Clo. DN5—3F 31
Rotherwood Cres. S66—5A 94
Rotherwood Rd. S31—2C 126
Rothesay Clo. DN5—4H 31
Rothey Gro. S40—6B 130
Rough La. S30—1H 73
Roughwood Grn. S61—4A 68
Roughwood Rd. S61—5G 67
Roughwood Way. S61—5G 67
Roundel St. S9—6B 88
Round Grn. La. S75—5D 22
Roundwood Ct. S70—5A 24
Roundwood Gro. S62—3G 69
Roundwood Way. S73—3D 26
Rowan Clo. S30—3E 65
Rowan Ct. DN2—3A 34

Rowan Dri. S66—4G 81
Rowan Dri. S75—4D 12
Rowan Garth. DN5—3A 32
Rowan Mt. DN2—3H 33
Rowan Rise. S66—4D 82
Rowan Rd. S31—6H 125
Rowan Tree Clo. S31—4A 126
Rowan Tree Dell. S17—6E 121
Rowan Tree Rd. S31—3H 125
Rowborn Dri. S30—5F 73
Rowdale Cres. S12—2F 113
Rowell La. S6—3B 84
Rowena Av. DN3—6D 20
Rowena Dri. DN5—3E 31
Rowena Dri. S66—4A 94
Rowena Rd. DN12—3D 58
Rowland Pl. DN1—1C 46
Rowland Rd. S2—5E 99
Rowland Rd. S75—4E 13
Rowland St. S3—6E 87
Rowland St. S71—1F 9
Rowms La. S64—2C 56
Rowsley Cres. S43—3A 134
Rowsley St. S2—4F 99
Row, The. DN3—2F 49
Roxby Clo. DN4—5B 48
Roxton Av. S8—1D 122
Roxton Rd. S8—6C 110
Royal Av. DN1—5E 33
Royale Clo. S31—6E 125
Royal St. S70—6G 13
Royalty La. DN5—1H 19
Royd Av. S72—1H 15
Royd Av. S75—4F 7
Royd Clo. S70—5H 23
Roydfield Clo. S19—5D 114
Roydfield Dri. S19—5D 114
Roydfield Gro. S19—5D 114
Royd La. S30—5F 141
Royd La. S75—4A 12
Royds Av. S60—1A 92
Royds Clo. Cres. S65—5C 70
Royds La. S74—6E 39
Royds Moor Hill. S60—2D 92
Royd, The. S30—5F 141
Royd View. S72—2G 11
Roy Kilner Rd. S73—5H 25 to
(in two parts)   5A 26
Royston Av. DN5—2A 32
Royston Av. S19—5A 114
Royston Clo. S19—5A 114
Royston Clo. S42—6D 136
Royston Cotts. S74—5H 37
Royston Croft. S19—5A 114
Royston Gro. S19—5A 114
(off Royston Clo.)
Royston Hill. S74—5H 37
Royston La. S71—3E 9
Royston Rd. S72—4A 10
Rubens Clo. S18—2D 128
Rubens Row. S2—3H 5
Rudyard Rd. S6—3A 86
Rufford Av. S71—5C 8
Rufford Clo. S40—4G 137
Rufford Ct. S19—5G 115
Rufford Pl. S65—1H 79
Rufford Rise. S19—5G 115
Rufford Rise. S63—5E 29
Rufford Rd. DN4—2F 47
Rufus La. DN11—4B 62
Rugby St. S3—5E 87
Rundle Dri. S7—6C 98
Rundle Rd. S7—6C 98
Rundle Rd. S30—3D 140
Runnymede Rd. DN2—5H 33
Rupert Rd. S7—2C 110
Rural Cres. DN3—3H 49
Rural La. S6—1F 85

Rushby St. S4—2H 87
Rushdale Av. S8—2E 111
Rushdale Mt. S8—2E 111
Rushdale Rd. S8—2E 111
Rushdale Ter. S8—2E 111
Rushen Mt. S40—6H 137
Rushey Clo. S62—5E 55
Rushleigh Ct. S17—2D 120
Rushley Av. S17—1D 120
Rushley Clo. S17—1D 120
Rushley Dri. S17—1D 120
Rushley Rd. S17—1D 120
Rushworth Clo. S75—5A 6
Ruskin Av. S64—5F 43
Ruskin Clo. S63—4C 40
Ruskin Dri. DN3—3G 35
Ruskin Rd. DN4—5A 46
Ruskin Sq. S8—1E 111
Russell Clo. S71—2B 14
Russell Ct. S11—5G 109
Russell Pl. S66—3G 83
Russell Rd. S62—6C 56
Russell St. S3—1E 5 & 6E 87
Russell St. S65—1E 79
Rustlings Ct. S10—5F 97
Rustlings Rd. S11—5G 97
Rustlings View. S11—5H 97
Ruston Clo. S40—5D 130
Ruthin St. S4—3A 88
Ruth Sq. S10—3C 98
Ruthven Dri. DN4—4F 45
Rutland Av. S31—6D 106
Rutland La. DN11—4B 62
Rutland Pk. S10—3A 98
Rutland Pl. S73—1D 38
Rutland Rd. S3—5D 86
Rutland Rd. S40—2H 137
Rutland St. DN1—5E 33
Rutland St. S3—5E 87
Rutland St. S41—1A 132
Rutland Way. S3—5D 86
Rutland Way. S75—4E 13
Ryan Pl. S62—3F 69
Rydal Clo. S18—2B 128
Rydal Clo. S31—6F 107
Rydal Cres. S41—3G 131
Rydalhurst Av. S6—1G 85
Rydall Pl. DN5—1H 31
Rydal Rd. S8—2C 110
Rydal Rd. S31—6F 107
Rydal Ter. S71—6A 14
Rydal Way. S64—5G 43
Rye Bank. S60—2B 92
Rye Ct. S60—1E 91
Rye Croft. DN12—3G 59
Rye Croft. S71—1A 14
Ryecroft Glen Rd. S17—1G 121
Ryecroft Rd. S62—1A 70
Ryecroft View. S17—1D 120
Ryedale Wlk. DN5—2E 31
Ryefield Gdns. S11—2G 109
Ryegate Cres. S10—2H 97
Ryegate Rd. S10—3G 97
Ryehill Av. S40—3C 136
Ryeview Gdns. S61—5B 68
Ryhill Dri. S19—5A 114
Ryle Rd. S7—6C 98
Rylstone Clo. S12—4B 114
Rylstone Gro. S12—5B 114
Rylstone Wlk. S70—3D 24
Ryton Av. S73—2H 39
Ryton Clo. S66—4G 83
Ryton Rd. S31—3F 119
Ryton Way. DN4—5E 49

Sackerville Ter. S31—3H 125
Sackup La. S75—4D 6

Sackville Clo. S42—5D 136
Sackville Rd. S10—1H 97
Sackville St. S70—5F 13
Saddler Av. S19—6D 114
Saddler Clo. S19—6D 114
Saddler Grn. S19—6D 114
Saddler Gro. S19—6D 114
Sadler Ga. S70—5G 13
Sadler's Ga. S73—5A 26
St Agnes Rd. DN4—1G 47
St Aidan's Av. S2—5H 99
St Aidan's Clo. S2—4A 100
St Aidan's Dri. S2—4A 100
St Aidan's Mt. S2—5A 100
St Aidan's Pl. S2—5A 100
St Aidan's Rd. S2—5A 100
St Aidan's Way. S2—5A 100
St Albans Clo. S10—4C 96
St Alban's Ct. S66—5F 81
St Albans Dri. S10—4B 96
St Albans Rd. S10—4B 96
St Alban's Way. S66—5E 81
St Andrew Rd. S30—4G 141
St Andrew's Clo. DN4—5F 49
St Andrew's Clo. S11—6B 98
St Andrew's Clo. S64—4B 56
St Andrew's Clo. S66—2G 81
St Andrews Cres. S74—5A 38
St Andrews Rise. S40—5E 137
St Andrew's Rd. DN12—4D 58
St Andrew's Rd. S11—6B 98
St Andrews Rd. S74—5A 38
St Andrew's Sq. S63—1A 42
St Andrew's Ter. DN4—2E 47
St Andrew's Wlk. S60—2A 90
St Andrew's Way. DN3—1E 21
St Andrews Way. S71—2G 25
St Anne's Dri. S71—6F 9
St Anne's Rd. DN4—1G 47
St Ann's Rd. S30—3F 141
St Ann's Rd. S65—1E 79
St Anthony Rd. S10—1G 97
St Augustines Av. S40—5A 138
St Augustines Cres. S40
                        —5A 138
St Augustines Dri. S40—4A 138
St Augustines Mt. S40—5A 138
St Augustines Rise. S40
                        —5A 138
St Augustine's Rd. DN4—2A 48
St Augustines Rd. S40—5H 137
St Austell Dri. S75—3A 12
St Barbara's Clo. S66—5E 83
St Barbara's Rd. S73—4D 26
St Barnabas La. S2—5E 99
St Barnabas Rd. S2—5E 99
St Bartholomew's Clo. S66
                        —5E 83
St Bart's Ter. S70—1H 23
St Bede's Rd. S60—3E 79
St Catherine's Av. DN4—3C 46
St Catherine's Way. S75—5D 12
St Cecilia's Rd. DN4—2G 47
St Chad's Sq. DN12—1B 58
St Chads Way. DN5—2E 45
St Charles St. S9—5A 88
St Christophers Clo. S71
                        —2G 25
St Christopher's Cres. DN5
                        —3G 31
St Christopher's Flats. DN4
(off Ashfield Rd.)   —4A 46
St Clement's Clo. DN5—3F 31
St Clements Clo. S71—2G 25
St David Rd. S30—4G 141
St David's Dri. DN5—3F 31
St David's Dri. S31—4F 119

St David's Dri. S71—1F 25
St David's Rise. S40—5F 137
St David's Rd. DN12—3D 58
St Dominic's Clo. DN5—3D 44
St Edmund's Av. S66—5A 94
St Edward's Av. S70—1F 23
St Elizabeth Clo. S2—5F 99
St Eric's Rd. DN4—3B 48
St Francis Boulevd. S71—6F 9
St Francis Clo. S66—2G 81
St George Ga. DN1—6C 32
St George Rd. S30—4G 141
St George's Av. S64—2A 56
St George's Clo. S3
                        —2A 4 & 2C 98
St George's Ct. S3—3B 4
St George's Dri. S60—3A 90
St George's Rd. DN4—2A 48
St George's Rd. S70—6G 13
St George's Ter. S3
                        —3B 4 & 2D 98
St Giles Clo. S40—5B 138
St Giles Ga. DN5—4F 31
St Giles Sq. S30—2D 64
St Helen Rd. S30—5G 141
St Helen's Av. S71—2B 14
St Helen's Boulevd. S71—1B 14
St Helen's Clo. S41—1A 138
St Helen's Clo. S60—2F 103
St Helens Clo. S63—1D 28
St Helens Ct. S74—5C 38
St Helen's Dri. S75—5D 12
St Helen's La. DN5—1H 43
St Helen's Rd. DN4—1G 47
St Helen's Sq. DN3—3D 20
St Helen's St. S41—1A 138
St Helen's View. S71—2C 14
St Helen's Way. S71—2D 14
St Hilda Av. S70—6E 13
St Hilda Clo. S30—5G 141
St Hilda's Rd. DN4—1G 47
St James Av. S31—3F 119
St James Clo. DN3—3D 20
St James Clo. S41—4C 138
St James Clo. S63—5G 41
St James' Clo. S70—5A 24
St James Ct. DN1—1D 46
St James' Dri. S65—4H 71
St James' Gdns. DN4—2B 46
St James' Row. S1
                        —3E 5 & 2E 99
St James's Bri. DN4—1C 46
St James Sq. S74—5A 38
(off High St. Hoyland)
St James St. DN1—1C 46
St James' View. S65—4H 71
St James Wlk. S13—5D 102
St Joan Av. S30—5G 141
St John's Av. S60—3B 78
St John's Av. S66—3G 81
St John's Av. S75—3A 12
St John's Clo. S2—1G 99
St John's Clo. S65—1G 79
St John's Cres. S73—2A 22
St John's Ct. S31—1E 107
St Johns Ct. S60—2B 78
St John's Gdns. S2—2G 99
St Johns Grn. S61—6G 67
St John's Mt. S41—3H 131
St Johns Pl. S43—2B 134
St John's Rd. DN4—3A 46
St John's Rd. DN12—3B 60
St John's Rd. S2—2G 99
St John's Rd. S30—4H 141
St John's Rd. S31—1E 107

St John's Rd. S41—4G to 3H 131
(in two parts)
St Johns Rd. S43—2A 134
St John's Rd. S64—2A 56
St John's Rd. S65—1G 79
St John's Rd. S70—1G 23
St John's Rd. S72—1H 15
St John's Wlk. S64—3D 42
St Joseph's Ct. S31—4F 107
St Joseph's Rd. S13—3H 101
St Lawrence Rd. S9—6G 77
St Lawrence Ter. DN6—1E 17
St Leger Av. S31—3C 106
St Leonard's Av. S65—5D 70
St Leonard's Clo. S31—5F 107
St Leonards Ct. S5—6F 75
St Leonards Dri. S41—4C 138
St Leonard's La. S65—2F 79
St Leonard's Lea. DN5—3G 31
St Leonard's Rd. S65—2E 79
St Leonards Way. S71—2G 25
St Lukes Way. S71—4C 14
St Margaret Av. S30—4G 141
St Margaret's Av. DN5—1G 43
St Margaret's Dri. S40—2H 137
St Margaret's Dri. S64—2H 55
St Margaret's Rd. DN4—2G 47
St Margarets Rd. S30—2F 75
St Mark Rd. S30—4G 141
St Mark's Cres. S10—3B 98
St Mark's Rd. S40—2G 137
St Martin Clo. S30—4G 141
St Martins Av. DN5—3G 31
St Martin's Clo. S75—6D 12
St Mary Cres. S30—5G 141
St Mary's Clo. S30—6E 65
St Mary's Clo. S72—6B 10
St Mary's Cres. DN1—5E 33
St Mary's Cres. S64—1A 56
St Mary's Dri. DN3—3G 35
St Mary's Dri. S60—5C 90
St Marys Gdns. S70—1E 37
St Mary's Ga. S2—4D 98
St Mary's Ga. S41—2B 138
St Mary's Ga. S70—5G 13
St Marys La. S30—6E 65
St Mary's Pl. S41—2B 138
St Mary's Pl. S70—5G 13
St Mary's Rd. DN1—4E 33
St Mary's Rd. DN12—4C 60
St Mary's Rd. S2—6F 5 & 4E 99
St Mary's Rd. S62—2G 69
St Mary's Rd. S63—3H 29
St Mary's Rd. S73—4F 27
(Darfield)
St Mary's Rd. S73—1E 39
(Wombwell)
St Mary's Ter. S30—6E 141
(off Walders La.)
St Mary's View. S61—4B 68
St Matthews Way. S71—4C 14
St Matthias Rd. S30—5G 141
St Michaels Av. DN11—3E 63
St Michael's Av. S64—1B 56
St Michael's Av. S71—1D 14
St Michaels Clo. S30—1F 75
St Michaels Cres. S30—2F 75
St Michael's Rd. DN4—2H 47
St Michaels Rd. S30—1F 75
St Nicholas Clo. S5—2C 20
St Nicolas Rd. S62—1G 69
St Nicolas Wlk. S62—2F 69
St Oswald's Dri. DN3—5D 20
St Owens Dri. S75—5D 12
St Patrick Rd. S30—4G 141
St Patrick's Rd. DN2—4G 33
St Patrick's Way. DN5—3F 31

St Paul Clo. S30—4G 141
St Paul Clo. S31—2A 118
St Pauls Av. S41—6D 138
St Paul's Pde. DN5—4F 31
St Paul's Pde. S1—4E 5
St Paul's Pde. S71—1F 25
St Peter Av. S30—4H 141
St Peter's Clo. S1—2E 5 & 1E 99
St Peter's Clo. S60—3A 90
St Peter's Dri. DN12—4D 58
St Peter's Rd. DN4—4G 45
St Peter's Rd. DN12—4D 58
St Peter's Ter. S70—1A 24
St Philip's Clo. S66—5E 83
St Philip's Dri. S41—5B 138
St Philip's La. S3—6D 86
St Philip's Rd. S3—2A 4 &
(in three parts) 1C 98 to 6D 86
St Quentin Clo. S17—4H 121
St Quentin Dri. S17—4H 121
St Quentin Mt. S17—4H 121
St Quentin Rise. S17—4H 121
St Quentin View. S17—4H 121
St Ronan's Rd. S7—6D 98
St Sepulchre Ga. DN1—6C 32
St Sepulchre Ga. W. DN4 & DN1
—1C 46
St Stephens Dri. S31—5B 104
St Stephen's Rd. S65—2E 79
St Stephens Wlk. DN5—4G 31
St Stephen's Wlk. S3—1C 98
St Thomas Rd. S10—2H 97
St Thomas's Clo. S30—5G 45
St Thomas's Rd. S75—3C 12
St Thomas St. S1—3C 4 & 2D 98
St Thomas St. S40—3E 137
St Ursula's Rd. DN4—1G 47
St Veronica Rd. S30—4H 141
St Vincent Av. DN1—5E 33
St Vincent Av. DN6—1B 16
St Vincent Rd. DN1—5E 33
St Vincent's Av. DN3—4G 49
St Wandrilles Clo. S30—6F 65
St Wilfrids Dri. DN4—4C 48
(off Masham Rd.)
St Wilfrids Rd. DN4—2A 48
St Wilfrid's Rd. S2—5E 99
St Withold Av. S66—5A 94
Salcey Sq. S40—4F 137
Sale Hill. S10—3H 97
Salerno Way. S73—3C 26
Sale St. S74—6F 37
Salisbury Av. S18—3E 129
Salisbury Av. S41—4G 131
Salisbury Cres. S41—4H 131
Salisbury Rd. DN4—2A 46
Salisbury Rd. S10—1H 97
Salisbury Rd. S18—4F 129
Salisbury Rd. S66—3F 83
Salisbury St. S75—4F 13
Salmon St. S11—5D 98
Salt Box La. S30—2A 74
Saltergate. S40—2H 137
Saltersbrook. S63—4F 29
Saltersbrook Rd. S73—2D 26
Samson St. S2—3G 99
Samuel Clo. S2—6H 99
Samuel Dri. S2—6H 99
Samuel Pl. S2—5H 99
Samuel Rd. S2—6H 99
Samuel Rd. S75—4D 12
Samuel Sq. S75—4D 12
Samuel St. DN4—5H 45
Sanctuary Fields. S31—6D 106
Sandall Beat La. DN2—3B 34
Sandall Beat Rd. DN4—6H 33
Sandall Carr Rd. DN3—4C 20
Sandall La. DN3—2B 20

Sandall Pk. Dri. DN2—2A 34
Sandall Rise. DN2—3H 33
Sandall Stones Rd. DN3—5B to
(in two parts) 4C 20
Sandall View. S31—2C 106
Sandal Rd. DN12—4C 58
Sandalwood Clo. DN2—1A 34
Sandalwood Rise. S64—5B 56
Sandbeck Clo. S71—4G 13
Sandbeck Ct. DN12—1B 58
Sandbeck Ho. DN1—1C 46
(off Grove Pl.)
Sandbeck Pl. S11—5B 98
Sandbeck Rd. DN4—1F 47
Sandbeck Way. S66—4A 82
Sandbed Rd. S3—4C 86
Sandbergh Rd. S61—5G 67
Sandby Ct. S14—5A 112
Sandby Croft. S14—5A 112
Sandby Dri. S14—5A 112
Sandcliffe Rd. DN2—3H 33
Sandcroft Clo. S74—6G 37
Sanderby Dri. S65—2H 81
Sanderson Rd. S9—1D 88
Sanderson St. S9—4B 88
Sandford Ct. S70—6F 13
Sandford Gro. Rd. S7—2C 110
Sandford Rd. DN4—5A 46
Sandhill Clo. S62—6H 55
Sandhill Ct. S72—1B 88
Sandhill Rd. S62—6H 55
Sandhurst Pl. S10—1A 98
Sandhurst Rd. DN4—4E 49
Sandiway. S40—5E 137
Sandon View. S10—6A 4
Sandown Clo. S31—6B 124
Sandown Gdns. DN4—1B 48
Sandown Rd. S64—5F 43
Sandpiper Rd. S61—1B 66
Sandringham Av. S60—2H 91
Sandringham Clo. S44—1G 139
Sandringham Pl. S65—1H 81
Sandringham Rd. DN2—6G 33
Sandringham Rd. S9—5C 76
Sandringham Dri. S44—1G 139
Sandrock Dri. DN4—4C 48
Sands Clo. S14—3A 112
Sandstone Av. S9—1B 88
Sandstone Rd. S42—4D 136
Sandstone Clo. S9—6C 76
Sandstone Dri. S9—1B 88
Sandstone Rd. S9—1B 88
Sandwith Rd. S31—2A 118
Sandy Acres Clo. S19—6F 115
Sandy Acres Dri. S19—6F 115
Sandybridge La. S72—1B 10
Sandy Flat La. S66—2E 93
Sandygate. S63—5F 41
Sandygate Ct. S10—3D 96
Sandygate Cres. S63—1F 53
Sandygate Grange Dri. S10
—3E 97
Sandygate Gro. S10—3D 96
Sandygate La. S10—3E 97
Sandygate Pk. S10—3D 96
Sandygate Pk. Cres. S10
—3D 96
Sandygate Pk. Rd. S10—3D 96
Sandygate Rd. S10—3D 96
Sandy La. DN4—2G 47
Sandy La. S66—6H 81 & 6A 82
(Bramley)
Sandy La. S66—4B 94
(Thurcroft)
Sandy La. S73—1A 38
Sandymount Rd. S63—5G 41
Sanforth St. S41—5A 132
Sankey Sq. S63—4F 29

Sarah St. S61—3B 78
Sarah St. S64—1E 57
Sark Rd. S2—6E 99
Saundby Clo. DN4—4A 48
Saunders Pl. S2—2A 100
Saunders Rd. S2—2A 100
Saunder's Row. S73—1E 39
Savage La. S17—2D 120
Savile St. S4—6G 87
Savile St. E. S4—5H 87
Savile Wlk. S72—2H 11
Saville Ct. S74—6F 37
Saville Hall La. S75—3B 22
Saville Rd. S60—2H 91
Saville Rd. S63—5E 41
Saville Rd. S75—3B 22
Saville St. S65—6A 70
Saville St. S72—6B 10
Saville Ter. S70—1G 23
Sawdon Rd. S11—4C 98
Sawn Moor Av. S66—5B 94
Sawn Moor Rd. S66—6B 94
Sawston Clo. DN4—1G 61
Saxon Cres. S70—4A 24
Saxonlea Av. S2—4D 100
Saxonlea Ct. S2—4E 101
Saxonlea Cres. S2—4E 101
Saxonlea Dri. S2—4D 100
Saxon Rd. S8—1E 111
Saxon Rd. S31—5B 118
Saxon St. S63—1G 29
Saxon St. S72—1H 15
Saxton Av. S30—3A 48
Saxton Clo. S74—5D 38
Saxton Dri. S60—2F 91
Sayers Clo. DN5—1G 43
Scafell Pl. S31—1H 119
Scaftworth Clo. DN4—4A 48
Scammadine Clo. S60—3D 90
Scamming La. S31—6H 95
Scampton Lodge. S5—1F 87
Scarborough Clo. S31—6E 107
Scarborough La. DN11—4B 62
Scarborough Rd. S9—6E 89
Scarbrough Cres. S66—5G 83
Scarbrough Farm Ct. S66
—4F 83
Scarbrough Rd. S66—4F 81
Scaresdale Rd. S41—3A 132
Scarfield Clo. S71—1F 25
Scargill Croft. S1—2F 5 & 1F 99
Scar La. S71—1F 25
Scarlet Oak M. S6—5C 84
Scarll Rd. DN4—2A 46
Scarsdale Clo. S18—3F 129
Scarsdale Cres. S43—4D 132
Scarsdale Cross. S18—2F 129
(off Scarsdale Rd.)
Scarsdale Rd. S8—4D 110
Scarsdale Rd. S18—2E 129
Scarsdale Rd. S41—3A 132
Scarsdale St. S31—4G 107
Scarth Av. DN4—3B 46
Scawsby La. DN5—1D 30
Scawthorpe Av. DN5—1F 31
Sceptone Gro. S72—2C 10
Sceptre Gro. DN11—6C 62
Schofield Dri. S73—3E 27
Schofield Pl. S73—3E 27
Schofield Rd. S30—3F 141
Schofield Rd. S73—3E 27
Schofield St. S64—6D 42
Scholes Grn. S61—3E 67
Scholes La. S61—4C to 1D 66
Scholes View. S30—6F 65
Scholes View. S74—6A 38
(Hoyland)

Scholes View. S74—4B 38
(Jump)
Scholey Rd. S66—4F 81
Scholey St. S3—6F 87
Scholfield Cres. S66—5H 83
School Av. S19—2E 125
School Board La. S40—2G 137
School Clo. S19—2F 125
School Clo. S31—5F 117
Schoolfield Dri. S62—6F 55
School Grn. La. S10—6B 96
School Gro. S31—6C 104
School Hill. S60—2A 92
School Hill. S72—6B 10
School La. DN3—3F 49
School La. S2—3H 5 & 2G 99
(in two parts)
School La. S6—6C 84
School La. S8—2D 122
(Greenhill)
School La. S8—6G 111
(Norton)
School La. S18—2E 129
School La. S30—6A 64
(Grenoside)
School La. S62—4E 69
School La. S65—4D 70
School La. Clo. S8—6G 111
School Rd S19—4G 115
School Rd. S10—2H 97
School Rd. S30—6C 50
School Rd. S31—1D 106
(Laughton)
School Rd. S31—5D 116
(Wales)
School Rd. S41—4A 132
School Rd. S66—5B 94
School St. S19—2D 124
School St. S31—4F 107
(Dinnington)
School St. S31—6D 124
(Eckington)
School St. S31—6A 104
(Swallownest)
School St. S63—1A 42
(Bolton-upon-Dearne)
School St. S63—1F 29
(Thurnscoe)
School St. S65—5C 70
School St. S70—1D 24
School St. S72—5B 10
School St. S73—3F 27
(Darfield)
School St. S73—3E 39
(Hemingfield)
School St. S73—6B 26
(Wombwell)
School St. S75—4F 13
(Barnsley)
School St. S75—4C 6
(Darton)
School St. S75—4G 7
(Mapplewell)
School St. Flats. S2—3H 5
School Wlk. DN12—1B 58
(Conisbrough)
School Wlk. DN12—6A 60
(Old Edlington)
School Wlk. S66—4F 83
Scorah's La. S64—2G 55
Scotia Clo. S2—5B 100
Scotia Dri. S2—5B 100
Scotland St. S3—1C 4 & 1D 98
Scot La. DN1—6D 32
Scott Av. DN5—1G 43
Scott Av. DN12—3C 58
Scott Clo. S66—5A 94

Scott Cres. DN3—4C 20
Scott Hill. DN5—3D 44
Scott Rd. S4—3G 87
Scott St. S4—3A 88
Scott Wlk. S66—3D 82
Scott Way. S30—3D 64
Scovell Av. S62—6D 54
Scowerdons Clo. S12—2H 113
Scowerdons Dri. S12—2H 113
Scraith Wood Dri. S5—1C 86
Scrooby Dri. S61—4C 68
Scrooby La. S62—4D 68
Scrooby Pl. S61—4C 68
Scrooby St. S61—4C 68
Sea Breeze Ter. S13—5G 101
Seabrook Rd. S2—3H 99
Seagrave Av. S12—3D 112
Seagrave Cres. S12—4C 112
Seagrave Dri. S12—3D 112
Seagrave Rd. S12—3D 112
Searby Rd. S66—2H 81
Seaton Clo. S2—3B 100
Seaton Cres. S2—3B 100
Seaton Gdns. DN11—6D 62
Seaton Pl. S2—3B 100
Seaton Way. S2—3B 100
Sebastian View. S60—1C 90
Second Av. DN6—3E 17
Second La. S31—4G 119
Second La. S66—1G 93
Sedan St. S4—4G 87
Sedbergh Cres. S41—4F 131
Sedge Clo. S66—5H 81
Sedgefield Way. S64—5F 43
Sedgeley Rd. S6—3B 86
Sedgemoor Clo. S40—1D 136
Sefton Ct. S10—6E 97
Sefton Rd. S10—6E 97
Selborne Rd. S10—3G 97
Selborne St. S9—6B 88
Selborne St. S65—1E 79
Selbourne Clo. S75—2A 12
Selby Clo. S31—6A 104
Selby Clo. S40—5E 137
Selby Rd. DN2—4G 33
Selby Rd. S4—2H 87
Selby Rd. S71—6B 8
Selhurst Cres. DN4—4C 48
Selhurst Rd. S41—6H 131
Selkirk Av. DN4—5F 45
Selkirk Rd. DN2—3A 34
Sellars Rd. S61—6G 67
Sellars Row. S30—5B 50
Sellers St. S8—6D 98
Selly Oak Gro. S8—3G 123
Selly Oak Rd. S8—3G 123
Selmer Cl. S43—3D 132
Selwood. S65—2F 79
Selwyn St. S65—1E 79
Senior Rd. DN4—1A 46
Senior Rd. S9—1F 101
Seniors Pl. S30—1E 65
Sennen Croft. S71—4B 14
Serlby Ho. DN1—1C 46
(off Grove Pl.)
Serpentine Wlk. S8—1E 123
Setcup La. S31—6H 125
Seth Ter. S70—1A 24
Setts Mkt. S1—2G 5
Sevenfields Ct. S6—2G 85
Sevenfields La. S6—2G 85
Severn Ct. S10—2B 98
Severn Rd. S10—2B 98
Severnside Dri. S13—6A 102
Severnside Gdns. S13—6A 102
Severnside Pl. S13—6A 102
Severnside Wlk. S13—6A 102
Sewell Rd. S19—3F 125

Sexton Dri. S66—5H 81
Seymore Rd. S31—1B 116
Seymour La. S43—2G 135
Seymour Rd. S66—4H 83
Shackleton Rd. DN2—6B 20
Shady Side. DN4—2H 45
(in two parts)
Shaftesbury Av. DN2—6H 33
Shaftesbury Av. DN6—1B 16
Shaftesbury Av. S40—2F 137
Shaftesbury Dri. S74—6H 37
Shaftesbury Ho. DN4—4A 34
Shaftesbury St. S70—1E 25
Shaftholme La. DN5—1B 18
Shaftholme Rd. DN5—2D 18
Shafton Hall Dri. S72—2B 10
Shafton Rd. S60—1H 91
Shakespeare Av. DN5—5H 31
Shakespeare Cres. S18
—3G 129
Shakespeare Dri. S31—5G 107
Shakespeare Rd. DN5—6B 18
Shakespeare Rd. S63—4D 40
Shakespeare Rd. S65—1F 79
Shaldon Gro. S31—6B 104
Shalesmoor. S3—6D 86
Shambles St. S70—6G 13
Shambles, The. S40—2A 138
Shap Clo. S42—6E 131
Shardlow Gdns. DN4—5D 48
Sharlston Gdns. DN11—4F 63
Sharpe Av. S8—1C 122
Sharpfield Av. S62—5E 55
Sharrard Clo. S12—2D 112
Sharrard Dri. S12—2D 112
Sharrard Gro. S12—1D 112
Sharrard Rd. S12—2D 112
Sharrow La. S11—5C 98
Sharrow Mt. S11—6B 98
Sharrow St. S11—5D 98
Sharrow Vale Rd. S11—5A 98
Sharrow View. S7—5C 98
Shaw Ct. DN3—4G 35
Shawfield Clo. DN3—1E 21
Shawfield Rd. S71—6F 9
Shaw La. DN2—1B 34
Shaw La. S70—6F 13
Shaw La. S71—4F 9
Shaw La. S75—3G 7
Shaw La. Ind. Est. DN2—1C 34
Shaw Rd. DN12—2C 60
Shaw Rd. S65—1G 79
Shawsfield Rd. S60—6F 79
Shaws Row. S40—3F 137
Shaw St. S9—1D 88
Shaw St. S18—5G 123
Shaw St. S41—3A 132
Shaw St. S70—6F 13
Shay Ho. La. S30—4D 140
Shay Rd. S30—3D 140
Shay, The. DN4—4C 48
Sheaf Bank. S2—6E 99
Sheaf Clo. DN12—4F 59
Sheaf Ct. S70—2D 24
Sheaf Cres. S63—2B 42
Sheaf Gdns. Ter. S2—4F 99
Sheaf Mkt. S1—2G 5
Sheaf Sq. S1—5F 5 & 3F 99
Sheaf St. S1—4G 5 & 2F 99
Sheardown St. DN4—1B 46
Sheards Clo. S18—1D 128
Sheards Dri. S18—2C 128
Sheards Way. S18—2D 128
Shearman Av. S61—5G 67
Shearwood Rd. S10—2B 98
Sheep Bri. La. DN11—3E 63
Sheepbridge La. S41—1G 131

Sheepcote Rd. S31—3A 126
Sheep Cote Rd. S60—6B 80
Sheep Dike La. S66—4G 93
Sheephill Rd. S11—4A 108
Sheep La. DN5—6A 30
Sheffield La. S60—6C 90
Sheffield Parkway. S2, S9 &
S60—2H 5 & 1G 99
Sheffield Rd. DN4—1B 60
Sheffield Rd. DN12—5B 58
Sheffield Rd. S9—2E 89 to 6H 77
Sheffield Rd. S12—5H 113
Sheffield Rd. S13—1A 114
(Woodhouse)
Sheffield Rd. S13 & S31—5E 103
(Woodhouse Mill)
Sheffield Rd. S18—6D 122
(Dronfield)
Sheffield Rd. S31—2F 119
(Anston)
Sheffield Rd. S31—1B 118
(Aston)
Sheffield Rd. S31—3D 124
(Eckington)
Sheffield Rd. S31—2H 125
(Killamarsh)
Sheffield Rd. S41
—5A 132 to 1H 131
Sheffield Rd. S60—6H 77
Sheffield Rd. S70—1H 23
(Barnsley)
Sheffield Rd. S70—2C 36
(Birdwell)
Sheffield Rd. S74—6E 37
Sheffield Rd. Business Pk. S9
—6G 77
Sheffield Technology Pk. S9
—5C 88
Sheldon Av. DN12—4F 59
Sheldon La. S6—5C 84
Sheldon Rd. S7—1C 110
Sheldon Rd. S30—3E 141
Sheldon Rd. S40—6D 130
Sheldon Row. S30—1G 5 & 1F 99
Sheldon St. S2—4E 99
Sheldrake Clo. S61—2B 66
Shelf St. S2—4F 99
Shelley Av. DN4—5B 46
Shelley Dri. DN3—3G 35
Shelley Dri. S18—4G 129
Shelley Dri. S31—5H 107
Shelley Dri. S65—4H 79
Shelley Dri. S71—4A 14
Shelley Gro. DN5—6H 31
Shelley Rise. DN6—1C 16
Shelley Rd. S65—3H 79
Shelley Way. S63—4C 40
Shenstone Dri. S65—5H 79
Shenstone Rd. S6—1A 86
Shenstone Rd. S65—5H 79
Shepcote La. S9—4E 89
Shepcote Way. S9—4E 89
Shephards Clo. DN12—2B 58
Shepherd Dri. S30—1C 64
Shepherd La. S63—2F 29
Shepherd St. S3—1C 4 & 1D 98
Shepherd St. S70—1H 23
Shepley Croft. S30—1C 64
Sheppard Rd. DN4—4A 46
Shepperson Rd. S6—2H 85
Sherbourne Av. S41—3G 131
Sherburn Ga. S30—1D 64
Sherburn Rd. S71—6A 8
Sherde Rd. S6—6C 86
Sheridan Av. DN4—5C 46
Sheridan Ct. S71—4B 14

Sheridan Dri. S65—3A 80
Sheridan Rd. DN3—1H 21
Sheringham Clo. S30—6B 50
Sheringham Gdns. S30—6B 50
(off Sheringham Clo.)
Sherwood Av. DN3—5D 20
Sherwood Av. DN5—3F 31
Sherwood Av. DN12—4C 58
Sherwood Chase. S17—4E 121
Sherwood Cres. S60—3E 79
Sherwood Dri. DN4—6G 45
Sherwood Glen. S7—6H 109
Sherwood Pl. S18—2B 128
Sherwood Rd. DN11—5E 63
Sherwood Rd. S18—2B 128
Sherwood Rd. S31—2C 126
Sherwood St. S40—4B 138
Sherwood St. S71—6A 14
Sherwood Way. S72—4A 10
Shetland Gdns. DN2—4A 34
Shetland Rd. S18—3F 129
Shield Av. S70—4A 24
Shinwell Av. S43—4H 133
Shipcroft Clo. S73—1G 39
Ship Hill. S60—3D 78
Shipman Ct. S19—2D 124
Shipton St. S6—6C 86
Shirburn Gdns. DN4—2D 48
Shirebrook Rd. S8—1E 111
Shirecliffe Clo. S3—3F 87
Shirecliffe La. S3—4E 87
Shirecliffe Rd. S5—1E 87
Shiregreen La. S5—5A to 6B 76
Shiregreen Ter. S5—4H 75
Shirehall Cres. S5—2H 75
Shirehall Rd. S5
—3H 75 to 2A 76
Shireoaks Rd. S18—1G 129
Shires Clo. DN5—2D 44
Shirland Av. S71—1A 14
Shirland La. S9—5C 88
Shirland St. S41—1A 138
Shirley Clo. S40—6D 130
Shirley Rd. DN4—2A 46
Shirley Rd. S3—4F 87
Shore Ct. S10—3H 97
Shoreham Av. S60—2G 91
Shoreham Dri. S60—2F 91
Shoreham Rd. S60—2F 91
Shoreham St. S2 & S1
—6F 5 & 5E 99
Shore La. S10—3G 97
Shore St. S73—1F 39
Shortbrook Bank. S19—1E 125
Shortbrook Clo. S19—1F 125
Shortbrook Croft. S19—1F 125
Shortbrook Dri. S19—1E 125
Shortbrook Rd. S19—1E 125
Shortbrook Wlk. S19—1F 125
(off Eastcroft Way.)
Shortbrook Way. S19—1E 125
Short Ga. DN11—6F 61
Short La. DN4—4H 47
Shortridge St. S9—5B 88
Short Rd. DN2—5A 34
Short Row. S71—2H 13
Shorts La. S17—3B 120
Short St. S74—6F 37
Short Wood Clo. S70—2D 36
Shortwood Vs. S74—3F 37
Shotton Wlk. DN1—1C 46
Shrewsbury Almshouses. S2
—5H 5 & 3G 99
Shrewsbury Clo. S64—6D 42
Shrewsbury Rd. S2
—6G 5 & 3F 99
Shrewsbury Ter. S17—5D 120
Shrewsbury Ter. S61—3H 77

Shrogs Wood Rd. S60—6B 80
Shubert Clo. S13—5B 102
Shude Hill. S1—2G 5
Sibbering Row. S30—4H 141
Sicey Av. S5—5H to 1H 75
Sicey La. S5—5H 75
Sidcop Rd. S72—5B 10
Siddall St. S1—3B 4 & 2D 98
Sidlaw Clo. S42—6E 131
Sidney Rd. DN2—5H 33
Sidney St. S1—6E 5 & 3E 99
Sidney St. S64—2B 56
Sidons Clo. S61—5G 67
Siemens Clo. S9—1G 89
Siena Clo. S73—4C 26
Sike Clo. S75—4A 6
Sikes Rd. S31—2F 119
Silkstone Clo. S12—3G 113
Silkstone Cres. S12—3G 113
Silkstone Dri. S12—3F 113
Silkstone Pl. S12—3G 113
Silkstone Rd. S12—3F 113
Silkstone View. S74—3A 38
Silver Birch Av. S10—6C 96
Silverdale Clo. DN3—3H 49
Silverdale Clo. S11—3G 109
Silverdale Clo. S41—2G 131
Silverdale Ct. S11—3H 109
(off Silverdale Gdns.)
Silverdale Cres. S11—2G 109
Silverdale Croft. S11—3G 109
Silverdale Dri. S71—2D 14
Silverdale Gdns. S11—3H 109
Silverdale Glade. S11—3H 109
Silverdale Rd. S11—2G 109
Silverdales. S31—4G 107
Silver Hill Rd. S11—2H 109
Silver Jubilee Clo. DN2—3A 34
Silver Mill Rd. S2—5E 99
Silvermoor Dri. S65—1H 81
Silverstone Av. S72—6C 10
Silver St. DN1—6D 32
Silver St. S1—2E 5 & 1E 99
Silver St. S65—5C 70
Silver St. S70—1G 23 to 6H 13
(in two parts)
Silver St. S75—3B 22
Silver St. Head. S1
—2D 4 & 1E 99
Silverwood Ho. DN1—2C 46
(off Elsworth Clo.)
Silverwood View. DN12—3D 58
Silverwood Wlk. S66—3F 81
Simcrest Av. S31—4B 126
Simmonite Rd. S61—5H 67
Simons Way. S73—4H 25
Simpson Pl. S64—6D 42
Sims St. S1—2D 4 & 1E 99
Sincil Way. DN4—4C 48
Singleton Cres. S6—4A 86
Singleton Gro. S6—4A 86
Singleton Rd. S6—4A 86
Sitka Clo. S71—2D 8
Sitwell. S19—1E 125
(off Shortbrook Way.)
Sitwell Av. S30—3C 140
Sitwell Av. S40—4H 137
Sitwell Dri. S60—6G 79
Sitwell Gro. S60—1G 91
Sitwell Gro. S64—3B 56
Sitwell La. S66—6F 81
Sitwell Pk. Rd. S60—6B 80
Sitwell Pl. S7—5D 98
Sitwell Rd. S7—5D 98
(in two parts)
Sitwell St. S31—6C 124
Sitwell Ter. S66—6F 81
(off Sitwell La.)

Sitwell Vale. S60—6F 79
Sitwell View. S60—2B 92
Sivilla Rd. S62—5B 56
Skeldale Dri. S40—5B 138
Skelton Av. S75—4F 7
Skelton Clo. S13—2B 114
Skelton Dri. S13—1C 114
Skelton Gro. S13—1B 114
Skelton La. S13—1B 114
Skelton La. S19—4F 115
Skelton Rise. S30—3D 72
Skelton Rd. S8—2E 111
Skelton Wlk. S13—1C 114
Skelton Way. S13—1B 114
Skelwith Clo. S4—2B 88
Skelwith Clo. S41—3F 131
Skelwith Dri. S4—1B 88
Skelwith Rd. S4—2B 88
Skew Hill. S30—2A 74
Skew Hill La. S30—1H 73
Skiddaw Clo. S40—5F 131
Skiers View Rd. S74—6G 37
Skiers Way. S74—6G 37
Skinnerthorpe Rd. S4—2H 87
Skipton Clo. DN12—2A 58
Skipton Rd. S4—3G 87
Skipton Rd. S31—6A 104
Skipwith Gdns. DN11—5C 62
Skye Edge Av. S2—3H 99
Skye Edge Rd. S2—3H 99
Slack Fields La. S30—1B 72
Slack La. S40—2D 136
Slacks La. S66—6H 81
Slade Rd. S64—3A 56
Slaidburn Av. S30—1D 64
Slate St. S2—6F 99
Slayleigh Av. S10—5C 96
Slayleigh Delph. S10—5C 96
Slayleigh Dri. S10—5D 96
Slayleigh La. S10—5C 96
Sleaford St. S9—5B 88
Sledgate Dri. S66—6D 80
Sledgate La. S66—6D 80
Sledmere Rd. DN5—3G 31
Slinn St. S10—6A 86
Slitting Mill La. S9—5B 88
Smallage La. S13—4F 103
Smalldale Rd. S12—3F 113
Smeaton Clo. S65—1H 81
Smeaton St. S11—5D 98
Smelter Wood Av. S13—6G 101
Smelter Wood Clo. S13—6G 101
Smelter Wood Ct. S13—6G 101
(off Smelter Wood Way)
Smelter Wood Cres. S13
—6H 101
Smelter Wood Dri. S13—6G 101
Smelter Wood La. S13—6G 101
Smelter Wood Pl. S13—6H 101
Smelter Wood Rise. S13
—6H 101
Smelter Wood Rd. S13—6G 101
Smelter Wood Way. S13
—6G 101
Smeltinghouse La. S18
—1A 130
Smillie Rd. DN11—5E 63
Smith Av. S43—4H 133
Smith Cres. S41—4D 138
Smithey Clo. S30—1B 64
Smithfield. S3—1D 4 & 1E 99
Smithfield Av. S41—6C 138
Smithfield Rd. S12—5C 112
Smithies La. S75 & S71—3G 13
Smithies Rd. S64—1B 56
Smithies St. S71—3G 13
Smithley La. S73—6F 25
Smith Rd. S30—3D 140

Smith Sq. DN4—4H 45
Smith St. DN4—4H 45
Smith St. S9—6E 89
Smith St. S30—2E 65
Smith St. S73—6C 26
Smithy Bri. La. S73
—4F to 5H 39
Smithy Carr Av. S30—2D 64
Smithy Carr Clo. S30—2D 64
Smithy Clo. S61—6H 67
Smithy Croft. S18—1A 128
Smithy Grn. Rd. S71—2H 13
Smithy Moor Av. S30—1A 140
Smithy Moor La. S30—1A 140
Smithy Wood Cres. S8—3C 110
(in two parts)
Smithy Wood La. S75—3B 22
Smithy Wood Rd. S8—3C 110
Smithy Wood Rd. S30—3H 65
Snail Hill. S60—3D 78
Snailsden Way. S75—5H 7
Snaithing La. S10—4E 97
Snaithing Pk. Clo. S10—4E 97
Snaithing Pk. Rd. S10—4E 97
Snake La. DN12—4F 59
Snape Hill. S18—1E 129
Snapehill Clo. S18—6E 123
Snapehill Cres. S18—6E 123
Snapehill Dri. S18—6E 123
Snape Hill La. S18—1E 129
Snape Hill Rd. S73—4D 26
Snelston Clo. S18—2A 128
Snetterton Clo. S72—6C 10
Snig Hill. S3—2F 5 & 1F 99
Snowberry Clo. S64—5A 56
Snowden Ter. S73—6B 26
Snowdon Way. S60—4D 90
Snow Hill. S75—3B 22
Snow Hill Row. S2—2H 5
Snow La. S3—1D 4 & 1E 99
Snydale Rd. S72—6B 10
Soaper La. S18—1E 129
Soap Ho. La. S13—1F 115
Society St. DN1—6D 32
Sokell Av. S73—1E 39
Solario Way. DN11—6C 62
Solferino St. S11—4D 98
Solly St. S1—3B 4 & 1D 98
Solway Rise. S18—1B 128
Somercotes Rd. S12—2F 113
Somersall Clo. S40—4C 136
Somersall Hall Dri. S40—5C 136
Somersall La. S40—5C 136
Somersall Pk. Rd. S40—4C 136
Somersby Av. DN5—5H 31
Somersby Av. S42—6D 136
Somerset Ct. S72—1H 15
Somerset Dri. S43—2F 133
Somerset Rd. DN1—1D 46
Somerset Rd. S3—5F 87
Somerset St. S3—5F 87
Somerset St. S66—5H 83
Somerset St. S70—5F 13
Somerset St. S72—1H 15
Somerton Dri. DN4—4C 48
Somerville Ter. S6—5B 86
Sopewell Rd. S61—3F 77
Sorby Hall. S10—4H 97
Sorby Rd. S31—6H 103
Sorby St. S4—6G 87
Sorby Way. S66—6E 81
Soresby St. S40—2A 138
Sorrel Rd. S66—3G 81
Sorrelsykes Clo. S60—3H 91
Sorrento Way. S73—2D 26
Sothall Clo. S19—4F 115
Sothall Ct. S19—4F 115
Sothall Grn. S19—4F 115

Sothall M. S19—4F 115
Sough Hall Av. S61—2B 66
Sough Hall Clo. S61—2B 66
Sough Hall Cres. S61—2B 66
Sough Hall Rd. S61—3B 66
Sousa St. S66—5H 83
Southall St. S8—1E 111
South Av. S64—3H 55
Southbourne Ct. S17—3D 120
Southbourne Hall. S10—3B 98
Southbourne Rd. S10—3A 98
South Clo. S71—3E 9
Southcote Dri. S18—2B 128
South Ct. S17—2E 121
South Cres. S31—2C 126
South Cres. S44—6E 135
South Cres. S65—2H 79
South Cres. S75—2B 22
Southcroft Gdns. S7—1D 110
Southcroft Wlk. S7—1D 110
(off Southcroft Gdns.)
Southdown Av. S40—1E 137
South Dri. S63—2H 41
South Dri. S71—3E 9
Southend Pl. S2—3A 100
Southend Rd. S2—3A 100
Southey Av. S5—6E 75
Southey Clo. S5—6D 74
Southey Cres. S5—6D 74
Southey Cres. S66—4G 83
Southey Dri. S5—6E 75
Southey Grn. Clo. S5—6D 74
Southey Grn. Rd. S5
—5B 74 to 5E 75
Southey Hall Clo. S61—2B 66
Southey Hall Dri. S5—6E 75
Southey Hall Rd. S5—6D 74
Southey Hill. S5—5C 74
Southey Pl. S5—6D 74
Southey Rise. S5—6D 74
Southey Rd. S66—4G 83
Southey Wlk. S5—6D 74
Southfield Av. S41—6D 108
Southfield Cotts. S71—4E 9
Southfield Cres. S63—2D 28
Southfield Dri. S18—3G 129
Southfield La. S63—3D 28
Southfield Mt. S18—3G 129
Southfield Rd. DN3—3E 35
Southgate. S31—6E 125
Southgate. S74—5A 38
Southgate. S75—4E 13
Southgrove Rd. S10—4B 98
Southlands Way. S31—6C 104
South La. S1—6C 4 & 4D 98
Southlea Av. S74—6B 38
Southlea Clo. S74—6B 38
Southlea Dri. S74—6A 38
Southlea Rd. S74—6B 38
South Lodge Ct. S40—2D 136
South Mall. DN1—6C 32
(off French Ga.)
Southmoor Av. DN3—3E 35
Southmoor Clo. S43—1F 139
South Pde. DN1—6E 33
South Pde. S3—6E 87
South Pl. S40—3F 137
(Barker La.)
South Pl. S40—3A 138
(South St.)
South Pl. S73—6H 25
South Pl. S75—4D 12
South Rd. S6—5A 86
South Rd. S30—6B 50
South Rd. S61—2G 77
South Rd. S75—2B 22
Southsea Rd. S13—1A 114
South St. DN4—2D 46

South St. DN6—5D 16
South St. S2—3H 5 & 2G 99
South St. S19—3D 124
South St. S31—4F 107
South St. S40—3A 138
South St. S61—4C 68
(Greasbrough)
South St. S61—4G 77
(Kimberworth & Rotherham)
South St. S62—1G 69
South St. S66—4B 94
South St. S70—6F 13
South St. S73—4E 27
South St. S75—3B 22
South St. N. S43—1D 132
South Ter. S31—4D 116
S. Vale Dri. S65—5D 70
South View. S19—2G 125
South View. S31—5H 117
South View. S72—6F 11
South View. S73—4E 27
S. View Clo. S6—2E 85
S. View Cres. S7—6D 98
S. View Rise. S6—2E 85
S. View Rd. S7—5D 98
S. View Rd. S74—6H 37
S. View Ter. S60—6C 90
Southway. S19—1E 125
Southwell Rise. S64—5F 43
Southwell Rd. DN2—3F 33
Southwell Rd. S4—2B 88
Southwell Rd. S62—1H 69
Southwell St. S75—5F 13
Southwood Av. S18—4E 129
Spa Brook Clo. S12—3H 113
Spa Brook Dri. S12—2H 113
(in two parts)
Spa La. S13—2C 114
Spa La. S41—2B to 3B 138
(in two parts)
Spa La. Croft. S13—1C 114
Spalton Rd. S62—3F 69
Spansyke St. DN4—1B 46
Sparkfields. S75—5F 7
Spark La. S75—6E 7
Spa View Av. S12—4H 113
Spa View Dri. S12—4H 113
Spa View Pl. S12—4H 113
Spa View Rd. S12—4H 113
Spa View Ter. S12—4H 113
Spa View Way. S12—4H 113
Spa Well Cres. S60—6E 91
Spa Well Ter. S71—5H 13
Speedwell Ind. Est. S43
—2C 134
Speeton Rd. S6—4A 86
Spencer Av. S43—1F 135
Spencer Ct. S60—2B 92
Spencer Dri. S65—7F 81
Spencer Grn. S60—2B 92
Spencer Rd. S2—6E 99
Spencer St. S40—1A 138
Spencer St. S64—6C 42
Spencer St. S70—6G 13
Spenser Rd. S65—4H 79
Spilsby Clo. DN4—5E 49
Spink Hall La. S30—4D 140
Spinkhill Av. S13—5E 101
Spinkhill Dri. S13—5F 101
Spinkhill Rd. S13—6E 101
Spinkhill Rd. S31—6B 126
Spinners Wlk. S60—4E 79
(off Warwick St.)
Spinney Clo. S60—6G 79
Spinneyfield. S60—1G 91
Spinney Hill. DN5—3D 44
Spinney, The. DN3—1E 21
Spinney, The. DN4—6H 45

Spinney, The. S43—3D 132
Spitalfields. S3—6F 87
Spital Gdns. S41—4C 138
Spital Gro. DN11—6E 63
Spital Hill. S4—6G 87
Spital La. S3—6G 87
Spital La. S41—3B 138 to 4E 139
Spital St. S4—6G 87
Spofforth Rd. S9—6C 88
Spooner Rd. S10—3A 98
Spoon Glade. S6—5C 84
Spoonhill Rd. S6—5F 85
Spoon La. S6—5A 84
Spoon M. S6—5C 84
Spoon Way. S6—5C 84
Spotswood Clo. S14—3A 112
Spotswood Dri. S14—2A 112
Spotswood Mt. S14—3H 111
Spotswood Pl. S14—3H 111
Spotswood Rd. S14—3H 111
Spout Copse. S6—5B 84
Spout La. S6—5B 84
Spout Spinney. S6—5B 84
Springbank. S73—4F 27
Springbank Clo. S71—5E 9
Spring Bank Rd. DN12—5D 58
Spring Bank Rd. S40—2H 137
Spring Clo. S60—2A 92
Spring Clo. Dell. S14—3B 112
Spring Clo. Mt. S14—3B 112
Spring Clo. View. S14—3A 112
Spring Cres. DN5—2D 44
Spring Croft. S61—6H 67
Springcroft Dri. DN5—1G 31
Springdale Rd. DN2—4G 33
Spring Dri. S73—3A 40
Springfield. S63—1G 41
Springfield Av. S7—2A 110
Springfield Av. S40—2F 137
Springfield Clo. DN3—4G 35
Springfield Clo. S7—3A 110
Springfield Clo. S31—6C 124
Springfield Clo. S61—6D 68
Springfield Clo. S73—4F 27
Springfield Ct. DN5—4G 31
Springfield Cres. S73—4F 27
Springfield Cres. S74—6G 37
Springfield Dri. S65—5E 71
Springfield Glen. S7—3H 109
Springfield Path. S64—1E 57
Springfield Pl. S70—6F 13
Springfield Rd. DN12—3C 60
Springfield Rd. S7—3A 110
Springfield Rd. S62—6C 56
Springfield Rd. S66—4E 81
Springfield Rd. S72—6F 11
Springfield Rd. S74—6F 37
Springfield St. S70—6F 13
Springfield Ter. S31—6C 106
Springfield Ter. S70—6F 13
Springfield Way. S30—2B 64
Spring Gdns. DN1—6C 32
Spring Gdns. S71—3C 14
Spring Gdns. S74—3A 38
Spring Hill. S10—1A 98
Springhill Av. S73—3A 40
Springhill Clo. DN5—2D 44
Spring Hill Rd. S10—1A 98
Spring Ho. Rd. S10—1A 98
Spring La. DN5—5D 30
Spring La. S2—5A 100
Spring La. S71—5E 9
Spring La. WF4—1G 7
Springmill Ter. S30—2D 140
Spring Pl. S40—2A 138
Spring St. S3—1E 5 & 1E 99
Spring St. S65—2E 79

Spring St. S70—1G 23
Spring Vale Av. S70—5H 23
Springvale Clo. S66—3F 83
Springvale Rd. S6 & S10—6B 86
Spring Vale Rd. S43—3D 132
Springvale Wlk. S6—6B 86
Spring View Rd. S10—1A 98
Spring Wlk. S65—2E 79
Spring Wlk. S73—5H 25
Spring Water Av. S12—4A 114
Spring Water Clo. S12—4H 113
Spring Water Dri. S12—4A 114
Springwell Clo. S66—3H 83
Springwell Gdns. DN4—5H 45
Springwell La. DN4 & DN11
—5H 45
Springwood. S5—1C 86
Springwood Av. S31—4A 104
Spring Wood Clo. S41—3E 131
Springwood Ho. DN1—1C 46
(off Elsworth Clo.)
Springwood La. S30—6A 50
Springwood Rd. DN5—1G 31
Springwood Rd. S8—1E 111
Springwood Rd. S74—6G 37
Sprink Hall La. S30—4D 140
Sprotbrough Rd. DN5—6H 31
Spruce Av. S66—4G 81
Spruce Av. S71—2D 8
Spruce Rise. S31—4A 126
Spurley Hey Gro. S30—4E 141
Spurr St. S2—5F 99
Square E., The. S66—2G 81
Square, The. S31—5F 117
Square, The. S42—4B 130
Square, The. S62—4H 51
Square, The. S70—1F 23
Square, The. S71—6E 15
Square W., The. S66—2F 81
Squirrel Croft. S61—3H 67
Stacey Cres. S72—6F 11
Stacey Dri. S65—4D 70
Stacye Av. S13—1D 114
Stacye Rise. S13—1D 114
Stadium Ct. S62—5E 69
Stadium Way. S9—6B 88
Stadium Way. S60—6F 69
Stafford Clo. S18—1A 128
Stafford Cres. S60—2F 91
Stafford Dri. S60—2F 91
Stafford La. S2—3H 99
Stafford M. S2—3H 99
(off Stafford La.)
Stafford Pl. DN12—2B 58
Stafford Rd. DN6—3E 17
Stafford Rd. S2—3H 99
Stafford St. S2—3G 99
Stafford Way. S30—2D 64
Stag Clo. S60—6A 80
Stag Cres. S60—6A 80
Stag La. S60—6H 79
Stainborough Clo. S75—3B 22
Stainborough La. S75—6A 22
Stainborough Rd. S75—3B 22
Stainborough View. S70
—4H 23
Stainborough View. S75—5B 36
Staincross Comn. S75—3F 7
Staindrop View. S30—1E 65
Stainforth Rd. DN3—2H 21
Stainley Clo. S75—3D 12
Stainmore Av. S19—5G 115
Stainton Clo. S71—1G 13
Stainton La. S66—2H 83
Stainton Rd. S11—5H 97
Stainton St. DN12—2B 58
Stairfoot Ind. Est. S70—2E 25
Stair Rd. S4—3G 87

196 Sheffield

Staithes Wlk. DN12—1C 58
Stalker Lees Rd. S11—5B 98
Stalker Wlk. S11—4C 98
Stamford St. S9—4B 88
Stamford Way. S75—3F 7
Stanage Rise. S12—2F 113
Stanage Way. S40—6C 130
Stanbury Clo. S75—3D 12
Standhill Cres. S71—6A 8
Standish Av. S5—3E 87
Standish Clo. S5—2E 87
Standish Dri. S5—2E 87
Standish Rd. S5—2E 87
Standon Cres. S9—4C 76
Standon Dri. S9—4C 76
Standon Rd. S9—4C 76
Stand Rd. S41—3H 131
Staneford Ct. S19—6D 114
Stanford Rd. S18—2A 128
Stanford Rd. S66—5H 83
Stanford Way. S42—5D 136
Stanground Rd. S2—4D 100
Stanhope Gdns. S75—4E 13
Stanhope Rd. DN1—4E 33
Stanhope Rd. S12—2E 113
Stanhope St. S70—6F 13
Staniforth Av. S31—6B 124
Staniforth Cres. S31—2A 118
Staniforth Rd. S9—6B 88
Stanley Av. S43—5H 133
Stanley Ct. S66—4D 82
Stanley Gdns. DN4—2B 46
Stanley Gro. S31—5D 104
  (in two parts)
Stanley La. S3—6F 87
Stanley Rd. S7—2F 31
Stanley Rd. S8—2F 111
Stanley Rd. S30—1B 64
  (Chapeltown)
Stanley Rd. S30—3E 141
  (Stocksbridge)
Stanley Rd. S70—2E 25
Stanley Sq. DN3—3D 20
Stanley St. S3—1G 5 & 6F 87
Stanley St. S31—2B 126
Stanley St. S41—3C 138
Stanley St. S60—3D 78
Stanley St. S70—6F 13
Stanley Ter. S66—4D 82
Stannington Rd. S6
                —5B 84 to 4H 85
Stannington View Rd. S10
                —1G 97
Stanton Cres. S12—3F 113
Stanwell Av. S9—5C 76
Stanwell Clo. S9—5C 76
Stanwell St. S9—5C 76
Stanwell Wlk. S9—5C 76
Stanwood Av. S6—5F 85
Stanwood Cres. S6—5F 85
Stanwood Dri. S6—5F 85
Stanwood Rd. S42—5D 136
Stanwood Rd. S6—5F 85
Staple Grn. S65—5E 71
Stapleton Rd. DN4—6F 45
Star La. DN12—3E 59
Starling Mead. S2—3A 100
Starnhill Clo. S30—6G 65
Station App. DN1—6C 32
  (off Factory La.)
Station Bk. La. S41—2B 138
Station Cotts. S75—4A 6
Station La. S9—1C 88
Station La. S30—2D 72
Station La. S41 & S43—1B 132
Station Rd. DN3—1D 20
Station Rd. DN5—6D 18
Station Rd. DN11—4E 63

Station Rd. DN12—2E 59
Station Rd. S9—1E 101
Station Rd. S13—1C 114
Station Rd. S19
                —2D 124 to 2H 125
Station Rd. S30—2F 65
  (Chapeltown)
Station Rd. S30—3H 141
  (Deepcar)
Station Rd. S30—6G 65
  (Ecclesfield)
Station Rd. S31—6E 125
  (Eckington)
Station Rd. S31—3H 125
  (Killamarsh)
Station Rd. S31—5H 117
  (Kiveton Park)
Station Rd. S31—2C 106
  (Laughton Comn., Dinnington)
Station Rd. S31—6B 126
  (Spinkhill)
Station Rd. S41—2B 138
  (Chesterfield)
Station Rd. S41—2A 132
  (Whittington Moor)
Station Rd. S43—3C 132
  (Brimington)
Station Rd. S43—2F 133
  (Hollingwood)
Station Rd. S60—5C 90
  (Catcliffe)
Station Rd. S60—3B 78
  (Rotherham)
Station Rd. S60—1E 103
  (Treeton)
Station Rd. S63—1A 42
  (Bolton-upon-Dearne)
Station Rd. S63—1F 29
  (Thurnscoe)
Station Rd. S63—4F 41
  (Wath upon Dearne)
Station Rd. S64—1E 57
  (in two parts)
Station Rd. S70—5F 13
  (Barnsley)
Station Rd. S70—5C 24
  (Worsbrough)
Station Rd. S71—2F 15
  (Lundwood)
Station Rd. S71—1D 8
  (Royston)
Station Rd. S73—6C 26
  (in two parts)
Station Rd. S75—4C 6
  (Darton)
Station Rd. S75—2A 22
  (Dodworth)
Station Rd. Ind. Est. S73—5C 26
Station St. S64—2B 56
Station Ter. S41—3C 132
Station Ter. S71—1G 9
Station Way. S31—2C 106
Staton Av. S19—3G 115
Staunton Rd. DN4—4E 49
Staveley La. S31—6E 125
Staveley Rd. S8—6E 99
Staveley Rd. S43—1E 133
  (New Whittington)
Staveley Rd. S43—3D 134
  (Poolsbrook)
Staveley Rd. S44—6C 134
Staveley St. DN12—2B 60
Steade Rd. S7—6D 98
Steadfield Rd. S74—6G 37
Steadfolds Clo. S66—5C 94
Steadfolds La. S66—5C 94
Steadfolds Rise. S66—5C 94
Steadlands, The. S62—6D 54

Stead La. S74—6F 37
Stead St. S31—6D 124
Steel City Trading Est. S9
                —6D 76
Steele Av. S43—5H 133
Steele St. S74—6E 37
Steelhouse La. S3—1E 5 & 1E 99
Steel Rd. S11—5A 98
Steel St. S61—4A 78
Steeping Clo. S43—3E 133
Steeton Ct. S74—5C 38
Stemp St. S11—5D 98
Stenson Ct. DN4—3A 46
Stenton Rd. S8—2D 122
Stentons Ter. S64—1F 57
Stephen Dri. S10—2F 97
Stephen Dri. S30—1H 73
Stephen Hill. S10—2F 97
Stephen Hill Rd. S10—2G 97
Stephen La. S30—1H 73
Stephenson Hall. S10—4A 98
Stephenson Pl. S40—2A 138
Stephenson Pl. S64—1B 56
Stephenson Rd. S43—2C 134
Stepney Row. S2—2H 5
Stepney St. S2—2H 5 & 1G 99
Stepping La. S30—1H 73
Sterland St. S40—2G 137
Sterndale Rd. S7—4A 110
Steven Cres. S30—2D 64
Stevenson Dri. S65—4H 79
Stevenson Dri. S75—3A 12
Stevenson Rd. DN4—5B 46
Stevenson Rd. S9—5A 88
Stevenson Way. S9—5B 88
Stevens Rd. DN4—2B 46
Steventon Rd. S65—5E 71
Stewart Rd. S11—5B 98
Stewarts Rd. S62—1H 69
Stewart St. DN1—1C 46
Sticking La. S64—4B 42
Stirling St. DN1—1C 46
Stockarth Clo. S30—5F 73
Stockarth La. S30—4E 73
Stockbridge Av. DN5—2A 32
Stockbridge La. DN5—6C 18
Stockil Rd. DN4—1E 47
Stock Rd. S2—4A 100
Stocks Grn. Ct. S17—5D 120
Stocks Grn. Dri. S17—5D 120
Stocks Hill. S30—6E 65
Stocks Hill Clo. S71—4E 9
Stock's La. S62—2F 69
Stock's La. S75—5E 13
Stockton Clo. S3—6F 87
Stockton Pl. S3—6F 87
Stockwell Av. S31—6G 117
Stockwell La. S31—6F 117
Stockwith La. S74—4F 37
Stoke St. S9—6A 88
Stoket La. S31—6D 92
Stokewell Rd. S63—4C 40
Stoneacre Av. S12—4B 114
Stoneacre Clo. S12—4B 114
Stoneacre Dri. S12—4B 114
Stoneacre Rise. S12—4B 114
Stonecliffe Clo. S2—4C 100
Stonecliffe Dri. S30—5D 140
Stonecliffe Pl. S2—4C 100
Stonecliffe Rd. S2—4C 100
Stonecliff Wlk. DN12—1C 58
Stone Clo. S18—6G 123
Stone Clo. S65—2H 81
Stone Clo. Av. DN4—1B 46
Stone Cotts. DN5—2H 17
Stone Cres. S66—4F 81
Stonecroft Rd. S17—4E 121
Stone Cross Dri. DN5—1D 44

Stonecross Gdns. DN4—3E 49
Stone Delf. S10—4C 96
Stone Font Gro. DN4—4D 48
Stonegarth Clo. S72—1H 15
Stonegravels Croft. S19
                —3E 125
Stonegravels La. S41—6A 132
Stonegravels Way. S19
                —3F 125
Stone Gro. S10—2B 98
Stone Hill Dri. S31—6B 104
Stonehill Rise. DN5—1G 31
Stonehill Rise. S72—1H 15
Stone La. S13—2A 114
Stoneley Clo. S12—6D 112
Stoneley Cres. S12—6D 112
Stonelow Ct. S18—1F 129
  (off Paddock Way)
Stonelow Cres. S18—1G 129
Stonelow Grn. S18—1F 129
Stonelow Rd. S18—1F 129
Stonely Brook. S65—3H 81
Stone Moor Rd. S30—4C 140
Stone Riding. DN12—4A 60
  (Edlington)
Stone Riding. DN12—6D 60
  (Edlington Wood)
Stone Rd. S18—5G 123
Stone Row. S40—3G 137
Stonerow Way. S60—6E 69
Stonesdale Clo. S19—2D 124
Stones Inge. S30—6B 50
Stone St. S19—2D 124
Stone St. S71—3G 13
Stonewood Ct. S10—3D 96
Stonewood Gro. S10—3D 96
Stoney Ga. S30—5B 50
Stonyford Rd. S73—5D 26
Stony La. S30—2B 72
Stony Wlk. S6—4A 86
Stoops La. DN4—4H 47
Stoops Rd. DN4—4B 48
Stopes Rd. S6—5A 84
Stoppard Row. S40—3E 137
Store St. S2—4F 99
Storey's Ga. S73—6H 25
Storey St. S64—2A 56
Storforth La. S40 & S41
                —6A 138
Storforth La. Ter. S41—5C 138
Storforth La. Trading Est S40
                —5B 138
Storrs Bri. S6—2A 84
Storrs Bri. La. S6—2A 84
Storrs Carr. S6—3A 84
Storrs Grn. S6—4A 84
Storrs Hall Rd. S6—5H 85
Storrs La. S6—4A 84
Storrs Rd. S40—3D 136
Storth Av. S10—5E 97
Storth La. S10—5E 97
Storth La. S31
                —4F 117 to 2A 118
Stortholme M. S10—4E 97
Storth Pk. S10—6D 96
Storthwood Ct. S10—4E 97
Stothard Rd. S10—1H 97
Stour Clo. S43—3E 133
Stour La. S6—1F 85
Stovin Dri. S9—5D 88
Stovin Gdns. S9—5D 88
  (in two parts)
Stovin Way. S9—4E 89
Stow Bri. La. S60—5C 92
Stowe Av. S7—3A 110
Stradbroke Av. S13—6F 101
Stradbroke Clo. S13—6G 101

Stradbroke Cres. S13—6G 101
Stradbroke Dri. S13—6G 101
Stradbroke Pl. S13—6G 101
Stradbroke Rise. S40—5E 137
Stradbroke Rd. S13
—6F 101 to 1B 114
Stradbroke Wlk. S13—6F 101
Stradbroke Way. S13—6G 101
Strafford Av. S70—3H 23
Strafford Av. S74—5D 36
Strafford Gro. S70—5D 36
Strafford Pl. S61—2A 66
Strafford Rd. DN2—4E 33
Strafford Rd. S61—5G 67
Strafford St. S75—5A 6
Strafford Wlk. S75—3B 22
Straight La. S63—4G 29
Straight Riding. DN12—5C 60
Strait La. S63—5E 41
Stratford Rd. S10—4D 96
Strathmore Gro. S63—5F 41
Strathmore Rd. DN2—6G 33
Strathtay Rd. S11—6H 97
Strauss Cres. S66—5H 83
Strawberry Av. S5—3F 75
Strawberry Gdns. S71—1E 9
Strawberry Lee La. S17
—4B 120
Straw La. S6—6C 86
Streatfield Cres. DN11—4C 62
Streetfield Cres. S19—3D 124
Streetfield La. S19—3E 125
Streetfields. S19—3E 125
Street La. S62—3F 53
Strelley Av. S8—6C 110
Strelley Rd. S8—6C 110
Strelley Rd. S71—5A 8
Stretton Clo. DN4—3E 49
Stretton Rd. S11—6A 98
Stretton Rd. S71—2A 14
Stride, The. S64—6H 137
Stringers Croft. S60—2B 92
Stringvale Clo. S66—1G 93
Stripe Rd. DN11—4E 63
Struan Rd. S7—2A 110
Strutt Rd. S3—4E 87
Stuart Clo. S41—5C 132
Stuart Gro. S30—3F 65
Stuart Rd. S30—3F 65
Stuart St. S63—1G 29
Stubbin Clo. S62—6D 54
Stubbing Ho. La. S6—2G 73
Stubbing La. S30—6C 72
Stubbing Rd. S40—6H 137
Stubbin La. S5—5G 75
Stubbin La. S62—5C 54
Stubbin Rd. S62—6B 54
Stubbins Hill. DN12—3B 60
Stubbins Riding. DN12—4C 60
Stubbs Cres. S61—6H 67
Stubbs Rd. S73—1E 39
Stubbs Wlk. S61—6H 67
Stubley Clo. S18—1C 128
Stubley Croft. S18—1B 128
Stubley Dri. S18—1C 128
Stubley Hollow. S18—6C 122
Stubley La. S18—1B 128
Stubley Pl. S18—1C 128
Studfield Cres. S6—3F 85
Studfield Dri. S6—2F 85
Studfield Gro. S6—3F 85
Studfield Hill. S6—3F 85
Studfield Rise. S6—2F 85
Studfield Rd. S6—3F 85
Studley Ct. S9—1E 101
Studmoor Rd. S61—5F 67
Studmoor Wlk. S61—5F 67
Stump Cross Gdns. S63—1H 41

Stump Cross Rd. S63—6E 41
Stumperlowe Av. S10—5E 97
Stumperlowe Clo. S10—5E 97
Stumperlowe Cres. Rd. S10
—5D 96
Stumperlowe Croft. S10—4D 96
Stumperlowe Hall Chase. S10
—4D 96
Stumperlowe Hall Rd. S10
—5D 96
Stumperlowe La. S10—5D 96
Stumperlowe Mans. S10
—5D 96
Stumperlowe Pk. Rd. S10
—4D 96
Stumperlowe View. S10—4D 96
Stupton Rd. S9—1C 88
Sturge Croft. S2—1F 111
Sturton Clo. DN4—5A 48
Sturton Croft. S65—6C 90
Sturton Rd. S4—3G 87
Sub-Station La. S41—3A 132
(off Queen St. N.)
Sudbury Clo. S40—6D 130
Sudbury Dri. S31—6C 104
Sudbury St. S3—6D 86
Sudhall Clo. S41—3F 131
Sudhall Ct. S41—3F 131
Suffolk Clo. S13—1G 119
Suffolk La. S2—6G 5
Suffolk Rd. DN4—5B 46
Suffolk Rd. S2—6F 5 & 3F 99
Suffolk View. DN12—3B 58
Sulby Gro. S70—3D 24
Summerdale Rd. S72—1G 15
Summerfield. S10—3A 98
Summerfield. S65—3E 79
Summerfield Cres. S43—3D 132
Summerfield Rd. S18—6F 123
Summerfield Rd. S40—4H 137
Summerfield St. S11—4C 98
Summer La. S17—5D 120
Summer La. S71—1D 8
Summer La. S73—6H 25
Summer La. S75 & S70—5F 13
Summerley Wlk. S40—6F 131
Summer Rd. S71—1D 8
Summerskill Grn. S43—4A 134
Summer St. S3—1C 98
Summer St. S70—5F 13
(in two parts)
Summerwood La. S18—6D 122
Summerwood Pl. S18—1D 128
Sumner Rd. S65—1F 79
Sunbury Ct. S10—3A 98
Sunderland St. S11—4C 98
Sunderland Ter. S70—1A 24
Sundew Croft. S30—5B 50
Sundew Gdns. S30—5B 50
Sundown Pl. S13—5H 101
Sundown Rd. S13—5H 101
Sunningdale Clo. DN4—5F 49
Sunningdale Clo. S40—5G 137
Sunningdale Clo. S64—4B 56
Sunningdale Dri. S72—5C 10
Sunningdale Mt. S11—2A 110
Sunningdale Rise. S40—5E 137
Sunningdale Rd. DN2—4G 33
Sunningdale Rd. S31—5F 107
Sunny Bank. DN3—6E 21
Sunny Bank. S10—4C 98
Sunny Bank. S30—6B 50
Sunnybank Cres. S60—3C 90
Sunnybank Dri. S72—2H 15
Sunny Bank La. S30—6E 141
Sunny Bank Rise. S74—5C 38
Sunny Bar. DN1—6D 32
Sunnyside. DN3—4C 20

Sunnyside Clo. S31—1G 119
Sunny Springs. S41—1A 138
Sunnyvale Av. S17—5D 120
Sunnyvale Rd. S17—5D 120
Sunny View Caravan Pk. DN11
—1F 61
Sunrise Mnr. S74—3A 38
Surbiton St. S9—3D 88
Surrey Clo. S70—2H 23
Surrey La. S1—4F 5 & 3F 99
(in two parts)
Surrey Pl. S1—4F 5 & 2E 99
Surrey St. DN4—4B 46
Surrey St. S1—4E 5 & 2E 99
Surtees Clo. S66—2E 83
Sussex Gdns. DN12—2B 58
Sussex Rd. S4—6G 87
Sussex Rd. S30—2E 65
Sussex St. DN4—4B 46
Sussex St. S4—1H 5 & 6G 87
Suthard Cross Rd. S10—1H 97
Sutherland Ho. DN2—3G 33
Sutherland Rd. S4—5G 87
Sutherland St. S4—5H 87
Sutton Av. S71—5B 8
Sutton Cres. S43—4A 134
Sutton Rd. DN3—2E 21
Sutton St. DN4—2A 46
Sutton St. S3—3A 4 & 1C 98
Swaddale Av. S41—5B 132
Swaddale Clo. S41—5B 132
Swaith Av. DN5—2H 31
Swaithedale. S70—4C 24
Swaithe View. S70—4D 24
Swalebank Clo. S40—5B 138
Swale Clo. S63—1B 42
Swale Ct. S60—1F 91
Swale Dri. S30—2C 64
Swale Gdns. S9—1E 101
Swale Rd. S61—4A 68
Swallow Clo. S70—3D 36
Swallow Clo. S75—5B 8
Swallow Ct. DN11—4E 63
Swallow Hill Rd. S75—6E 7
Swallow La. S31—1C 116
Swallow's La. S19—1C 124
Swallow Wood Ct. S13—1A 114
Swamp Wlk. S6—4B 86
Swanbourne Clo. S5—5C 138
Swanbourne Pl. S5—5G 75
Swanbourne Rd. S5—4G 75
Swanee Rd. S70—2B 24
Swannington Clo. DN4—4F 49
Swan Rd. S31—1C 116
Swan St. DN5—5B 18
Swan St. S60—4D 78
Swanwick St. S41—1A 132
Swarcliffe Rd. S9—6C 88
Sweet La. DN11—6H 61
Sweyn Croft. S70—4A 24
Swifte Rd. S60—6G 79
Swift Rise. S61—1C 66
Swift Rd. S30—1B 74
Swift St. S75—5F 13
Swift Way. S2—4A 100
Swinburne Av. DN4—5B 46
Swinburne Av. DN6—2C 16
Swinburne Clo. DN3—1H 21
Swinburne Pl. S65—4H 79
Swinburne Rd. S65—4H 79
Swinscoe Way. S40—6C 130
Swinston Hill Rd. S31—5F 107
Swinton Meadows Ind. Est. S64
—2D 56
Swinton Rd. S64—1D 56
(in two parts)
Swinton St. S3—6E 87

Sycamore Av. DN3—2G 35
Sycamore Av. S18—6E 123
Sycamore Av. S31—5F 117
Sycamore Av. S40—4G 137
Sycamore Av. S66—4G 81
Sycamore Av. S72—6B 10
Sycamore Cres. S63—6G 41
Sycamore Dri. S31—4A 126
Sycamore Dri. S71—2C 8
Sycamore Farm Clo. S66
—6F 81
Sycamore Gro. DN4—3D 48
Sycamore Gro. DN12—4C 58
Sycamore Ho. Rd. S5—3B 76
Sycamore La. S43—2G 133
Sycamore Rd. DN3—2H 21
Sycamore Rd. S30—1F 75
(Ecclesfield)
Sycamore Rd. S30—4C 140
(Stocksbridge)
Sycamore Rd. S43—2F 133
Sycamore Rd. S64—6C 42
Sycamore Rd. S65—6H 69
Sycamores, The. DN5—1F 31
Sycamore St. S19—3F 115
(Beighton)
Sycamore St. S19—1C 124
(Mosborough)
Sycamore St. S75—5E 13
Sycamore Wlk. S63—1F 29
Sydney Rd. S6—1B 98
Sydney St. S40—2G 137
Sydney Ter. S70—1H 23
Sykes Av. S75—5F 13
Sykes Ct. S64—4B 56
Sykes St. S70—2F 23
Sylvan Clo. S41—4B 138
Sylvan Clo. S66—3H 83
Sylvester Av. DN4—2C 46
Sylvester Gdns. S1
—6E 5 & 3E 99
Sylvester St. S1—6E 5 & 3E 99
Sylvestria Ct. DN11—4E 63
Sylvia Clo. S13—6D 102
Sylvia Rd. S18—5H 129
Symes Gdns. DN4—2D 48
Symonds Av. S62—5C 54
Symons Cres. S5—5D 74

Tadcaster Clo. DN12—3A 58
Tadcaster Cres. S8—3D 110
Tadcaster Rd. S8—3D 110
Tadcaster Way. S8—3D 110
Taddington Rd. S40—6D 130
Tait Av. DN12—5B 60
Talbot Av. DN3—2H 21
Talbot Circle. DN3—2H 21
Talbot Cres. S2—5H 5 & 3G 99
Talbot Cres. S42—6D 138
Talbot Gdns. S2—5H 5 & 3G 99
Talbot Pl. S2—3G 99
Talbot Rd. S2—3G 99
Talbot Rd. S64—2D 56
Talbot St. S2—5H 5 & 3G 99
Talbot St. S41—6D 138
Talmont Rd. S11—1H 109
Tamar Clo. S75—4A 12
Tanfield Clo. S71—5C 8
Tanfield Rd. S6—2B 86
Tanfield Way. S66—5F 81
Tankersley La. S74—1D 50
Tank Row. S71—6D 14
Tannery Clo. S13—1B 114
Tannery St. S13—1B 114
Tan Pit La. S63—6F 29
Tansley Dri. S9—5D 76
Tansley St. S9—5D 76

Tansley Way. S43—5A 134
Tap La. S40—2G 137
Taplin Rd. S6—3H 85
Tapton. S10—2A 98
Tapton Bank. S10—3G 97
Tapton Ct. S10—3H 97
Tapton Cres. Rd. S10—3H 97
Tapton Grange. S43—6E 133
Tapton Gro. S43—6E 133
Tapton Hill Rd. S10—2G 97
Tapton Ho. Rd. S10—3H 97
Tapton La. S41—2B 138
Tapton Pk. S41—6C 132
Tapton Pk. Rd. S10—4F 97
Tapton Ter. S41—1B 138
Tapton Vale. S41—6C 131
Tapton View Rd. S41—6H 131
Taptonville Cres. S10—3A 98
Taptonville Rd. S10—2A 98
Tapton Wlk. S10—3H 97
Tapton Way. S44—2F 139
Tarleton Clo. DN3—3E 21
Tasker Rd. S10—1H 97
Tasman Gro. S8—3E 83
Tatenhill Gdns. DN4—4E 49
Taunton Av. S9—5D 76
Taunton Gdns. S64—5G 43
Taunton Gro. S9—5D 76
Taverner Clo. S30—4B 50
Taverner Croft. S30—5C 50
(off Taverner Way.)
Taverner Way. S30—5B 50
Tavistock Rd. S7—1D 110
Tay Clo. S18—1B 128
Taylor Cres. S41—4D 138
Taylor Row. S70—1H 23
Taylor's Clo. S62—5E 69
Taylor's La. S62—5E 69
Taylor St. DN12—3F 59
Taylor St. S63—1F 29
(in two parts)
Taylor Wlk. S64—4A 56
Tay St. S6—1B 98
Teesdale Clo. S12—6H 113
Teesdale Rd. S61—4H 67
Teeside Clo. DN5—4F 31
Telford Cres. S43—1D 134
Telford Rd. DN5—4A 32
Telson Clo. S64—2G 55
Temperance St. S64—2B 56
Tempest Av. S73—2E 27
Templar Clo. S66—5H 93
Temple Cres. S66—5H 81
Temple Gdns. DN4—4E 49
Temple Rd. S60—6H 77
Temple Way. S71—4D 14
Ten Acre Rd. S61—1H 77
Tenby Gdns. DN4—4A 46
Tennyson Av. DN3—3F 35
Tennyson Av. DN5—5H 31
Tennyson Av. S40—2H 137
Tennyson Av. S64—5F 43
Tennyson Clo. S31—5G 107
Tennyson Rise. S63—3C 40
Tennyson Rd. DN5—6B 18
Tennyson Rd. S6—5B 86
Tennyson Rd. S65—4G 79
Tennyson Rd. S66—5G 83
Tennyson Rd. S71—3B 14
Ten Pound Wlk. DN4—3C 46
Tenter Balk La. DN6—2C 16
Tenterden Rd. S5—5B 76
Tenter La. DN4—5E 45
Tenter Rd. DN4—5E 45
Tenters Grn. S70—5H 23
Tenter St. S1—2D 4 & 1E 99
Tenter St. S60—2C 78
Terminus Rd. S7—4A 110

Terrace Rd. S62—3F 69
Terrace, The. S5—6A 76
Terrace Wlk. S11—5A 98
Terrey Rd. S17—4E 121
Terry St. S9—3D 88
Tetney Rd. S10—3F 97
Teynham Dri. S5—1D 86
Teynham Rd. S5—1C 86
Thackeray Av. S62—6H 55
Thames St. S60—2C 78
Thatch Pl. S61—4A 68
Thealby Gdns. DN4—4A 48
Theatre La. S41—2B 138
Thellusson Av. DN5—3E 31
Theobald Av. DN4—2F 47
Theobald Clo. DN4—2E 47
Thicket Dri. S66—3H 83
Thicket La. S70—5C 24
Third Av. DN6—3E 17
Thirlmere Clo. S63—2A 42
Thirlmere Ct. S64—5H 43
Thirlmere Dri. S18—1E 129
Thirlmere Dri. S31—1H 119
Thirlmere Gdns. DN3—4D 20
Thirlmere Rd. S8—2C 110
Thirlmere Rd. S41—4E 131
Thirlmere Rd. S71—6A 14
Thirlwall Av. DN12—3C 58
Thirlwell Rd. S8—1E 111
Thirsk Clo. DN12—3A 58
Thirza St. S6—5C 86
Thomas St. DN12—4B 60
Thomas St. S1—5C 4 & 3D 98
(in two parts)
Thomas St. S31—5H 117
Thomas St. S62—6D 56
Thomas St. S64—1B 56
Thomas St. S70—1H 23
(Barnsley)
Thomas St. S70—4A 24
(Worsbrough)
Thomas St. S73—4F 27
Thompson Clo. S41—3A 132
Thompson Clo. S62—5C 54
Thompson Clo. S63—5F 41
Thompson Clo. S66—2E 83
Thompson Dri. S64—4A 56
Thompson Gdns. S30—5A 50
Thompson Hill. S30—6A 50
Thompson Rd. S11—4B 98
Thompson Rd. S73—1F 39
Thompson St. S41—4A 132
Thomson Av. DN4—4H 45
Thomson Av. DN12—3A 60
Thoresby Av. DN4—2F 47
Thoresby Av. S71—4C 14
Thoresby Clo. S31—6D 104
Thoresby Pl. S43—5A 134
Thoresby Pl. S65—1H 79
Thoresby Rd. S6—4A 86
Thornborough Clo. S2—6G 99
Thornborough Pl. S2—6G 99
Thornborough Rd. S2—6F 99
Thornbridge Av. S12—4F 113
Thornbridge Clo. S12—4F 113
Thornbridge Cres. S12—4G 113
Thornbridge Cres. S40—6H 137
Thornbridge Dri. S12—4F 113
Thornbridge Gro. S12—4F 113
Thornbridge Pl. S12—4F 113
Thornbridge Rise. S12—4G 113
Thornbridge Rd. S12—5F 113
Thornbridge Way. S12—4G 113
Thornbrook Gdns. S30—1F 65
Thornbrook M. S30—1E 65
Thorncliff Cres. S40—6A 138
Thorncliffe Ind. Est. S30—5D 50
Thorncliffe La. S30—6D 50

Thorncliffe Vs. S30—6D 50
Thorndale Rise. S60—3D 90
Thorndene Clo. S41—5A 132
Thorndon Way. S40—5E 137
Thorne Clo. S42—1B 136
Thorne Clo. S71—6A 8
Thorne End Rd. S75—3F 7
Thornely Av. S75—1B 22
Thornely Cres. S63—1E 29
Thorne Rd. DN1, DN2 & DN3
—6D 32
Thorne Rd. S7—2C 110
Thornfield Av. S40—4D 136
Thornfield Ct. S41—6A 132
Thorn Garth. DN5—3A 32
Thornham Clo. DN3—4F 35
Thornhill Av. DN2—3H 33
Thornhill Av. S60—4B 90
Thornhill Edge. S60—2C 78
Thornhill Pl. S63—5E 41
Thorn La. DN2—5B 20
Thornlea Ct. DN12—4A 60
Thornley Cotts. S75—2B 22
Thornley Sq. S63—1D 28
Thornley Sq. S75—2B 22
Thornley Vs. S70—4C 36
Thorn Rd. S62—4B 56
Thornsett Ct. S11—5C 98
Thornsett Gdns. S17—2F 121
Thornsett Rd. S7—5C 98
Thorntondale Rd. DN5—2F 31
Thornton Pl. S18—2A 128
Thornton Rd. S70—2C 24
Thornton St. S61—4G 77
Thornton Ter. S41—4G 77
Thornton Ter. S70—2C 24
Thorntree Clo. S61—3B 66
Thorntree Clo. S40—6H 137
Thorntree La. S47—4F 13
Thorntree Rd. S61—4B 66
Thornwell La. S61—1B 66
Thorogate. S62—6E 55
Thorold Pl. DN3—2D 20
Thorp Clo. S2—5E 99
Thorpe Av. S18—5G 123
Thorpe Bridle St. S31—6F 119
Thorpe Clo. S41—3H 131
Thorpe Dri. S19—6E 115
Thorpefield Clo. S61—2B 66
Thorpefield Dri. S61—2B 66
Thorpe Grn. S19—6D 114
Thorpehall Rd. DN3—4E 21
Thorpe Ho. Av. S8—3E 111
Thorpe Ho. Rise. S8—3E 111
Thorpe Ho. Rd. S8—3E 111
Thorpe La. DN5—2D 44
Thorpe St. S61—2B 66
Thorpleigh Rd. S43—1F 135
Threatre Yd. S40—2A 138
(off Low Pavement)
Three Hills Clo. S65—4D 70
Three Nooks La. S72—4B 10
Threshfield Way. S12—4B 114
Thrumpton Rd. S71—4B 8
Thrush Av. S60—3D 90
Thrush St. S6—5H 85
Thruxton Clo. S72—5C 10
Thrybergh Ct. DN12—2D 58
Thrybergh Hall Rd. S62—1H 69
Thrybergh La. S65—4E 71
Thunderclffe Rd. S61—2D 76
Thurcroft Ho. DN1—1C 46
(off St James St.)
Thurcroft Ind. Est. S66—3A 94
Thurnscoe Bri. La. S63—3F 29
Thurnscoe La. S72—1B 28
Thurnscoe Rd. S63—1A 42
Thurstan Av. S8—1C 122

Tiber View. S60—2C 90
Tickhill Rd. DN4 & DN11—4A 46
Tickhill Rd. S66—4H 83
Tickhill Sq. DN12—2B 58
Tickhill St. DN12—1B 58
Tidswell Clo. S43—3A 134
Tideswell Rd. S5—6G to 5H 75
Tiercel M. S31—4E 107
Tilford Rd. S13—1C 114
Tillotson Clo. S8—1E 111
Tillotson Rise. S8—1E 111
Tillotson Rd. S8—1E 111
Tiltshills La. DN5—1B 18
Tilts La. DN5—1D 18
Timothy Wood Av. S70—3D 36
Tingle Bri. Av. S73—4E 39
Tingle Bri. Cres. S73—4E 39
Tingle Bri. La. S73—4E 39
Tingle Clo. S73—4E 39
Tinker La. S6 & S10—6H 85
Tinker La. S74—5E 37
Tinker Rd. S12—1G 69
Tinsley Ind. Est. S9—5E 89
Tinsley Pk. Clo. S9—4E 89
Tinsley Pk. Rd. S9—4D 88
Tinsley Rd. S74—4H 37
Tipsey Hill. S75—4H 7
Tipton St. S9—1C 88
Tissington Clo. S40—6D 130
Tithe Barn Av. S13—6C 102
Tithe Barn Clo. S13—6C 102
Tithe Barn La. S13—6C 102
Tithe Barn Way. S13—6B 102
Tithe Laithe. S74—5A 38
Titterton Clo. S9—5C 88
Titterton St. S9—5C 88
Tiverton Clo. S64—6C 6
Tivydale Dri. S75—6C 6
Toad La. S66—6H 93
Tockwith Rd. S9—6D 88
Todmorden Clo. DN12—2A 58
Todwick Ho. Gdns. S31—1A 118
Todwick Rd. S8—4C 110
Todwick Rd. S31—5A 106
Todwick Rd. Ind. Est. S31
—4B 106
Toecroft La. DN5—2B 44
Tofield Rd. DN11—5G 61
Tofts La. S6—1C 96
Toftstead. DN3—4F 35
Toftwood Av. S10—1G 97
Toftwood Rd. S10—1H 97
Togo Bldgs. S63—2E 29
Togo St. S63—2E 29
Toll Bar Av. S12—2A 112
Toll Bar Clo. S12—2A 112
Toll Bar Dri. S12—2B 112
Toll Bar Rd. S12—2A 112
Toll Bar Rd. S64—3H 55
Toll Bar Rd. S65—5C 80
Tollbridge Rd. S43—1F 135
Tollgate Ct. S3—4F 87
Tom La. S10—4D 96
Tom La. S44—6C 134
Tomlinson Rd. S74—5B 38
Tontine Rd. S40—2A 138
Tooker Rd. S60—4E 79
Topcliffe Rd. S71—2A 14
Topcliffe Rd. S10—1H 97
Top Fold. S71—1G 25
Top Field La. S65—1B 80
Top Fold. S71—1G 25
Top Hall Rd. DN4—5D 48
Top La. DN4—4F 47
Toppham Dri. S8—3D 122
Toppham Rd. S8—3D 122
Toppham Way. S8—3D 122
Top Pingle Clo. S43—4E 133
Top Rd. DN3—2H 21
Top Rd. S30—4D 72

Top Rd. S44—3F 139
Top Row. S75—2C 6
Top Side. S30—1H 73
Tops, The. S62—1C 68
Top Ter. S10—2A 98
(off Parker's La.)
Top Tree Way. S65—4D 70
Top View Cres. DN12—5B 60
Top Warren. S30—5F 51
Torbay Rd. S4—4H 87
Tor Clo. S71—2B 14
Torksey Clo. DN4—6C 48
Torksey Rd. S5—5H 75
Torne Clo. DN4—5E 49
Torrington Clo. DN6—1C 16
Torry Ct. S13—1C 114
Tortmayns. S31—2A 118
Tor Way. S60—3D 90
Tor Wood Dri. S8—2C 122
Totley Brook Clo. S17—4D 120
Totley Brook Croft. S17
—4D 120
Totley Brook Glen. S17—4D 120
Totley Brook Gro. S17—4D 120
Totley Brook Rd. S17
—3D 120 to 4F 121
Totley Brook Way. S17—4D 120
Totley Clo. S71—6D 8
Totley Grange Clo. S17—5D 120
Totley Grange Dri. S17—5D 120
Totley Grange Rd. S17—5D 120
Totley Hall La. S17—5D 120
Totley La. S17—5F & 4H 121
(in three parts)
Totley Mt. S43—3D 132
Towcester Way. S64—5G 43
Tower Clo. DN5—6F 17
Tower Clo. S2—5G 99
Tower Dri. S2—5G 99
Tower St. S70—2G 23
Town End. DN5—5B 32
Town End Av. S31—5C 104
Townend Clo. S60—1E 103
Townend La. S30—5G 141
Town End Rd. S30—1D 74
Townend St. S10—6A 86
Town Fields Av. S30—1G 75
Town Field Vs. DN1—6E 33
Towngate. S75—4F 7
Towngate Rd. S30—4C 72
Townhead Rd. S17—2C 120
Townhead St. S1—3D 4 & 2E 99
Town La. S61—5F 67 to 3A 68
Town Moor Av. DN2—5F 33
Town St. S9—1F 89
Town St. S60—5D 78
Town View Av. DN5—1D 30
Town Wells. S31—2F 119
Toyne St. S10—1H 97
Trafalgar Rd. S6—5A 74
Trafalgar St. S1—4C 4 & 2D 98
Traffic Ter. S41—6B 138
Trafford Ct. DN1—6C 32
Trafford Way. DN1—6C 32
Tranmoor Av. DN4—4C 48
Tranmoor Ct. S74—6F 37
Tranmoor La. DN3—4F 35
Tranquil Wlk. DN11—5B 62
Trap La. S11—1E 109
Travey Rd. S2—6C 100
Travis Gdns. DN4—2H 45 &
(in three parts)   2A 46
Travis Pl. S10—6A 4 & 3C 98
Tredis Clo. S71—4B 14
Treecrest Rise. S75—3G 13
Treefield Clo. S61—4A 68
Treelands. S75—4D 12

Treeneuk Clo. S40—2D 136
Tree Root Wlk. S10—2B 98
Treeton Cres. S60—6E 91
Treeton Ho. DN1—1C 46
(off St James St.)
Treeton La. S31—3A 104
Treeton La. S60—6D 90
Treherne Rd. S60—4F 79
Trelawney Wlk. S70—4H 23
Trent Gro. S18—6F 123
Trentham Clo. S60—3D 90
Trenton Clo. S13—1D 114
Trenton Rise. S13—1D 114
Trent St. S9—5A 88
Trent Ter. DN12—2E 59
Trent Vs. S31—5H 117
Treswell Cres. S6—3A 86
Trevose Clo. S40—6E 137
Trewan Ct. S71—4B 14
Triangle Est. S9—2G 101
Trickett Clo. S64—4B 56
Trickett Rd. S6—4A 86
Trickett Rd. S30—5A 50
Trinity Clo. S41—1H 137
Trinity Rd. S31—5B 118
Trinity St. S31—1D 4 & 1E 99
Trippet Ct. S10—5G 97
Trippet La. S1—3C 4 & 2D 98
Tristford Clo. S60—5D 90
Troon Clo. S40—5E 137
Troon Wlk. S31—5F 107
Troughbrook Hill. S43—3A 134
Troughbrook Rd. S43—2H 133
Trough Dri. S65—5E 71
Troutbeck Clo. S63—2E 29
Troutbeck Rd. S7—3C 110
Troutbeck Way. DN11—6C 62
Trowell Way. S71—5B 8
Trueman Grn. S66—3E 83
Trueman Ter. S71—5E 15
Truman Gro. S30—3H 141
Truman St. DN5—6A 18
Truro Av. DN2—1H 33
Truro Ct. S71—4B 14
Truswell Av. S10—1G 97
Truswell Rd. S10—2G 97
Tudor Ct. DN3—1D 20
Tudor Pl. S1—4F 5 & 2E 99
Tudor Rd. DN2—5G 33
Tudor Rd. DN6—4E 17
Tudor St. DN11—5D 62
Tudor St. S1—4F 5 & 2F 99
Tudor St. S43—1D 134
Tudor St. S63—1G 29
Tudor Way. S1—4F 5 & 2F 99
Tudor Way. S70—4A 24
Tuffolds Clo. S2—6C 100
Tulip Tree Clo. S19—2G 115
Tullibardine Rd. S11—1H 109
Tulyar Clo. DN11—6D 62
Tumbling La. S71—1F 15
Tummon Rd. S2—3A 100
Tummon St. S61—3B 78
Tune St. S70—1A 24
Tune St. S13—1E 39
Tunstall Grn. S40—4F 137
Tunstall Way. S40—4F 137
Tunwell Av. S5—2F 75
Tunwell Dri. S5—2F 75
Tunwell Greave. S5—2F 75
Tunwell Rd. S66—2E 95
Turie Av. S5—3E 75
Turie Cres. S5—3E 75
Turnberry Clo. S40—5E 137
Turnberry Gro. S2—4C 10
Turnberry Way. S31—6F 107
Turner Av. S73—6H 25
Turner Clo. S18—2D 128

Turner Clo. S62—3G 69
Turner Dri. S43—3H 133
Turner La. S60—2H 91
Turner's Clo. S74—4C 38
Turners La. S10—3A 98
Turner St. S2—5G 5 & 3F 99
Turner St. S72—1A 28
Turnesc Gro. S63—2F 29
Turnoaks La. S40—6A 138
Turnpike Croft. S30—6A 64
Turnshaw Av. S31—4A 104
Turnshaw Rd. S31—4C 104
Tutbury Gdns. DN4—4E 49
Tuxford Cres. S71—5D 14
Tuxford Rd. S9—3C 88
Tween Woods La. DN11—4F 61
Twelve O'Clock Ct. S4—6G 87
Twenty Lands, The. S60
—2E 103
Twentywell Dri. S17—3H 121
Twentywell La. S17—2G 121
Twentywell Rise. S17—3H 121
Twentywell Rd. S17—4H 121
Twentywell View. S17—4H 121
Twibell St. S71—4A 14
Twickenham Clo. S19—3E 125
Twickenham Ct. S19—3E 125
Twickenham Cres. S19—3E 125
Twickenham Glade. S19
—3E 125
Twickenham Glen. S19—4F 125
Twickenham Gro. S19—4E 125
Twitchill Dri. S13—1B 114
Twyford Clo. S64—2G 55
Tyas Pl. S64—6G 43
Tyas Rd. S5—2E 75
Tye Rd. S19—4G 115
Tyler St. S9—1D 88
Tyler Way. S9—1D 76
Tylney Rd. S2—3H 99
Tylney Rd. S40—5D 136
Tynker Av. S19—4G 115
Tyzack Rd. S8—5C 110

Ulley Cres. S13—6D 100
Ulley La. S31—4C 104
(Aston)
Ulley La. S31—3B 104
(Aughton & Ulley)
Ulley Rd. S13—6D 100
Ulley View. S31—3B 104
Ullswater Av. S19—3E 125
Ullswater Clo. S18—1C 128
Ullswater Clo. S19—3E 125
Ullswater Clo. S31—6E 107
Ullswater Clo. S63—2A 42
Ullswater Dri. S18—2C 128
Ullswater Pk. S18—1C 128
Ullswater Pl. S18—1C 128
Ullswater Rd. S64—5H 43
Ullswater Rd. S71—1H 25
Ullswater Wlk. DN5—2E 31
Ulrica Dri. S66—5A 94
Ulverston Rd. S8—3C 110
Ulverston Rd. S41—4F 131
Underbank La. S30—1A 140
Undercliffe Rd. S6—5F 85
Underhill. S70—5B 24
Underhill La. S6—4H 73
Underwood Av. S70—3B 24
Underwood Rd. S8—3D 110
Union Ct. S70—1H 23
Union La. S1—5E 5 & 3E 99
(in two parts)
Union Rd. S11—1B 110
Union St. DN1—1C 46
Union St. S1—5E 5 & 3E 99

Union St. S61—3B 78
Union St. S70—1H 23
Union Wlk. S30—2A 138
Unity Pl. S60—3D 78
Unsliven Rd. S30—1A 140
Unstone-Dronfield By-Pass S18
—2D 128
Unstone St. S2—4E 99
Upland Rise. S40—4F 137
Uplands Av. S75—5A 6
Uplands Dri. DN3—3G 35
Uplands Way. S62—1E 69
Up. Albert Rd. S8—3E 111
Up. Allen St. S3—2B 4 & 1D 98
Up. Castle Folds. S1—2G 5
Up. Charter Arc. S70—6H 13
(off Cheapside)
Up. Clara St. S61—3H 77
Up. Croft Clo. S43—4E 133
Upperfield Clo. S66—3F 83
Upperfield Rd. S66—3E 83
Uppergate Rd. S6—6B 84
Up. Hanover St. S3—5A 4 &
(in two parts)   3C 98
Up. Hoyland Rd. S74—3F 37
Up. Ley Ct. S30—3E 65
Up. Ley Dell. S30—2E 65
Up. May Day Grn. Arc. S70
(off Cheapside)   —6H 13
Up. Millgate. S60—3D 78
Up. Moor St. S40—3D 136
Up. Newbold Clo. S41—4D 130
Up. Rye Clo. S60—2B 92
Up. School La. S18—2E 129
Up. Sheffield Rd. S70—2A 24
Upperthorpe Glen. S6—6B 86
Upperthorpe Rd. S6—6C 86
Upperthorpe Rd. S31—4B 126
Upperthorpe Vs. S31—4B 126
Up. Valley Rd. S8—2E 111
Up. Whiston La. S60—4A 92
Upperwood Rd. S73—3C 26
Upperwood Shopping Precinct.
S73—3D 26
Up. Wortley Rd. S61
—3A 66 to 1F 77
Upton Clo. S66—2E 83
Upton Clo. S73—5H 25
Upwell Hill. S4—2A 88
Upwell La. S4—2A 88
Upwell St. S4—2B 88
Upwood Clo. S40—6C 130
Upwood Rd. DN14—2A 46
Urban Rd. DN14—2A 46
Urch Clo. DN2—4E 59
Utah Ter. S12—4C 114
Uttley Clo. S9—5D 88
Uttley Croft. S9—5D 88
Uttley Dri. S9—5D 88
Uttoxeter Av. S64—5G 43

Vaal St. S70—1B 24
Vainor Rd. S6—1G 85
Vale Av. S65—5D 70
Vale Clo. S18—2E 129
Vale Cres. S65—5D 70
Vale Gro. S6—3E 85
Valentine Clo. S5—4G 75
Valentine Cres. S5—4G 75
(in two parts)
Valentine Rd. S5—4G 75
Vale Rd. S3—4D 86
Vale Rd. S65—5D 70
Valiant Gdns. DN5—6G 31
Valley Cres. S41—3C 138
Valley Dri. DN3—3H 49
Valley Dri. S31—2B 126

Valley Dri. S63—5E 41
Valley Rd. S8—1E 111
Valley Rd. S12—4C 114
Valley Rd. S30—1C 64
Valley Rd. S31—2B 126
Valley Rd. S41—3C 138
Valley Rd. S64—3H 55
Valley Rd. S73—5C 26
Valley Rd. S75—4E 7
Valley View Clo. S31—6H 125
Valley Way. S74—5A 38
Vancouver Dri. S63—1H 41
Vanguard Trading Est. S40
—6B 138
Varley Gdns. S66—3F 81
Varney Rd. S63—6E 41
Vaughan Av. DN1—5D 32
Vaughon Rd. S75—4D 12
Vaughton Hill. S30—3H 141
Vauxhall Clo. S9—5D 76
Vauxhall Rd. S9—5D 76
Velvet Wood Clo. S74—6F 37
Venetian Cres. S73—4D 26
Ventnor Clo. DN4—4H 45
Ventnor Ct. S7—5D 98
Ventnor Pl. S7—5D 98
Venus Ct. S60—1C 90
Verdant Way. S5—4H 75
Verdon St. S3—5F 87
Verelst Av. S31—4B 104
Vere Rd. S6—1A 86
Verger Clo. DN11—4F 63
Vernon Av. S70—2H 23
Vernon Clo. S70—2H 23
Vernon Cres. S70—4H 23
Vernon Delph. S10—2F 97
Vernon Dri. S30—2E 65
Vernon Rd. S17—3E 121
Vernon Rd. S40—2F 137
Vernon Rd. S60—6H 79
Vernon Rd. S70—4H 23
Vernon St. S70—5D 36
Vernon St. S71—5H 13
Vernon St. S74—6H 37
Vernon St. N. S71—5H 13
Vernon Ter. S10—3G 97
Vernon Ter. S70—1A 24
(off Gold St.)
Vernon Way. S66—3E 83
Vernon Way. S75—4D 12
Verona Rise. S73—4E 27
Vesey St. S62—3F 69
Vicarage Clo. DN4—4E 49
Vicarage Clo. S64—1G 57
Vicarage Clo. S65—1B 80
Vicarage Clo. S74—5A 38
Vicarage Cres. S30—1A 74
Vicarage La. S17—2D 120
Vicarage La. S65—3D 78
Vicarage La. S71—2E 9
Vicarage Rd. S9—4B 88
Vicarage Rd. S30—1A 74
Vicarage Way. DN5—5E 19
Vicar Cres. S73—4F 27
Vicar La. S1—3E 5 & 2E 99
Vicar La. S13—6B 102
Vicar La. S40—2A 138
Vicar Rd. S63—4E 41
Vicar Rd. S73—4F 27
Vickers Dri. S5—6H 75
Vickers Rd. S5—1H 87
Vickers Rd. S30—6B 50
Victoria Av. S43—1D 134
Victoria Av. S65—3F 79
Victoria Av. S70—5G 13
Victoria Clo. S30—3D 140
Victoria Clo. S31—5A 118
Victoria Ct. DN5—4B 18

Victoria Cres. S70—4C 36
(off Chapel St.)
Victoria Cres. S75—5F 13
Victoria Cres. W. S75—5F 13
Victoria Gro. S43—6F 133
Victoria La. DN11—4C 62
Victorian Cres. DN2—5F 33
Victoria Pk. Rd. S43—6F 133
Victoria Rd. DN4—3B 46
Victoria Rd. DN5—5B 18
Victoria Rd. DN6—1F 17
Victoria Rd. DN12—2B 60
Victoria Rd. S10—6A 4 & 4C 98
Victoria Rd. S19—3F 115
Victoria Rd. S30—3D 140
Victoria Rd. S62—3F 69
(in two parts)
Victoria Rd. S63—4D 40
Victoria Rd. S64—6E 43
Victoria Rd. S70—5G 13
Victoria Rd. S71—1F 9
Victoria Rd. S73—6B 26
Victoria Sta. Rd. S4
—1G 5 & 1F 99
Victoria St. S3—4B 4 & 2D 98
Victoria St. S18—1D 128
Victoria St. S30—3D 140
Victoria St. S31—4G 107
Victoria St. S41—1A 138
Victoria St. S43—2F 133
Victoria St. S60—5D 90
(Catcliffe)
Victoria St. S60—3B 78
(Rotherham, in two parts)
Victoria St. S62—6C 56
Victoria St. S63—4G 29
Victoria St. S64—6C 42
Victoria St. S66—6G 83
Victoria St. S70—5G 13
(Barnsley)
Victoria St. S70—1D 24
(Stairfoot)
Victoria St. S72—6B 10
Victoria St. S73—3F 27
Victoria St. S74—5B 38
Victoria St. N. S41—1H 131
Victoria St. W. S40—3E 137
Victoria Ter. S10—2A 98
(off Parker's La.)
Victoria Ter. S70—1A 24
Victoria Vs. S6—6C 86
(off Blake Gro. Rd.)
Victor Rd. S17—2F 121
Victor St. S6—4B 86
Victor Ter. S70—1A 24
Viewland Clo. S72—2H 15
View Rd. S2—6E 99
View Rd. S65—1G 79
Viewtree Clo. S62—4H 51
Viking Way. S31—4B 118
Villa Gdns. DN5—2A 18
Village St. DN5—4F 31
Village St. DN6—1D 16
Villa Pk. Rd. DN4—3C 48
Villa Rd. DN6—2D 16
Villiers Clo. S2—1A 112
Villiers Dri. S2—1A 112
Vincent Cres. S40—3D 136
Vincent Rd. S7—5D 98
Vincent Rd. S65—2H 81
Vincent Rd. S71—4F 15
Vincent Ter. S63—2H 29
Vine Clo. S60—3C 78
Vine Clo. S71—3C 14
Viola Bank. S30—3D 140
Violet Av. DN12—4B 60
Violet Av. S19—4E 115
Violet Bank Rd. S7—1C 110

Vivian Rd. S5—1H 87
Vizard Rd. S74—5C 38
Vulcan Ho. S65—2G 79
Vulcan St. S9—1E 89

Wadbrough Rd. S11—4B 98
Waddington Rd. S75—5D 12
Waddington Ter. S64—1F 57
Wade Clo. S60—5F 79
Wade Meadow. S6—2G 85
Wade St. S4—2A 88
Wade St. S75—5D 12
Wadsley La. S6—1G 85
Wadsley Pk. Cres. S6—2G 85
Wadsworth Av. S12—2E 113
Wadsworth Clo. S12—1F 113
Wadsworth Dri. S12—2E 113
(in two parts)
Wadsworth Dri. S62—5C 54
Wadsworth Rd. S12—2E 113
Wadsworth Rd. S66—5H 81
Wadworth Av. DN11—4F 63
Wadworth Hall La. DN11
—6G 61
Wadworth Hill. DN11—6H 61
Wadworth Rise. S65—6C 70
Wadworth St. DN12—2C 58
Wager La. S72—2G 11
Wagon Rd. S61—5B 68
Waingate. S3—2F 5 & 1F 99
Wainscott Clo. S71—2D 14
Wainwright Av. S13—5F 101
Wainwright Av. S73—6H 25
Wainwright Cres. S13—5F 101
Wainwright Pl. S73—6H 25
Wainwright Rd. S61—6H 67
Wakefield Rd. WF4, S75 & S71
—1G 7
Wake Rd. S7—6C 98
Walbank Rd. DN3—3G 35
Walbert Av. S63—2E 29
Walbrook. S70—5B 24
Walden Av. DN5—6G 17
Walden Rd. S2—6F 99
Walders Av. S6—1G 85
Walders La. S30—6E 141
Walesmoor Av. S3—3F 127
Wales Pl. S6—5B 86
Wales Rd. S31—5F 117
Waleswood Ind. Est. S31
—3D 116
Waleswood Rd. S31—2H 115
(Beighton)
Waleswood Rd. S31—3D 116
(Wales)
Waleswood View. S31—1B 116
Waleswood Vs. S31—4D 116
Walford Rd. S31—3A 126
Walgrove Av. S40—4F 137
Walgrove Rd. S40—4F 137
Walker Clo. S30—1A 74
Walker La. S65—2E 79
Walker Pl. S65—2E 79
Walker Rd. S61—6H 67
Walker Rd. S75—6D 36
Walker's La. S31—3B 126
Walkers Ter. S71—2C 14
Walker St. S3—6F 87
Walker St. S62—1H 69
Walker St. S64—2C 56
Walker View. S62—1H 69
Walkley Bank Clo. S6—4A 86
Walkley Bank Rd. S6
—5G 85 to 5A 86
Walkley Cres. Rd. S6—5H 85
Walkley La. S6—3A 86
Walkley Rd. S6—5A 86

Walkley St. S6—5A 86
Walkley Ter. S6—5G 85
Walk, The. S65—2H 79
Walk, The. S70—5C 36
Wallace Rd. DN4—5G 45
Wallace Rd. S3—4D 86
Waller Rd. S6—5G 85
Walling Clo. S9—1D 88
Walling Rd. S9—1D 88
Wall St. S70—1G 23
Walney Fold. S71—1D 14
Walnut Dri. S31—5F 107
(Dinnington)
Walnut Dri. S31—4A 126
(Killamarsh)
Walnut Gro. S64—5D 42
Walnut Pl. S30—3D 64
(in two parts)
Walnut Tree Hill. DN11—6H 61
Walpole Clo. DN4—6H 45
Walpole Gro. S31—4B 104
Walseker La. S31—1G 127
Walsham Dri. DN5—4G 31
Walshaw Rd. S30—4D 72
Walters Rd. S66—4H 83
Walter St. S6—4B 86
Walter St. S60—2C 78
Waltham Gdns. S19—5G 115
Waltham St. S70—1A 24
Waltheof Rd. S2—5C 100
Walton Back La. S42—6A 136
Walton Clo. S18—1A 128
Walton Clo. S30—5A 50
Walton Clo. S40—5D 136
Walton Ct. S8—1C 122
Walton Cres. S40—4G 137
Walton Dri. S40—4G 137
Walton Dri. Ct. S40—4G 137
Waltonfields Rd. S40—3F 137
Walton Ho. DN1—1C 46
(off Grove Pl.)
Walton Rd. S11—4B 98
Walton Rd. S40—3F 137
Walton St. S75—4E 13
Walton St. N. S75—4E 13
Walton Wlk. S40—3G 137
Wannop St. S62—4F 69
Wansfell Rd. S4—2B 88
Wansfell Ter. S71—6A 14
Wapping, The. S65—6H 57
Warburton Clo. S2—6G 99
Warburton Gdns. S2—6G 99
Warburton Rd. S2—6G 99
Warde Aldam Cres. S66—4E 81
Warde Av. DN4—5H 45
Warden Clo. DN4—3E 49
Warden St. S60—6D 78
Wardgate Way. S40—6C 130
Wardlow Clo. S40—5H 137
Wardlow Rd. S12—2F 113
Ward Pl. S7—5D 98
Wardsend Rd. S6—1B 86
Wardsend Rd. N. S6—6A 74
Ward St. S3—6E 87
Wareham Ct. S19—5G 115
Warehouse La. S63—5E 41
Warley Rd. S2—4A 100
Warminster Clo. S8—3E 111
Warminster Cres. S8—4F 111
Warminster Dri. S8—4F 111
Warminster Gdns. S8—4E 111
Warminster Pl. S8—5F 111
Warminster Rd. S8—3E 111
Warmsworth Halt. DN4—1B 60
Warmsworth Halt Ind. Est. DN4
—1C 60
Warmsworth Rd. DN4—5G 45
Warner Av. S75—5D 12

Warner Pl. S75—5E 13
Warner Rd. S6—2H 85
Warner Rd. S75—5D 12
Warner St. S41—4B 138
Warnington Dri. DN4—6E 49
Warning Tongue La. DN3 & DN4
—3F 49
Warren Av. S62—6E 55
Warren Clo. DN2—5G 33
Warren Cres. S70—2H 23
Warren Dri. S61—1H 77
Warreners Dri. S65—5D 70
Warren Gdns. S30—5F 51
Warren Hill. S30—5E 51
Warren Ho. Clo. S66—4H 81
Warren La. DN4—6D 48
Warren La. S30—4D 50 to 5F 51
(in two parts)
Warren La. S75—2F 7
Warren Mt. S61—1H 77
Warren Pl. S70—2H 23
Warren Quarry La. S70—2H 23
Warren Rise. S18—6G 123
Warren Rd. DN12—4D 58
Warren Rd. S66—4F 81
Warren St. S4—6H 87 & 6A 88
(in two parts)
Warren, The. S31—6D 104
Warren Vale. S62 & S64—6G 55
Warren Vale Rd. S64—2G 55
Warren View. S70—1H 23
Warren View. S74—1G 51
Warren Wlk. S71—1F 9
Warrington Rd. S10—1B 98
Warris Clo. S61—6G 67
Warris Pl. S2—2H 99
Warsop Rd. S71—4A 8
Warwick Rd. DN2—6H 33
Warwick Rd. S71—3B 14
Warwick St. S10—1A 98
Warwick St. S40—6B 138
Warwick St. S60—4E 79
Warwick St. S. S60—4E 79
Warwick Ter. S10—1A 98
Warwick Way. S31—6E 107
Wasdale Av. S19—3E 125
Wasdale Clo. S19—3E 125
Washfield Cres. S60—1E 103
Washfield La. S60—1E 103
Washford Rd. S9—5A 88
Wash Ho. S40—3E 137
Washington Av. DN12—3B 58
Washington Av. S73—1D 38
Washington Gro. DN5—2A 32
Washington Rd. DN6—2D 16
Washington Rd. S11—5D 98
Washington Rd. S30—6F 65
Washington Rd. S63—2F 29
Washington St. S64—6F 43
Wasteneys Rd. S31—2B 118
Watch Ho. La. DN5—3H 31
Watch St. S13—5E 103
Waterdale. DN1—1D 46
Waterdale Rd. S70—5H 23
Waterdale Shopping Centre.
(off Waterdale) DN1—6D 32
Waterfall Rd. S9—6E 89
Waterfield Pl. S70—1E 25
Wateringbury Gro. S43—1D 134
Watering La. S71—1A 26
Water La. S17—2F 121
Water La. S60—4D 78
Water La. S62—2C 52
Water La. S65—1G 71
Waterloo Rd. S3—4C 86
Waterloo Rd. S70—6F 13
Waterloo Wlk. S6—6D 86
Watermead. S63—2B 42

Watermeade. S31—6G 125
Water Meadow La. S41—4D 130
Water Slacks Clo. S13—1B 114
Water Slacks Dri. S13—1B 114
Water Slacks La. S13—1A.114
Water Slacks Rd. S13—1B 114
Water Slacks Wlk. S13—1B 114
Water Slacks Way. S13
—1B 114
Watersmeet Rd. S6—4H 85
Water St. S3—1E 5 & 1E 99
Waterthorpe Clo. S19—1F 125
Waterthorpe Cres. S19—1F 125
Waterthorpe Gdns. S19—1F 125
Waterthorpe Glade. S19
—1F 125
Waterthorpe Glen. S19—1F 125
Waterthorpe Greenway. S19
—4D 114
Waterthorpe Rise. S19—6F 115
Watery St. S3—6D 86
Wath E. Ind. Est. S63—5H 41
Wath Rd. S7—1C 110
(Bolton-upon-Dearne)
Wath Rd. S63—1A 42
(Wath upon Dearne)
Wath Rd. S64—5B 42
Wath Rd. S73—1H 39
(Brampton)
Wath Rd. S73—4E 39
(Hemingfield)
Wath Rd. S74—1D 52
Wath W. Ind. Est. S63—3C 40
Wath Wood Bottom. S63—2E 55
Wath Wood Dri. S64—2F 55
Wath Wood Rd. S63—1F 55
Watkinson Gdns. S19—6E 115
Watnall Rd. S71—5B 8
Watson Clo. S61—1H 77
Watson Glen. S61—1E 77
Watson Rd. S10—3A 98
Watson Rd. S61—1H 77
Watson St. S74—6F 37
Watsons Wlk. S1—2F 5
Watt La. S10—3F 97
Waveney Dri. S75—4A 12
Waverley Av. DN4—4G 45
Waverley Av. DN12—3E 59
Waverley Av. S31—4A 118
Waverley Av. S66—5B 94
Waverley Cotts. S13—2H 101
Waverley La. S13—2H 101
Waverley Rd. S9—1E 101
Waverley View. S66—6C 90
Waycliffe. S71—4C 14
Wayford Av. S41—4B 138
Wayford Av. S66—3H 81
Wayland Av. S70—4H 23
Wayland Rd. S11—5B 98
Wayside. S43—3D 132
Weakland Clo. S12—5H 113
Weakland Cres. S12—4H 113
Weakland Dri. S12—4H 113
Weakland Way. S12—4H 113
Weaver Clo. S75—4A 12
Weavers Clo. S30—6A 64
Webb Av. S30—4G 141
Webbs Av. S6—5E 85
Webley Clo. DN2—4A 34
Webster Clo. S61—1E 77
Webster Cres. S61—1F 77
Webster Croft. S41—1B 132
Webster St. S9—2D 88
Wedgewood Clo. S62—2F 69
Weedon St. S9—2D 88
Weet Shaw La. S72—4A 10
Weetwood Dri. S11—2G 109

Weetwood Rd. S60—1G 91
Weigh La. S2—2G 99
Weir Clo. S74—6A 38
Weir Head. S9—2D 88
Welbeck Clo. S18—1A 128
Welbeck Clo. S43—5B 134
Welbeck Dri. S31—6D 104
Welbeck Pl. S65—1H 79
Welbeck Rd. DN4—1F 47
Welbeck Rd. S6—5H 85
Welbeck St. S75—5F 13
Welbourne Clo. S30—3G 65
Welbury Gdns. S19—3E 125
Welby Pl. S8—2D 110
Welfare Av. DN12—3C 58
Welfare Av. S40—2F 137
Welfare Rd. DN6—4D 16
Welfare Rd. S8—1F 29
Welfare View. S63—5F 29
Welfare View. S75—1B 22
Welham Dri. S60—5E 79
Welland Clo. S3—5D 86
Welland Ct. S75—4A 12
Welland Cres. S74—5C 38
Wellcarr Rd. S8—5E 111
Wellcliffe Clo. S66—3G 81
Well Ct. S12—4B 114
Well Croft. S30—6B 50
Wellcroft Clo. DN2—3A 34
Well Dri. S65—5E 71
Wellesley Rd. S10—2B 98
Wellfield Clo. S12—6G 113
Wellfield Rd. S6—6B 86
Wellfield Rd. S61—5G 67
Wellfield Rd. S75—4F 13
Wellgate. DN12—3E 59
Wellgate. S60—3E 79
Wellgate. S75—4F 7
Wellgate Mt. S60—3E 79
Wellgate Ter. S60—3E 79
Well Grn. Rd. S6—6B 84
Wellhead Rd. S8—1E 111
Well Hill Gro. S71—1E 9
Well Hill Rd. S30—1H 141
Wellington Av. S31—6D 106
Wellington Clo. S71—3B 14
Wellington Cres. S70—3C 24
Wellington Gro. DN5—2A 32
Wellington Pl. S9—1E 101
Wellington Pl. S70—6H 13
Wellington Rd. DN12—3B 60
Wellington Rd. S6—5E 85
Wellington St. S1—5C 4 & 3D 98
Wellington St. S63—4G 29
Wellington St. S64—6E 43
Wellington St. S70—6G 13
Welling Way. S61—2G 77
Well La. DN11—6H 61
Well La. S6—1F 85
Well La. S12—3B 114
Well La. S30—6A 64
Well La. S31—3A 104
Well La. S60—1E 103
(Treeton)
Well La. S60—4B 92
(Upper Whiston)
Well La. S60—2H 91
(Whiston)
Well La. S71—2C 14
Well Meadow Dri. S3—2B 4
Well Meadow St. S3
—1B 4 & 1D 98
Well Rd. S8—1E 111
Wells Rd. DN2—3F 33
Wells St. S72—1H 15
Well's St. S75—5C 6
Wells, The. S31—2F 119
Well St. S70—6F 13

Well View Rd. S61—1F 77
Wellway, The. S66—2F 81
Welney Pl. S6—5A 74
Welshpool Pl. S40—2F 137
Welshpool Yd. S40—3F 137
Welton Clo. DN4—5A 48
Welwyn Clo. S12—3D 112
Welwyn Clo. S40—2F 137
Welwyn Rd. S12—3D 112
Wembley Av. DN12—3C 58
Wembley Clo. DN2—4A 34
Wendel Gro. S74—5D 38
Wenlock Clo. S40—1F 137
Wenlock Cres. S40—1E 137
Wenlock St. S13—4H 101
Wensley Clo. S4—2A 88
Wensley Ct. S4—1A 88
Wensley Ct. S60—1F 91
Wensley Ct. S71—6A 8
Wensley Cres. DN4—4D 48
Wensley Croft. S4—1A 88
Wensleydale Dri. S60—4D 90
Wensleydale Rd. DN5—2F 31
Wensleydale Rd. S61—4H 67
Wensley Dri. S4—1A 88
Wensley Gdns. S4—1A 88
Wensley Grn. S4—1A 88
Wensley Rd. S71—6A 8
Wensley St. S4—1A 88
Wensley St. S63—1D 28
Wensley Way. S43—3A 134
Wentworth Av. S11—5F 109
Wentworth Av. S31—1D 116
Wentworth Av. S40—5G 137
Wentworth Clo. S61—2A 66
Wentworth Cres. S75—5H 7
Wentworth Gdns. S64—4A 56
Wentworth Ho. DN1—1C 46
(off St James St.)
Wentworth Ind. Pk. S75—1B 50
Wentworth Pk. S62—6E 53
Wentworth Pl. S61—5E 67
Wentworth Rd. DN2—4E 33
Wentworth Rd. S18—2A 128
Wentworth Rd. S61—2B 66
Wentworth Rd. S62 & S64
—4C 54
Wentworth Rd. S74—2H 37
(Blacker Hill)
Wentworth Rd. S74—1C 52
(Elsecar)
Wentworth Rd. S74—4C 38
(Jump)
Wentworth Rd. S75—5B 6
(Darton)
Wentworth Rd. S75—5G 7
(Mapplewell)
Wentworth St. S70—4C 36
Wentworth St. S71—4G 13
Wentworth View. S73—2F 39
Wentworth View. S74—6A 38
Wentworth Way. S31—6G 107
Wentworth Way. S75—3B 22
(Dodworth)
Wentworth Way. S75—1B 50
(Tankersley)
Wentworth Woodhouse. S62
—5E 53
Wescoe Av. S72—1A 28
Wesley Av. S31—5B 104
Wesley Ct. S61—2B 66
Wesley La. S10—2H 97
Wesley Pl. S31—3F 119
Wesley Rd. S30—6A 50
(in two parts)
Wesley Rd. S31—4H 117
Wessenden Clo. S75—6C 12
Wessex Gdns. S17—4D 120

West Av. DN4—4A 46
West Av. DN6—2B 16
West Av. S62—1F 69
West Av. S63—2H 41
West Av. S71—1F 9
West Av. S73—6H 25
Westbank Clo. S18—5F 123
Westbank Ct. S18—5G 123
Westbank Dri. S31—3E 119
W. Bank La. S1—3D 4 & 2E 99
W. Bank Rise. S31—3F 119
West Bar. S3—1E 5 & 1E 99
Westbar Grn. S1—2D 4 & 1E 99
West Bars. S40—2H 137
West Bawtry Rd. S60—2D 90
Westbourne Gdns. DN4—6H 45
Westbourne Gro. S40—2D 136
Westbourne Gro. S75—4F 13
Westbourne Rd. S10—4A 98
Westbourne Ter. S70—6E 13
Westbrook Bank. S11—5B 98
Westbrook Clo. S40—3B 136
Westbrook Dri. S40—3B 136
Westbrook Rd. S30—2E 65
Westbury Av. S30—3F 65
Westbury Clo. S75—3D 12
Westbury St. S9—6B 88
Westby Cres. S60—2H 91
West Clo. S61—1G 77
West Cres. S30—3C 140
West Cres. S44—6E 135
Westcroft Cres. S19—1E 125
Westcroft Dri. S19—2E 125
Westcroft Gdns. S19—1E 125
Westcroft Glen. S19—2E 125
Westcroft Gro. S19—2E 125
W. Don St. S6—5C 86
W. End Av. DN5—2A 32
W. End Av. S71—2C 8
W. End Cres. S71—2C 8
W. End La. DN11—4A 62
W. End Rd. S63—4B 40
W. End View. S31—6H 125
Westerdale Rd. DN5—2F 31
Western Av. S31—5F 107
Western Bank. S10—2B 98
Western Clo. S31—5F 107
Western Rd. S10—1A 98
Western Rd. S65—2G 79
Western St. S70—5G 13
Western Ter. S73—6A 26
Westfield. S19—1E 125
Westfield Av. S12—4C 114
Westfield Av. S31—4A 104
Westfield Av. S40—4D 136
Westfield Centre. S19—1E 125
Westfield Clo. S40—3D 136
Westfield Cres. S19—1C 124
Westfield Cres. S63—1D 28
Westfield Gdns. S40—3E 137
Westfield Gro. S12—4B 114
Westfield La. DN5—1F 43
Westfield La. S75—2A 12
Westfield Northway. S19
—1E 125
Westfield Rd. DN3—3E 35
Westfield Rd. DN4—3B 46
Westfield Rd. S18—3G 129
Westfield Rd. S31—4A 126
Westfield Rd. S62—4E 69
Westfield Rd. S66—4H 81
Westfield Rd. S73 & S63—5A 40
Westfields. S70—5A 24
Westfields. S71—1C 8
Westfield Southway. S19
—1E 125
Westfield St. S70—6F 13
Westfield Ter. S1—4C 4 & 2D 98

Westgate. S60—4D 78
West Ga. S64—6G 43
Westgate. S70—6G 13
Westgate. S71—3B 14
West Gro. DN2—4G 33
West Gro. S71—1C 8
Westhaven. S72—2H 15
West Hill. S61—3E 77
Westhill La. S3—4B 4 & 2D 98
Westholme Rd. DN4—2B 46
W. Kirk La. S72—2A 28
W. Laith Ga. DN1—6C 32
Westland Clo. S19—6E 115
Westland Gdns. S19—6E 115
Westland Gro. S19—1E 125
Westland Rd. S19—1E 125
West La. S6—1A 84
West La. S31—4H 103
West Lea. S66—2D 94
West Lea. S40—3D 136
Westleigh Ct. S40—6G 131
West Mall. DN1—6C 32
(off French Ga.)
West Mall. S19—6E 115
Westminster Av. S10—4B 96
Westminster Clo. S10—4B 96
Westminster Cres. DN2—4H 33
Westminster Cres. S10—4B 96
Westminster Ho. DN2—4A 34
W. Moor Cres. S75—6C 12
W. Moor La. DN3—1H 35
W. Moor La. S63 & DN5—1D 42
Westmoor Rd. S43—1F 139
Westmoreland St. S6—6C 86
Westmoreland Way. DN5
—2C 44
Westmorland La. DN12—2B 58
Westmorland St. DN4—5H 45
W. Mount Av. S63—3C 40
Westnall Ho. S30—2D 72
(off Glossop Row.)
Westnall Rd. S5—2H 75
Westnall Ter. S5—2H 75
Weston Clo. S40—5C 130
Weston Rd. DN4—5A 46
Weston St. S3—2A 4 & 1C 98
Westover Rd. S10—3E 97
W. Park Dri. S31—6H 103
W. Pinfold. S71—2E 9
Westpit Hill. S63—4A 40
West Pl. DN5—6B 18
W. Quadrant. S5—6H 75
West Rd. S64—6D 42
West Rd. S75—5D 12
West St. DN1—6C 32
West St. DN12—3E 59
West St. S1—4B 4 & 2D 98
West St. S18—1D 128
West St. S19—4F 115
West St. S31—3F 119
(Anston)
West St. S31—6H 125
(Eckington)
West St. S40—1H 137
West St. S63—4G 29
(Goldthorpe)
West St. S63—5E 41
(in two parts,
Wath upon Dearne)
West St. S64—1E 57
West St. S66—4B 94
West St. S70—5A 24
West St. S71—1F 9
West St. S73—4E 27
(Darfield)
West St. S73—6A 26
(Wombwell)
West St. S74—5G 37

West St. La. S1—3D 4 & 2E 99
Westthorpe Rd. S31—4B 126
W. Vale Rd. S65—5D 70
West View. S43—2B 134
West View. S70—2G 23
W. View Clo. S17—4F 121
W. View Cres. S63—5E 29
W. View La. S17—3F 121
W. View Rd. S41—5G 131
W. View Rd. S61—3E 77
W. View Rd. S64—1E 57
W. View Ter. S70—5B 24
Westville Rd. S75—4F 13
Westwell Pl. S19—3D 124
Westwick Cres. S8—2B 122
Westwick Gro. S8—2C 122
Westwick La. S42—2A 136
Westwick Rd. S8—3B 122
Westwood Av. S43—3A 134
Westwood Ct. S70—5G 13
Westwood La. S30—1A 50
Westwood La. S43—1F 139
Westwood New Rd. S30 & S75
—6A 50
Westwood New Rd. S70—6D 36
(off Sheffield Rd.)
Westwood Rd. S11—5F 97
Westwood Rd. S30—5B 50
Westwood Rd. S44—1G 139
Wetherby Clo. DN5—4F 31
Wetherby Ct. S9—1E 101
Wetherby Dri. S31—6A 104
Wetherby Dri. S64—5F 43
Wetlands La. S41—1D 138
Wet Moor La. S63—4D 40
Whaley Rd. S75—2B 12
Wharf Clo. S64—2C 56
Wharfe Ct. S60—1F 91
Wharfedale Dri. S20—2C 64
Wharfedale Rd. S75—5C 12
Wharf La. S41—1A 138
Wharf La. S43—1D 134
Wharf Rd. DN1—4D 32
Wharf Rd. S9—6F 77
Wharf Rd. S62—6C 56
Wharf St. S2—2H 5 & 1G 99
Wharf St. S64—2C 56
Wharf St. S71—4A 14
Wharncliffe. S75—3C 22
Wharncliffe Av. S31—5C 104
Wharncliffe Av. S63—5F 41
Wharncliffe Clo. S62—5D 54
Wharncliffe Clo. S74—1H 51
Wharncliffe Rd. S10
—6A 4 & 3C 98
Wharncliffe Rd. S30—6B 50
Wharncliffe St. DN4—1A 46
Wharncliffe St. S65—2E 79
Wharncliffe St. S70—6F 13
Wharncliffe St. S71—5F 9
Wharton Av. S31—4B 104
Wheatacre Rd. S30—3E 141
Wheata Dri. S5—2F 75
Wheata Pl. S5—2F 75
Wheata Rd. S5—3E 75
Wheatbridge Rd. S40—2G 137
Wheat Croft. DN12—3G 59
Wheatcroft Rd. S62—1H 69
Wheatfield Clo. DN6—1E 21
Wheatfield Cres. S5—3H 75
Wheatfield Way. S42—6B 130
Wheathill Clo. S42—6B 130
Wheathill Clo. S43—1F 139
Wheathill La. S41—1D 138
Wheatley Clo. S71—3H 13
Wheatley Gro. S13—4G 101
Wheatley Hall Rd. DN2
—3E 33 to 1B 34

Wheatley La. DN1—5E 33
Wheatley Pk. Rd. DN5—5A 18
Wheatley Pl. DN12—2B 58
Wheatley Rise. S75—3F 7
Wheatley Rd. S61—6G 67
Wheatley Rd. S62—6C 56
Wheatley Rd. S70—2E 25
Wheatley St. DN12—2B 58
Wheats La. S1—2E 5
Wheeldon Cres. S43—3D 132
Wheeldon La. S40—2A 138
Wheeldon St. S1—3B 4 & 2D 98
Wheel La. S30—1B 74
(Grenoside)
Wheel La. S30—2B 72
(Oughtibridge)
Wheel, The. S30—1D 74
Wheldrake Rd. S5—1H 87
Whernside Av. S30—1D 64
Whinacre Clo. S8—3F 123
Whinacre Pl. S8—3E 123
Whinacre Wlk. S8—3E 123
Whinfell Clo. DN6—1D 16
Whinfell Ct. S11—5E 109
Whin Hill Rd. DN4—3D 48
Whinmoor Rd. S5—6B 76
Whinmoor Rd. S30—6A 50
Whinnifred Rd. S63—5H 41
Whins, The. S62—2C 68
Whiphill Clo. DN4—4C 48
Whiphill La. DN3—4G 35
Whiphill Top La. DN3—1H 49
Whirlow Ct. Rd. S11—5F 109
Whirlowdale Clo. S11—5F 109
Whirlowdale Cres. S7—4H 109
Whirlowdale Rise. S11—5F 109
Whirlowdale Rd. S11 & S7
—5E 109
Whirlow Farm M. S11—4F 109
Whirlow Gro. S11—5F 109
Whirlow La. S11—4E 109
Whirlow Pk. Rd. S11—5F 109
Whiston Brook View. S60
—2A 92
Whiston Grange. S60—2G 91
Whiston Grn. S60—3H 91
Whiston Gro. S60—5F 79
Whiston Vale. S60—3H 91
Whitaker Clo. DN11—6D 62
Whitaker Sq. DN11—5C 62
Whitbeck Clo. DN11—6H 61
Whitburn Rd. DN1—1E 47
Whitby Rd. DN11—5C 62
Whitby Rd. S9—6E 89
Whitcomb Dri. DN11—6D 62
Whitebank Clo. S41—4B 138
Whitecotes Clo. S40—5G 137
Whitecotes La. S40—5F 137
White Croft. S1—2D 4 & 1E 99
Whitecroft Cres. S60—3C 90
White Cross La. DN11—4G 61
White Cross La. S70—4D 24
White Cross Rise. S70—4D 24
White Cross Rd. S72—2H 15
White Edge Clo. S40—6F 131
White Farm Clo. DN5—6C 18
White Ga. S31—1H 119
Whitegate Wlk. S61—4G 67
Whitehall Rd. S61—3A 67
Whitehall Way. S61—4A 68
Whitehead Av. S30—3F 141
Whitehead St. S43—1D 134
Whitehill Av. S60—3C 90
White Hill Av. S70—6C 12
Whitehill Dri. S60—4C 90
White Hill Gro. S70—6D 12
Whitehill La. S60—2C 90
Whitehill Rd. S60—3C 90

White Hill Ter. S70—6C 12
Whitehouse La. S6—5B 86
Whitehouse Rd. S6—5B 86
Whitehouses. S41—4B 138
White La. S12—4C 112 to 6G 113
White La. S30—6F 51
Whitelea Gro. S64—1D 56
Whitelea Gro. Trading Est S64
—1D 56
White Leas. S40—1D 136
Whitelee Rd. S64—2C 56
Whiteley La. S10—6C 96
Whiteleys Av. S62—6E 55
Whiteley Wood Clo. S11—6F 97
Whiteley Wood Rd. S11—1E 109
Whitelow La. S17—1A 120
White Rd. S43—1E 135
White Rose Ho. S60—4D 78
White Rose Way. DN4 & DN11
—2D 46
White's La. S2—2H 99
White Thorns Clo. S8—3F 123
White Thorns Dri. S8—4F 123
White Thorns View. S8—3F 123
White Towers Caravan Site.
DN2—3C 34
Whiteways Clo. S4—3H 87
Whiteways Dri. S4—3H 87
Whiteways Gro. S4—3H 87
Whiteways Rd. S4—3H 87
Whitewood Clo. S71—2D 8
Whitfield Rd. S10—6C 96
Whitfield Rd. S62—6D 54
Whitham Rd. S10—3A 98
Whiting St. S8—1E 111
Whitley La. S30—6B 64 to 5F 65
Whitley View Rd. S61—4D 76
Whitney Clo. DN4—6G 45
Whittier Rd. DN4—5A 46
Whittington Hill. S41—2A 132
Whittington St. DN1—4D 32
Whiting Valley Rd. S41
—2A 132
Whitton Clo. DN4—5A 48
Whitton Pl. S44—6E 135
Whitwell Cres. S30—3D 140
Whitwell La. S30—4C 140
Whitwell St. S9—1F 101
Whitwell View. DN11—4F 63
Whitworth Bldgs. S63—1G 29
(off Clarke St.)
Whitworth Croft. S10—3F 97
Whitworth La. S9—4C 88
Whitworth Rd. S10—4E 97
Whitworth Rd. S41—5A 132
Whitworth St. S63—4G 29
Whitworth Way. S63—4E 41
Whixley Rd. S9—6D 88
Whybourne Gro. S60—4E 79
Whybourne Ter. S60—3E 79
Whyn View. S63—1E 29
Wicker. S3—1G 5 & 1D 98
Wicker La. S3—1G 5 & 1F 99
Wickersley Rd. S60—5G 79
Wickett Hern Rd. DN3—3H 35
Wickfield Clo. S12—2H 113
Wickfield Dri. S12—2H 113
Wickfield Gro. S12—3G 113
Wickfield Pl. S12—2G 113
Wickfield Rd. S12—3H 113
Wicklow Rd. DN2—4G 33
Widdop Clo. S13—5F 101
Widdop Croft. S13—5F 101
Wigfield Dri. S70—4H 23
Wigfull Rd. S11—4A 98
Wigley Rd. S43—5A 134
Wignall Av. S66—5D 80
Wikeley Way. S43—3D 132

Wike Rd. S71—5E 15
Wilberforce Rd. DN2—6B 20
Wilberforce Rd. S31—2F 119
Wilbrook Rise. S75—3C 12
Wilby La. S70—1A 24
Wilcox Clo. S6—4B 74
Wilcox Grn. S61—3A 68
Wilcox Rd. S6—4A 74
Wild Av. S62—6C 54
Wildflower Clo. DN11—6C 62
Wilding Clo. S61—1G 77
Wilding Way. S61—1G 77
Wilford Rd. S71—4A 8
Wilfred St. S60—3D 78
Wilfred Ter. S70—1G 23
Wilfrid Rd. S9—6C 88
Wilkin Hill. S18—2A 130
Wilkinson Av. DN11—5E 63
Wilkinson Dri. S43—4H 133
Wilkinson La. S10
—4A 4 & 2C 98
Wilkinson Rd. S74—6C 38
Wilkinson St. S10—4A 4 & 2C 98
Wilkinson St. S70—1H 23
Willan Dri. S60—6C 90
Willbury Dri. S12—1C 112
Willey St. S3—1G 5 & 1D 98
William Clo. S19—3D 124
William Cres. S19—2D 124
William La. DN3—3B 62
Williamson Rd. S11—6B 98
Williams Rd. DN5—3H 31
William St. S10—6A 4 & 3C 98
William St. S31—6D 124
William St. S41—5A 132
William St. S60—3E 79
William St. S62—3G 69
William St. S63—4E 29
(Goldthorpe)
William St. S63—5F 41
(Wath upon Dearne)
William St. S64—2C 56
William St. S73—6A 26
William St. N. S41—1H 131
Willingham Clo. S19—6G 115
Willingham Gdns. S19—6G 115
Willington Rd. S5—5G 75
Willis Rd. S6—2H 85
Willman Rd. S71—4F 15
Willoughby St. S4—1A 88
Willow Av. DN4—3D 48
Willow Av. S62—2G 69
Willow Bank. S71 & S75—2F 13
Willow Bri. Caravan Site. DN5
—4B 32
Willow Bri. Rd. DN5—4B 32
Willow Clo. S31—4F 119
Willow Clo. S60—4D 90
Willow Clo. S66—3G 81
Willow Clo. S72—6B 10
Willow Clo. S74—6G 37
Willow Ct. S44—2G 139
Willow Ct. S63—6E 41
Willow Cres. S30—3E 65
Willow Dene Rd. S72—6G 11
Willow Dri. S9—2G 101
Willow Dri. S64—6D 42
Willow Dri. S66—3G 81
Willow Garth. S62—1G 69
Willowgarth Av. S60—3C 90
Willow Garth Rd. S41—3E 131
Willow Glen. DN3—3H 49
Willow Gro. S31—5D 104
Willow La. DN11—4E 63
Willow La. S63—2B 42
Willow Rd. DN3—2G 35
Willow Rd. S30—5D 140
Willow Rd. S31—4A 126

Willow Rd. S63—1F 29
(Thurnscoe)
Willow Rd. S63—1G 55
(Wath upon Dearne)
Willow Rd. S66—4D 82
Willows, The. S61—5F 67
Willow St. DN12—3F 59
Willow St. S70—1F 23
Willow Wlk. S05—4A 18
Wilsden Gro. S75—4D 12
Wilsic Ho. DN1—1C 46
(off Grove Pl.)
Wilson Av. S62—1E 69
Wilson Dri. S65—6C 70
Wilson Gro. S71—3F 15
Wilson Pl. S8—1E 111
Wilson Rd. S11—5A 98
Wilson Rd. S18—5G 123
Wilson Rd. S30—4H 141
Wilson St. S3—5E 87
Wilson St. S18—3F 129
Wilson St. S73—6H 25
Wilson Wlk. S75—3C 22
Wilstrop Rd. S9—6D 88
Wilthorpe Av. S75—3E 13
Wilthorpe Cres. S75—3E 13
Wilthorpe Farm Rd. S75—3E 13
Wilthorpe Gdns. S19—4A 114
Wilthorpe Grn. S75—3E 13
Wilthorpe La. S75—3D 12
Wilthorpe Rd. S75—3C 12
Wilton Clo. S62—2F 69
Wilton Ct. S61—2A 78
Wilton Gdns. S61—2A 78
Wilton La. S61—3A 78
Wilton Pl. S10—3C 98
Wiltshire Av. DN12—2B 58
Wiltshire Rd. DN2—5A 34
Wimborne Cres. S41—4G 131
Winberry Av. S31—2G 119
Wincanton Clo. S64—5F 43
Winchester Av. DN2—3G 33
Winchester Av. S10—5B 96
Winchester Ct. S65—2E 79
(off Nottingham St.)
Winchester Cres. S10—5B 96
Winchester Dri. S10—5B 96
Winchester Ho. DN3—3F 31
Winchester Rd. S10—5B 96
Winchester Rd. S41—4G 131
Winchester Way. DN5—3G 31
Winchester Way. S60—2A 90
Winchester Way. S71—2G 25
Wincobank Av. S5—6A 76
Wincobank Clo. S5—6B 76
Wincobank La. S4—2B 88
Wincobank Rd. S5—6B 76
Winco Rd. S4—2B 88
Winco Wood La. S9—6B 76
Windam Dri. DN3—1H 21
Windermere Av. DN2—4A 34
Windermere Av. S18—2C 128
Windermere Av. S63—5G 29
Windermere Clo. S64—5H 43
Windermere Ct. S31—1G 119
Windermere Cres. DN3—3D 20
Windermere Grange. DN12
—4B 60
Windermere Rd. S8—2C 110
Windermere Rd. S41—4E 131
Windermere Rd. S71—6A 14
Winders Pl. S73—1F 39
Windgate Hill. DN12—2F 59
Windham Clo. S71—4H 13
Windhill Av. S64—6G 43
Windhill Av. S75—2E 7
Windhill Cres. S64—5G 43
Windhill Cres. S75—2E 7

Windhill Dri. S75—2E 7
Windhill La. S75—2E 7
Windhill Mt. S75—2E 7
Windhill Ter. S64—5G 43
Windle Rd. DN4—2A 46
Windle Sq. DN3—3D 20
Windmill Av. DN12—4F 59
Windmill Av. S72—5G 11
Windmill Balk La. DN6—3C 16
Windmill Dri. DN11—6H 61
Windmill Est. DN12—4F 59
Windmill Greenway. S19
—4E 125
Windmill Hill La. S30—3C 64
Windmill La. S5—5A 76
Windmill Rd. S31—1G 119
Windmill Rd. S73—1D 38
Windmill Ter. S71—1D 8
Windsor Av. S75—5A 6
Windsor Clo. DN5—1G 43
Windsor Clo. S40—4E 137
Windsor Clo. S66—3H 81
Windsor Ct. S11—3F 109
Windsor Ct. S63—1G 29
Windsor Cres. S71—4B 14
Windsor Cres. S72—2H 27
Windsor Dri. S18—2A 128
Windsor Dri. S64—5G 43
Windsor Dri. S75—2B 22
Windsor Rise. S31—1C 116
Windsor Rd. DN2—5F 33
Windsor Rd. DN12—2D 58
Windsor Rd. S8—1D 110
Windsor Rd. S61—3B 66
Windsor Sq. S63—1G 29
Windsor St. S4—5H 87 & 6A 88
(in two parts)
Windsor St. S63—1G 29
Windsor St. S74—4H 37
Windsor Wlk. DN5—3G 31
Windsor Wlk. S31—4E 119
Windsor Wlk. S41—4C 138
Windy Ho. La. S2—6C 100
Windy Ridge. S31—4A 104
Winfield Rd. S63—6F 41
Wingerworth Av. S8—1B 122
Wingerworth Way. S40
—6H 137
Wingfield Clo. S18—3A 128
Wingfield Clo. S61—4A 68
Wingfield Cres. S12—2E 113
Wingfield Rd. S61—4H 67
Wingfield Rd. S71—1A 14
Winholme. DN3—3F 35
Winifred St. S60—3C 78
Winkley Ter. S5—4A 76
Winlea Av. S65—5C 80
Winnat Pl. S43—4A 134
Winnats Clo. S40—6E 131
Winn Clo. S6—6H 73
Winn Dri. S6—6H 73
Winn Gdns. S6—6H 73
Winn Gro. S6—6H 73
Winnipeg Rd. DN5—6B 18
Winsford Rd. S6—4A 74
Winster Clo. S70—3D 36
Winster Ct. S41—1A 138
Winster Rd. S6—1A 86
Winster Rd. S43—3A 134
Winston Av. S30—2B 140
Winter Av. S75—5E 13
Winter Hill La. S61—2G 77
Winterhill Rd. S61—3F 77
Winter Rd. S75—5E 13
Winter St. S3—1C 98
Winter Ter. S75—5E 13
Winterton Clo. DN4—5B 48
Winterton Gdns. S12—4C 114

Printed and bound in Great Britain by
BPCC Paperbacks Ltd
Member of BPCC Ltd